Cognition and Intelligence

In 1957, Lee Cronbach called on the membership of the American Psychological Association to bring together experimental and differential approaches to the study of cognition. The field of intelligence research is an example of a response to that call, and *Cognition and Intelligence: Identifying the Mechanisms of the Mind* investigates the progress of this research program in the literature of the past several decades. With contributions from formative experts in the field, including Earl Hunt and Robert Sternberg, this volume reviews the research on the study of intelligence from diverse cognitive approaches, from the most bottom-up to the most top-down. The authors present their findings on the underlying cognitive aspects of intelligence based on their studies of neuroscience, reaction time, artificial intelligence, problem solving, metacognition, and development. The book summarizes and synthesizes the literature reviewed and makes recommendations for the pursuit of future research in the field.

Robert J. Sternberg is IBM Professor of Psychology and Education at Yale, Director of the PACE Center at Yale, and 2003 President of the American Psychological Association. He is the author of more than 1,000 publications on topics related to cognition and intelligence and has received over $18 million in grants for his research. He has won numerous awards from professional associations and holds five honorary doctorates.

Jean E. Pretz received her B.A. from Wittenberg University in Springfield, Ohio, and her M.A., M.Phil., and Ph.D. from Yale University. She is Assistant Professor of Psychology at Illinois Wesleyan University in Bloomington, Illinois. Her doctoral work examines the role of intuition and expertise in practical problem solving from both an experimental and a differential perspective. This project has received the American Psychological Foundation/Council of Graduate Departments of Psychology (APF/COGDOP) Graduate Research Scholarship Award, the American Psychological Association Dissertation Research Award, as well as a Yale University Dissertation Fellowship. Her research on the role of implicit processes in insight problem solving received two awards from the American Psychological Society Graduate Student Caucus. She has also received a Fulbright fellowship to study the psychology of religion in the former East Germany. Dr. Pretz has co-authored a book on creativity titled, *The Creativity Conundrum*, with Dr. Sternberg and Dr. James Kaufman.

Cognition and Intelligence

Identifying the Mechanisms of the Mind

Edited by

ROBERT J. STERNBERG
Yale University

JEAN E. PRETZ
Yale University

CAMBRIDGE
UNIVERSITY PRESS

2008

PUBLISHED BY THE PRESS SYNDICATE OF THE UNIVERSITY OF CAMBRIDGE
The Pitt Building, Trumpington Street, Cambridge, United Kingdom

CAMBRIDGE UNIVERSITY PRESS
The Edinburgh Building, Cambridge CB2 2RU, UK
40 West 20th Street, New York, NY 10011-4211, USA
477 Williamstown Road, Port Melbourne, VIC 3207, Australia
Ruiz de Alarcón 13, 28014 Madrid, Spain
Dock House, The Waterfront, Cape Town 8001, South Africa

http://www.cambridge.org

First published 2005

Printed in the United States of America

Typeface Palatino 10/12 pt.   *System* LaTeX 2_ε [TB]

A catalog record for this book is available from the British Library.

Library of Congress Cataloging in Publication Data
Cognition and intelligence : identifying the mechanisms of the mind /
edited by Robert J. Sternberg, Jean Pretz.
   p. cm.
Includes bibliographical references and index.
ISBN 0-521-82744-2 – ISBN 0-521-53479-8 (pbk.)
   1. Cognition. 2. Intelligence. I. Sternberg, Robert J. II. Pretz, Jean E.
BF311.C5478 2004
153 – dc22   2004043565

ISBN 0 521 82744 2 hardback
ISBN 0 521 53479 8 paperback

Contents

Preface

How did the study of cognition and intelligence get started? Although some psychologists in the nineteenth century were interested in cognitive processing (e.g., Donders, 1868/1869), the connection between information processing and intelligence seems first to have been explicitly drawn by Charles Spearman (1923), the same individual known for initiating serious psychometric theorizing about intelligence with his theory of the general factor of intelligence (Spearman, 1927).

Spearman (1923) proposed what he believed to be three fundamental qualitative principles of cognition. The first, *apprehension of experience*, is what today might be called the encoding of stimuli (see Sternberg, 1977). It involves perceiving the stimuli and their properties. The second principle, *eduction of relations*, is what today might be labeled inference. It is the inferring of a relation between two or more concepts. The third principle, *eduction of correlates*, is what today might be called application. It is the application of an inferred rule to a new situation.

Spearman was not the only early psychologist interested in the relationship between cognition and intelligence. Thorndike et al. (1926) proposed a quite similar theory based on Thorndike's theory of learning. According to this theory, learned connections are what underlie individual differences in intelligence. Some early researchers tried to integrate cognition and biology in studying intelligence. For example, the Russian psychologist Alexander Luria (1973, 1980) believed that the brain is a highly differentiated system whose parts are responsible for different aspects of a unified whole. In other words, separate cortical regions act together to produce thoughts and actions of various kinds. Luria (1980) suggested that the brain comprises three main units. The first, a unit of arousal, contains the brain stem and midbrain structures, including the medulla, reticular activating system, pons, thalamus, and hypothalamus. The second unit of the brain is a sensori-input unit, which comprises the temporal, parietal, and occipital lobes. The third unit is the frontal cortex, which is involved in organization and planning. It comprises cortical structures anterior to the central sulcus. Luria's theory remains of interest to researchers even today (Naglieri & Das, 1990, 1997).

In general, early approaches to cognition and intelligence came in fits and starts. Lee Cronbach (1957) tried to revive interest in the cognitive approach with an article on "the two disciplines of scientific psychology," and there were some fits and starts during the 1960s in an effort to revive this approach. But systematic work was to wait until the 1970s.

Serious revival can probably be credited in large part to the work of Earl Hunt (1978, 1980; Hunt, Frost, & Lunneborg, 1973; Hunt, Lunneborg, & Lewis, 1975), who was the originator of what has come to be called the cognitive-correlates approach to integrating the study of cognitive processing with the study of intelligence (Pellegrino & Glaser, 1979). It examined basic (sometimes called "lower order") processes of intelligence.

The proximal goal of this research is to estimate parameters representing the durations of performance for information processing components constituting experimental tasks commonly used in the laboratories of cognitive psychologists. These parameters are then used to investigate the extent to which cognitive components correlate across participants with each other and with scores on psychometric measures commonly believed to measure intelligence, such as the Raven Progressive Matrices tests.

For example, Hunt and his colleagues used the Posner and Mitchell (1967) task as one of their cognitive tasks. This task requires individuals to recognize whether two letters match physically or (in another variant of the task) in name. The goal of such a task is to estimate the amount of time a given participant takes to access lexical information – letter names – in memory. The physical-match condition is included to subtract out (control for) sheer time to perceive the letters and respond to questions. The difference between name and physical-match times thus provides the parameter estimate of interest for the task. Hunt and his colleagues found that this parameter and similar parameters in other experimental tasks typically correlate about −.3 with scores on psychometric tests of verbal ability.

The precise tasks used in such research have varied. The letter-matching task has been a particularly popular one, as has been the short-term memory scanning task originally proposed by S. Sternberg (1969). Other researchers have preferred simple and choice reaction time tasks (e.g., Jensen, 1979, 1982). Most such studies have been conducted with adults, but some have been conducted developmentally with children of various ages (e.g., Keating & Bobbitt, 1978).

An alternative approach came to be called the cognitive-components approach (Pellegrino & Glaser, 1979). This approach focused on higher-order components of intelligence. In this approach, participants are tested on their ability to perform tasks of the kinds actually found on standard psychometric tests of mental abilities – for example, analogies, series completions, mental rotations, and syllogisms. Participants typically are timed and response time is the principal dependent variable, with error rate and pattern-of-response choices serving as further dependent variables. This approach was suggested by Sternberg (1977; see also Royer, 1971).

The proximal goal in this research is, first, to formulate a model of information processing in performance on the types of tasks found in conventional psychometric tests of intelligence. Second, it is to test the model while estimating parameters for the model. Finally, it is to investigate the extent to which these components correlate across participants with each other and with scores on standard psychometric tests. Because the tasks that are analyzed are usually taken directly from psychometric tests of intelligence or are very similar to such tasks, the major issue in this kind of research is not whether there is any correlation at all between cognitive task and psychometric test scores. Rather, the issue is one of isolating the locus or loci of the correlations that are obtained. One seeks to discover what components of information processing are the critical ones from the standpoint of the theory of intelligence (Carroll, 1981; Pellegrino & Glaser, 1979, 1980, 1982; Royer, 1971; Sternberg, 1977, 1980, 1983; Sternberg & Gardner, 1983). An example of a component would be inference, which refers to the conceiving of a relationship between two items (such as words, numbers, or pictures).

Thus, Hunt and his successors focused on lower-order processes, whereas Sternberg and his successors focused on higher-order processes. A third approach focused on developmental processes. Jean Piaget (1952, 1972) was never very interested in individual differences. He viewed intelligence as arising from cognitive schemas, or structures that mature as a function of the interaction of the organism with the environment. Piaget (1926, 1928, 1952, 1972), like many other theorists of intelligence, recognized the importance of adaptation to intelligence. Indeed, he believed adaptation to be its most important principle. In adaptation, individuals learn from the environment and learn to address the changes in the environment. Adjustment consists of two complementary processes: assimilation and accommodation. *Assimilation* is the process of absorbing new information and fitting it into an already existing cognitive structure about what the world is like. The complementary process, *accommodation*, involves forming a new cognitive structure in order to understand information. In other words, if no existing cognitive structure seems adequate to understand new information, a new cognitive structure must be formed through the accommodation process.

The complementary processes of assimilation and accommodation, taken together in an interaction, constitute what Piaget referred to as equilibration. *Equilibration* is the balancing of the two and it is through this balance that people either add to old schemas or form new ones. A *schema*, for Piaget, is a mental image or action pattern. It is essentially a way of organizing sensory information. For example, we have schemas for going to the bank, riding a bicycle, eating a meal, visiting a doctor's office, and the like. Equilibration unfolds through four stages of cognitive development: sensori-motor, preoperational, concrete-operational, and formal-operational.

Whereas Piaget emphasized primarily biological maturation in the development of intelligence, other theorists interested in structures, such as Vygotsky (1978), emphasized more the role of interactions of individuals with the environment. Vygotsky suggested that basic to intelligence is *internalization*, which is the internal reconstruction of an external operation. The basic notion is that we observe those in the social environment around us acting in certain ways and we internalize their actions so that they become a part of us.

Vygotsky also proposed the important notion of a *zone of proximal development*, which refers to functions that have not yet matured but are in the process of maturation. The basic idea is to look not only at developed abilities but also at abilities that are developing. This zone is often measured as the difference between performance before and after instruction. Thus, instruction is given at the time of testing to measure the individual's ability to learn in the testing environment (Brown & French, 1979; Grigorenko & Sternberg, 1998; Feuerstein, 1980). The research suggests that tests of the zone of proximal development tap abilities not measured by conventional tests.

By the 1980s, it was clear that there were *many* ways in which intelligence could be examined through cognitive means. Many of these are summarized in various handbooks of intelligence (Sternberg, 1982, 2000) as well as an encyclopedia of intelligence (Sternberg, 1994). The field has progressed by leaps and bounds since the work in the 1970s and 1980s, and the goal of this volume is to document that progress, concentrating particularly on research that is ongoing or that has been conducted in the last 10 years.

The organization of this book is in terms of the three main approaches described here. Within these approaches, there are diverse points of view. One approach looks at biological and basic processes. A second looks at higher-order processes. And a third concentrates on developmental processes. Students of intelligence will find all three approaches represented here.

This book is written for upper division undergraduate students, graduate students, career professionals, and anyone else who wishes to understand the current landscape with respect to the study of cognition and intelligence. The book contains chapters by many of the leading contemporary figures in this field.

We are grateful to Alejandro Isgut and Cheri Stahl for assistance in the preparation of the manuscript. Preparation of the book was supported in part under Grant REC-9979843 from the U.S. National Science Foundation and the Javits Act Program (Grant No. R206R000001) as administered by the U.S. Institute of Educational Sciences, U.S. Department of Education. Grantees undertaking such projects are encouraged to express freely their professional judgment. This book, therefore, does not necessarily represent the position or policies of the National Science Foundation or the Institute of Educational Sciences, and no official endorsement should be inferred.

References

Brown, A. L., & French, A. L. (1979). The zone of potential development: Implications for intelligence testing in the year 2000. In R. J. Sternberg & D. K. Detterman (Eds.), *Human intelligence: Perspectives on its theory and measurement* (pp. 217–235). Norwood, NJ: Ablex.

Carroll, J. B. (1981). Ability and task difficulty in cognitive psychology. *Educational Researcher, 10*, 11–21.

Cronbach, L. J. (1957). The two disciplines of scientific psychology. *American Psychologist, 12*, 671–684.

Donders, F. C. (1868/1869). Over de snelheid van psychische processen. Onderzoekingen gedaan in het Physiologisch Laboratorium der Utrechtsche Hoogeschool. *Tweede reeks, II*, 92–120.

Feuerstein, R. (1980). *Instrumental enrichment: An intervention program for cognitive modifiability.* Baltimore, MD: University Park Press.

Grigorenko, E. L., & Sternberg, R. J. (1998). Dynamic testing. *Psychological Bulletin, 124*, 75–111.

Hunt, E. B. (1978). Mechanics of verbal ability. *Psychological Review, 85*, 109–130.

Hunt, E. B. (1980). Intelligence as an information-processing concept. *British Journal of Psychology, 71*, 449–474.

Hunt, E., Frost, N., & Lunneborg, C. (1973). Individual differences in cognition: A new approach to intelligence. In G. Bower (Ed.), *The psychology of learning and motivation* (Vol. 7, pp. 87–122). New York: Academic Press.

Hunt, E. B., Lunneborg, C., & Lewis, J. (1975). What does it mean to be high verbal? *Cognitive Psychology, 7*, 194–227.

Jensen, A. R. (1979). *g*: Outmoded theory of unconquered frontier? *Creative Science and Technology, 2*, 16–29.

Jensen, A. R. (1982). Reaction time and psychometric *g*. In H. J. Eysenck (Ed.), *A model for intelligence.* Heidelberg: Springer-Verlag.

Keating, D. P., & Bobbit, B. (1978). Individual and developmental differences in cognitive processing components of mental ability. *Child Development, 49*, 155–169.

Luria, A. R. (1973). *The working brain.* New York: Basic Books.

Luria, A. R. (1980). *Higher cortical functions in man* (2nd ed., revised & expanded). New York: Basic Books.

Naglieri, J. A., & Das, J. P. (1990). Planning, attention, simultaneous, and successive cognitive processes as a model for intelligence. *Journal of Psychoeducational Assessment, 8,* 303–337.

Naglieri, J. A., & Das, J. P. (1997). *Cognitive assessment system.* Itasca, IL: Riverside.

Pellegrino, J. W., & Glaser, R. (1979). Cognitive correlates and components in the analysis of individual differences. In R. J. Sternberg & D. K. Detterman (Eds.), *Human intelligence: Perspectives on its theory and measurement* (pp. 61–88). Norwood, NJ: Ablex.

Pellegrino, J. W., & Glaser, R. (1980). Components of inductive reasoning. In R. E. Snow, P. A. Federico, & W. E. Montague (Eds.), *Aptitude, learning, and instruction: Cognitive process analyses of aptitude* (Vol. 1, pp. 177–217). Hillsdale, NJ: Erlbaum.

Pellegrino, J. W., & Glaser, R. (1982). Analyzing aptitudes for learning: Inductive reasoning. In R. Glaser (Ed.), *Advances in instructional psychology* (Vol. 2). Hillsdale, NJ: Erlbaum.

Piaget, J. (1926). *The language and thought of the child.* New York: Harcourt, Brace.

Piaget, J. (1928). *Judgment and reasoning in the child.* London: Routledge & Kegan Paul.

Piaget, J. (1952). *The origins of intelligence in children.* New York: International Universities Press.

Piaget, J. (1972). *The psychology of intelligence.* Totowa, NJ: Littlefield Adams.

Posner, M. I., & Mitchell, R. F. (1967). Chronometric analysis of classification. *Psychological Review, 74,* 392–409.

Royer, F. L. (1971). Information processing of visual figures in the digit symbol substitution task. *Journal of Experimental Psychology, 87,* 335–342.

Spearman, C. (1923). *The nature of "intelligence" and the principles of cognition* (2nd ed.). London: Macmillan. (1923 edition reprinted in 1973 by Arno Press, New York.)

Spearman, C. (1927). *The abilities of man.* London: Macmillan.

Sternberg, R. J. (1977). *Intelligence, information processing, and analogical reasoning: The componential analysis of human abilities.* Hillsdale, NJ: Erlbaum.

Sternberg, R. J. (1980). Factor theories of intelligence are all right almost. *Educational Researcher, 9,* 6–13, 18.

Sternberg, R. J. (1982). Natural, unnatural, and supernatural concepts. *Cognitive Psychology, 14,* 451–488.

Sternberg, R. J. (1983). Components of human intelligence. *Cognition, 15,* 1–48.

Sternberg, R. J. (Ed.) (1994). *Encyclopedia of human intelligence.* New York: Macmillan.

Sternberg, R. J. (Ed.) (2000). *Handbook of intelligence.* New York: Cambridge University Press.

Sternberg, R. J., & Gardner, M. K. (1983). Unities in inductive reasoning. *Journal of Experimental Psychology: General, 112,* 80–116.

Sternberg, S. (1969). Memory-scanning: Mental processes revealed by reaction-time experiments. *American Scientist, 4,* 421–457.

Thorndike, E. L., Bregman, E. D., Cobb, M. V., & Woodyard, E. I. (1926). *The measurement of intelligence.* New York: Teachers College.

Vygotsky, L. S. (1978). *Mind in society: The development of higher psychological processes.* Cambridge, MA: Harvard University Press.

1

Information Processing and Intelligence

Where We Are and Where We Are Going

Earl Hunt

INTRODUCTION

Intelligence tests are about one hundred years old. If you agree with Boring (1923) that intelligence is what the intelligence tests measure, then the science of intelligence is one hundred years old. I will call this *psychometrically defined intelligence*. Empirically the study of psychometric intelligence is a booming field, for it has led to a very large literature, impressive technological developments, and coherent relationships among test scores (Carroll, 1993). However, it has a weakness.

A purely psychometric approach to intelligence lets the technology of measurement define the concept, rather than the concept defining an appropriate measurement technology. Along with many others, I prefer a more conceptual, less boring approach. The conceptual definition of intelligence as individual variation in mental competence has a longer history. In the sixteenth century the Spanish philosopher Juan Huarte de San Juan (Huarte, 1575/1991) proposed a multifaceted theory of intelligence that was not too far from today's crystallized–fluid distinction. In the nineteenth century, Galton (1883) used laboratory techniques for measuring individual differences in basic mental processes that are recognizable ancestors of paradigms used in today's laboratories. And for that matter, Binet, the founder of modern testing, was not entirely atheoretic (Sternberg, 1990). All interesting theories of intelligence try to go beyond test scores to connect individual differences with a theory of how the mind works. Developing such a theory is the province of cognitive psychology.

Nevertheless, for the first seventy or so years of the twentieth century intelligence testing and cognitive psychology followed paths that, if not orthogonal, were not closer than 60 degrees to each other. At mid-century Cronbach (1957) called for a reorientation. Psychometricians and cognitive psychologists agreed, but, like supertankers turning, it took about twenty years to see either discipline change its course.

Switching metaphors gloriously, it now appears that troop movements in response to Cronbach's trumpet call did not occur until the 1970s. At that time my colleagues and I (Hunt, Frost, & Lunneborg, 1973; Hunt, Lunneborg, & Lewis, 1975) conducted a series of studies in which we related the parameters of information processing theories, as measured by a variety of paradigms, to performance on conventional paper and pencil tests of verbal and mathematical reasoning. Foreshadowing much future research, we found that in university student populations there was a correlation in the −.3 range between the test scores and estimates of the performance parameters of models of reaction time for the paradigms that we used. The negative correlation is to be expected because the model parameters were all estimates of how long it took a person to perform a basic mental operation, such as looking up a word in a mental lexicon. Somewhat later Arthur Jensen (1982) conducted similar studies in which he related intelligence test scores to various parameters of choice reaction times. Once again the raw correlations were on the order of −.3.

Sternberg (1977) responded to Cronbach's call in a somewhat different way. Analogy problems were known to be good markers of general intelligence. Sternberg showed that the time required to solve analogies problems could be fractionated into different stages, such as encoding, mapping from one analogy to another, and verification of a hypothesized relation. In retrospect, it seems fair to say that Hunt et al. and Jensen were attempting to relate individual differences in information processing parameters to overall performance on the tests, while Sternberg was analyzing performance within test items.

At that point the dam broke. There is now a huge literature on individual differences in information processing. The topic is studied both for its own sake and because of the relation between information processing measures and scores on conventional intelligence tests, the psychometric definition of intelligence. The success of the effort is shown by the fact that some of the most active laboratories in the field are headed by people whose academic histories are completely independent of the original protagonists. Articles on individual differences in information processing appear regularly in all the major journals and constitute staple items for several of them.

The publication of this volume provides an opportunity to look back at what has been done and, with somewhat more hesitation, to attempt to identify what more needs to be done. Like any large intellectual movement, the study of information processing and intelligence has split into several subareas. The most important ones are reviewed in individual chapters in the current volume. I will try to take a larger view.

Cronbach wanted to establish a unity between two different ways of looking at human behavior. To understand what success we have had, we must know what these views are. They certainly are not the views that were held when Cronbach wrote.

Up to about 1957 behaviorism dominated human experimental psychology. This view did not lend itself to being connected to the factor-analytic view of differential psychologists. That connection had to wait for the replacement of behaviorism by information processing psychology. Modern cognitive psychology has now subsumed information processing, although information processing remains an important part of the expanded field. Similarly, differential psychology has moved well beyond the rigid view of counting factors that was implied by the data processing technology of half a century ago. To understand our present progress and future challenges, we need to see how cognitive and differential psychology look today.

THE CONCEPTS OF COGNITIVE PSYCHOLOGY

Theories and issues in cognitive psychology can be stated at the biological, information processing, or representational levels (Hunt, 2002). To understand the relation between cognitive psychology and theories of intelligence, we have to understand what these levels are.

At the biological level cognitive neuroscience attempts to associate information processing functions with brain mechanisms and processes. The idea is that the brain provides the mind with a toolkit of neural mechanisms to be used to build the functions of the mind: the ability to control attention, short- and long-term memory, maintenance of spatial orientation, and the like. The relevant mechanisms are to be located by direct observation or physiological intervention in the brain itself.

One level of abstraction higher, information processing psychology, a subset of cognitive psychology, attempts to characterize the mental functions themselves. To illustrate, memory is one of the most important aspects of human cognition; who we are is intimately tied to our imperfect remembrances of past experience. In 1957, when Cronbach wrote, memory was thought of as a unitary ability. By the 1970s the distinction between short-term and long-term memory was a basic tenet of cognitive psychology. Today we distinguish between at least half a dozen types of memories and make a strong distinction between storage and retrieval processes. The relation between the information processing and biological level is illustrated by modern attempts to identify the brain structures and processes that produce each of these different functional aspects of memory (Schacter, 1996). Because information processing measures can and have profitably been related to biological measures, information processing can be used to develop a link between biological measures and intelligence test scores.

Cognitive psychology is also concerned with higher levels of thinking, such as how people understand causation, solve logical and mathematical problems, and choose between alternative courses of action and even how religious upbringing influences one's understanding of evolutionary principles. This is cognition at the representational level because the issues to be studied are how people represent the world to themselves and how these representations influence their behavior. Representational-level thinking emerges from the brain, for the mind cannot have a thought that the brain cannot support. However, it turns out that this is a conceptual "bridge too far." It is more useful to think of representational-level thinking as emerging from the interaction between information processing capacities and the individual's social environment.

Outside of psychology the term "thinking" almost always refers to thought at the representational level. To a layperson psychological investigation of what eyewitnesses (or physics students) can be counted on to remember seems immanently reasonable. A psychological investigation of how people remember lists of arbitrary paired associates requires a bit more justification. The layperson has a point; ultimately we are interested in the thinking that reflects what people do, not how people behave in a laboratory setting.

What might cognitive psychology tell us about representational-level thinking? First, representational-level thinking emerges from the interaction between information processing capacities and an individual's social and physical environment. Accordingly, some common themes, dictated by information processing capacities, should apply to everyone. On the other hand, understanding the individual requires an understanding of both the format in which the information is held and the content of the information itself. The content is obviously a product of the individual's life history.

To remove the discussion from complete abstraction, I offer two examples. My treatment will be brief. For further discussion of these topics, see Hunt (2002, Chaps. 8–11).

The first, and clearest, is language. Modern linguistic theories assume that all human languages follow rather restricted information processing principles that govern, for instance, the permissible types of transformations from deep to surface structure. On the other hand, the natural languages are clearly different in many ways. The extent to which the form and content of a natural language influence the thought of its speakers (the *Whorfian hypothesis*) is a matter of debate. It would take us too far afield to explore the topic here. My point is solely that this is a reasonable topic for investigation, and one that could have considerable implications for individual variations in mental competence.

The second example involves the names of common animals. Cognitive psychologists interested in "thinking in general" have often investigated how American college students represent animal names as a way of understanding how classes are represented, and understanding how properties of classes and of individuals within a class influence both inductive and deductive reasoning. Lopez et al. (1997) developed models of knowledge about animals held by American college students and by the Itzaj Maya, a Central American group of forest dwellers. They found that the formal mechanisms for holding information about animals were similar for both groups. Animals were categorized by size, ferocity, certain biological properties, and ecological niche. However the weight placed on different dimensions of similarity varied. (The Maya placed more weight on ecological niche.) Furthermore, these differences led to understandable between-group differences in the conclusions that Americans and Maya reached when presented with evidence about new properties of animals, for example, that a certain animal was susceptible to an exotic disease. You could not understand the thinking of the groups unless you had an understanding both of culture-general "data structure" showing how information about animals was held and the culture-specific information about what each group knew, and what they regarded as important.

The sorts of issues I have just raised are ones that probably would not have even occurred to a behaviorist. By 1970 information processing psychology was a step beyond the behaviorist's insistence on unitary mechanisms of learning. As of the early twenty-first century the expansion had gone beyond information processing to look at brain processes in one direction and social–cultural correlates in another.

What had happened to theories of psychometric intelligence?

THEORIES OF PSYCHOMETRIC INTELLIGENCE

Psychometric intelligence has been buttressed by, and sometimes plagued by, the success or failure of technology. In the nineteenth century Galton attempted to account for individual differences in mental competence in terms of what we would now call information processing measures. He and his immediate successors failed, at least in their own eyes, because they could not find high correlations between their information processing tests and other indicators of intellectual competence, such as school grades. Interestingly, the correlations they did find are in the range observed in modern studies relating intelligence tests to information processing measures (Sternberg, 1990). The facts have not changed, but our definition of success has!

When Binet and Simon introduced the modern intelligence test, performance on such tests and in academics related to the test became the de facto definition of intelligence. For instance, Spearman's original argument for a general factor in intelligence was based on the analysis of the grades of English schoolchildren (Carroll, 1993). By 1957 when Cronbach sounded his trumpet, discussions of theories of intelligence had devolved into a debate over the factor structure of representative batteries of such tests: Do have a single general factor (g) or are there multiple dimensions of individual differences *within the constraints of what had come, by convention, to be called "intelligence tests"*?

The one-factor versus multifactor debate has very largely been settled. Carroll (1993) showed that the best fit to the psychometric data is a three-layer model, very close to the one developed by Cattell (1971) and Horn (Horn, 1985; Horn & Noll, 1994). The Cattell–Horn model is based on the idea that there are three broad abilities: fluid intelligence (g_f), crystallized intelligence (g_c) and spatial-visual intelligence (g_v). Loosely speaking, g_f is the ability to develop solutions to relatively novel problems, g_c is the ability to apply previously learned solution methods to the current problem, and g_v is the ability to reason spatially. In most populations g_c and g_f are correlated, with the degree of correlation ranging anywhere from .5 to nearly 1.0. However, g_v tends to stand further apart, having correlations generally in the .4 to .5 range, or even lower, with g_c and g_f measures.

Because g_c and g_f are correlated, and often highly correlated, a number of authors (most notably Jensen, 1998; but see also Gottfredson, 1997) have argued that they are all manifestations of a single underlying construct, general intelligence (g). The argument is usually accompanied by a codicil in which it is stated that g_f and g are virtually identical, a point that is questioned immediately below.

The correlation between g_c and g_f could arise in two different ways. One, of course, is that something called general intelligence exists, and that tests of g_f and g_c are different manifestations of the same thing. The alternative is a sort of investment theory, first maintained by Cattell (1971), in which people invest their fluid intelligence in different learning experiences, and thus acquire g_c. A less-than-perfect correlation would be expected because different people, with identical g_f capabilities, might have different experiences and thus would acquire different levels of g_c.

Detterman and Daniel (1989), and since them several other authors in independent studies (Abad et al., 2003; Deary et al., 1996; Hunt, 1995b), discovered a fact that is important for this debate. Correlations between different intelligence tests are higher in populations of generally lower intellectual competence. With the exceptions of a few special syndromes (e.g., Turner's syndrome cases, where there is a selective loss of spatial-visual ability), correlations between test scores of mentally retarded individuals are quite high. By contrast, a great deal of differentiation of ability is seen in examinations of people whose ability is relatively high overall. Statistically, at low levels of ability a wide variety of tests load on a general factor, while at high levels of ability there is a pronounced g_c–g_f differentiation. Going still further, we would expect that people whose educational and life experiences differ (e.g., college students who pursue different majors, adults following different professions) would show distinctions within the

g_c field, depending upon precisely what aspects of previously acquired knowledge and problem-solving methods are being evaluated.

Today's definition of psychometric intelligence features (a) a strong general intelligence factor for the lower ranges of ability in the population, with a possible distinction between g and g_f and (b) differentiation along the g_f–g_c lines at higher levels of ability.

This theory is clearly well amplified beyond theories of intelligence circa 1957 and even circa 1975. The amplifications are very important for an attempt to unite the concepts of cognitive psychology to the concepts of intelligence theory. Three points stand out.

The first point is that the population matters. Information processing measures that depend upon fairly mechanistic performance, such as well-practiced reaction time measures or measures of perceptual speed, would be expected to have their greatest effect in populations where g is an important variable, because these measures presumably tap neural efficiency properties that apply to virtually all cognition. On the other hand, as specialized performance becomes more important, basic information processing capacity may be less important than the knowledge a person has and the strategies by which a person utilizes his or her capacity. Therefore correlations between simple information processing measures and intelligence test scores should increase when the sample is drawn from a population of lower general mental ability. Indeed, that is what Detterman and Daniel (1989) found.

The second point is that the test matters, especially when dealing with populations of average and above-average abilities. This caution is particularly important when intelligence theorists try to go outside of test scores to relate intelligence, as defined by a test, to the broader definition of intelligence defined by individual differences in competence in socially important areas. Much of the evidence for a connection between test scores and indices of success is drawn from studies using either the Wechsler Adult Intelligence Scale (WAIS), the Armed Services Vocational Aptitude Battery (ASVAB), or the Scholastic Assessment Test (SAT). The conclusion is usually that "general intelligence matters." See, for instance, discussions by Gottfredson (1997) and Herrnstein and Murray (1994). However, in the populations for which they were intended these tests load on crystallized intelligence (g_c), not g or g_f (Horn, 1985; Roberts et al., 2000). The importance of this distinction for the debate over whether intelligence counts "in the real world" is obvious. The importance of the distinction for the relation between cognitive psychology and the study of intelligence will be discussed later, when we look to the future of the relationship.

The third point has to do with the recurrent debate over whether intelligence is inherited. Present findings, based upon many studies of adoption and pedigree, show clearly that within the variety of environments that occur in the developed industrial societies, intelligence test scores behave as if they have heritability coefficients in the .5 to .8 range. Sadly, that convoluted sentence is necessary. Were studies to be conducted in societies with greater social heterogeneity (e.g., societies in which some groups are close to starvation or where some children's educations have been disrupted by war) or in societies with less genetic heterogeneity, we would expect the heritability coefficient to go down. What the present studies clearly do show is that under the conditions that apply to well over half the world, genetics does matter.

Tracing the information processing–test score link and tracing the genetic composition–test score link are both reductionist enterprises. Obviously no one inherits a test score in the same sense that a person inherits eye color. However, one might inherit information processing capabilities that would then, in appropriate environments, predispose a person to have a particular test score. Discouragingly, though, there has been relatively little exploration of this link.

Most attempts to respond to Cronbach's call have accepted the psychometric definition of intelligence. However, there are three major exceptions to this trend. Gardner (1983; Gardner, Kornhaber, & Wake, 1996) has argued for a much broader view. Gardner includes under intelligence such topics as individual differences in musical, social, and physical (motor control) skills. Sternberg and his colleagues in many writings (Sternberg, 1988, 1996; Sternberg et al., 2000) have been somewhat less catholic. They argue that conventional tests tap skills required in academic settings but fail to reflect individual differences in creativity (creative intelligence) and cognitive competence in everyday, nonacademic settings (practical intelligence). Goleman (1995) has argued for the existence of emotional intelligence, which he defines both as self-awareness of, and control over, one's own emotional reactions and an ability to recognize and react to other people's emotional state.

These movements have stricken a chord with a public that is somewhat wary of the idea that it is possible to evaluate a person's mental competence using a test that takes less than three hours to complete. A complete analysis of all the ramifications of these expansions of the "intelligence is what the tests measure" view is beyond the scope of this chapter. A few words are in order about how these expansions of the term "intelligence" might influence attempts to understand intelligence in terms of variations in individual information processing capacities.

Plato is supposed to have advised that in attempting to understand nature we should carve it at its joints. This is usually taken to mean that when we define a field of study, that field should be constrained along some recognizable lines. More formally, if x, y, and z are measurements of behaviors that are within a specific field (e.g., intelligence), then x should be sensitive to perturbations in y and z, and similarly for all other pairings. At the same time, x, y, and z should be relatively insensitive to, or should be responsive in the same way, to perturbations in a fourth variable, w, that is defined to be outside the field. Note that this implies that measurements of w, x, y, and z exist. Philosophy ~~may be able to~~ exist without measurement but science cannot. *can*

As discussed later, we have a rather good idea of what information processing capacities are related to cognitive competence. We are also well on the way to identifying the brain structures that provide these capacities. Similarly, we are also well on the way to understanding the brain structures that underlie emotional responses (LeDoux, 2002). Most importantly, we know that the brain structures underlying cognition and emotion are not identical. This suggests that it might be a good idea to make a fairly strong distinction between individual differences in emotional sensitivity and individual differences in more "cold-blooded" cognitive skills. Of course, this conclusion mirrors the long-time practice in psychometrics, where a distinction is drawn between intelligence and personality tests.

Goleman's emotional intelligence and several of Gardner's multiple intelligences seem to fall more in the personality than the intelligence realm. This conclusion in no way diminishes the importance of studying these variables or of studying the interaction between traits identified in the personality and intelligence realms. It is a good idea to remember that personality and cognitive competence may well be two separate systems of individual variation.

Sternberg's expansion of intelligence, on the other hand, does retain a distinctly cognitive flavor. The measures that Sternberg and his colleagues have designed measure people's ability to identify culturally acceptable solutions to problems that (a) lie outside of problems that can be addressed using information that is typically taught in schools and (b) do not ask examinees to deal with virtually content-free problems in pattern induction. Sternberg et al. make two claims. They contend that performance on practical and creative problems should be considered in the definition of intelligence and they further contend that they have developed appropriate tests of creative and practical intelligence.

The first contention is a matter of definition, and I suspect that virtually no one would disagree. See, for instance, Gottfredson's (1997) discussion of the practicality of general intelligence, as measured by conventional tests.

The second contention is an empirical claim about tests that exist at a particular point in time. There are two ways that this contention could be rejected. One would be to show that *all* reliable variance in cognitive performance outside the testing arena is related to variance on conventional test scores. This is patently not true. The strongest advocates for the use of tests of general intelligence in personnel selection claim, at most, a correlation of .5 between test performance and job performance (Hunt, 1995a; Schmidt and Hunter, 1998).

Panel A

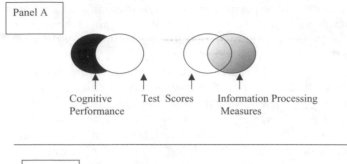

Cognitive   Test Scores   Information Processing
Performance   Measures

Panel B

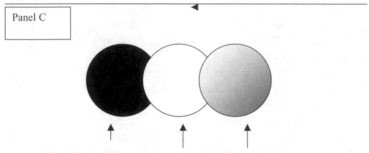

Cognitive Performance Information Processing Test Scores
                       Measures

Panel C

Cognitive Performance Test Scores Information Processing
                                    Measures

FIGURE 1. Possible configurations of shared variation between information processing measures, extra-laboratory performance, and conventional intelligence tests. The configuration in Panel A must exist, but it could be produced by the configurations in either Panels B or C.

Another way to reject the contention would be to show that all variation in cognitive performance not associated with test scores is associated with properties of the situation in which performance is assessed, rather than properties of the person being assessed. While this is not impossible in principle, at present no such demonstration exists.

Given that the contention cannot be rejected, can it be affirmed? This issue has to be settled on a case-by-case basis. See, for instance, the exchange between Brody (2003) and Sternberg (2003). The essence of that exchange was that Brody showed that a particular set of results that had been put forward as evidence for measured cognitive performance "outside of general intelligence" had a variety of defects and could not be used as proof that the contention was correct. Sternberg, in his reply, referred to as-yet-unpublished data that he hoped would provide proof that measurements exist that both relate to cognitive performance outside the laboratory and are not part of conventional test theory. When these data are published they will, of course, be critiqued and may or may not be accepted as evidence that practical intelligence has been identified and measured. If accepted, the issue will be settled. If not, we can always go on to the next measurement.

This controversy has implications for discussions of the role of individual differences in information processing as indicators of intelligence, in the broad sense of intellectual competence, rather than in the narrower sense of predicting test scores. The possibilities are shown in Figure 1. Panel A of Figure 1 shows what we know: that intelligence test scores are reliably but less than perfectly related to individual differences in information processing and that cognitive performance, outside of the laboratory, is reliably but less than perfectly related to test scores. Panel B of Figure 1 shows one interpretation of these facts; that individual differences in information processing provide a substantial part of the link between test scores and extra-laboratory performance. Panel C shows another, less interesting possibility. The variance in test scores that is related to general cognitive performance (the whole point of having the test) might be separate from the variance related to individual differences in information processing ability.

We can then ask where practical intelligence, or any other personal property related to cognitive performance, would fit in. Some possibilities are shown in Figure 2. By definition, the practical intelligence–performance

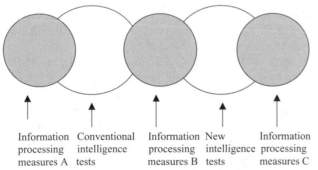

Information	Conventional	Information	New	Information
processing	intelligence	processing	intelligence	processing
measures A	tests	measures B	tests	measures C

FIGURE 2. Possible configurations of information processing measures, conventional intelligence tests, and hypothetical new measures, such as practical intelligence. Based on our present knowledge, either information processing measures in set A or set B or both must exist. There is no information concerning the existence or nonexistence of set C.

link has to be outside the conventional intelligence–performance link. Individual differences in information processing might be related only to test scores, or there might be two sets of information processing measures, one set related to intelligence as conventionally assessed and the other set related to the new measures. At present we do not have any information that discriminates between these and other configurations of shared variation.

Let us now move from theory to discussion of some specific findings.

EARLY ATTEMPTS: RELATING THE PARAMETERS OF INFORMATION PROCESSING MODELS TO SPECIFIC DIMENSIONS OF PSYCHOMETRIC INTELLIGENCE

Information processing models specify a process by which some action is taken (e.g., identification of a word or decision to choose one of several responses) and then specify methods for estimating parameters of the process. One way to develop a theory of individual differences in information processing is to determine which parameters do (or do not) show substantial individual differences and to relate these individual differences to other properties of the individual, including intelligence test scores.

To illustrate, one of the basic processes in reading a phonetic language is associating names with arbitrary symbols, such as associating the word form CAT with the English word "Cat." Posner et al. (1969) developed a technique for measuring this process. Respondents were asked to determine, as quickly as possible, whether two symbols had identical names. Suppose that the two symbols are "A..A." These symbols are physically identical (PI). Therefore they must have the same name, whatever that name is. Suppose, though, that the symbols are "A..a." These symbols are name identical (NI) but not physically identical. Posner et al. found that college students took, on the average, about 80 milliseconds more to respond to an NI than to a PI pair. This came to be called the NI–PI difference score. It was taken as a measure of the time it takes to associate a visual symbol with a name. Reading, an important cognitive skill, is based on the ability to make such associations.

Hunt and his colleagues (Hunt, Frost, & Lunneborg, 1973; Hunt, Lunneborg, & Lewis, 1975) extended this finding, showing that college students with high scores on a test of verbal comprehension (similar to the SAT verbal scale) showed a difference of only 60 milliseconds between name and physical identification, while students with low verbal comprehension scores showed a difference of about 100 milliseconds. More generally, the NI–PI score had a correlation of about −.3 with verbal comprehension test scores in a college population. Speculatively, this could indicate that part of the variation in very complex verbal tasks, such as those that make up psychometric tests of verbal ability, is due to the speed with which people access their mental lexicon.

Subsequent studies tested this hypothesis more directly. For instance, Palmer et al. (1985), once again using a college population, showed that there was a correlation of −.4 between scores on reading tests and the time required to distinguish between common English words such as CART and pronounceable nonwords such as TARC.

Access to the lexicon is an important part of verbal comprehension, but it is not all of it. In addition to retrieving word meanings, the comprehender must combine them to make sense out of sentences and paragraphs. This requires the manipulation of information in working memory. Research on "span tasks," in which people are asked to comprehend sentences while simultaneously holding unrelated information in memory, has shown that individual differences in the ability to hold information in immediate memory are also very clearly associated with performance on more complicated linguistic tasks, such as sentence and paragraph comprehension. See Daneman and Merikle (1996) for a review of much of this research, and MacDonald, Just, and Carpenter (1992) for a particularly good example of how individual differences in working memory can be related to the act of parsing a sentence.

Verbal comprehension depends upon a number of controlled, conscious processes, such as recognizing the name of a word form or gaining the gist of a sentence. These processes, in turn, rely partly upon automatic processes for arranging information in a timely fashion and for resolving ambiguities. One of the most important of the automatic processes is the spread of activation from a recognized item to other items that are associated with it either semantically or statistically. One of the questions we can ask, then, is whether both automatic and controlled processes exhibit substantial individual differences.

Apparently they do not. To see this, let us look again at the Palmer et al. (1985) paper, which indicated that there are substantial individual differences in lexical identification, as explained above. Palmer et al. also evaluated an automatic phenomenon called priming, in which the exposure of a visual word facilitates the recognition of semantically related words. For instance, the word DOCTOR is recognized more quickly if it is preceded by NURSE than if it is preceded by BUTTER. Although the existence of priming is not in question – indeed it was demonstrated in the Palmer et al. study – priming does not display large individual differences.

This observation is interesting in light of later research, which has led to the conclusion that human reasoning can be divided into two broad systems: automatic processes that proceed rapidly, on the basis of statistical associations between and temporal contiguity of stimuli, and controlled processes that proceed much more slowly and are under conscious control (Hunt, 2002; Sloman, 1996). This distinction has largely been ignored in studies of the relation between information processing measures and intelligence. However, it may explain an important phenomenon; the relation between intelligence measures and expertise in a particular field. Ackerman (Chap. 8 in this volume) points out that intelligence tests are generally not good predictors of individual differences in performance after asymptotic performance levels have been reached. This may be true because experts, who have benefited from extensive practice, rely more on automated than controlled processing.

The research on verbal comprehension was not an attempt to "explain intelligence." It was an attempt to relate an important and definable dimension of human variability, the ability to comprehend language, to individual differences in the information processing components that underlie performance along this dimension. There was no claim that individual differences in information processing account for all verbal comprehension; obviously environmental variables (predominantly schooling) will be important. Nevertheless, understanding individual differences in those information processing tasks that are part of any act of verbal comprehension is an important goal.

Similar attempts have been made to fractionate visual reasoning into its information processing components. Space does not permit a review of this interesting line of research. Suffice it to say that three correlated abilities have been identified. They are the ability to (1) imagine movement or distortion of an object, (2) isolate a figure against a complicated background, and (3) deal with an actual perception of motion. It is also of interest that other research, not primarily aimed at individual differences, has shown that working memory for spatial-visual tasks is somewhat different from working memory for verbal tasks (Logie, 1995). This finding is consistent with brain imaging studies that identified different regions for verbal and spatial-visual working memories (Smith & Jonides, 1997).

SPEED OF INFORMATION PROCESSING AND GENERAL INTELLIGENCE

The research just described represents an attempt to connect information processing models of specific areas of cognition to demonstrated individual differences in those areas. There has also been considerable progress in connecting information processing measures to indices of general intelligence (g) and fluid intelligence (g_f). Indeed these terms are often used synonymously, although, as noted above, there is question about whether this is appropriate, especially at higher levels of general competence.

Tests of general intelligence appear to evaluate several cognitive abilities at once. This is obvious for tests made up of a battery of subtests, such as the Wechsler Adult Intelligence Scale. It is equally true, albeit less explicitly obvious, for tests that appear to consist of homogeneous items, such as a progressive matrix test or numerical analogies tests. In this case the items themselves are complicated, draw on different information processing capacities (e.g., short-term memory or the ability to abstract features from a perceptual display), and are often amenable to several strategies. See, for instance, the analysis of different types of test items by Carpenter, Just, and Shell (1990), Embretson (Chap. 13, this volume), Hunt (1974), and Sternberg (1977). If individual differences in mental competence, that is, intelligence in the conceptual sense, depends upon the ability to deploy a variety of information processing capacities, attempts to relate intelligence to any one of these capacities will have only limited success unless this capacity is either pervasive throughout the nervous system or refers to a component of information processing that is used in a wide variety of tasks.

Two candidate information processing capacities have been suggested. One is simply neural processing speed. The argument is that the nervous system is essentially an information transmission system, so therefore the efficiency of the cabling should be reflected in the system's performance on virtually any task. Jensen (Chap. 2, this volume) has been a prominent advocate of this proposition.

In his early work Jensen (1982) attempted to find a "pure" measure of information processing speed. Hick (1952), and since then many others, found that in a choice reaction time (CRT) task, when people are asked to identify a stimulus as being one of a set of N familiar stimuli (e.g., identifying a number as being either 1, 5, or 7, or indicating that one of $N < 9$ lamps has been lit) the time required to do so is a linear function of the logarithm of the set size. This is interesting because it suggests an extremely efficient process for searching long-term memory. The key measure is the slope of the function relating choice time to the logarithm of the number of possible alternatives. Jensen took this parameter as a measure of internal neural efficiency and, in a number of studies, related the slope measure to scores on measures of general intelligence (g). There is indeed a reliable correlation between the slope measure and measures of general intelligence, but it is only $-.17$ (Jensen, 1998, p. 212). As in the case of the NI–PI measure, a negative correlation is expected because latency is being related to intelligence, with long latencies associated with lower test scores.

A closer examination of research related to CRT latency presents some interesting results. The latency of a choice can be broken down into two components, one (choice time) that is supposed to reflect the time required to determine what response is appropriate and another (movement time) that reflects the time required to make the response. To the extent that choice is "cognitive" and movement is "motor," one would expect intelligence test scores to be related to choice time but not to movement time. In practice, though, the results are highly varied. It appears that the choice time–intelligence correlation is only slightly higher than the movement

...ne–intelligence correlation. This suggests that the key variable is some general property of the nervous system, such as neural efficiency, that is involved in both choice and movement times. Therefore, more recently Jensen (Chap. 2, this volume) has suggested that the overall decision time or CRT, especially for choices involving several alternatives, may be the most appropriate measure. When this is done the correlations can rise to the .2–.4 range (in absolute magnitude).

There is a good argument for using the overall CRT latency measure. Suppose that the observed latency (time to make a choice) is divided into three components: the time required to make the decision, the time required to make the response, and a random measurement error component whose variance is independent of the other two processes. The more complex the decision, the longer the time required to make it. Therefore the percentage of variance in the observed latency that might be expected to be due to individual differences in cognition will be larger, relative to the measurement error, for complex, time-consuming decisions than it will be for simple decisions.

Jensen has also argued that the within individual variance in choice reaction time reflects, in part, inconsistent neural processing. Therefore the variance should be negatively related to general intelligence test scores. While this is a reasonable argument, the evidence for it seems to be, as it were, variable. It is also worth noting, though, that Jensen's argument assumes that estimates of the expected time to make a decision and estimates of the variance of that time are independent. It has long been known that an individual's reaction times are not normally distributed. Some of the models used to analyze reaction times assume distributions in which the expectation and the variance are functions of the same underlying parameter (Luce, 1986; McGill, 1963). If these models are correct, then including the variance as well as the mean as a predictor of an intelligence test score simply increases the reliability of the predictor rather than sampling a different process.

Choice reaction time tasks have two undesirable characteristics. First, it can take a large number of training trials before reaction times stabilize. This may not be appreciated by researchers on individual differences, who have often used far fewer training trials than is customary in research on information processing models per se. Research by Ackerman and others (see Chap. 8, this volume) on tasks very similar to the CRT task has shown that the correlation between latencies and tests of general intelligence is higher in the earlier stages of training than in the later ones. This suggests that the correlations reported by Jensen, and by the many others who have used his procedure, may have more to do with the participant's speed at figuring out how to deal with the apparatus (e.g., establishing a response set) than with the efficiency of neural processing.

The second undesirable property is reliability. As Jensen (Chap. 2, this volume) points out, choice reaction latencies are highly reliable ($r \sim .9$) within a single session. However, the correlation between individual reaction times, taken in sessions as little as five days apart, falls to about .6. The discrepancy between these two statistics indicates that the problem is not measurement error. Instead, the process being measured by the CRT paradigm is itself somewhat variable over time. On the one hand, this suggests that the correlation between intelligence test scores (which are stable over a period of more than a year) and the "true, consistent" component of choice reaction time is even higher than the observed .2–.4. This is interesting on theoretical grounds. On practical grounds, though, the day-to-day variability in reaction times is enough to rule out the CRT paradigm as a replacement for intelligence tests in any practical setting.

An alternative approach to measuring general processing speed is to utilize a perceptual task that is less amenable to the examinee's response strategies. The *inspection time paradigm* (Nettlebeck, 1987) has been widely used for this purpose. Two stimuli are presented for a brief, experimenter-controlled time. They differ on a single physical dimension (e.g., two lines of different length or two successive tones of different pitch). The observer's task is to detect which of the stimuli is longer or higher. The minimum exposure time needed to make a reliable judgment is taken as a measure of the observer's internal processing speed. The initial results with this measure were extremely promising, but appear to have been heavily influenced by the inclusion of extreme groups, such as combined analyses of data from college students and mental retardates. A meta-analysis of subsequent studies (Grudnik & Kranzler, 2001) has shown an uncorrected correlation of about $-.3$ between inspection time and a variety of intelligence test scores. (If one is willing to make various statistical assumptions the "true score," disregarding both unreliability of measurement and possible restriction in range of the population being tested, the correlation is $-.51$.) Insofar as this author knows, there are little data concerning day-to-day variability in the inspection time measure. Analyses of inspection time in multivariate studies (e.g., Nettlebeck, 2001) indicate that this measure loads on a general perceptual speed factor and, through it, on a general intelligence factor.

On the whole, measures that we can reasonably regard as evaluations of "mental speed" seem to account for 10 to 15% of the variance of scores on intelligence tests, as measured in a typical study. If we are willing to make various statistical corrections, especially for the restricted range of test scores in any one study, the estimate rises to 25% of the variance. These corrections depend upon assumptions about the relation of the measured distribution to the distribution in a hypothetical "general population," and in particular, depend upon the assumption that scores on both the information processing and intelligence variables are multivariate normally distributed in the unmeasured general population. In fact, though, as was pointed out earlier, the multivariate normal assumption is false. Intelligence test scores become more differentiated as the general level of intelligence increases, and the relation between intelligence test scores and information processing measures increases as the general intelligence level falls.

Therefore the safest thing to say is that (1) the 10–15% figure holds for most young adult populations of average to slightly above average general ability, (2) the figure would certainly rise if the entire range of the population were to be sampled, and (3) the figure is probably higher for populations in the lower IQ ranges and lower in populations with exceptionally high general intelligence scores.

A straightforward interpretation of these results is that some people simply have brains that work faster than other people. This hypothesis has received striking, albeit indirect, support from observations of neural processing as people are asked to solve problems. In the late 1980s brain imaging techniques were developed that make it possible to measure metabolic activity in various areas of the brain as a person attempts to attack a cognitive problem. This work, which is discussed later by Neubauer and Fink (Chap. 4) and by Newman and Just (Chap. 5), has shown that better problem solvers and more intelligent individuals, as indicated by test scores, show less metabolic activity than do individuals with poorer problem-solving abilities. This could happen in two different ways. It could be that the better problem solvers simply have more efficient neural systems. That is, when faced with a problem, their brains perform more efficiently at a fixed level of organization. Alternatively it could be that better problem solvers have developed a better organization of brain systems, analogous to smooth motion in motor systems, so that less neural processing is required to achieve the same information processing result. At present there is no evidence to indicate which of these hypotheses is correct. The distinction is important because more efficient organization could be achieved by more rapid learning (Garlick, 2002). At present, though, there is no evidence that would discriminate between the performance and learning explanation for the test score–processing speed correlation.

To close this section, two caveats are in order. One is about what we do not know. The argument that neural efficiency and/or neural processing speed accounts for the relation between general intelligence and information processing measures of speediness implies that the new measures of brain metabolism account for the same portion of variance in test scores as do information processing measures, such as the CRT and inspection time measures. Put another way, the partial correlation between test scores and metabolic measures should vanish once behavioral measures of speediness are held constant. This hypothesis has not yet been tested.

The second caveat concerns a misinterpretation of the speediness–test score relation. Several critics of neural speediness as an explanation for intelligence have pointed out that it is not always good to be fast. Indeed, while rapid responding is valued in some cultures, such as questioning the speaker at a graduate colloquium or responding to a challenge in a debate, in other cultures rapid responding is seen as a sign of immaturity and foolhardiness. This objection to speed measures misses the point. What the speediness studies have shown is that individuals with higher test scores have the ability to make simple decisions more rapidly than individuals with low test scores. The extent to which a person would exercise that ability in a particular situation is an entirely different issue. Indeed, the ability to inhibit a response, when appropriate, turns out to be an important part of intelligence. We now turn to this issue.

LOOKING FOR A PERVASIVE FUNCTION: WORKING MEMORY

The research on reaction time and inspection time measures was motivated by the idea that a pervasive neural process might explain intelligence. An alternative approach is to examine individual differences in an information processing function and ultimately a brain function that is required by practically all intellectual acts. Consider the following analogy. Suppose that we observed two carpenters, one of whom was markedly quicker and more accurate in building furniture. It could be that the more adept carpenter had quicker, more accurate motor movements. However, it could be that the more adept carpenter had a larger, better organized workbench. Or both explanations could be true. Keeping this analogy in mind may help the reader follow the argument in the rest of this section.

Modern theories of cognition emphasize working memory as a pervasive component of reasoning. As the name suggests, working memory refers to the ability to keep in mind different aspects of a currently active problem, for example, a driver's being aware that there is a vehicle to the left rear, where it cannot be seen. Much of the evidence for the importance of working memory rests upon tasks that demand control of attention, either to switch back and forth from one stream of information to another (think of a person listening to the radio while driving) or that require people to perform one task while ignoring irrelevant stimuli (think of carrying on a conversation at a cocktail party) (Baddely, 1986, 1992).

Working memory is required for many tasks that we normally think of as displaying intelligence. Spearman's (1923) definition of general intelligence stressed the importance of seeing common patterns and relations in multiple cases. If a person is going to compare two or more pieces of information, it must be possible to keep them both in mind at the same time.

iven the importance of working memory in general theories of cognition, it is natural to investigate the relationship between measures of working memory and psychometric intelligence test scores. One of the earliest modern studies of information processing and intelligence reported a correlation between the speed of scanning information in immediate memory and scores on tests of mathematical ability (Hunt et al., 1973). Hunt (1980) also noted that groups of individuals of widely varying mental capacity differed markedly in the speed with which they scanned short-term memory. Unfortunately these findings were not developed at the time.

 Kyllonen and his colleagues (Kyllonen & Christal, 1990; Kyllonen & Stephens, 1990) deserve credit for the first substantial findings tying working memory capacity to abstract reasoning. They showed that individual variation on tests of abstract reasoning could almost entirely be accounted for, statistically, by measures of working memory capacity. Subsequent research tied working memory capacity to models of performance on the well-known Raven's Progressive Matrices test (Carpenter et al., 1990) and to models of sentence comprehension (MacDonald et al., 1992).

Engle and his colleagues have carried this research forward in an important way by more precisely defining working memory (Hambrick, Kane, & Engle, Chap. 6, this volume). The gist of their findings is that the ability to keep several pieces of information in mind at once depends upon the ability to suppress responding to those aspects of a situation that are irrelevant to the problem at hand. It is worth noting that this finding is consistent with findings on attention deficit disorder, a syndrome in which schoolchildren (and in some cases adults) are unable to function well because they cannot concentrate their attention in the face of distractions.

Unlike response time measures, working memory measures do not show much fluctuation over time, at least when the measurement situation is "normal."

So, does whatever underlies intelligence test scores depend upon working memory capacity or general processing speed? The answer appears to be that both are important. Schretlen et al. (2000), in a well-designed study involving participants varying across the entire adult range, found that combined measures of speed, working memory, and frontal lobe volume could account for almost 60% of the variance in scores on a measure of fluid intelligence.

PROSPECTUS

Cognitive psychologists may have taken twenty years to respond to Cronbach's call to study individual differences, but once the response movement began it met with success. The research reviewed here is the tip of a very large iceberg of research papers relating individual differences in information processing to measures of general intellectual functioning, such as intelligence test scores. It is now clear that individual differences in information processing are responsible for a substantial part, but not all, of general mental competence. The relationship is particularly strong for measures of abstract, analytical reasoning. Lohman in Chapter 12 points out correctly that this is an important function, but that understanding analytic reasoning does not explain all human thought because a substantial part of our mental power depends upon combining reasoning ability with the possession of specific knowledge.

But where do we go from here? The answer to this question depends upon which of the two research goals is meant. Is the goal of research the reductionist one of understanding the link among brain mechanisms, information processing, and intelligence, in the conceptual sense? Or is it the expansionist goal of understanding the relation between individual differences in cognition and success in the world outside of the laboratory?

Work toward the reductionist goal is well advanced. For instance, we now know that structures in the dorsolateral prefrontal cortex are active during tasks that involve working memory, which suggests strongly that differences in the efficiency of this structure underlie some individual differences in human reasoning capacity (Kane & Engle, 2002). We do not know how the process by which the prefrontal cortex and other related structures achieve working memory functions, but that knowledge will come. We are similarly aware of the structures involved in memory storage, spatial reasoning, and a variety of linguistic functions, but we do not know how these structures work in an information processing sense.

It is reasonable to expect that in the next fifty years there will be substantial advances in understanding how the brain produces differences in information processing capacity. If we couple these advances with advances in molecular genetics, we are very likely to understand how nurture makes its contribution to the product of nature and nurture that we call intelligence, especially that part of intelligence that can be measured by conventional tests.

What is much less clear, though, is how the study of information processing is going to contribute to the expansionist goal of understanding individual differences in cognitive performance in "real life." Theories of intelligence have, of late, tended to concentrate on measures of "general intelligence" (cf. Jensen, 1998). In fact, the picture is more complicated. The closest real picture for intelligence is the g_c–g_f–g_v hierarchy. Furthermore the tests that appear to be the highest correlates of performance in school and the workplace are tests of crystallized intelligence, such as the SAT, ASVAB, and WAIS, rather than tests of fluid intelligence. As was pointed out earlier, these are tests of g_c, not g_f of g. And what is g_c? The ability to apply previously acquired information and problem-solving methods to the current problem. Knowledge counts.

What is needed is a better understanding of how information processing capacities are involved in the process of knowledge acquisition and use. These studies need to go beyond studies of the application of knowledge to include understanding of strategies of problem solving. This research will inevitably involve understanding particular situations. It is going to be difficult to draw general principles across applications. In spite of the difficulty, though, the task must be done. Understanding what drives performance on an intelligence test is not interesting in itself. It is interesting only if the finding assists us in understanding variations in cognitive competence in life.

References

Abad, F. J., Colom, R., Juan-Espinosa, M., & Garcia, L. F. (2003). Intelligence differentiation in adult samples. *Intelligence, 31*(2), 157–166.

Baddeley, A. D. (1986). *Working memory*. Oxford: Oxford University Press.

Baddeley, A. D. (1992). Working memory. *Science, 255*, 556–559.

Boring, E. G. (1923). Intelligence as the tests test it. *New Republic, 35*(June 6), 35–37.

Brody, N. (2003). Construct validation of the Sternberg Triarchic Abilities Test: Comment and reanalysis. *Intelligence, 31*(4), 319–330.

Carpenter, P. A., Just, M. A., & Shell, P. (1990). What one intelligence test measures. A theoretical account of processing in the Raven Progressive Matrix Test. *Psychological Review, 97*(3), 404–431.

Carroll, J. B. (1993). *Human cognitive abilities*. Cambridge, UK: Cambridge University Press.

Cattell, R. B. (1971). *Abilities: Their structure, growth, and action*. Boston: Houghton Mifflin.

Cronbach, L. J. (1957). The two disciplines of scientific psychology. *American Psychologist, 12*, 671–684.

Daneman, M., & Merikle, P. M. (1996). Working memory and language comprehension: A meta-analysis. *Psychonomic Bulletin & Review, 3*(4), 422–433.

Deary, I. J., Egan, V., Gibson, G. J., Austin, E. J., Brand, C. R., & Kellaghan, T. (1996). Intelligence and the differentiation hypothesis. *Intelligence, 23*(2), 105–132.

Detterman, D. K., & Daniel, M. H. (1989). Correlations of mental tests with each other and with cognitive variables are highest in low IQ groups. *Intelligence, 13*, 349–360.

Galton, F. (1883). *Inquiry into human faculty and its development*. London: MacMillan.

Gardner, H. (1983). *Frames of mind: The theory of multiple intelligences*. New York: Basic Books.

Gardner, H., Kornhaber, M. L., & Wake, W. K. (1996). *Intelligence: Multiple Perspectives*. New York: Harcourt Brace.

Garlick, D. (2002). Understanding the nature of the general factor of intelligence: The role of individual differences in neural plasticity as an explanatory mechanism. *Psychological Review, 109*, 116–136.

Goleman, D. (1995). *Emotional intelligence*. New York: Bantam Books.

Gottfredson, L. S. (1997). Why *g* matters: The complexity of everyday life. *Intelligence, 24*(1), 79–132.

Grudnik, J. L., & Kranzler, J. H. (2001). Meta-analysis of the relationship between intelligence and inspection time. *Intelligence, 29*, 523–535.

Herrnstein, R. J., & Murray, C. (1994). *The Bell Curve: Intelligence and Class Structure in American Life*. New York: The Free Press.

Hick, W. E. (1952). On the rate of gain of information. *Quarterly Journal of Experimental Psychology, 4*, 11–26.

Horn, J. L. (1985). Remodeling old models of intelligence. In B. B. Wolman (Ed.), *Handbook of intelligence. Theories, measurements, and applications* (pp. 267–300). New York: Wiley.

Horn, J. L., & Noll, J. (1994). A system for understanding cognitive capabilities: A theory and the evidence on which it is based. In D. Detterman (Ed.), *Current Topics in Human Intelligence: Vol. 4. Theories of Intelligence* (pp. 151–204). Norwood, NJ: Ablex.

Huarte de San Juan, J. (1575/1991). *Examen de ingenios para las ciencias (Edicion Felisa Fresco Otero)*. Madrid: Espasa-Calpe S.A.

Hunt, E. (1974). Quote the Raven? Nevermore! In L. W. Gregg (Ed.), *Knowledge and cognition* (pp. 129–157). Potomac, MD: Erlbaum.

Hunt, E. (1980). Intelligence as an information processing concept. *British Journal of Psychology, 71*(4), 449–474.

Hunt, E. (1995a). *Will we be smart enough? A cognitive analysis of the coming workforce*. New York: Russell Sage.

Hunt, E. (1995b). The role of intelligence in modern society. *American Scientist 83*, July-August, 356–368.

Hunt, E. (2002). *Thoughts on thought*. Mahwah, NJ: Erlbaum.

Hunt, E., Frost, N., & Lunneborg, C. E. (1973). Individual differences in cognition: A new approach to intelligence. In G. S. Bower (Ed.), *Advances in learning and motivation* (Vol. 7, pp. 87–123). New York: Academic Press.

Hunt, E., Lunneborg, C. E., & Lewis, J. (1975). What does it mean to be high verbal? *Cognitive Psychology, 7*, 194–227.

Jensen, A. R. (1982). The chronometry of intelligence. In R. J. Sternberg (Ed.), *Advances in the psychology of human intelligence* (Vol. 1, pp. 235–310). Hilldale, NJ: Erlbaum.

Jensen, A. R. (1987). Individual differences in the Hick paradigm. In P. A. Vernon (Ed.), *Speed of information processing and intelligence* (pp. 101–176). Norwood, NJ: Ablex.

Jensen, A. R. (1998). *The g factor: The science of mental ability*. Westport, CT: Praeger.

Kane, M. J., & Engle, R. W. (2002). The role of prefrontal cortex in working memory capacity, executive attention, and general fluid intelligence: An individual differences perspective. *Psychonomic Bulletin and Review, 9*(4), 637–671.

Kyllonen, P. C., & Christal, R. E. (1990). Reasoning ability is (little more than) working memory capacity?! *Intelligence, 14*, 389–433.

Kyllonen, P. C., & Stephens, D. L. (1990). Cognitive abilities as determinants of success in acquiring logic skills. *Learning and Individual Differences, 2*(2), 129–160.

LeDoux, J. (2002). *The synaptic self. How our brains become who we are*. New York: Viking.

Logie, R. H. (1995). *Visuo-spatial working memory*. Hove, UK: Erlbaum.

Lopez, A., Atran, S., Coley, J. D., Medin, D. L., & Smith, E. E. (1997). The tree of life: Universal and cultural features of folkbiological taxonomies and inductions. *Cognitive Psychology, 32*(3), 251–295.

Luce, R. D. (1986). *Response times: Their role in inferring elementary mental organization.* New York: Oxford University Press.

MacDonald, M. C., Just, M. A., & Carpenter, P. A. (1992). Working memory constraints on the processing of syntactic ambiguity. *Cognitive Psychology, 24,* 56–98.

McGill, W. J. (1963). Stochastic latency mechanisms. In R. D. Luce, R. R. Bush, & E. Galanter (Eds.), *Handbook of mathematical psychology: Volume I* (pp. 309–360). New York: Wiley.

Nettlebeck, T. (1987). Inspection time and intelligence. In P. A. Vernon (Ed.), *Speed of information processing and intelligence* (pp. 295–346). Norwood, NJ: Ablex.

Nettlebeck, T. (2001). Correlations between inspection time and psychometric ability: A personal interpretation. *Intelligence, 29,* 459–474.

Palmer, J., MacLeod, C. M., Hunt, E., & Davidson, J. (1985). Information processing correlates of reading. *Journal of Memory and Language, 24,* 59–88.

Posner, M. I., Boies, S. E., Eichelman, W. H., & Taylor, R. L. (1969). Retention of visual and name codes of single letters. *Journal of Experimental Psychological Monographs 79,* 1–16.

Posner, M. I., & Raichle, M. E. (1994). *Images of mind.* San Francisco: Freeman.

Roberts, R. D., Goff, G. N., Anjoul, F., Kyllonen, P. C., Pallier, G., & Stankov, L. (2000). The Armed Services Vocational Aptitude Battery (ASVAB): Little more than acculturated learning (Gc)!? *Learning and Individual Differences, 12*(1), 81–103.

Schacter, D. L. (1996). *Searching for memory: The brain, the mind, and the past.* New York: Basic Books.

Schmidt, F. L., & Hunter, J. E. (1998). The validity and utility of selection methods in personnel psychology: Practical and theoretical implications of 85 years of research findings. *Psychological Bulletin, 124*(2), 262–274.

Schretlen, D., Pearlson, G. D., Anthony, J. C., Aylward, E. H., Augustine, A. M., Davis, A., & Barta, P. (2000). Elucidating the contributions of processing speed, executive ability, and frontal lobe volume to normal age-related differences in fluid intelligence. *Journal of the International Neuropsychological Society, 6,* 52–61.

Sloman, S. A. (1996). The empirical case for two systems of reasoning. *Psychological Bulletin, 119*(1), 3–22.

Smith, E. E., & Jonides, J. J. (1997). Working memory: A view from neuroimaging. *Cognitive Psychology, 33*(1), 5–42.

Spearman, C. (1923). *The nature of "intelligence" and the principles of cognition.* London: Methuen.

Sternberg, R. J. (1977). Component processes in analogical reasoning. *Psychological Review, 84,* 353–378.

Sternberg, R. J. (1988). *The triarchic mind: A new theory of human intelligence.* New York: Viking.

Sternberg, R. J. (1990). *Metaphors of mind.* Cambridge, UK: Cambridge University Press.

Sternberg, R. J. (1996). *Successful intelligence: How practical and creative intelligence determines success in life*. New York: Simon & Schuster.

Sternberg, R. J. (2003). Issues in the theory and measurement of successful intelligence: A reply to Brody. *Intelligence, 31*(4), 331–338.

Sternberg, R. J., Forsythe, G. B., Hedlund, J., Horvath, J. A., Wagner, R. K., Williams, W. M., Snook, S. A., & Grigorenko, E. L. (2000). *Practical intelligence in everyday life*. New York: Cambridge University Press.

2

Mental Chronometry and the Unification of Differential Psychology

Arthur R. Jensen

Mental chronometry is the measurement of cognitive speed. It is the actual time taken to process information of different types and degrees of complexity. The basic measurements are an individual's response time (RT) to a visual or auditory stimulus that calls for a particular response, choice, or decision.

Since at least the time of Sir Francis Galton (1822–1911), the father of differential psychology, it has been hypothesized by him and many others that mental speed is a major aspect of general intelligence. What we now know for sure is that RT can be a highly precise, reliable, and sensitive measure of individual differences. Its relationship to other psychological and ecological variables, however, is a complex affair just recently being explored.

Research on RT has a venerable history. Not only was it the earliest measurement technique used in empirical psychology, but also its scientific use as a measure of individual differences preceded the beginning of experimental psychology by at least half a century. The first published research on RT appeared in astronomy journals. Time, as measured by the Earth's rotation with reference to a star's moment of transit across a hairline in the lens of a telescope, had to be measured as accurately as possible. In 1796 it was accidentally discovered by the Astronomer Royal at the Greenwich Observatory that astronomers showed individual differences in RT to the star's transit across the hairline. So it was decided that each astronomer's RT had to be "corrected" for any given individual's "personal equation," that is, the deviation of the individual's mean RT from the mean RT based on the observations made by a number of astronomers. Before then, it had been assumed that such simple RT was virtually instantaneous. RT was later taken up as a basic tool in experimental psychology. Shortly thereafter, the measurement of individual differences in RT, along with other measures of human capacities, became a subject of interest in its own right to Galton, who tested simple RT on thousands of people (Jensen, 1982b, 1994). Unfortunately, by the early 1900s the purely technical inadequacies of this early work in mental chronometry caused the near demise of this field of investigation, and subsequent developments in mental testing were dominated for nearly a century by the psychometric model based on the famous intelligence test devised by Alfred Binet in 1905. In recent years, however, the premature abandonment of chronometric methods in differential psychology has been rectified by a rapidly burgeoning research literature in this field, particularly related to the nature of intelligence conceived theoretically as the speed and efficiency of information processing (Vernon, 1987).

This chapter explains the important differences between conventional psychometric measurement and mental chronometry and points out the particular advantages of chronometry and its future prospects for the advancement of differential psychology as a natural science.

PSYCHOMETRY AND CHRONOMETRY COMPARED

The practical success of psychometrics is unquestionably one of the triumphs of applied psychology. When nothing more than ordinal measurement is required, there can be little dispute about the practical usefulness of item-based mental tests. These are composed of a number of separate items on which the subject's responses are scored either right or wrong (R/W) or pass/fail (P/F). Given the variation in items' p values (the proportion of the normative sample passing the item) and given a range of individual differences in the ability to pass the items, the distribution of total scores (e.g., the number right) constitutes an ordinal scale. An individual's score on such a scale is interpreted in terms of its location in the distribution of scores obtained in some specified group, so the scores are "norm referenced." The interpretation of normative scores is facilitated by various forms of scaling, such as ranking, percentile ranks, standardized scores (e.g., z, T, IQ), normalized scores, and various Rasch-type scales.

To suppose that any kind of transformation of the raw scores' rank order represents a true *interval* scale or a *ratio* scale, rather than merely an ordinal scale, depends entirely on an assumption. Plausible and practical though this assumption may be, it remains just an assumption. We have to assume that the distribution of the essential variable, or latent trait, measured by the test has a particular form in the normative population. Psychologists usually assume that the trait has a normal (Gaussian) distribution, so the ordinal score distribution, whatever its form, is mathematically transformed to conform to this assumption. Or items may be specially selected for difficulty level and item intercorrelations that will produce an approximately normal distribution of scores. The transformed or manipulated test scores contain no new information that was not present in the rank-ordered raw scores; the form of the distribution simply reflects the initial assumption.

Ordinal scales have many shortcomings. Without a true *interval* scale, but armed with only our faith in the unproved distribution assumption, we cannot make really meaningful statements about many things we want to know in differential and developmental psychology. For example, there are obvious questions about the form of the population distribution of a given trait, or the form of the growth curve for that trait, and its rate of change across the lifespan. Knowing these things depends on having equal interval measurements throughout the full range of variation in the characteristic of interest. For the same reason, meaningful comparison of the within-group variance between different groups whose score distributions are centered in different ranges of the scale depends on measures having equal units across the whole scale. Otherwise a difference of X points between two scores near the high end of the scale is not assuredly equivalent to a difference of X points near the low end. The precision of covariance and of both the Pearson r and intraclass correlation (but not Spearman's rank correlation) depends on equal-interval measurements of both variates. Without an interval scale the specific form of any functional relationship, as might be shown on a graph, say, in which mental test scores (y axis) are plotted as a function of drug dosages (x axis), provides no dependable information over what could be expressed by the rank correlation coefficient between the x and y variables.

A *ratio* scale, with both a natural zero point and equal intervals, is even less attainable by any plausible assumptions based on item statistics than is an interval scale. Yet a ratio scale is essential for any valid mathematical manipulations of data beyond simple additivity. Without ratio scale properties, multiplicative or ratio properties of the data cannot be known. About 35 years ago, for instance, some psychologists proclaimed that children, on average, acquire one-half of their mental growth potential by four years of age. But psychometrics has no measurement scales that could test this interesting claim. Answering this kind of question about height, or weight, poses no problem at all. It would be scientifically useful if psychologists could determine the functional relationship of various mental measurements to the precisely known growth curves for certain structures of the brain. But our psychometric tests cannot do this meaningfully. At best, they cannot really provide anything more informative than a rank correlation between any mental ability and any metrical property of the brain.

This absence of ratio scales in differential psychology is most unfortunate, as many psychological variables behave multiplicatively, exponentially, or logarithmically in relation to internal and external physical variables, as has been discovered in sensory psychophysics, probably the most advanced branch of psychology where measurement is concerned.

The noted limitations of the scale properties of psychological tests and the claimed advantages of true interval and ratio scales might be dismissed as a trivial issue for most aspects of applied psychometrics, for which reliable ordinality is sufficient for the practical predictive validity of tests. It is not sufficient, however, for the advancement of differential psychology as a natural science, especially the study of individual variation in the domain of cognitive abilities, including the well-established dimensions, such as g, verbal, and spatial factors. With only ordinal scales we do not know the true form of the population distribution of each of these different factors or the true amount of variance attributable to each one. Nor can we know or compare their growth curves or their rates of decline with age. The future of reductionist research in this field, which aims to be explanatory, will necessarily be focused on discovering functional relationships between behaviorally measured cognitive abilities and their causal physical properties and processes in the brain. A main scientific purpose of measurement is the discovery and description of how one measured variable is related to some other measured variable. Ideally, and often necessarily, the measurements on *both* sides of the equation should be ratio scales. The physical measurements in brain research per se are of course ratio scales. Arguably the most natural scale for the behavioral measurement of mental activity is *time*, a physical ratio scale of international standardized units.

ADVANTAGES OF MENTAL CHRONOMETRY

Mental chronometry (MC) has two main classes of paradigms: (1) the measurement of an individual's *response time* (RT) to a *reaction stimulus* (RS) that elicits some form of mental activity and (2) the measurement of an individual's *inspection time* (IT), or the minimum length of exposure needed by the subject to discriminate between stimuli that differ on some dimension. MC also includes *derived* measures obtained from mathematical relationships (sums, products, ratios, etc.) between various RTs (or ITs), and these also have the scale properties of physical measurements. Nowadays RT is measured by an electronic apparatus that accurately registers intervals of time in milliseconds (ms). Besides the undisputed virtue that *time* is a ratio scale measurement, what are some of the most general advantages of MC for advancing a true science of differential psychology?

RELIABILITY. RTs are always measured over a number of trials. The internal consistency reliability (e.g., Cronbach's coefficient alpha) of individual differences in the mean RT obtained from a given number of trials can be made as high as may be required for a particular purpose simply by increasing the number of test trials. Reliability coefficients as high as those of most good psychometric tests can be obtained in as few as 20 to 30 trials, taking only a few minutes. The alpha reliability coefficients for different numbers of trials conform near perfectly to the values predicted by the

Spearman–Brown prophecy formula because the essential condition on which the S–B formula depends is perfectly met, i.e., every RS is randomly sampled from the same pool of RSs.

REPEATABILITY. Most chronometric tests can be repeated in identical form over and over again. There is virtually an infinite supply of equivalent forms of a specific test that are truly equivalent across administrations. Practice effects are typically small compared to individual differences; they approach asymptote after a certain number of trials (depending on RS complexity), and they have relatively little effect on the reliability of individual differences across trials or occasions. Repeatability of measurement is a great advantage for a test that is used over an extended period of days, weeks, or months to monitor a behavioral or cognitive effect of a drug or other treatment. Repeatability is also a boon to the study of drug-dosage curves; a given cognitive effect can be functionally related to differing dosages of the drug. Because of this advantage, MC is now of interest to pharmaceutical firms and treatment hospitals, as more and more new drugs unintentionally have side effects on cognitive performance that cannot be monitored repeatedly by ordinary item-based tests.

RANGE OF EQUIVALENCY. Conventional psychometric tests typically have a very narrow range of equivalency compared to chronometric tests. The IQs of low-scoring individuals on a test like the Wechsler Adult Intelligence Scale (WAIS) are based on a largely different set of items than are the IQs of high scoring individuals. Thus because of the limited range of a given item's p values for individuals in different segments of the score distribution, strictly speaking the same test cannot be given to low, medium, and high scoring persons. Without Rasch scaling, at least, it is even questionable whether the same variable is being measured in the different ability groups. The same problem applies to children of different ages. Even though a five-year-old and a ten-year-old are given nominally the same test, they have actually been tested on entirely different discriminating items, unless they obtain nearly the same raw score. The range of ability or age within which the same test items are discriminative is remarkably narrow. In contrast, one and the same chronometric test, with a set number of trials, can discriminate as reliably among preschool children as among university students, and among gifted as among mentally retarded children. Moreover, in all of these groups the chronometric measures have shown similar correlations with IQ. The groups differ markedly in mean RT, of course, and one can describe the differences in mathematically meaningful terms. But with ordinary item-based tests given to such diverse groups we could only rank the group means and estimate the statistical significance of their differences. Direct comparisons of ability levels would be meaningless or impossible.

SENSITIVITY OF MEASUREMENT. RT is an extraordinarily sensitive measure, showing reliable individual differences and within-subject differences in the cognitive demands of various elementary tasks that are virtually undetectable by psychometric tests. A classic example is a chronometric analysis that shows how schoolchildren in the first grade perform the simple arithmetic task of adding two single digit numbers (Groen & Parkman, 1972). On each test trial the subject is shown two integers that always sum to values from 0 to 9. The subject responds by pressing one of ten keys labeled with the digits 0 to 9, and the RT is measured in milliseconds. Analysis of the RTs revealed what the children were doing mentally: First they selected the larger (L) number in the given pair; then they counted up the smaller (S) number (perhaps using their fingers). The RTs measured on the various problems increased as a linear function of S, indicating that even simple addition is not merely the unitary recall of a memorized number fact but is a strategic construction. The contrast between this constructive effect and sheer memorization is seen in the finding that when both numbers in the pair are the same, there is no systematic variation in RT. This suggests that the sum of any two identical digits has been memorized as a unit and RT simply reflects the time for retrieval of this item of information from long-term memory. The RT for retrieval averages less than the RT for construction.

It is most interesting that these very same strategic and memorial phenomena are found also in young adult college students, although their RTs average only about one-fourth the RTs of first-grade children. But the college students are still constructing addends from pairs of single digits in the same way as first graders, only much faster. But college-age students are also much faster than young children on every kind of RT. Studies of elementary schoolchildren selected for ability to perform perfectly on simple addition, subtraction, and multiplication problems given as untimed paper-and-pencil tests have shown significant individual differences when RTs are measured on the same problems. There are also consistent mean differences between RTs for addition, subtraction, and multiplication, indicating differences in complexity of processing for the three types of arithmetic (Jensen, 1998a, see references to Jensen & Whang). These pupils' RTs on such simple arithmetic problems predicted their ability in more advanced types of arithmetic problem solving, consistent with the hypothesis that success in complex problem solving depends in part on the speed with which elementary components of the problem can be processed. Indeed a whole psychology of arithmetic cognition could be ferreted out of cleverly designed experiments based on chronometric analysis.

Other evidence of sensitivity is that chronometric measures detect variation in physiological state associated with an individual's metabolic diurnal cycle, changes in body temperature, effects of exercise, stimulant and depressant drugs, medical conditions, and the presence of genes that are risk factors for the development of Alzheimer's disease, such as the apolipoprotein (APOE) e4 allele, even before its cognitive effects are clinically detectable by psychometric tests specifically designed for this purpose (O'Hara, Sommer, & Morgan, 2001).

The sensitivity of RT can also be a disadvantage in that it is a source of variance that acts as a measurement error in studies of individual differences. In studies of *intra*-individual differences, the sensitivity of RT can be taken into account by obtaining repeated measures always at the same time of day and monitoring indicators of physiological state at the time of testing and the time since the last meal, body temperature, drug usage, and time in the menstrual cycle.

THE PSYCHOMETRIC MISCONCEPTION OF MENTAL SPEED

Psychometric measures of mental speed, such as the digit symbol or coding subtest of the Wechsler scales and the clerical checking subtest of the Armed Services Vocational Aptitude Battery, are mentally very easy tests on which virtually all subjects would obtain a perfect score if the tests were not highly speeded. The score is the number of items completed within a given time limit. Such speeded tests have often been included in factor analyses with many other more complex mental tests, such as vocabulary, verbal and figural analogies, problem arithmetic, matrices, and block designs, to name a few. In a hierarchical factor analysis these speeded tests typically show up as rather small first-order factors; they have little variance in common with other tests as shown by the fact that they have smaller loadings than other tests on any of the higher-order factors, least of all on the most general factor, psychometric *g*. This has resulted in a long held and strongly entrenched misconception in psychometrics that mental speed is a minor factor in the abilities hierarchy and has little relevance to higher mental abilities or the *g* factor.

The kinds of tests identifying this psychometric speed factor are decidedly different from the chronometric methods used to measure RT and IT, which behave quite differently from the speeded tests used in psychometrics. RT measured in various chronometric paradigms generally has its largest correlations with the nonspeeded and most highly *g* loaded tests, whereas its lowest correlations are with the most speeded tests like the digit symbol subtest in the Wechsler scales. Moreover, the correlations of various RT measures with each other and with various nonspeeded psychometric tests are generally similar to the correlations among the various subscales of standard test batteries. More generally, we should realize that the traditional distinction between *speed* and *power* in describing psychometric tests is strictly a formal distinction. It is a mistake to attribute these purely descriptive terms to categorically different cognitive processes.

STANDARDIZING CHRONOMETRIC METHODS

The study of individual differences in RT originated in astronomy, when extremely precise measurement of individual differences in RT, the so-called personal equation, was critical in measuring the instant a star's transit crossed a hairline in the telescope. The units of time have been standardized throughout the history of MC. Today these units, measured electronically in milliseconds, are the same in all laboratories. What is seldom realized, however, is that the testing conditions for obtaining these measurements in different laboratories are not at all well standardized. This is most unfortunate for the development of a unified science. Under a comparable handicap the physical or biological sciences could not have progressed to their present level. This condition has seemed tolerable where MC is used in experimental psychology, but it will prove a severe hindrance to differential psychology. This is because the former is concerned with the effects of experimentally varying task parameters and measuring the effects on RT *within* subjects, while variation *between* subjects is treated as unwanted error, to be minimized by averaging RTs over a number of subjects or over many test trials in a single subject. Only the direction and relative magnitudes of the experimental effects are of interest. Thus it is not a critical disadvantage that the exact numerical values of RT vary from one lab to another, so long as the relative effects of experimental manipulations are replicable across different labs.

Because differential psychology is concerned with differences *between* subjects, the *absolute* values of RT become important. This calls for standardization of the methods by which RT is measured, unless we limit our uses of chronometry to discovering purely relative effects and performing only correlation analyses, methods for which measures of central tendency and variance are irrelevant. Without standardization MC loses many of its advantages. The failure of one lab to replicate the specific findings of another lab using nominally the same paradigm can be due either to differences between the subject samples or to differences in the test instruments themselves, although both are measuring and comparing, say, simple RT and 2-choice RT to visual stimuli. Unless the same apparatus (or perfect clones), as well as the instructions and the number of practice trials, are used in both labs, a true replication is not possible.

The sensitivity of RT makes for considerable differences when nominally the same variable is measured by different, though equally accurate, apparatuses. The difference arises not in the timing mechanism per se, but in subtleties of the stimulus and response demands of the task. Given the same testing conditions, any significant difference in results should be solely attributable to a difference between the subject samples, not to the conditions of measurement. Regardless of the RT data collected for a particular study, an important element in describing the subject sample (besides the usual descriptors such as age, sex, and education) should consist of descriptive statistics based on, say, at least 20 trials of both simple RT and 2-choice RT measured on the standard RT apparatus. Without such methodological standardization in differential research, the cumulation of archival data from different laboratories is hardly worthwhile. Such fundamental standardization has been essential for progress in the so-called exact sciences, and it is equally important for the advancement of a science of differential mental chronometry. Decisions about the design of standard apparatuses, methods, and procedures that should be required in every chronometric laboratory will need to be worked out and agreed on by an international consortium of researchers in this field. This agreement would also include recommendations for electronically recording and archiving chronometric data from labs using the standardized equipment and procedures. I find it hard to imagine a greater boon to the advancement of differential psychology, with its present aim of discovering how behavioral measurements of cognition are related to the physical properties of the brain.

CHRONOMETRY AS A PRIMARY TOOL FOR RESEARCH ON INTELLIGENCE

The century of progress in the psychometric approach to the study of mental abilities, beginning with Spearman and Binet, has reached a consensus regarding their factor structure. Relatively few factors, or latent variables, account for most of the individual differences variance in practically all psychometric tests. John B. Carroll's (1993) systematic factor analysis of the huge number of test intercorrelations reported in virtually the entire psychometric literature shows that they are best represented by a hierarchical factor structure. Carroll named it the *three-stratum model*. It comprises some forty first-order factors in the first stratum, eight second-order factors in the second stratum, and one factor (psychometric g) in the third stratum. The challenge now is to discover the causal basis of the individual differences from which these factors arise. Researchers now want to understand them in terms of cognitive processes and brain physiology. The greatest interest so far is focused on g, the most general component of the common factor variance. It is also the most mysterious, as it cannot be characterized in terms of the information content of mental tests or in terms of any observable types of behavior. As its discoverer Charles Spearman noted, g is known not by its nature but by the variation in its loadings on a wide variety of mental tests. But psychometric tests with the same g loadings are so highly varied in their specific information content and the particular mental skills called for as to defy a unitary classification in lexical terms. The g factor itself is best thought of not as a verbally describable mental ability, or even as an ability of any kind, but rather as an aspect of individual differences that causes positive correlations between virtually all measurable cognitive abilities.

The individual assessment of g is always problematic, not because g is a chimera, but because its psychometric measurement as a factor score is always attached to a *g*-weighted average of a relatively small number of diverse tests. Therefore, the psychometric "vehicles" of *g* also unavoidably carry other factors besides *g*, including variance unique to each test. We can only minimize these sources of non-*g* variance in the obtained *g* factor scores. But because the contamination of *g* factor scores by the vehicles of *g* is unavoidable, this attempt can only be more or less successful for different individuals. Fortunately for research on the nature of *g*, it is unnecessary to have a direct measure of *g* for each individual in a study. One can indirectly determine the correlation of *g* with other psychological and physical variables by the methods of factor analysis or other latent trait models.

The advancement of intelligence research along scientific lines now requires extending its traditional methodology beyond the use of item-based psychometric tests and the factor analysis of the virtually unlimited variety of tests. During the past two decades, chronometric methods have gained prominence in research probing the nature of *g* and other components of psychometric variance. It is now well established that many types of RT and IT are correlated with psychometric *g* and with IQ or other highly *g*-loaded tests. The correlations for single elementary cognitive tasks (ECTs) with RTs in the range from simple RT (about 200 ms) to more complex tasks (not exceeding 2,000 ms in young adults) the correlations with IQ range from about .10 to .50. The general factor extracted from a battery of several diverse ECTs has correlations with the general factor of a battery of psychometric tests (e.g., the Wechsler scales) ranging between .60 and .90. Studies of the RT/IQ relationship based on multiple regression, factor analysis, canonical correlation, and structural equation models suggest that chronometric and psychometric tests have much the same general factor in common. Reviews of the empirical evidence and bibliographic entries to virtually the entire literature on this subject can be found elsewhere (Caryl et al., 1999; Deary, 2000a, b; Jensen, 1982a, b, 1985, 1987a, 1998a, Chap. 8; Lohman, 2000; Neubauer, 1997; Vernon, 1987). So here I will not reiterate the evidence proving that RT and IT are related to *g*. Rather, I shall point out some of the collateral phenomena that have turned up in this field of investigation. Their investigation is important for advancing this line of research. A true theory of *g* and its neural basis will have to account for each of these phenomena, unless future research finally dismisses them as unreliable or as experimental artifacts.

But first let me emphasize that the eventual explanation of *g*, as marvelous an achievement as that might be, is not the main purpose of mental chronometry. Its scope is far wider. It is a general tool for measuring all aspects of cognition. Our conventional psychometric tests, whatever their practical usefulness, are not a higher court to which mental chronometry must appeal for its scientific importance. Chronometric methods have generated a universe of psychological phenomena for study in its own right.

That some of these phenomena happen to be related to psychometric test scores is simply a fortunate discovery, helping us understand individual differences in more functionally analytic terms than is possible with the factor analysis or multidimensional scaling of item-based tests. We recognize, of course, that these psychometric methods have served a necessary taxonomic purpose in describing the whole domain of psychometric abilities in terms of a quite limited number of latent variables.

FUNDAMENTAL FINDINGS IN THE RELATIONSHIP OF CHRONOMETRICS TO PSYCHOMETRIC g

Speeded Psychometric Tests
The RT–g correlation is not in the least explained by the time limits or speed instructions given to the subjects taking the mental tests. In fact, the types of tests that are usually the most speeded, such as clerical checking and digit-symbol coding tests, have lower correlations with RT than do so-called power tests, in which subjects are encouraged to attempt all the items and to take all the time they need.

Tests' g Loadings
Tests with larger g loadings generally show higher correlations with RT, indicating that g is the main psychometric factor in the RT–IQ correlation.

Complexity of the RT Task
The absolute size of the RT–IQ correlation (which is always a negative r) generally has an inverted-U-shaped relationship to the complexity of the RT task. Simple RT (i.e., one stimulus–one response) with RTs of about 300 ms for young adults shows *small* correlations ($-.10$ to $-.20$); moderate tasks (RTs around 500–900 ms) show *moderate* correlations of ($-.40$ to $-.50$); and difficult RT tasks (above 1200 ms) show *small* correlations ($-.20$ to $-.30$). One hypothesis proposed to explain this phenomenon holds that the simplest RT tasks have a smaller cognitive component relative to a larger perceptual-motor component, which does not reflect g. As the RT task demands are increased in cognitive complexity beyond some optimal point, a wider range of individual differences in an increasingly greater variety of performance strategies comes into play. These include task-specific factors that are uncorrelated with psychometric factors and therefore attenuate the RT–g correlation. Also, when task complexity increases to the point that response errors become a reliable source of individual differences, fewer subjects are processing the RT task in the same way. Interestingly, those forms of both RT and IT tasks that are the most liable to allow subjects to adopt different strategies show the weakest correlations with IQ. Evidently it is the sheer speed of processing, rather than the subject's choice of a strategy, that is most related to g.

Because we are often without an independent interval scale of task complexity, task complexity is often measured by RT itself. Such RT measures on simple tasks, though differing only in tens of milliseconds (i.e., time intervals below the threshold of visual or auditory detection), have considerable subjective validity as measures of task complexity. This was shown when a group of university students was asked simply to rank the complexity (or difficulty) of fourteen different items in a Semantic Verification Test (SVT, described in the following section). Their subjective ranking of item complexity, from least complex (=1) to most complex (=14), correlated +.61 with the item's average RTs obtained in another university sample (Paul, 1984; Jensen, Larson, & Paul, 1988). It could well be that RT provides the best measure of item complexity and could be used in the process of item selection in the design of ordinary paper-and-pencil tests for children. Simple test items can be scaled on a ratio scale of difficulty according to their average RTs obtained in a group of bright university students who can answer the items without error. Reliable discrepancies between the item p values for children and the item RTs for university students would indicate that p and RT are not scaling item difficulty (or complexity) on the same dimension. I predict, however, that this would very seldom occur.

Correlation Trade-Off and Convertibility Between RT and Error Responses

As RT tasks increase in complexity, there is a rise in response errors. The correlation between RT and IQ *decreases* with a rise in response errors, whereas the correlation between response errors and IQ *increases*. This reciprocal trade-off suggests a breakdown in information processing at higher levels of task complexity. The point of breakdown on the continuum of difficulty or complexity and the resulting response error determine the correlation of single test items (scored pass/fail) with IQ.

Untimed psychometric tests based on right/wrong scoring of items with little or no prior-learned knowledge, such as the Raven matrices and number series tests, are an example of this; the average item scores (p values) reflect differences in item complexity or difficulty. If items are so easy that nobody misses them (i.e., all item p values = 100%), differences in their difficulty levels can still be determined by measuring the RTs for solving the items.

The convertibility between item RTs and item error rates can be shown by means of a simple Semantic Verification Test (SVT) (Paul, 1984). Each item in the test consists of a simple statement about the relative positions of just the three letters **A, B, C**. There are 14 different statements, such as **B after A**, or **B not before A**, or **B between A and C**, etc., with a total of 84 presentations. Immediately following a 3-second presentation of one of these statements on the display screen, three letters (e.g., **A C B**) are presented simultaneously in an order that either affirms or disaffirms the statement.

The subject, instructed to respond as accurately and quickly as possible, presses one of two pushbuttons labeled **YES** or **NO**. The SVT was very easy for Berkeley undergraduates whose average rate of response errors over 84 test trials was 7%. But their mean RTs on the 14 SVT items varied widely, between 600 and 1,300 ms. Obviously the items differ in complexity or difficulty. (The correlation of subjects' mean RTs with scores on the Raven Advanced Progressive Matrices was −.45 in Berkeley undergraduates.)

To obtain reliable measures of variation in item difficulty among the fourteen SVT conditions measured as the p values of the SVT items, these items had to be given to schoolchildren (ages 8 and 9 years) as an *untimed* paper-and-pencil test, with an average item p value of 82%. The children's p values on the fourteen SVT items had a rank-order correlation of −.79 with the mean RTs of the corresponding SVT items in the adult sample. The more difficult an SVT item was for the children, the greater was its average RT for university students. Thus an index of item difficulty (p) for average third-grade schoolchildren is convertible into processing time (RTs) for university students all in the top quartile of the nationally normed IQ.

Primary versus Derived Measures in Chronometric Paradigms

Primary measures are the central tendency (*mean* or *median*) of an individual's RTs over a given number (n) of trials. Derived measures are (1) the *standard deviation* of an individual's RTs over n trials (RTSD), (2) the *intercept* of the regression of mean RTs on task difficulty, and (3) the *slope* of the linear regression relating the individual's mean RT on two or more tasks to their differences in complexity (hence in RT). The slope parameter is a key feature of three classic RT paradigms: the Hick paradigm (linear slope of RT over four levels of complexity measured in bits), the Saul Sternberg paradigm (linear slope of RTs over 1 to 5 or more digits to be scanned in short-term memory), and the Posner paradigm, where the slope is the difference between only two means (Name Identity RT *minus* Physical Identity RT). These slope parameters are of considerable theoretical interest, as the steepness of the slope is a prima facie measure of the *rate* of information processing as a function of increasing information load. An index of *skewness* of an individual's RT distribution over n trials is another derived measure that has more recently become of interest in connection with the "worst performance rule" (discussed later).

The derived measures typically show lower correlations with IQ than do the primary measures, which at least in the case of the slope parameter is definitely contrary to the theoretical prediction. But the prima facie evidence against the theoretical prediction that the slope parameter should be correlated (negatively) with IQ at least as much if not more than the mean RT was a premature and technically mistaken judgment. Two statistical artifacts work against the overly simple analysis typically used to test the prediction, namely, a simple (zero-order) correlation between slope and

IQ: (1) the low reliability of the slope measurement and (2) the intercept measurement acts as a suppressor variable in the slope–IQ correlation (because the intercept and slope share the same measurement errors but in opposite directions). These unwanted statistical effects are not intrinsic to the theoretical prediction, but they can be taken into account by an appropriate statistical analysis based on disattenuating the slope measure and partialling out the intercept from the IQ–slope correlation. When such an analysis is applied to the Hick paradigm, the theoretical prediction of the slope–IQ correlation is significantly borne out (Jensen, 1998b).

It should always be remembered that any derived measures, if based on difference scores, $X - Y$, will have lower reliabilities than either X or Y to the degree that X and Y are correlated with each other. This is sometimes forgotten in studies of individual differences in the Posner paradigm and other difference scores such as the difference between choice RT and simple RT. Not taking proper account of reliability in different derived measures is often the reason why derived scores in RT studies result in weaker correlations with external variables like IQ than do the primary RT variables.

The Problematic Meaning of Inter-Trial Variability of RT

Inter-trial variability, also referred to as intra-individual variability, is measured as the standard deviation of an individual's RTs over n trials, abbreviated RTSD. Its interest inheres in the hypothesis that RTSD measures individual differences in "neural noise" or the result of random effects in the transmission of information in the brain, and that the amount of neural noise is a causal factor in intelligence differences. RTSD is negatively correlated with IQ in various paradigms to at least the same degree as the median RT, even though RTSD usually has somewhat lower reliability than RT, so that when all of the statistical parameters of the RT performance are corrected for attenuation, RTSD has the largest correlation with IQ. It therefore commands attention in the chronometric study of cognitive differences.

RTSD has two problematic aspects, as yet unresolved. First is the question of redundancy of the mean RT and RTSD. The near-perfect constancy of the proportionality between the mean RT and RTSD, measured as the coefficient of variation ($C_V = \sigma/\mu$), both for individuals and for different tasks is well established. It implies a perfect correlation between RT and RTSD, corrected for measurement error. Therefore it is mysterious that these two measures do not have the same correlation with IQ and that they show significant interactions with race and sex differences (Jensen, 1992a). Furthermore, analysis of several sets of median RT and RTSD showed that the true-score correlation between the two variables is very high (averaging +0.81), but that still leaves a significant 36% of the variance that the two measures do not have in common. This noncommon variance could result from the fact that all these analyses were based on median RT over n,

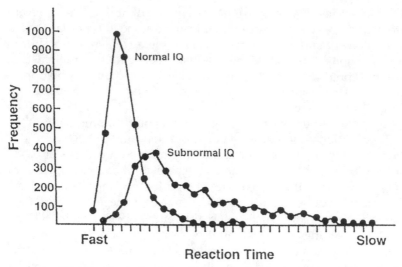

FIGURE 1. Distributions of reaction times of individuals with normal and subnormal IQs. (From Baumeister, 1998, p. 260, with permission of Ablex.)

not the mean RT. Because the RT distribution is always positively skewed, the mean is always somewhat larger than the median. But it has not yet been determined whether a perfect true-score correlation exists between the *mean* RT and RTSD. If there is a perfect correlation, a purely statistical theory could account for it, as follows: (1) Every individual, at a given time, has a physiological limit for the speed of reaction, determined by the minimum times for sensory transduction of the stimulus and the nerve conduction velocity and synaptic delays going to and from the relevant sensory and motor regions of the brain. (2) On a given RT task, the range of individual differences in the physiological limit is much smaller than the range of individual differences in the central tendency (particularly the mean) of RTs measured over many trials. (3) The location of the mean RT, therefore, is determined by the distribution of RT deviations above the physiological limit. (4) Because these deviations can only go in one direction, their distribution is skewed to the right. (5) Whatever causes the variable deviations in RTs thus has three perfectly correlated effects on the first three moments (mean, *SD*, and skew) of the individual's RT distribution. Empirically, over many trials, the correlations among individual differences in the mean RT, the RTSD, and skewness would approach unity. Theoretically, then, the parameters of an individual's RT distribution would all result from the individual's physiological limit plus positive deviations of RT from that limit. This deviation phenomenon would be more or less equally reflected by any one of these moments of the individual's RT distribution. This phenomenon is illustrated in Figure 1.

This hypothesis reduces the problem of explaining the RT–IQ relationship to that of explaining the cause(s) of the RT deviations above threshold. Is it "neural noise," implying true randomness, in which individuals would differ? Or could it be a regular oscillation in neural receptivity, the periodicity of which differs across individuals? A regular oscillation of excitatory potential would simply appear to be random if on each test trial the experimenter-controlled presentation of the reaction stimulus (RS) was seldom synchronized with the individual's period of oscillations above and below the threshold of excitation for the given stimulus. We know that increasing the intensity of the RS correspondingly decreases both the mean RT and the RTSD, indicating that the threshold for the activation of a response operates as a gradient or wave, not as dichotomous on/off levels of stimulus receptivity.

ANOTHER MEASURE OF RT VARIABILITY. For researching this hypothesis, RTSD is not an ideal measure of individual variation in RT across trials. It is liable to include any systematic variation or trend in RTs across trials, such as a practice effect. It would be more desirable to measure an individual's RT deviations across trials in a way that would determine if successive deviations look as if they were produced by a random numbers generator, given the lower limit and the mean of the individual's RT distribution.

Such a measure of random variability, that does not reflect systematic trends in the trial-to-trial RT measures, is provided by Von Neumann's (1941) *mean square successive difference* (MSSD), or its square root. The MSSD is defined as $\delta^2 = [\Sigma(X_i - X_{i+1})^2/(n-1)$, where X_i and X_{i+1} are all sequentially adjacent values (e.g., RTs on Trials 1 and 2, 2 and 3, etc.) and n is the number of trials. It is most commonly used in time series analysis in economics, where it is desirable to distinguish between random fluctuations and systematic trends in financial data. The *Von Neumann ratio* ($R = \delta^2/\sigma^2$) provides one of the strongest statistical tests of randomness in a series of n numbers. [The chance probabilities (p) of R for different values of n are given by Hart (1942).] Although this statistic can indicate randomness of RTs, it cannot, of course, distinguish between randomness due to neural noise and randomness due to asynchrony between a regular oscillation in neural excitatory potential and the intervals between presentations of the RS. That distinction would have to be discovered experimentally by pacing test trials to determine if the subject's minimal RTs can be systematically synchronized in accord with a regularly fluctuating oscillation of neural excitatory potential.

The "Worst Performance Rule"

This RT phenomenon was named by Larson and Alderton (1990), who defined it as follows: "The worst RT trials reveal more about intelligence than do other portions of the RT distribution." Their quite robust finding, based on Navy recruits, was replicated with college students on different

RT tasks (Kranzler, 1992); the phenomenon is also observed in comparing persons with relatively low and high IQs (Jensen, 1982a). However, a study by Salthouse (1998) based on very heterogeneous age groups (18 to 88 years) did not show the worst performance rule (to be discussed later).

The analysis for demonstrating the phenomenon consists of rank ordering each individual's RTs on every trial from fastest to slowest RTs and, *within* each rank, obtaining the correlation between the individual's RTs and ability measures (e.g., IQ). The RT–IQ correlations are seen to increase monotonically from the fastest to the slowest RT trials.

This finding, however, appears not to be a new, independent RT phenomenon. It is best viewed as a statistical consequence of the RT variance phenomena described in the preceding section. Individual differences are least in the smallest RT deviations above a physiological limit, and there is an increasing variance of individual differences for larger deviations. The phenomenon is most clearly seen in comparing groups of normal and mildly retarded young adults on simple RT, shown in Figure 2. Even within a normal group of young adults (Navy recruits) there is a monotonically increasing coefficient of variation ($C_V = SD$/mean), going from the fastest to the slowest RTs (e.g., Larson & Alderton, 1990, Table 4). (The same phenomenon is clearly seen in the study by Salthouse, 1998, Table 1.) Consequently, the larger deviations have less restriction of range, therefore higher reliability and higher correlation with individual differences in IQ. The coefficients of variation across the RT ranks going from the fastest to the slowest RTs, in fact, were correlated .998 with the RT–IQ correlations within the ranks. Therefore the essential phenomenon calling for theoretical explanation is not the derivative worst performance rule itself, but the fact that higher IQ subjects have consistently smaller RT deviations above their physiological limit than do lower IQ subjects. The more basic question is not yet answered: What causes individual differences in the magnitude of these intra-individual RT deviations? The relationship of the various RT parameters (mean, median, SD, $MSSD$, skew) to IQ and psychometric g all derive from this one fundamental phenomenon.

Although the RT data per se in the study by Salthouse (1998) show essentially the same features as those in other studies, the Salthouse results differ markedly from the others by not conforming to the worst performance rule with respect to ability. Going from the fastest to the slowest RT, the correlations between RT and scores on various cognitive tests (with age partialled out) show no upward trend. And there is a marked downward trend in the correlations between age and RT, going from fast to slow RT. Salthouse (1998, p. 165) attributes this discrepancy between his and the other studies to several method differences – in the RT tasks, the range of RTs elicited, the types of psychometric tests, the subjects' ages, the number of practice trials, and other procedural differences. So many variations simply rule out any possibility of a specific explanation for the

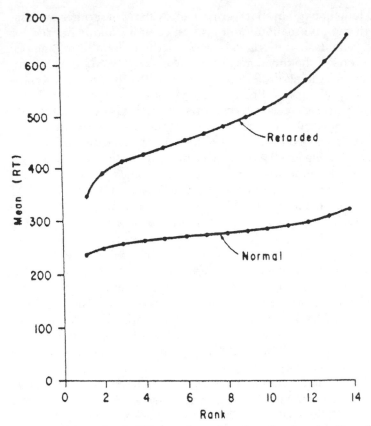

FIGURE 2. Mean simple RT plotted as a function of rank order (from fastest to slowest) of each individual's RTs, for groups of young adults with normal intelligence (mean IQ 120) and with mental retardation (mean IQ 70). (From Jensen, 1982a, p. 291, with permission of Springer-Verlag.)

discrepant results. Each of these studies appears methodologically sound and the results in every instance must be taken seriously, yet each study is so unique methodologically that they can scarcely be regarded as attempts to replicate the same phenomenon. So the worst performance rule is not brought into question, but the limits of its generality is questioned. The importance of true replications of research findings emphasizes the need for standardizing RT apparatuses and procedures in all laboratories engaged in chronometric research.

Working Memory (WM) and Speed of Processing (SP)

Memory is a crucial phenomenon in normal cognition. However, it is not a unitary construct. Stimuli (i.e., information) must be preserved in the neural processing system after their physical presence has ceased, and they must be held long enough in short-term memory (STM) for other process-ing to occur. If the information input is at all complex and is needed for getting on with the task, it needs to be processed into long-term memory (LTM). That is one of the functions of *working memory* (WM), which is in-volved in many reasoning tasks and has been called the "mind's scratch pad." WM is a hypothetical ability that (1) rehearses information in STM for storage in LTM, or (2) encodes or transforms information, or (3) simultane-ously does 1 or 2 (or both) while processing newly arrived information from the sensorium or retrieved from LTM (Baddeley, 1986). Backward memory span, for example, engages WM capacity more than does forward digit span; the same is true for arithmetic problem solving as compared with mechanical arithmetic. The elements of a problem must be held in WM long enough, or retrieved from the LTM store of past acquired information and cognitive skills, to achieve solution. The *capacity* of WM refers to the quantity of information it can juggle simultaneously without becoming overloaded, causing a breakdown in processing due to the rapid decay of STM traces and the consequent loss of information.

Quite simple laboratory measures of WM have remarkably high corre-lations with IQ, and it has even been claimed that psychometric g (or fluid intelligence, g_f, which is highly correlated with g) is little, if anything, other than WM capacity. It is hard, however, to evaluate this seeming identity between WM and g. It may be a matter of giving different names to the same construct, as many of the tests of WM are indistinguishable from the highly g-loaded items in psychometric tests. There is no sound basis for pitting WM against mental processing speed as the more fundamental explanation of g. Both constructs – WM and processing speed – are theo-retically necessary. The essential question concerns how the two constructs are related. It is a fact that RT derived from simple paradigms is at least as correlated with tests of WM as with nonspeeded g-loaded psychometric tests. RT derives its correlation with various psychometric tests almost en-tirely through their mutual g loading; when g is statistically removed from a test battery, it has a near-zero correlation with RT. The same is true for WM.

Kyllonen (1993) tested 202 college students on nine diverse WM mea-sures composed either of verbal, numerical, or spatial content and scored as the percentage of correct responses; he also measured 2-choice reaction time (CRT): subjects were presented an alphanumeric stimulus that was either preceded or followed by an asterisk (e.g., *7) and they indicated as quickly as possible which side the asterisk was on by pressing one of two keys positioned 5 inches apart on the left- and right-hand sides of the re-sponse console. The average correlation (reflected) between CRT and each of the nine WM tests is .32; the average of all the correlations among just the WM tests is .45. This small difference (.45 − .32) would likely vanish if a slightly more complex CRT paradigm were used. The RT–IQ correlation is increased by including some demand on WM in the RT task. This is done with a *dual task* paradigm, which interposes a different RT task between the first reaction stimulus (RS_1) and the response to it (RT_1), thus: $RS_1 \rightarrow RS_2 \rightarrow RT_2 \rightarrow$ cue for $RS_1 \rightarrow RT_1$, where $RS_2 \rightarrow RT_2$ is the interposed task. Both RT_1 and RT_2 are lengthened by this demand on WM, and both RT_1 and RT_2 show larger correlations with *g* than when either task is presented alone (Jensen, 1987b, pp. 115–118). Thus both processing speed and WM are essential components of individual differences in *g*.

A plausible working hypothesis of the RT–WM correlation is that information processing speed *amplifies* the capacity of WM by a multiplicative factor in which there are consistent individual differences. Here is a brief summary of the points I have elaborated on elsewhere (Jensen, 1982b, 1992b, 1993): (1) The conscious brain typically acts as a *single-channel* processor with *limited capacity*, (2) this restricts the amount of information that can be dealt with simultaneously and the *number of operations* that can be simultaneously performed on it, (3) there is a *rapid decay of information* in STM, which limits the time allowed for manipulating the input or consolidating new information into LTM by rehearsal, (4) overloading the capacity of WM results in a *breakdown in processing*, i.e., some loss of information essential for correctly responding to the task, (5) a faster *speed of processing* allows more operations to be performed on the input per unit of time, thereby increasing the chances of reaching a successful response before the point of overload and breakdown due to loss of information, (6) because of individual differences in speed of processing, a series of novel tasks of increasing *complexity* will show corresponding individual differences in the point of breakdown on the complexity continuum, (7) psychometric tests with items scored right/wrong depend on the complexity continuum (item *p* values) for measuring *g*, (8) therefore, individual differences in speed of processing and its amplification of WM capacity are the cause of psychometric *g*. The specific neural mechanisms involved are not yet known.

Brinley Plots and the Generality of Processing Speed

Differential psychology is mainly concerned with individual differences. But aggregated data, such as mean differences between groups selected to differ on a given trait, afford an essential tool for discovering the common features of the group difference, which consists simply of aggregated individual differences. By aggregating the measurements of many individuals one can distinguish the particular variable of interest from the "noise" caused by other, usually unknown and probably unique, sources of individual variation.

The aggregation principle has been most informative in recent chronometric research studies using a graphical method known as a *Brinley plot*. Originally used in the study of cognitive aging (Brinley, 1965), it consists

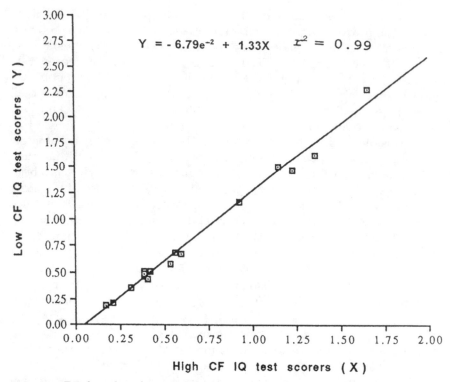

FIGURE 3. Brinley plot of processing speed measures (in seconds) on 15 different RT tasks given to adults in the lower (Low CF IQ) and upper (High CF IQ) halves of the distribution of scores on the Cattell Culture Fair Intelligence Test. The data points are well fitted by the linear regression ($r^2 = 0.99$). (From Rabbitt, 1996, with permission of Ablex.)

of a bivariate plot of the RT means for each of a number of diverse RT tasks in two selected groups (e.g., low IQ and high IQ). One group is plotted on the x axis, the other on the y axis, and the regression line of y on x goes through the bivariate data points. If the contrasted groups should differ in processing strategies on the various tasks, indicating an interaction between groups and tasks, the plotted bivariate means fall off the regression line. The goodness of fit of the RT means to the regression line is indicated by r^2_{xy}, i.e., the proportion of variance in one variate predicted by the other.

An example of a Brinley plot is given by Rabbitt (1996). Cattell's Culture Fair Test of IQ was given to adults who then were divided into the lower and upper halves (called Low CF IQ and High CF IQ) of the total distribution of CF test scores. They also took fifteen chronometric tasks with quite diverse but simple cognitive demands. Figure 3 shows a Brinley plot of the mean RTs on the fifteen tasks. All the data points closely fit a linear function. The squared correlation ($r^2 = .99$) between the RTs of the High and Low IQ groups indicates that 99% of the variance in the fifteen data points of the Low IQ group is predicted by the data points of the High IQ group (and vice versa). The slope of the regression line is indicated by the raw regression coefficient of 1.33, which approximates the average ratio of Low IQ RTs/High IQ RTs across all of the 15 tasks. (The standardized regression coefficient is $r = \sqrt{.99}$.) Rabbitt (1996) interpreted this result as evidence that individual differences in CF test scores (which are highly *g*-loaded) "facilitate all decisions [in the various RT tasks] in close proportion to the times needed to make them, irrespective of their durations (relative difficulty) and of the qualitative nature of the comparisons, and so of the mental processes, that they involve" (p. 79). RT increases *multiplicatively* with task complexity in direct proportion to the number of operations or processing steps involved in the task.

Although a Brinley plot reflects the large global factor (probably *g*) that both the psychometric and chronometric variables have in common, Rabbitt notes that the plot does not capture the fine grain of variation between specific RT tasks. Any given task may differ in the simple ratio of the means of the contrasted groups, thus departing from the common regression line (i.e., the average ratio for all of the RT tasks). Granted this relative insensitivity of Brinley plots for highlighting reliable task specificity (i.e., its interaction with group differences on a second variable such as IQ), it is the multiplicative or *ratio* property, not the additivity, of task differences that is the seminal discovery. It would have been impossible to discover, much less prove, this ratio property of task difficulty without chronometric methods, as they have the theoretical benefit of a true ratio scale. With psychometric test scores, on the other hand, ratios and proportions are meaningless.

Other examples of the Brinley-plot phenomenon are also displayed in Rabbitt's 1996 article and in other chronometric studies of group differences, particularly changes in cognitive abilities across the lifespan. Brinley plots all look much alike, indicating the broad generality of processing speed across a wide variety of elementary cognitive tasks (ECTs) for various kinds of group differences. In every study, the RTs of the slower group are predicted by a single constant multiplier of the corresponding RTs of the faster group. The correlation (predictive validity) is typically in the high .90s. Studies of mental development have compared RTs of children in different grades in school (Fry & Hale, 1996; Hale 1990; Hale & Jansen, 1994; Kail, 1991a, b). Academically gifted 13-year-old students were compared with age-matched average children and with university students on eight RT tasks (Cohn, Carlson, & Jensen, 1985), resulting in Brinley plots averaging a correlation of .96. Studies of cognitive aging used Brinley plots to compare adult groups of different ages (Cerella, 1985; Cerella & Hale, 1994). Brinley plots of RT differences showing the typical global effect of differences in processing speed have also been found in contrasting the following conditions with control groups: brain injury, multiple sclerosis, and clinical depression (references in Myerson et al., 2003). Changes or differences in ability associated with cognitive development, cognitive aging, health conditions, giftedness, and IQ differences at a given age all reflect global differences in speed of processing in a wide variety of RT tasks.

The impressively thought-out article by Myerson et al. (2003) provides the most sophisticated theoretical and quantitative development of this global speed of processing phenomenon. It will prove heuristic to hypothesize that this same global process is the basis of g and affects every form of information processing encountered by individuals throughout life.

What ultimately needs to be discovered is the physical basis of differences in cognitive processing speed. Current research based on positron emission tomography (PET scan) and functional magnetic resonance imaging (fMRI) have proven valuable in discovering the specific regions of brain localization for certain cognitive functions, including the areas of cortical activation (mainly in the frontal lobes) associated with performance on high g-loaded tests (Duncan et al., 2000; Thomson et al., 2001). Of course, it is important to determine whether the very same cortical areas are activated in performance on the general factor of various chronometric tasks. But the next step in achieving a complete physical account of the causal mechanisms involved in g must go beyond studies of brain localization. It must eventually deal with the neural networks in the activated areas on the brain indicated by PET and fMRI. Research strategy in this frontier, similar to the research strategy in particle physics, calls for experimentally testing hypotheses about the known neurophysiological processes that could account for specific behavioral manifestations of g, as measured under standardized laboratory conditions. For the reasons outlined earlier in this chapter, I believe that the methods of mental chronometry should prove to be a most valuable research tool for advancing toward this ultimate goal.

References

Baddeley, A. (1986). *Working memory*. Oxford, UK: Clarendon Press.

Baumeister, A. A. (1998). Intelligence and the "personal equation." *Intelligence, 26,* 255–265.

Brinley, J. F. (1965). Cognitive sets, speed and accuracy in the elderly. In A. T. Welford & J. E. Birren (Eds.), *Behavior, aging, and the nervous system* (pp. 114–149). New York: Springer-Verlag.

Carroll, J. B. (1993). *Human cognitive abilities: A survey of factor-analytic studies*. Cambridge, UK: Cambridge University Press.

Caryl, P. G., Deary, I. J., Jensen, A. R., Neubauer, A. C., & Vickers, D. (1999). Information processing approaches to intelligence: Progress and prospects. In I. Mervielde, I. Deary, F. de Fruyt, & F. Ostendorf (Eds.), *Personality psychology in Europe* (Vol. 7, pp. 181–219). Tilburg, Netherlands: Tilburg University Press.

Cerella, J. (1985). Information processing in the elderly. *Psychological Bulletin, 98,* 67–83.

Cerella, J., & Hale, S. (1994). The rise and fall in information-processing rates over the life span. *Acta Psychologica, 86,* 109–197.

Cohn, S. J., Carlson, J. S., & Jensen, A. R. (1985). Speed of information processing in academically gifted youths. *Personality and Individual Differences, 6,* 621–629.

Deary, I. J. (2000a). *Looking down on human intelligence: From psychometrics to the brain.* Oxford, UK: Oxford University Press.

Deary, I. J. (2000b). Simple information processing and intelligence. In R. J. Sternberg (Ed.), *Handbook of intelligence* (pp. 267–284). Cambridge, UK: Cambridge University Press.

Duncan, J., Seitz, R. J., Kolodny, J., Bor, D., Herzong, H., Ahmed, A., Newell, F. N., & Emslie, H. (2000). A neural basis for intelligence. *Science, 289,* 457–460.

Fry, A. F., & Hale, S. (1996). Processing speed, working memory, and fluid intelligence: Evidence for a developmental cascade. *Psychological Science, 7,* 237–241.

Groen, G. J., & Parkman, J. M. (1972). A chronometric analysis of simple addition. *Psychological Review, 79,* 329–343.

Hale, S. (1990). A global developmental trend in cognitive processing speed. *Child Development, 61,* 653–663.

Hale, S., & Jansen, J. (1994). Global processing-time coefficients characterize individual and group differences in cognitive speed. *Psychological Science, 5,* 384–389.

Hart, B. R. (1942). Tabulation of the probabilities for the ratio of the mean square successive difference to the variance. *Annals of Mathematical Statistics, 13,* 207–214.

Jensen, A. R. (1982a). The chronometry of intelligence. In R. J. Sternberg (Ed.), *Advances in the psychology of human intelligence* (Vol. 1, pp. 93–132). Hillsdale, NJ: Erlbaum.

Jensen, A. R. (1982b). Reaction time and psychometric *g.* In H. J. Eysenck (Ed.), *A model for intelligence* (pp. 93–132). New York: Springer.

Jensen, A. R. (1985). Methodological and statistical techniques for the chronometric study of mental abilities. In C. R. Reynolds & V. L. Wilson (Eds.), *Methodological and statistical advances in the study of individual differences* (pp. 51–116). New York: Plenum.

Jensen, A. R. (1987a). Individual differences in the Hick paradigm. In P. A. Vernon (Ed.), *Speed of information processing and intelligence* (pp. 101–175). Norwood, NJ: Ablex.

Jensen, A. R. (1987b). The *g* beyond factor analysis. In R. R. Ronning, J. A. Glover, J. C. Conoley, & J. C. Witt (Eds.), *The influence of cognitive psychology on testing* (pp. 87–142). Hillsdale, NJ: Erlbaum.

Jensen, A. R. (1992a). The importance of intraindividual variability in reaction time. *Personality and Individual Differences, 13,* 869–882.

Jensen, A. R. (1992b). The relation between information processing time and right/wrong responses. *American Journal on Mental Retardation, 97,* 290–292.

Jensen, A. R. (1993). Why is reaction time correlated with psychometric *g? Current Directions in Psychological Science, 2,* 9–10.

Jensen, A. R. (1994). Reaction time. In R. J. Corsini (Ed.), *Encyclopedia of Psychology,* 2nd ed. (Vol. 3, pp. 282–285). New York: Wiley.

Jensen, A. R. (1998a). *The g factor.* Westport, CT: Praeger.

Jensen, A. R. (1998b). The suppressed relationship between IQ and the reaction time slope parameter of the Hick function. *Intelligence, 26,* 43–52.

Jensen, A. R., Larson, G. E., & Paul, S. M. (1988). Psychometric *g* and mental processing speed on a semantic verification test. *Personality and Individual Differences, 9,* 243–255.

Kail, R. (1991a). Developmental change in speed of processing during childhood and adolescence. *Psychological Bulletin, 109,* 490–501.

Kail, R. (1991b). Development of processing speed in childhood and adolescence. *Advances in Child Development and Behavior, 23,* 151–185.

Kranzler, J. H. (1992). A test of Larson and Alderton's (1990) worst performance rule of reaction time variability. *Personality and Individual Differences, 13,* 255–261.

Kyllonen, P. C. (1993). Aptitude testing inspired by information processing: A test of the four-sources model. *Journal of General Psychology, 120,* 375–405.

Larson, G. E., & Alderton, D. L. (1990). Reaction time variability and intelligence: A "worst performance" analysis of individual differences. *Intelligence, 14,* 309–325.

Lohman, D. F. (2000). Complex information processing and intelligence. In R. J. Sternberg (Ed.), *Handbook of intelligence* (pp. 285–340). Cambridge, UK: Cambridge University Press.

Myerson, J., Zheng, Y., Hale, S, Jenkins, L., & Widaman, K. (2003). Difference engines: Mathematical models of diversity in speeded cognitive performance. *Psychonomic Bulletin and Review, 10,* 262–288.

Neubauer, A. C. (1997). The mental speed approach to the assessment of intelligence. In J. S. Carlson, J. Kingma, & W. Tomic (Eds.), *Advances in cognition and educational practice: Reflections on the concept of intelligence* (Vol. 4, pp. 149–173). Greenwich, CT: JAI Press Inc.

O'Hara, R., Sommer, B., & Morgan, K. (2001). Reaction time but not performance on cognitive tasks identifies individuals at risk for Alzheimer's disease: A preliminary report. Unpublished manuscript, Department of Psychiatry and Behavioral Sciences, Stanford University School of Medicine, Stanford University, Stanford, CA.

Paul, S. M. (1984). Speed of information processing: The Semantic Verification Test and general mental ability. Unpublished Ph.D. dissertation, University of California, Berkeley.

Rabbitt, P. (1996). Do individual differences in speed reflect "global" or "local" differences in mental abilities? *Intelligence, 22,* 69–88.

Salthouse, T. A. (1998). Relation of successive percentiles of reaction time distributions to cognitive variables and adult age. *Intelligence, 26,* 153–166.

Thompson, P. M., Cannon, T. D., Narr, K. L., van Erp, T., Poutanen, V.-P., Huttunen, M., Longqvist, J., Standertkjold-Nordenstam, C.-G., Kaprio, J., Khaledy, M., Dail, R., Zoumalan, C. I., & Toga, A. W. (2001). Genetic influences on brain structure. *Nature: Neuroscience, 4*(No. 12), 1253–1258.

Vernon, P. A. (Ed.) (1987). *Speed of information processing and intelligence* (pp. 101–175). Norwood, NJ: Ablex.

Von Neumann, J. (1941). Distribution of the ratio of the mean square successive difference to the variance. *Annals of Mathematical Statistics, 14,* 378–388.

3

Reductionism versus Charting

Ways of Examining the Role of Lower-Order Cognitive Processes in Intelligence

Lazar Stankov

Following on Locke's theory that the senses are the building blocks of thinking and knowledge, Galton (1883) proposed that fine differences in sensory discrimination should be related to individual differences in cognitive ability. Although the evidence accumulated by the beginning of the twentieth century strongly rejected this proposal, near the end of that same century, there was a reemergence of related views. These views have always been motivated by a desire to uncover the biological roots of intelligence.

The groundwork for a renewed interest in the relationship between lower-order processes and intelligence was set in the 1970s with developments that eventually crystallized into different programmatic orientations and aims. One of these was frankly *reductionist* and very much in a Galtonian tradition. The other approach – *charting* – was motivated by a realization that, for historical and technical reasons, the domain of cognition was far from being covered in all its breadth in psychometric studies of intelligence; the task of mapping it out is far from being finished. In the late 1980s research on cognitive aging, which is somewhat removed from the traditional area of intelligence, also moved in the direction of linking lower-order processes and intelligence. This work, however, *combined* both reductionist and charting features. My aim in this chapter is to review recent developments within these three orientations and consider implications for psychometric theories of intelligence.

Contemporary work in all three orientations has been influenced by developments that saw changes in the interpretation of "sensory." The shift was away from acuity measures of sensory discrimination (i.e., absolute and differential thresholds), which were seen as crucial to the meaning of sensory in the pre-Binet test times, and toward a variety of simple cognitive processes that are presumed to be the ingredients of more complex cognitive processes of the kind involved in typical tests of intelligence. Associated with this new focus was an increased reliance on timed (i.e., speed) measures of mental processing that was facilitated by the availability of microcomputers. Initially, it appeared as if the "cognitive components" approach (the breaking down of, say, an analogical reasoning task into its ingredient processes), as advocated by R. Sternberg, and the "cognitive correlates" approach of E. Hunt (correlating a parameter of a well-understood cognitive task, like sentence–picture verification, with intelligence test scores) are conceptually different. It was quickly realized that they are not. At about the same time (i.e., the late 1970s), A. Jensen became interested in the relationship between simple and choice reaction time and intelligence and initiated a large number of studies utilizing the Hick paradigm. Cognitive components and correlates, as well as aspects of simple and choice reaction times, rapidly became known as "elementary cognitive tasks" (ECTs, Carroll, 1976).[1] Carroll's (1976) list of ECTs was expanded in the ensuing years, but without a systematic framework for sampling of the tasks from the cognitive domain being instituted. In other words, the theoretical background that was evident in the original (i.e., components and correlates approaches) attempts to link cognitive psychology to the study of intelligence has largely disappeared and the choice of the ECTs seems to have become related to the whim of the researcher. In effect, any elementary cognitive task that showed a glimmer of correlation with higher-order processes was quickly placed onto somebody's research agenda.

REDUCTIONISM: PSYCHOLOGY AS A SCIENCE SANDWICHED AMONG THE "TURTLES-ALL-THE-WAY-DOWN"

The most pronounced current in today's attempts to link lower-order processes to intelligence is contained within a reductionist agenda. Ultimately, the hope is that it will be possible to show that physical characteristics of the organism can account for at least a part, perhaps a significant part, of the individual differences in higher-order cognitive processes. An anecdote that inspired the above subtitle, as retold by Stephen Hawking in the "Brief History of Time," is about a well-known scientist who delivered a public lecture on astronomy. He described how the Earth orbits around the

---

[1] Carroll (1976) was quite enthusiastic about these developments. He proposed a taxonomy of cognitive processes and embarked on the task of classifying measures of primary mental abilities like those contained within the Educational Testing Services' Kit of Reference tests (French, Ekstrom, & Price, 1963). The title of Carroll's report "New Structure of Intellect" harked back to Guilford's taxonomic ideas from the preceding decade, but by that time, the "cognitive revolution" has made its impact on studies of intelligence, and the taxonomy of ECTs looked relatively modern by comparison. In retrospect, it is perhaps interesting that Stankov (1980) employed cluster analysis to show that the hierarchical structure that emerges from Carroll's taxonomy approximates quite well the structure that is postulated by the theory of fluid and crystallized intelligence. One may lament over the fact that a similar taxonomy of currently popular ECTs does not exist.

sun and how the sun, in turn, orbits around the center of a vast collection of stars called our galaxy. At the end of the lecture, a little old lady stood up and said: "What you have told us is rubbish. The world is really a flat plate supported on the back of a giant tortoise." When the scientist replied with a question, "What is the tortoise standing on?," the answer came back quickly "But, of course, it's the turtles all the way down." Reductionism is based on the notion of sciences being ordered hierarchically.[2] One such hierarchy places sociology on the top, followed by psychology, biology, chemistry, and atomic physics.

Deary (2000) is perhaps the most vocal advocate of a reductionist position in psychology. After downplaying attempts to understand intelligence in terms of its predictive validity (i.e., in terms of "still more molar processes"), he states that "potentially more important and profound, though, are attempts to explain intelligence by appealing to differences in lower-level psychological and biological processes" (Deary, 2000, p. 32). Thus, Deary distinguishes between two kinds of reductionist explanations. I believe that one of these – biological reductionism – can be useful in providing additional, and perhaps even more profound, explanations of some (hopefully, for the sake of our science, never all) psychological phenomena. Measures of brain functions as detected by EEG recordings, various kinds of brain imaging, and the like promise to provide interesting new hypotheses about the nature of psychological processing that takes place in the course of carrying out cognitive activities.[3] For example, our recent work (Stankov et al., 2002, in preparation) focuses on the gamma-band frequency range (centered on 40 Hz) of EEG recordings. This frequency range has been implicated in discussions about what is known as the "binding problem" in neuropsychology. This has to do with the fact that quite distinct and geographically separated brain areas may be engaged almost simultaneously in any act of cognitive processing. The suggestion has been made that gamma-band frequency provides information about this synchronicity.

The notion of binding and related ideas of psychological tuning-in of processes from distinct brain areas are, of course, related to Hebb's (1949) conception of cell assemblies that underpins his theory of intelligence. Our own interest in this topic derived from a suggestion that individual differences in measures of synchronicity, such as the speed with which different brain regions achieve synchronous activity or the amplitude (strength) of joint activity of different brain regions, may be related to scores on intelligence tests. Our findings to date are encouraging. There are indeed

---

[2] There are also references to the world resting on turtles' backs in Indian mythology.

[3] It is necessary to stress at this point that "promise" is the operative word. Despite considerable effort over the past half century or more at linking physical substrata to intelligence, precious little useful information can be extracted from a large, but often inconclusive and contradictory, body of research.

significant correlations between measures of synchronicity across different brain regions and scores on tests of intelligence. The number of significant correlations and their sizes rule out the interpretation that the effects are due to experimental or sampling errors. Thus, people who have higher IQs appear to show quicker and stronger tuning-in of brain regions that are responsible for carrying out particular cognitive acts.

If replicated, these findings may have important implications for the nature of fluid (g_f, Hebb's intelligence A) and crystallized (g_c, Hebb's intelligence B) abilities. This may include demonstrations that g_f, g_c, and other broad abilities involve different brain regions, which may corroborate brain imaging data. More importantly, the work may shed light on the issues that were of major interest to Hebb: how do g_f and g_c (and other broad abilities) develop during childhood and what happens in the process of recovery from prolonged sensory deprivation or after brain injury. Indeed, the work may provide us with a window for looking at changes in neural plasticity during the whole of human lifespan and therefore provide a sophisticated and sensible understanding of the interplay between nature and nurture. This is because the measurement of synchronous activity in different brain regions can be used to study the formation of new neuronal networks through repeated stimulation that arises from experience. This is the basis of learning and therefore of both fluid and crystallized intelligence.

However, Deary's (2000) alternative type of reductionism – the use of lower-level psychological processes such as sensory processes and the ECTs – as explanations of individual differences in intelligence test performance I take with a large dose of scepticism mainly because the division into lower-order and higher-order processes is arbitrary. There have been numerous instances of a process that initially seemed to belong to the lower order proving to be, on closer scrutiny, complex and therefore belonging to the higher-order category. It may therefore be wise to wait for the charting of the cognitive domain to be completed before we embark on the reductionist explanation based on lower-order psychological processes.[4]

Nevertheless, the main reason for studying ECTs within the reductionist framework clearly resides in a desire to get closer to the biological level of explanation. As pointed out by Stankov (2002a, b), the reductionist approach is closely linked to a research program that is strongly influenced by theories of intelligence that emphasize a general factor g and, as a rule, pays only lip service to other broad and primary mental ability factors sometimes mislabeled as "specific" factors. An important line of argument

---

[4] Even if the hierarchy of cognitive processes were to be shown to exist, it would not necessarily follow that lower-order processes can explain everything about the higher-order processes, as reductionists seem to want to argue.

is an attempt to show that the genetic part of variance in intelligence tests is identical, or perhaps closely linked to, the genetic component of elementary cognitive tasks. A corollary of this argument is the assumption that a general factor that can be extracted from a battery of ECTs is linked to the general factor of intelligence. A study reported by Luo and Petrill (1999) is one in a series of studies with this general agenda. To gain a feel for the type of tasks employed in this line of research, consider a couple of ECTs used by these researchers:

> Stimulus Discrimination. "Subjects in the Sensory Discrimination task were presented with six blank windows in the bottom portion of the screen, and a probe window in the upper portion of the screen. The six windows would each display a different diagram, and the probe window would present a diagram identical to one of the six diagrams below. The subject's task was to find the match to the probe in the windows below, and indicate it as quickly as possible."
>
> Inspection Time. "Two diagrams were presented simultaneously for a very brief duration and were then masked, and subjects were asked to determine whether they were the same. The presentation time varied until a threshold duration for correct identification was determined" (Luo & Petrill, 1999, p. 160).

Altogether, Luo and Petrill (1999) employed six different simple tasks from which nine ECT measures were derived. They also administered Wechsler's Intelligence Scale for Children (WISC) scores, as well as scholastic achievement measures. Stankov (2002b) pointed out that a general factor obtained from the WISC scores became weaker if the nine ECT measures were added to the battery. Furthermore, a separate chronometric factor with loadings from the ECT measures emerged as well. This weaker general factor is simply a consequence of the inclusion of the ECTs – simple tasks that have low correlations among themselves and with the general factor. However, Stankov (2002b) did not comment on the main point of Luo and Petrill's 1999 paper, which was that the correlation between the g-factor and scholastic achievement measures did not change with the addition of the ECTs to the battery. Thus, if you have a general factor from the WISC and a general factor that is derived from the WISC plus ECTs, correlations of both these general factors with scholastic achievement are about the same. This too may be a consequence of low correlations between the ECTs and all other measures; they have poor predictive validity.[5]

---

5 But in this particular case it is likely that a somewhat different situation obtains. For technical reasons Luo and Petrill (1999) could not test directly whether their chronometric factor by itself predicted scholastic achievement. Since ECT correlations with school achievement are small but not totally insignificant (they range from .13 to .32, with median of .24), it is quite possible that ECTs do indeed add to the prediction equation an aspect that is different from

It is interesting to observe that one of the driving forces behind study-ing lower-order processes in relation to intelligence – the hope of showing strong genetic links between them – may not be borne out strongly in empirical research. Thus, a generic version of the inspection time (IT) mea-sure, similar to the one described earlier, was employed in a recent study reported by Luciano et al. (2001). Curiously, the findings indicate that heri-tability estimates for IT are smaller than those for intelligence itself. If men-tal speed and inspection time are "basic" – that is, they reflect processes that are closer to physical aspects of the organism than IQ measures – one would expect that the heritability estimate for IT would be as high as the heritability of IQ. It may be that heritabilities of EEGs (or measures used in brain imaging) are considerably lower than those of intelligence itself. With this in mind, one may be tempted to argue that small correlations be-tween lower-order processes and intelligence are due to low heritability of the lower-order processes. Biological reductionism, contrary to its driving force, is not necessarily linked to either nature or nurture.

A large body of literature exists on two ECTs. One of these is the inspec-tion time paradigm that has been of particular interest to Deary (2000). Over 90 articles are based on IT, and one whole 2001 issue of the journal *Intelligence* is devoted to the same topic. In the most recent meta-analysis by Grudnik and Kranzler (2001), the average raw correlation between IT and IQ is −.30 (or −.51 when corrected for the presumed artifactual effects). Traditionally, IT has been interpreted as a measure of mental speed which, in turn, is seen as the basic process that underlies individual differences in intelligence. Nettelbeck (2001) is one of the initial contributors to the study of IT and, to this day, one of the main figures in IT research. His most recent interpretation of the correlation between inspection time and psychometric abilities is at variance with the prevailing view. He claims that IT is sensitive both to focused attentional capacities and to decision processes that monitor responding. Furthermore, he points out that in a young adult group, IT is correlated with the g_s (broad speediness) func-tion and, in the case of visual IT, to broad visualization (g_v) abilities. Con-trary to the common assumption, in this group of participants IT is not re-lated to fluid intelligence (g_f). Yet again, what might have been seen as an "elementary" and simple process escapes simple interpretation and turns out not to be easily tractable, a familiar story in psychology.

Another popular ECT paradigm involves the measurement of sim-ple and choice reaction time as frequently employed by Jensen and his

the general factor. To the extent that they do, the role of the general factor is undermined. In other words, since there are correlations between the ECTs and school achievement and the general factor does not account for them, it is logical to conclude that these correlations are due to the chronometric factor. This possibility was not discussed by Luo and Petrill (1999).

collaborators (see Jensen, 1998). Both these measures of mental speed tend to have lower correlations with the general factor than does IT, around .20 overall. It is hard to understand the importance that is sometimes attached to such low, and frequently insignificant, correlations. Roberts and Stankov (1999) measured choice reaction time using the card-sorting paradigm. This procedure places a greater demand on decision processes than the typical Hick's paradigm employed in Jensen's work. Their data point out that it is the decision time, calculated from card sorting and several other measures of mental speed, that has *the* central role in linking mental speed to intelligence. The decision process itself is certainly more complex than processes underlying most of the ECTs. This finding, together with the tendency for choice reaction time to correlate higher with intelligence as the number of choices increases, suggest that the study of complexity, not "elementarity," is likely to be a more crucial aspect of intelligence.

Research employing elementary cognitive tasks has shown that nothing of substance has really changed since the beginning of the last century. In fact, a recent study by Acton and Schroeder (2001) revisited the original sensory discrimination interpretations of Galton. Based on a rather large sample of almost 900 participants, they report correlations of .21 between pitch discrimination and g and .31 between color discrimination and g. These authors suggest that sensory discrimination is relatively distinct from general intelligence, and that their results cast doubts on a strong form of the sensory discrimination explanation of g.

I suspect that one of the reasons for Deary's (2000) claim that reductionism may provide "more important and profound" explanations derives from concerns about psychology's status as a scientific discipline. It is often claimed that if we can understand psychological phenomena in terms of biological processes, we are on a firmer, more scientific, ground. The popularity of neurosciences and related fields today derives in part from such concerns about psychology. Clearly, this is a weak argument. After all, biology itself is not a science because it can be understood in terms of chemistry. As described earlier, the reductionist view of science is akin to a series of turtles standing on top of each other, with each lower-level turtle representing a science that is a basis, and therefore an explanation, for a higher-level science. However, a branch of science is defined primarily in terms of the existence of a unique subject matter and method, not in terms of its position within the turtle hierarchy. Psychology is fine from the former point of view; turtles cannot be a justification for calling something science.

In the long run, recent attempts to link lower-order ECTs to intelligence are likely to be seen as useful, but not for reasons hoped for by the current advocates of reductionism. A large body of literature on IT, choice reaction time, and ECTs, similar to those studied by Roberts and Stankov (1999), is certainly a contribution to the overall aim of psychometric charting the cognitive domain in its entirety. However, explanatory aspects derived from ECTs are probably better kept in the background.

CHARTING AS A WAY OF BREAKING THE CHAINS OF THE PAPER-AND-PENCIL TESTING MEDIUM

Psychometric testing, to this day, has been dominated by the medium used for test administration. To the extent to which current theories of intelligence focus on verbal (usually written), quantitative, and spatial (two-dimensional drawing) abilities, we can say that "the medium is the message." The predominant use of a single testing medium is usually justified by the argument that higher-order processes can be measured about equally well irrespective of the input modality. This is sometimes referred to as the "irrelevance of the indicator." But, although the focus on these areas may encompass a large part of the cognitive domain, much is left untouched. An increased use of multimedia (dynamic stimuli, color, photos, and moving pictures with sound) facilities for contemporary test development would be one way to remove this limitation within the visual modality itself.

Another way is to accept the fact that sensory modalities other than vision have remained largely unexplored in psychometric literature and use them as a broad framework that can provide for a systematic exploration of new areas. From this perspective, lower-order processes become important for two reasons. First, given the importance of complexity for our understanding of intelligence, it may be profitable to combine tasks based on different sensory modalities into competing versions, both dual and multiple. Exploring the unique feature of each modality can be the first step in the direction of developing competing multiple tasks, and thus expanding the study of cognitive complexity. Second, and most important, is the plausible assumption that each sensory modality has a unique set of processes that have hitherto been left out of studies of individual differences. These cognitive processes may be simple and similar to the ECTs, but some of them may be complex and therefore need to be classified as parts of broader abilities like g_f and g_c.

The study of auditory abilities can provide illustrations for both these points. Sensory and perceptual processes in audition were brought into the realm of intelligence testing in the late 1970s. Prior to that decade psychometric studies in the area of listening did exist, of course, but much of their importance derived from the practical needs to select candidates for musical training on the one hand and for military duties (e.g., radiotelegraphers and sonarmen) on the other. Systematic studies of musical and listening abilities within the realm of intelligence research pointed to the existence of several primary auditory abilities that were not a part of previous structural accounts of intelligence (see Stankov & Horn, 1980). These abilities include perception of rhythmic patterns and perception of auditory material under various forms of distraction and distortion that define a broad auditory function (g_a) at the second stratum. These also include tonal memory, which proved to be distinct from short-term memory that is measured by nonmusical material, although the time interval for retention and recognition is approximately the same. Tonal memory is also distinct from short-term memory in other modalities because it is more closely related to auditory sensory discrimination. g_a is, therefore, a broad perceptual function similar to broad visualization (g_v) in the visual domain.

Another primary ability, temporal tracking, is not strongly dependant on sensory processing. Tasks that measure this ability require keeping in mind previously presented stimuli and either ignoring them or taking some specific action when presented with the same stimuli again. Since its main feature is a sequential presentation of information, stimuli that are not auditory in nature can be easily employed for its measurement. But sequential presentation was previously ubiquitous to auditory stimulation. Its importance was not fully realized in studies based on the typical paper-and-pencil medium. In fact, processes captured by the construct of working memory, which subsequently became popular in accounts of reasoning and fluid intelligence, are largely sequential in nature. Furthermore, the identification of primary abilities within the auditory area paved the way for the selection of component tasks in dual or competing tasks studies. These tasks can be interpreted in terms of divided attention and as manipulations of complexity par excellence.

Our recent work has examined the structure of tactile, kinaesthetic, and olfactory abilities with the primary aim of charting the domain and, hopefully, uncovering neglected cognitive processes that are unique to each domain but may be important for intelligent behavior (see Roberts, Pallier, & Goff, 1999). Two studies of tactile/kinaesthetic abilities have been carried out over the past several years. Within traditional intelligence research and related areas of personnel selection, tactile and kinaesthetic abilities, particularly the latter, are treated within the context of the psychomotor abilities. Our work, however, was motivated by neuropsychological findings. In the first study (Roberts et al., 1997) marker tests of g_f, g_c, and g_v were given together with several measures from the Halstead–Reitan Neuropsychological Test Battery and other measures of tactile and kinaesthetic sensory and perceptual processes. An interesting finding emanating from this research was that complex Halstead–Reitan tasks could not be separated from broad visualization (g_v, Pallier, Roberts, & Stankov, 2000). In other words, the processes involved in complex tactile and kinaesthetic tasks seem to activate spatial visualization abilities during their performance. This finding, of course, augurs well with the practice encouraged by the sport coaches and puppetry performers who use visualization as a form of practice of skilled movements. It was also apparent that tactile and kinaesthetic tests used in neuropsychological research may be, in fact, measuring fluid intelligence. In other words, the tasks that are used for the detection of brain damage but do not depend on the verbal or written medium are effectively measuring higher-order cognitive processes.

On the basis of the experiences gained with auditory stimuli, we reasoned that the inclusion of simpler tactile and kinaesthetic tasks in a battery of neurological tests may bring out either a broad perceptual factor encompassing both these modalities or separate broad tactile and kinaesthetic factors analogous to g_a and the spatial-visualization factor, g_v. This reasoning led to the design of a second study in which several lower-order tactile and kinaesthetic tasks were employed. In the outcome, two factors – one in the tactile and another in the kinaesthetic domain – were found (Stankov, Seizova-Cajic, & Roberts, 2000). Tactile abilities require processing that depends on fine discrimination of pressure on the skin. Kinaesthetic abilities involve the awareness of (passive) movements of upper limbs and the ability to visually recognize a path that individuals follow while blindfolded.

It is important to keep in mind that the charting of cognitive abilities with sensory modalities as a framework for exploration is not an empty academic exercise. At least one contemporary theory of intelligence, albeit based on more limited empirical evidence than the psychometric work reviewed in this chapter, points to the complex processes indicative of high artistic and sporting achievement, and therefore of intelligence, that are at least as dependent on tactile and kinaesthetic abilities as they are on higher-order cognition (Gardner, 1983). A similar claim can be made with respect to the olfactory and gustatory abilities, since there are people with highly developed skills in perfume detection, wine tasting, and cooking whose expertise simply cannot be detected with traditional paper-and-pencil tests.

The olfactory sensory modality has attracted little interest among students of cognitive abilities working within the psychometric tradition. Evidence from within experimental cognitive psychology suggests that olfactory memory is distinct from memory processes in other sensory modalities, including vision and audition. In a study reported by Danthiir et al. (2001), participants were tested with a battery of twelve psychometric tests, four putative cognitive olfactory tasks, and one olfactory discrimination measure. Results indicate the possible existence of an olfactory memory factor (OM), which is structurally independent of the established higher-order abilities (g_f, g_v, g_c, and short-term acquisition and retrieval or SAR) and unrelated to simple olfactory sensitivity. It is also unrelated to the processes of tonal memory that are unique to auditory processes. The OM factor is defined only by the olfactory tasks, all of which have a strong memory component. Importantly, the tests defining this factor contain elements of memory systems that are ordinarily seen as separate – that is, short-term and long-term memory measures. In other words, olfactory memory appears unusual in the sense that it blurs the distinction between long-term and short-term memory.

It appears that gustatory processes have been studied even less than olfaction. Given the importance of food experiences in contemporary societies and high levels of expertise that can be achieved by epicures, the paucity of research in this area is lamentable.

Over the past five years sensory abilities have also been studied because of considerable interest in decision processes and, specifically, in the role that self-confidence plays in the situations with high degrees of uncertainty. Predictions of future states of affairs (e.g., in economic forecasting, medical diagnosis, and the like) always involve a degree of guesswork. It is interesting that a certain amount of uncertainty always exists in psychophysical measurements of performance at the threshold levels. Indeed, psychophysical assessment has traditionally relied on measures of confidence. Although somewhat outside the immediate purpose of charting the cognitive domain, this aspect of our work provided impetus for the study of sensory processes in modalities that would have not been studied otherwise.

Self-confidence in sensory processes has been studied because of the interest in two issues. First, are individual differences in self-confidence on complex cognitive tasks related to individual differences in self-confidence on sensory tasks? Our findings clearly indicate that the answer to this question is positive. In other words, there is a strong, apparently general, trait of self-confidence that is not restricted to general knowledge, perceptual, or nonverbal intelligence tasks (see Kleitman & Stankov, 2001; Pallier et al., 2002; Stankov, 1998). Curiously, when cast in this light, self-confidence in performance on sensory tasks can be seen as being related not to the physical bases of the organism but rather to metacognition, the process Deary (2000) would most likely want to dismiss as being too "molar." This is because the importance of self-confidence derives from its relationship to actual performance. Some people are accurate (i.e., they are neither over- nor under-confident) in knowing how good (or bad) their performance is, whereas others tend to be biased in either direction. Second, there have been claims that sensory processes are fundamentally different from more complex processes in that, on a group level, sensory processes tend to show under-confidence (i.e., people tend to perform better than they think they are capable of doing) and complex processes tend to show over-confidence. The initial enthusiasm for this conceptually interesting distinction has evaporated since, in our work, only one type of visual task (line length comparison) showed under-confidence; most other sensory tasks showed over-confidence or reasonable accuracy.

Perhaps the goal of charting (i.e., description) of the cognitive sphere is not as lofty an enterprise as the goal of reductionist interpretation (i.e., explanation) of behavior. As mentioned earlier, with respect to the use of lower-order psychological processes for the latter purpose, it is advisable to wait at least until the charting is complete or more advanced than it is at present. But charting by itself holds promise of being highly profitable since it may uncover cognitive processes that have been neglected due to the slavish adherence to the paper-and-pencil medium in psychological testing practices.

It is interesting to contemplate that the reductionist agenda has nevertheless helped the task of charting. Thus, the underlying aim of this activity has not been so much to understand the diversity of cognitive processes, but rather to show that they all have the same core in the *g* factor. Paradoxically, a consequence of the pursuit of reductionist goals has been a diminution of the strength of the *g* factor itself due to low correlations between lower-order processes with complex measures of intelligence.

COGNITIVE AGING IN BETWEEN CHARTING AND REDUCTIONIST AGENDAS

Throughout most of the lifespan (until retirement age), sensory processes and intelligence are minimally correlated. Thus, Li, Jordanova, and Lindenberger (1998) report that among 30–50 year olds, fluid intelligence correlates .20 with visual and .15 with auditory acuity. However, a pronounced decline occurs in both sensory processes and intelligence in old age. It was therefore natural to ask whether their relationship becomes stronger with age and, if so, what are the nature and the cause of this change. With respect to vision and hearing, it is generally acknowledged following the report of Baltes and Lindenberger (1997) that the link between these two kinds of sensory functioning and cognitive processing, as captured by the fluid intelligence tests, is about 20% stronger in the older than in the younger segments of the population. However, their work is based on a cross-sectional design. As is often the case in lifespan developmental work, at least some longitudinal studies question the causal nature of this relationship. For example Anstey, Luszcz, and Sanchez (2001) show that a decline in hearing is not associated with a decline in any higher-order cognitive function, while a decline in visual acuity is associated only with a decline in memory, but not with a decline in verbal ability or processing speed.

Both charting and reductionist agendas are in the background of the current interest in the sensory–cognition links at the later stages of life. However, an ideologically tainted distinction that mars mainstream intelligence research is not as apparent in cognitive aging studies.

With respect to charting, examination of sensory processes was driven by practical consideration of the difficulties that impede coping with everyday demands of life among the elderly. As shown by Marsiske, Klumb, and M. Baltes (1997), auditory and visual acuity measures are powerful predictors of competence with basic activities of daily living and the amount of participation in social and leisure activities. Similarly, consideration has to be given to the conditions that cause accidents and therefore injuries and perhaps even death. For example, body damage caused by falls is a more common reason for hospitalization among the aged than it is among younger people. Such damage can be fatal due to complications that may be a consequence of diabetes or osteoporosis, the incidence of which is pronounced among those older than 65. The circumstances that lead to falls and fractures implicate the sense of vision for sure but other senses as well. These include tactile and kinaesthetic abilities and the proprioceptive sense that provide information about body balance–gait in addition to the information provided by the vestibular system. Thus, the charting had to be moved into a new territory that is outside the traditional domains and, to some, still untouched by mainstream studies of intelligence.

Anstey, Stankov, and Lord (1993) and Stankov and Anstey (1997) employed a battery of sensory tests that measured, among others, processes linked to the detection of vibrations on the skin, the stability of upright posture with eyes closed, the precision of movement, and the strength of upper and lower limbs. Li et al. (1998) measured roughness discrimination, part-whole discrimination (i.e., matching of an arc to the circle from which the arc is excised), and tactile pressure sensitivity. Corroborating some of the findings from mainstream research, Li et al. (1998) demonstrated that the two discrimination tasks, being more complex, have higher correlation with intelligence than tactile pressure sensitivity. The selection of these tasks was clearly influenced by neuropsychological considerations and was therefore focused on functions that are distinct from those emphasized by personnel selection issues that often drive mainstream research in intelligence.

Most studies of the sensory–cognitive link during lifespan development are based on large samples. There is, however, an indication from neuropsychology that decline in olfactory ability appears linked to Alzheimer's disease and perhaps other kinds of dementia. This certainly suggests that aging research should expand its focus beyond the modalities studied up until now and consider the chemical senses as well.

With respect to the reductionist accounts, Baltes and Lindenberger (1997) and their coworkers have proposed a "common cause" hypothesis that is supposed to account for the increased sensory–cognitive link. The hypothesis states that lower-level sensory processing and high-level cognitive functioning are both expressions of a third common factor, namely, the efficacy of neural information processing in the central nervous system. Since aging compromises brain efficiency, which, in turn, imparts on both sensory and cognitive processes, performances in these two areas become increasingly intercorrelated. This, of course, is a plausible account. Li et al. (1998) took pains to point out that this hypothesis, although in accord with Galton's ideas, differs from his account in that age acts as a mediating factor.

In my opinion, the jury is still out as far as the status of the common-cause hypothesis is concerned. While the link between sensory measures of intelligence may exist in later stages of life, the actual strength of the correlation may be open to dispute and indeed is likely to vary depending on the actual measures employed and between modalities. Furthermore, whatever the strength of this relationship, the common-cause hypothesis needs to be tested more thoroughly than it has been up until now. Modular hypothesis that postulates a separate aging process for sensory function (peripheral) and a separate aging process for the cognitive function (central) is still a serious option.

There is little doubt, however, that a strong reductionist hypothesis that postulates a causal link between sensory processes and intelligence and claims that decline in intelligence is caused by the decline in sensory processes is unlikely to succeed. An attempt to have a closer look at this option was made by Stankov and Anstey (1997). That study compared two structural equation models that differed with respect to the treatment of the sensory variables. One model assumed that sensory variables are a part of the structure of intelligence that had causal paths *from* nonability variables of age, education, and health. The other model moved sensory measures to the causal side under the assumption that, if sensory variables affect the performance on cognitive tasks in the way variables like age and education do, the fit of the latter model would be superior. In the outcome, both models had an equally good fit to the data. This can be interpreted to imply the lack of support for a strong reductionist position.

SENSORY PROCESSES AND PSYCHOMETRIC THEORIES OF INTELLIGENCE

Lower-order sensory and other cognitive processes captured by elementary cognitive tasks are a part of cognition and therefore an aspect of intelligence. Many of them, particularly those related to modalities other than vision, have been neglected. The primary aim of any attempt to bring sensory processes and ECTs into structural studies of intelligence is the completion of charting of the domain. Occasionally, as a bonus, this may bring into focus hitherto unknown complex processes like those related to sequential presentation of stimuli within the auditory domain, the importance of olfactory memory, and new tactile and kinaesthetic processes. All these processes are likely to have features similar to the second-stratum factors like g_f and g_c, but, in particular, they are similar to broad perceptual processes such as g_v and g_a. Some of these new processes may become a part of the g_f or of some other broad factor.

The study of lower-order psychological processes with the reductionist aim in mind is untenable at present because the attempts to classify cognitive processes into lower-order and higher-order have been fraught with difficulties.

The interpretation of the hierarchical structure of human abilities that is based on factor analysis remains as always. Part of the variance is due to the general factor, part of it to the unique factor. Empirical studies have also shown that very few, if any, cognitive tests measure only a general and a unique factor. As argued by Stankov (2002a), the strength of the general factor is weaker than its proponents are telling us. The indications are that sensory tasks from different modalities will define factors reflective of that modality. To be meaningful, the design of studies of intelligence has to be multivariate. Shortcuts like having a single measure of intelligence (e.g., Raven's Progressive Matrices Test) and a single ECT (e.g., a measure of inspection time) can lead to confusion since the latter may be primarily related to, say, the visualization process (g_v) or an aspect of mental speed (g_s) and only through these to g itself.

Although at first blush it may appear that the study of ECTs and sensory tasks is rather boring and less glamorous than some other popular areas of study (e.g., the so-called emotional intelligence), it is unlikely that their use in research on intelligence will diminish in the foreseeable future, if ever, for several reasons: The study of the role of complexity in intelligence can benefit from the delineation of the ingredient processes, biological reductionism will continue to prefer ECTs to any molar measure of intelligence, and the outcomes of charting to date have brought into the picture several interesting new factors and there is promise for more.

References

Acton, G. S., & Schroeder, D. H. (2001). Sensory discrimination as related to general intelligence. *Intelligence, 29*, 263–271.

Anstey, K. J., Luszcz, M. A., & Sanchez, L. (2001). Two-year decline in vision but not hearing is associated with memory decline in very old adults in a population-based sample. *Gerontology, 47*, 289–293.

Anstey, K., Stankov, L., & Lord, S. (1993). Primary aging, secondary aging and intelligence. *Psychology and Aging, 8*, 562–570.

Baltes, P. B., & Lindenberger, U. (1997). Emergence of a powerful connection between sensory and cognitive functions across the adult lifespan: A new window to the study of cognitive aging? *Psychology and Aging, 12*, 12–21.

Carroll, J. B. (1976). Psychometric tests as cognitive tasks: A new "Structure of Intellect." In L. Resnick (Ed.), *The nature of intelligence* (pp. 27–56). Hillsdale, NJ: Erlbaum.

Danthiir, V., Roberts, R. D., Pallier, G., & Stankov, L. (2001). What the nose knows: Olfaction and cognitive abilities. *Intelligence, 29*, 337–361.

Deary, I. J. (2000). *Looking down on human intelligence*. Oxford, UK: Oxford University Press.

French, J. W., Ekstrom, R. B., & Price, L. A. (1963). *Manual and kit of reference tests for cognitive factors*. Princeton, NJ: Educational Testing Service.

Galton, F. (1883). *Inquiries into human faculty*. London: Dent.

Gardner, H. (1983). *Frames of mind: The theory of multiple intelligences*. New York: Basic Books.

Grudnik, J. L., & Kranzler, J. H. (2001). Meta-analysis of the relationship between intelligence and inspection time. *Intelligence, 29*, 523–535.

Hebb, D. O. (1949). *The Organization of Behaviour: A neuropsychological theory*. New York: Wiley.

Jensen, A. R. (1998). *The "g" factor*. Westport, CT: Praeger.

Kleitman, S., & Stankov, L. (2001). Ecological and person-driven aspects of metacognitive processes in test-taking. *Applied Cognitive Psychology, 15*, 321–341.

Li, S.-H., Jordanova, & Lindenberger, U. (1998). From good senses to good sense: A link between tactile information processing and intelligence. *Intelligence, 26*, 99–122.

Luciano, M., Smith, G. A., Wright, M. J., Geffen, G. M., Geffen, L. B., & Martin, N. (2001). On the heritability of inspection time and its correlation with IQ: Twin study. *Intelligence, 29*, 443–458.

Luo, D., & Petrill, S. A. (1999). Elementary cognitive tasks and their roles in "g" estimates. *Intelligence, 27*, 157–174.

Marsiske, M., Klumb, P., & Baltes, J. M. (1997). Everyday activity patterns and sensory functioning in old age. *Psychology and Aging, 12*, 444–457.

Nettelbeck, T. (2001). Correlation between inspection time and psychometric abilities: A personal interpretation. *Intelligence, 29*, 459–474.

Pallier, G., Roberts, R., & Stankov, L. (2000). Biological vs. psychometric intelligence: Halstead's (1947) distinction re-visited. *Archives of Clinical Neuropsychology, 15*(3), 205–226.

Pallier, G., Wilkinson, R., Danthiir, V., Kleitman, S., Knezevic, G., Stankov, L., & Roberts, R. (2002). The role of individual differences in the realism of confidence judgments. *Journal of General Psychology, 122*, 1–39.

Roberts, R. D., & Stankov, L. (1999). Individual differences in speed of mental processing and human cognitive abilities: Towards a taxonomic model. *Learning and Individual Differences, 11*, 1–120.

Roberts, R. D., Pallier, G., & Goff, G. N. (1999). Sensory processes within the structure of human abilities. In P. L. Ackerman, P. C. Kyllonen, & R. D. Roberts (Eds.), *Learning and individual differences: Process, trait, and content determinants* (pp. 339–370). Washington, DC: American Psychological Association.

Roberts, R. D., Stankov, L., Pallier, G., & Dolph, B. (1997). Charting the cognitive sphere: Tactile/kinesthetic performance within the structure of intelligence. *Intelligence, 25*, 111–148.

Stankov, L. (1980). Psychometric factors as cognitive tasks: A note on Carroll's "New Structure of Intellect". *Intelligence, 4*, 65–71.

Stankov, L. (1998). Calibration curves, scatterplots and the distinction between general knowledge and perceptual tests. *Learning and Individual Differences, 8,* 28–51.

Stankov, L. (2002a). "g": A diminutive general. In R. Sternberg & E. Grigorenko (Eds.), *General factor of intelligence: How general is it?* Los Angeles: Erlbaum.

Stankov, L. (2002b). Complexity in intelligence. In R. Sternberg & T. Lubart (Eds), *Models of intelligence for the new millennium.* Washington, DC: American Psychological Association.

Stankov, L., & Anstey, K. (1997). Health and cognitive aging in Australia. *Australian Journal on Aging, 16,* 34–40.

Stankov, L., & Horn, J. L. (1980). Human abilities revealed through auditory tests. *Journal of Educational Psychology, 72,* 19–42.

Stankov, L., Seizova-Cajic, T., & Roberts, R. (2001). Tactile and kinesthetic perceptual processes within the taxonomy of human abilities. *Intelligence, 29,* 1–29.

4

Basic Information Processing and the Psychophysiology of Intelligence

Aljoscha C. Neubauer and Andreas Fink

BASIC INFORMATION PROCESSING AND INTELLIGENCE

Research on individual differences in human cognitive abilities or intelligence has a long history in scientific psychology. After decades of psychometric research into the structure of human cognitive abilities, the last 20 to 30 years have been characterized also by attempts to analyze cognitive components and correlates of psychometric intelligence. In this realm an important approach has been the attempt to relate the individual speed of information processing to psychometric intelligence (the so-called mental speed approach). This approach traces back to the idea that human cognitive or intellectual functioning might be decomposed in elementary cognitive processes, which are assumed to constitute an important basis of intellectual functioning. In the last two decades important progress has been made in this field of research: In using so-called elementary cognitive tasks (ECTs), which put only minimal requirements on the participants and are, thus, less likely prone to differential strategy usage, dozens of studies have provided converging evidence that shorter reaction times in these tasks are associated with higher psychometric intelligence, indicating a higher speed of information processing in brighter individuals.

The ECTs that have been used most extensively in this field of research are the Hick and the inspection time (IT) paradigm (see Fig. 1). In the IT paradigm (cf. Vickers, Nettelbeck, & Wilson, 1972) participants are tachistoscopically (i.e., for very short exposure durations) shown two vertical lines of different length. Immediately after their exposure, the lines are masked by two thicker vertical lines of equal length. Subsequently, the participant's task is to decide which one of the two lines is longer. A procedure is employed, in which the probability of correct responses to varying

The preparation of this chapter was partially supported by grants from the Austrian Science Foundation (Fonds zur Förderung wissenschaftlicher Forschung; FWF).

A)

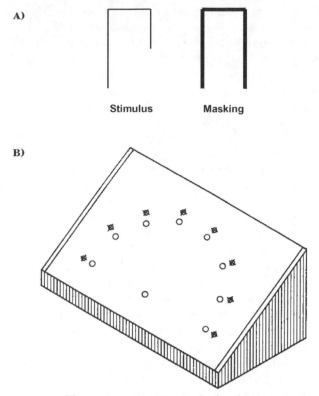

Stimulus   Masking

B)

FIGURE 1. Elementary cognitive tasks for the assessment of speed of information processing: a) inspection time paradigm, b) Hick apparatus.

stimulus exposure times (usually ranging from 10 to 200 ms) is assessed, by which the so-called inspection time can be determined (the minimum time required for a near-perfect, for instance, 95%-correct visual discrimination). From a meta-analysis ($N > 4100$) of IT–intelligence studies, Grudnik and Kranzler (2001) reported a mean negative correlation of $r = -.30$; therefore, a short inspection time (i.e., time to discriminate the lines) is associated with higher cognitive ability. Correcting for the effects of sampling error, attenuation, and range restriction, they estimated the "true" IT–intelligence correlation to be $r = -.51$.

Another ECT that is frequently used in mental speed research is the simple and choice reaction time task based on Hick's (1952) observation of a linear relationship between the amount of information (bits) processed in a visual reaction time task and the performance (i.e., reaction time) of a participant. The Hick task is employed using an apparatus consisting of eight semicircularly arranged buttons around a so-called home button on which the participant's index finger of the preferred hand is placed at the start of a trial (see Fig. 1b). In each trial, one of the lamps above each response button is switched on and the participant's task is to move his/her finger as quickly as possible from the home button to the response button adjacent to the light. In the so-called simple reaction time task, participants are required to respond as fast as possible to a single stimulus (0 bits of information). If a decision between two alternatives (visual stimuli) is necessary, one binary decision (1 bit) is involved, when four alternatives are presented two binary decisions (2 bit) are necessary, and so on. A review of studies relating parameters of the Hick paradigm to psychometrically determined intelligence is given by Jensen (1987): On the basis of 33 independent samples comprising a total of 2,317 participants, he reported mean correlations between −.12 and −.28 for various parameters of the Hick paradigm; that is, a high speed in the simple and choice reaction tasks (i.e., shorter reaction times) is associated with a high psychometric intelligence.

Both the IT and the Hick paradigms primarily measure the speed of perception and encoding of visual stimulus information. To explore the idea that speed of memory retrieval might also contribute to human intelligence differences (cf. Jensen, 1982), mental speed research also employs elementary cognitive memory tasks to assess the speed with which individuals are able to scan or retrieve information from short- or long-term memory. For example, the speed of retrieval from short-term memory (STM) is assessed by means of Saul Sternberg's (1966, 1969) memory scanning. In this task, participants are sequentially shown a random sequence of one to six digits, which have to be kept in STM (i.e., the memory set). After a warning signal, participants are asked to indicate as fast as possible whether a single digit was present in the previously shown memory set or not. An increase in the number of elements in the memory set typically leads to a linear increase of reaction time as more elements have to be kept in STM. On the basis of this linear relationship between reaction time and memory set size, the regression of reaction times on the number of items in STM can be calculated. According to this procedure, two parameters of the Sternberg paradigm are of special interest: First, the slope of this regression should be indicative of the time needed for STM retrieval of a single element; second, the intercept of this regression should indicate the duration of stimulus encoding and motoric response processes.

Neubauer (1995, 1997) reviewed studies that focused on the relationship between parameters of Sternberg's memory scanning and psychometrically determined intelligence. Averaged across ten studies with a total N of 972, the following average N-weighted correlations with intelligence test scores were found: $r = -.27$ for mean reaction time, $r = -.35$ for the variability of reaction time, $r = -.30$ for the intercept, and $r = -.11$ for the slope parameter of the Sternberg task.

Similarly, the speed of retrieval from long-term memory (LTM) is assessed by means of Posner's (Posner & Mitchell, 1967) letter matching paradigm. In this task participants are shown two letters per trial, which are either physically the same (e.g., "AA"), semantically the same, but physically different ("Aa"), or semantically different ("Ab"). In one condition participants judge the physical identity (PI) of the presented stimuli by pressing a "YES"-button to stimuli of the type "aa" or "BB" or a "NO"-button to stimuli of the type "Ab" or "Aa." In the more complex name identity (NI) condition, the participant's task is to indicate whether the presented letters are of identical name or not (e.g., answer "YES" to stimuli of the type "Aa" or "bB" and answer "NO" to stimuli of the type "Ab" or "Ba"). While the PI-condition necessitates only a visual discrimination the NI-condition additionally requires an access to highly overlearned material stored in the LTM (i.e., the letters of the alphabet). According to Hunt's (1980) suggestion, the difference between the mean reaction time in the NI and PI condition (NI − PI) should reflect the time needed for LTM retrieval.

A survey of studies, which related parameters of the Posner paradigm to psychometrically determined intelligence, is given by Neubauer (1995, 1997). Based on a total N of 1,064 participants in 11 independent studies, he reported an average N-weighted correlation of $r = -.23$ between the mean reaction time in the PI condition and intelligence test scores and a mean N-weighted correlation of $r = -.33$ between the mean reaction time in the NI condition and intelligence test scores. The NI − PI difference, the measure for LTM retrieval, correlates also negatively with psychometrically determined intelligence (mean $r = -.27$).

On the whole, the mental speed approach to human intelligence suggests a robust relationship between speed of information processing in elementary cognitive tasks and psychometrically determined intelligence; that is, a high psychometric intelligence is associated with a fast execution of elementary cognitive processes. The rather low (although consistent) negative correlations between reaction times in ECTs and psychometrically determined intelligence observed in the majority of studies (up to −.30, or at best −.40) gave several authors reason to conclude that the speed of information processing in single ECTs cannot explain more than 10% of variance in intelligence tests (see, e.g., Hunt, 1980; Stankov & Roberts, 1997). However, most of the critics ignore the fact that the relatively low RT–intelligence correlations are partially due to the homogeneity of the samples tested; about 90% of the studies in this field of research used samples of university or college students. As shown in some recent studies conducted in our own laboratory (Neubauer & Bucik, 1996; Neubauer & Knorr, 1997, 1998) much higher correlations – even between *single* ECT parameters and psychometrically determined intelligence – can be observed (of about −.50) when using more representative or heterogeneous samples with respect to the distribution of intellectual ability (cf. also Vernon, 1990).

In addition to this, when a comprehensive test battery composed of different ECTs is used, e.g., an ECT battery composed of Sternberg's memory scanning, Posner's letter matching, and Lindley and Smith's (1992) coding test (see Neubauer & Knorr, 1998), it is even possible to obtain multiple correlations up to $R = .77$, indicating that almost 60% of intellectual variance can be accounted for by mental speed.

Critics of the mental speed approach have also emphasized the role of high-level cognitive processes and prefer top-down explanations of the speed–intelligence relationship (rather than bottom-up explanations): Brighter individuals might be more strongly motivated to perform quickly in RT tasks, they might be faster in understanding the task instructions, or they might devote more attentional resources to the elementary cognitive task. These and other top-down explanations have been empirically tested in a series of studies (for a review see Neubauer, 1995, 1997; cf. also Deary, 2000), for example, by controlling for the level of attention, by systematically varying motivation (e.g., using incentives or feedback on reaction times), by varying instructions, or by allowing deliberate practice on the reaction time task. However, most of these studies found no empirical support for these alternative interpretations of the RT–intelligence relationship; therefore, it seems not unreasonable to attach importance to so-called bottom-up explanations, which originate from the idea that this relationship must by caused by one or more physiological properties of the human central nervous system.

PHYSIOLOGICAL CORRELATES OF HUMAN INTELLIGENCE

When trying to explain this relationship between speed of information processing and psychometrically determined intelligence by means of central nervous system characteristics, some proponents refer to the concept of *neural efficiency* (e.g., Vernon, 1993) – a concept that assumes that more intelligent individuals use their brains more efficiently when engaged in cognitive task performance. But what is high neural efficiency? Research on the basic processes underlying efficient performance in a variety of cognitive ability or intelligence tests – especially on the role of speed of information processing as a basic constituent in individual differences in human intelligence – has taken a conspicuous turning point. Starting in the late 1960s, the first research efforts were undertaken to find a physiological (biological) basis for individual differences in cognitive ability. In the first stage of this physiologically oriented research on human intelligence differences, most of the studies focused – in direct conjunction to the mental speed research tradition – on several speed parameters of the human electroencephalogram (EEG), for example, the latency of different components of the event-related or evoked potential (EP).

Although the expected negative EP latency–intelligence relationship has been observed in a multitude of studies (for reviews see Deary & Caryl, 1993; Neubauer, 1995), many other studies showed no such relationship.

Therefore, the relation of the EP parameter to psychometrically determined intelligence remains unclear. This might at least partly be due to the weak stability (i.e., low test–retest reliability) of many physiological measures as well as to the great number of experimental and technical variations in EP measurement (sensory modalities, stimulus intensity and timing, electrode positioning, etc.). In addition to this, most of the studies used only a very small number of cortical derivations, and, therefore, it seems unjustifiable to generalize the findings, that is, to assume similar EP–intelligence relationships for different cortical areas.

Another physiological approach is the measurement of the so-called peripheral nerve conduction velocity (PNCV) – a measure for the speed of conductance in the peripheral nervous system, which involves no obvious cognitive activity. Similar to the measurement of EP latencies, this approach also has roots in the mental speed approach to human intelligence differences, which underpins the role of speed of information processing as a basic constituent of human intelligence differences. However, attempts to relate PNCV to psychometrically determined intelligence have proven unsuccessful in a series of studies (e.g., Barrett, Daum, & Eysenck, 1990; Barrett & Eysenck, 1992; Reed & Jensen, 1991, 1992; Wickett & Vernon, 1994). Only one study (Vernon & Mori, 1992) reported empirical evidence in favor of the expected positive relationship between PNCV and intelligence.

However, in contrast to these comparatively unsuccessful attempts in relating EP and PNCV parameters to psychometrically determined intelligence, other physiological approaches have had more promising results. A method that has been used in a variety of studies dealing with physiological correlates of human intelligence differences is the measurement of the glucose metabolism rate (GMR) of the brain using positron emission tomography (PET). Like every other human organ, the brain consumes energy, especially in cognitively demanding situations, and this consumption of energy is compensated by metabolizing glucose. In measuring the GMR of the brain, individuals are injected with a metabolic tracer and the effects of cognitive activity on the GMR of different brain regions can be analyzed during a so-called uptake phase, a period of several minutes during which the metabolic tracer is taken up by the brain. Finally, the individuals are moved to the PET scanner where the GMR of the brain is measured.

In using this measurement method, mostly negative relationships between GMR and psychometrically determined intelligence have been observed: brighter individuals displayed a lower GMR during cognitive task performance than did lower IQ individuals. For instance, Haier et al. (1988) observed that brighter individuals displayed less glucose metabolism during performance of Raven's Advanced Progressive Matrices (IQ–GMR correlations between −.44 and −.84 for various brain regions). Similarly, Parks et al. (1988) presented a word fluency test during the uptake phase and found substantial negative correlations between GMR and test performance (*r* between −.50 and −.54). In further studies Haier et al. (1992a, b) replicated this finding of a more efficient use of the brain in brighter individuals. In these studies participants were required to perform and practice a complex computer game (Tetris) during the uptake period. The authors confirmed the hypothesized negative intelligence–GMR relationship (−.68 for Raven's Advanced Progressive Matrices and −.43 for the Wechsler scales). Additionally, they found the largest glucose metabolism decreases (resulting from increasing practice on the task) in individuals who improved their Tetris performance after practice the most – suggesting that practice or learning may result in decreased use of extraneous or inefficient brain areas.

However, even if the PET method facilitates the analysis of the activity of the whole brain during cognitive task performance, it has the disadvantage of a rather low temporal resolution. The PET scan only shows cumulative effects of brain functions over longer uptake phases, during which a metabolic tracer (i.e., a radioactive substance) is taken up by the brain (usually in the range of minutes). A more fine-grained temporal analysis of brain activation, which would be necessary when studying activation during the performance of an elementary cognitive task, cannot be obtained with the PET method.

To analyze phasic (i.e., short-lasting) changes of cortical activation during the performance of cognitively demanding tasks, we used another psychophysiological measurement method, the so-called event-related desynchronization (ERD) in the human EEG. The ERD method, originally proposed by Pfurtscheller and Aranibar (1977; see also Pfurtscheller & Lopes da Silva, 1999), is based on the well-known phenomenon of a blocking or desynchronization of rhythmic EEG background activity within the alpha band (from 8 to 12 Hz). In a series of trials of a cognitive task, the EEG background activity is measured in a reference interval (R; not involving any cognitive activity) as well as in an activation interval (A), during which individuals process stimulus information (immediately before participants' response, see Fig. 2). The ERD is then quantified by calculating the percentage of decrease of power in defined frequency bands (mostly alpha bands) from the reference (R) to the activation interval (A) using the formula $\%\text{ERD} = [(R - A)/R] \times 100$. Thus, changes in EEG alpha power are given as a percentage of the reference power, with positive %ERDs for decreases of alpha power (reflecting a cortical activation) and with negative %ERDs for increases of alpha power (indicative of a cortical deactivation).

As we are primarily interested in psychophysiological correlates of elementary cognitive processes (as assessed by elementary cognitive tasks) that are less likely to permit alternative interpretations as compared to more complex tasks (e.g., assuming individual differences in strategies during complex task performance), the ERD method seems especially suited here, since it allows the study of phasic changes of cortical activation (by

ERD (Event-Related Desynchronization)

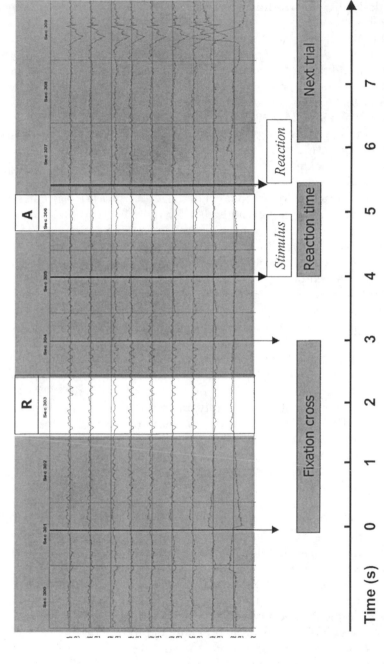

FIGURE 2. Measuring the extent of event-related desynchronization (ERD) in the EEG: schematic display of the EEG measurement intervals.

providing a very fine-grained temporal resolution of cortical activation). Thus, we employed the ERD method to analyze spatio-temporal patterns of cortical activation during performance of several well-known elementary cognitive tasks.

In a first study (Neubauer, Freudenthaler, & Pfurtscheller, 1995), we analyzed spatio-temporal patterns of cortical activation during performance of the well-known sentence verification test (SVT; Carpenter & Just, 1975; Clark & Chase, 1972) – which correlates substantially with psychometric intelligence (e.g., Neubauer & Freudenthaler, 1994). In this test participants are shown a simple sentence on the computer screen (e.g., "star is above plus") followed by the presentation of a picture showing the star above the plus or the inverse constellation. Participants were required to indicate whether the sentence was a true or false description of the picture. In analyzing the extent of ERD in the EEG during performance of the SVT, we found empirical evidence in favor of the *neural efficiency* concept of human intelligence: Lower IQ individuals were more likely to display a comparatively unspecific and stronger cortical activation as compared to brighter individuals, whereas the latter were more likely to display a more specific (i.e., more focused) cortical activation, presumably restricted to those cortical regions required for task performance, resulting in less overall cortical activation than displayed by lower IQ individuals.

In a second study (Neubauer, Sange, & Pfurtscheller, 1999), we tried to replicate these findings with another well-known elementary cognitive task, Posner's letter matching (Posner & Mitchell, 1967). As already mentioned, in the Posner task participants are shown two letters in each trial, which are physically the same (e.g., "AA"), semantically the same but physically different ("Aa"), or semantically different ("Ab"). In the first condition participants simply judge the physical identity (PI) of the presented stimuli (i.e., visual discrimination), whereas in the more complex name identity (NI)-condition, which additionally requires an access to highly overlearned material stored in the LTM (i.e., the letters of the alphabet), the participant's task was to judge the semantical or name identity of the stimuli.

As depicted in Figure 3, the findings of Neubauer et al. (1999) are again in line with the neural efficiency hypothesis. We found brighter individuals, who scored high on Raven's Advanced Progressive Matrices (APM; Raven, 1958), again displaying a more focused cortical activation (resulting in a lower total cortical activation) as compared to lower IQ individuals (i.e., lower APM scores). Most interestingly, these IQ group differences were much more prominent in the more complex NI condition; in the relatively simple PI condition only marginal and nonsignificant IQ group differences with respect to the level and topographical distribution of cortical activation were observed. It seems that for a corroboration of the neural efficiency phenomenon, obviously a certain level of task difficulty (as in the NI

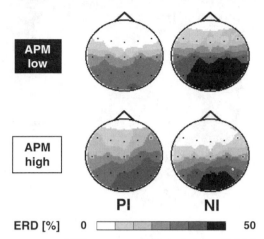

FIGURE 3. ERD maps separately for the APM low and APM high group. Black and dark gray areas in these maps symbolize a large extent of ERD; brighter areas depict no or only weak ERD.

condition) is required, whereas the PI condition is possibly too simple to allow for group differences.

To more thoroughly study this latter issue, we further investigated the influence of task complexity on the relationship between cortical activation patterns and intelligence. For the latter variable we additionally distinguished between fluid and crystallized intelligence (Neubauer & Fink, 2003). We employed a modified version of Stankov's (2000; cf. also Stankov & Crawford, 1993; Stankov & Raykov, 1995) Triplet Numbers test, which consists of five increasingly complex conditions differing with respect to the number of mental steps that are required to perform successfully the given task. Participants are simultaneously shown three one-digit numbers on a computer screen (e.g., "3 9 4") and their task is to indicate (by pressing either the "YES" or "NO" buttons) whether these digits match a specific rule or not (e.g., "Is the first digit the largest?"). The five increasingly complex Triplet versions differ with respect to the instructions given to the participants, e.g., "Is digit 5 contained within the triplet?" in Triplet 1 or "Is the second digit the smallest and an even number or is the third digit the largest and an odd number?" in the most complex Triplet 5 condition.

Interestingly, the task complexity had only a general effect on cortical activation (more complex tasks evoking stronger activation), but this effect did not interact with the intelligence level.

Rather, the most interesting finding of the (Neubauer & Fink, 2003) study is that the distinction between fluid and crystallized intelligence differentially affects physiological differences between individuals low versus high in cognitive ability. The neural efficiency phenomenon seems to be more strongly related to individual differences in fluid intelligence than

GF - LOW   GF - HIGH

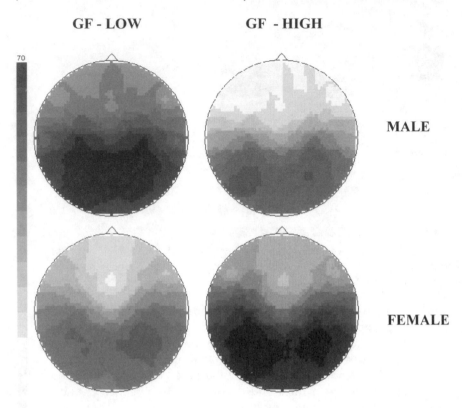

MALE

FEMALE

FIGURE 4. ERD maps for both g_f group (g_f low vs. g_f high) and sexes (male vs. female).

to crystallized intelligence. Moreover, males and females seem to produce different patterns of cortical activation. In Figure 4 the ERD maps are plotted separately for both ability groups (i.e., high fluid intelligence g_f vs. low fluid intelligence) and sexes. Most interestingly, the male sample was more likely to show activation patterns in line with the neural efficiency hypothesis (less activation in brighter than in less intelligent individuals), whereas the females showed no significant intelligence-related differences with respect to cortical activation patterns.

However, the finding that males and females display different patterns of cortical activation (as assessed by means of the ERD method) is not exclusively restricted to the (Neubauer & Fink, 2003) study. Similarly, in Neubauer, Fink, and Schrausser (2002) we found male and female brains again displaying different activation patterns during cognitive task performance. Here, we tried to analyze the neural efficiency phenomenon with respect to possible effects of stimulus or material content. Instead of just

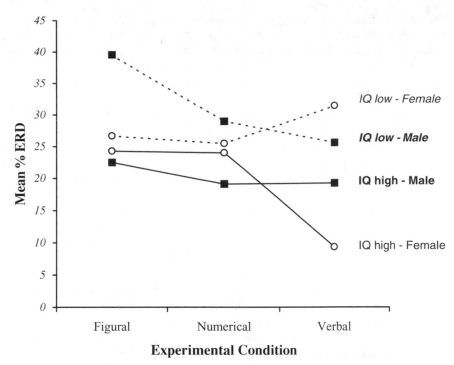

FIGURE 5. Mean %ERD in the verbal, numerical, and figural letter matching task separately for both sexes and IQ groups.

using one type of stimulus material, we used three variants (i.e., verbal, numerical, and figural-spatial) of Posner's letter matching test. This was done because most studies within the mental speed approach to human intelligence employed the elementary cognitive tasks in their classical form, for example, using pairs of letters in the Posner paradigm or digits in Sternberg's memory scanning task. Possible influences of content or material specificity factors have been largely ignored in this research tradition. This might be problematic since differences in physiological parameters might not only be traced to differences in cognitive task requirements but also to a topographic specialization of the cortex for certain types of stimulus material (e.g., specialization of the left hemisphere for verbal material). Therefore, we employed ECTs consisting of verbal, numerical, and figural stimulus elements. In addition to this, we endeavored to analyze possible sex differences with respect to cortical activation patterns.

Our findings (Neubauer et al., 2002) can be summarized as follows: First, we replicated and corroborated existing findings of a more efficient use of the cortex (resulting in a lower total cortical activation) in brighter as compared to less intelligent individuals (i.e., neural efficiency hypothesis). Second, as illustrated in Figure 5, we found both sexes displaying different patterns of cortical activation when comparing activation during performance of the verbal, numerical, and figural-spatial Posner variant. Most interestingly, both sexes displayed the expected activation patterns (i.e., neural efficiency patterns) in that domain in which they usually perform better – the females in the verbal Posner task and the males in the figural-spatial Posner task.

Summarizing the empirical work on physiological correlates of human intelligence, we can conclude that there is sound evidence for more intelligent individuals displaying a higher neural efficiency as indicated by less and topographically more focused cortical activation (for converging evidence from studies using other EEG methods, cf. e.g., Jausovec, 1996; Vitouch et al., 1997).

However, as Sternberg and Kaufman (1998) noted, this relationship does not necessarily imply the causation neural efficiency → intelligence, which is more or less implicitly assumed by most researchers in this area. It would also be conceivable that brighter subjects have to expend less effort when solving cognitive tasks and this would account for their lower metabolism/cortical activation. As the presently available empirical evidence on the neural efficiency–intelligence relationship is purely correlational this alternative explanation cannot be ruled out. It should be noted that correlations cannot only be explained in an A → B or B → A direction; rather a third variable C could drive individual differences in A and B. Actually there is no experimental evidence that could inform us about the direction of causation. Considering that both neural efficiency and human intelligence are based on the same biological substrate (i.e., the brain), it is readily conceivable that the relationship is caused by one or more fundamental (e.g., anatomical) properties of the brain.

BIOLOGICAL BASIS OF HUMAN INTELLIGENCE: THREE HYPOTHESES

What might be such a general property of the brain? As Britt Anderson (1995) argued, "From neuropsychological data, it can be shown that no single brain region or psychological process is essential for normal intelligence" (p. 602), rather "the mathematical entity g is the consequence of there being a biological feature with a general influence on cognitive performance" (p. 603). He proposed (and analyzed) six hypotheses that assume individual differences in

1. brain size
2. nerve conduction velocity (myelination)
3. neuron number
4. dendritic arborization
5. synapse number
6. synaptic efficiency

Most of these anatomical features cannot be determined reliably and validly in the living human brain; therefore hypotheses on biological features actually are more or less plausible hypotheses. Three hypotheses are elaborated in more detail in the following discussion.

The *myelination hypothesis* (Miller, 1994) starts from the following assumptions: As already mentioned, higher psychometric intelligence is associated with shorter reaction times in elementary cognitive tasks and with shorter latencies in the evoked potential. Higher IQ is correlated with larger brain size, with higher neural efficiency (as shown by less cortical glucose metabolism under cognitive load and less and more strongly focused cortical EEG activation), and, finally, with a higher nerve conduction velocity.

Stronger myelination of axons in the brain produces a higher speed of neural conduction, less leakage of signals, less "cross-talk" errors between neurons, and anatomically larger brains.

In addition, there is converging evidence regarding the development of intelligence, processing speed, and myelin with age. Intelligence increases during childhood and decreases in old age. Reaction times show a similar development; they decrease during childhood indicating an increase of speed of processing and increase in old age (i.e., slowing of processing speed). Similar findings have been obtained for the P300 latency of the evoked potential, and we also know that the process of brain myelination develops during childhood whereas demyelination takes place in old age. By integrating all these findings, Miller concluded that a stronger myelination might be an anatomical cause for higher intelligence.

A second approach, the *neural pruning hypothesis* of human intelligence, has been put forward by Richard Haier (1993). He started from the observation by Huttenlocher (1979) that the number of synapses in the brain increases rapidly during the first five years of life and then until the early teen years around 11 or 12 a dramatic decrease in synaptic density can be observed; it is assumed that during that time redundant synaptic connections are eliminated, a process termed *neural pruning*. Empirical evidence for this phenomenon, however, is only indirect. Cerebral glucose use increases in the first five years and displays a decrease afterward, resulting in the finding that glucose use in five-year-olds is twice that of normal adults (as synaptic activity requires energy consumption, this finding could reflect the process of increase and subsequent decrease of synapses).

Additional evidence relates synaptic density to the phenomena of mental retardation: Higher synaptic densities have been found in mentally retarded persons (postmortem analyses); in living subjects higher glucose use has been found in those with mental retardation, Down's syndrome, and autism (cf. the references provided by Haier, 1993). From these findings Haier derived the hypothesis that a failure in neural pruning could lead to mental retardation or lower cognitive ability, whereas an overpruning (i.e., an extremely efficient pruning process) would lead to giftedness.

Finally, the most recent hypothesis advocates the growth of dendritic trees and axon branches as a neural basis underlying individual differences in human intelligence. In explaining the nature of the general factor of intelligence, Garlick (2002) presupposes some kind of *neural plasticity* of the brain that paraphrases the brain's ability to adapt to environmental stimuli. He bolsters his presumption with neurophysiological data suggesting that a neural system will exhibit both axonal and dendritic plasticity; that is, neurons will change their connections with other neurons in response to environmental stimulation. In this context Garlick also focuses on the ontogenetic development of the brain (i.e., increase of cells, axons, and synapses) and argues that "the development of intelligence over childhood is due to this long-term process whereby the brain gradually alters its connections to allow for the processing of more complex environmental stimuli" (p. 120).

Garlick (2002) further argues that a brain which is more able to adapt its connections to environmental stimuli (i.e., the more "intelligent" brain) might also show other characteristics. With this in mind, he explains individual differences in speed and neural efficiency by assuming that a neural network consisting of stronger and more appropriate connections (the "fine-tuned" neural network) would also be able to process even relatively simple tasks (e.g., elementary cognitive tasks) at a faster rate. Moreover, a fine-tuned neural network that is able to differentiate between different inputs might also be able to selectively activate the appropriate relations in the brain. This might be the reason why brighter individuals usually display shorter reaction times in a variety of cognitive tasks or why the brains of brighter individuals are less active when performing cognitively demanding tasks (i.e., the neural efficiency hypothesis).

A BRAIN AREA FOR INTELLIGENCE?

Beneath these general properties of the brain (myelination, neural pruning, and neural plasticity) that might be treated as more or less plausible hypotheses for individual differences in the level of general intelligence, one might also look for a special brain area as a neural basis of intelligence.

Presently, from the viewpoint of the general cognitive neuroscientist the answer to this question seems straightforward: the frontal lobe. PET and fMRI studies comparing spatial patterns of cortical activation during performance of (highly *g*-loaded) intelligence, especially fluid reasoning tasks, as compared to other cognitive tasks (with low *g*-loadings) found an increased involvement of the frontal cortex for the former tasks (Prabhakaran et al., 1997; Duncan et al., 2000). The frontal lobe receives inputs from all major sensory afferent systems (e.g., thalamus, hypothalamus) and is believed to be responsible for many important aspects of human behavior, in particular for the so-called higher cognitive functions such as planning, goal-directed behavior, or complex problem solving. The predominant role of the frontal brain in this domain has been underpinned by neuropsychological data which congruently suggest that frontal lobe lesions are associated with impairments or dysfunctions in a variety of cognitive processes such as planning, selective attention, decision making, goal-directed behavior (i.e., scheduling processes in complex task performance), or monitoring of ongoing activity that all constitute important prerequisites for complex task performance (cf. Duncan, Burgess, & Emslie, 1995; for recent reviews see Fiez, 2001; Gabrieli, 1998; Kessels et al., 2000).

As the brain regions activated during performance of highly g-loaded, fluid reasoning tasks (like Raven's Progressive Matrices) largely match those found in neuroimaging working memory studies (cf. Smith & Jonides, 1999), we can conclude that performance in fluid reasoning tasks is mediated by a composite of different working memory abilities. This finding is not surprising in view of the close relationship between working memory capacity and reasoning (Kyllonen & Christal, 1990).

It should be emphasized, however, that the role of the frontal lobe in fluid reasoning has been only studied from the perspective of a general neuroscientist, that is, it has been demonstrated only by employing comparisons of tasks. What we need is research on the "differential perspective" showing that subjects high in fluid reasoning ability (or in g) display differential involvement of the frontal cortex than subjects low in such abilities.

If that could be demonstrated, what could we then conclude about the biological "basis" of human intelligence? Is it the "quality" of the frontal cortex or is it a general brain property like myelination, synapse number, or dendritic arborization?

Presently, a clear-cut answer to this question is not possible. Maybe the answer is not "either or" but rather "as well as": On the one hand, the role of the frontal lobe in areas of intellectual functioning seems to be attributable mainly to the working memory involvement of the intelligence tasks. On the other hand the other important elementary cognitive basis for human intelligence, namely speed of information processing – as well as neural efficiency findings – can probably more plausibly be explained by a general property of the brain like myelination, synapse number, or dendritic branching. Just as the quality of a performance of a symphony is surely dependent upon the quality of the conductor as well as the quality of the musicians in the orchestra, human cognitive ability might likewise be a product of the efficiency of the frontal brain (as the "conductor" of the cortex) as well as the performance of the neurons, synapses, axons, and dendrites (as the musicians in the orchestra).

References

Anderson, B. (1995). *G* explained. *Medical Hypotheses, 45*, 602–604.

Barrett, P. T., Daum, I., & Eysenck, H. J. (1990). Sensory nerve conduction and intelligence: A methodological study. *Journal of Psychophysiology, 4*, 1–13.

Barrett, P. T., & Eysenck, H. J. (1992). Brain electrical potentials and intelligence. In A. Gale & H. J. Eysenck (Eds.), *Handbook of individual differences: Biological perspectives*. New York: Wiley.

Carpenter, P. A., & Just, M. (1975). Sentence comprehension: A psycholinguistic processing model of verification. *Psychological Review, 82*, 45–73.

Clark, H. H., & Chase, W. G. (1972). On the process of comparing sentences against pictures. *Cognitive Psychology, 3*, 472–517.

Deary, I. J. (2000). *Looking down on human intelligence*. Oxford, UK: Oxford University Press.

Deary, I. J., & Caryl, P. G. (1993). Intelligence, EEG, and evoked potentials. In P. A. Vernon (Ed.), *Biological approaches to the study of human intelligence* (pp. 259–315). Norwood, NJ: Ablex.

Duncan, J., Burgess, P., & Emslie, H. (1995). Fluid intelligence after frontal lobe lesions. *Neuropsychologia, 33*, 261–268.

Duncan, J., Seitz, R. J., Kolodny, J., Bor, D., Herzog, H., Ahmed, A., Newell, F. N., & Emslie, H. (2000). A neural basis for general intelligence. *Science, 289*, 457–460.

Fiez, J. A. (2001). Bridging the gap between neuroimaging and neuropsychology: Using working memory as a case study. *Journal of Clinical and Experimental Neuropsychology, 23*, 19–31.

Gabrieli, J. D. E. (1998). Cognitive neuroscience of human memory. *Annual Review of Psychology, 49*, 87–115.

Garlick, D. (2002). Understanding the nature of the general factor of intelligence: The role of individual differences in neural plasticity as an explanatory mechanism. *Psychological Review, 109*, 116–136.

Grudnik, J. L., & Kranzler, J. H. (2001). Meta-analysis of the relationship between intelligence and inspection time. *Intelligence, 29*, 523–535.

Haier, R. J. (1993). Cerebral glucose metabolism and intelligence. In P. A. Vernon (Ed.), *Biological approaches to the study of human intelligence* (pp. 317–332). Norwood, NJ: Ablex.

Haier, R. J., Siegel, B. V., Nuechterlein, K. H., Hazlett, E., Wu, J. C., Paek, J., Browning, H. L., & Buchsbaum, M. S. (1988). Cortical glucose metabolic rate correlates of abstract reasoning and attention studied with positron emission tomography. *Intelligence, 12*, 199–217.

Haier, R. J., Siegel, B. V., MacLachlan, A., Soderling, E., Lottenberg, S., & Buchsbaum, M. S. (1992a). Regional glucose metabolic changes after learning a complex visuospatial/motor task: A positron emission topographic study. *Brain Research, 570*, 134–143.

Haier, R. J., Siegel, B., Tang, C., Abel, L., & Buchsbaum, M. S. (1992b). Intelligence and changes in regional cerebral glucose metabolic rate following learning. *Intelligence, 16*, 415–426.

Hick, W. E. (1952). On the rate of gain of information. *Quarterly Journal of Experimental Psychology, 4*, 11–26.

Hunt (1980). Intelligence as an information processing concept. *British Journal of Psychology, 71,* 449–474.

Huttenlocher, P. R. (1979). Synaptic density in human frontal cortex – Developmental changes and effects of aging. *Brain Research, 163,* 195–205.

Jausovec, N. (1996). Differences in EEG alpha activity related to giftedness. *Intelligence, 23,* 159–173.

Jensen, A. R. (1982). Reaction time and psychometric *g*. In H. J. Eysenck (Ed.), *A model for intelligence* (pp. 93–132). Heidelberg: Springer.

Jensen, A. R. (1987). Individual differences in the Hick paradigm. In P. A. Vernon (Ed.), *Speed of information processing and intelligence* (pp. 101–176). Norwood, NJ: Ablex.

Kessels, R. P. C., Postma, A., Wijnalda, E. M., & de Haan, H. F. (2000). Frontal-lobe involvement in spatial memory: Evidence from PET, fMRI, and lesion studies. *Neuropsychology Review, 10,* 101–113.

Kyllonen, P. C., & Christal, R. E. (1990). Reasoning ability is (little more than) working-memory capacity? *Intelligence, 14,* 389–433.

Lindley, R. H., & Smith, W. R. (1992). Coding tests as measures of IQ: Cognition or motivation? *Personality and Individual Differences, 13,* 25–29.

Miller, E. M. (1994). Intelligence and brain myelination: A hypothesis. *Personality and Individual Differences, 17,* 803–832.

Neubauer, A. C. (1995). *Intelligenz und Geschwindigkeit der Informationsverarbeitung.* Vienna: Springer.

Neubauer, A. C. (1997). The mental speed approach to the assessment of intelligence. In J. Kingma & W. Tomic (Eds.), *Advances in cognition and educational practice: Reflections on the concept of intelligence* (pp. 149–174). Greenwich, CT: JAI Press.

Neubauer, A. C., & Bucik, V. (1996). The mental speed–IQ relationship: Unitary or modular? *Intelligence, 22,* 23–48.

Neubauer, A. C., & Fink, A. (2003). Fluid intelligence and neural efficiency: Effects of task complexity and sex. *Personality and Individual Differences, 35,* 811–827.

Neubauer, A. C., & Freudenthaler, H. H. (1994). Reaction times in a sentence–picture verification test and intelligence: Individual strategies and effects of extended practice. *Intelligence, 19,* 193–218.

Neubauer, A. C., & Knorr, E. (1997). Elementary cognitive processes in choice reaction time tasks and their correlation with intelligence. *Personality and Individual Differences, 23,* 715–728.

Neubauer, A. C., & Knorr, E. (1998). Three paper-and-pencil tests for speed of information processing: Psychometric properties and correlations with intelligence. *Intelligence, 26,* 123–151.

Neubauer, A. C., Fink, A., & Schrausser, D. G. (2002). Intelligence and neural efficiency: The influence of task content and sex on the brain–IQ relationship. *Intelligence, 30,* 515–536.

Neubauer, A. C., Freudenthaler, H. H., & Pfurtscheller, G. (1995). Intelligence and spatio-temporal patterns of event related desynchronization. *Intelligence, 20,* 249–267.

Neubauer, A. C., Sange, G., & Pfurtscheller, G. (1999). Psychometric intelligence and event-related desynchronisation during perfomance of a letter matching task. In

G. Pfurtscheller & F. H. Lopes da Silva (Eds.), *Event-Related Desynchronization (ERD) – And related oscillatory EEG-phenomena of the awake brain, Handbook of EEG and Clinical Neurophysiology, Revised Series* (Vol. 6, pp. 219–231). Amsterdam: Elsevier.

Parks, R. W., Loewenstein, D. A., Dodrill, K. L., Barker, W. W., Yoshii, F., Chang, J. Y., Emran, A., Apicella, A., Sheramata, W. A., & Duara, R. (1988). Cerebral metabolic effects of a verbal fluency test: A PET scan study. *Journal of Clinical Experimental Neuropsychology, 10,* 565–575.

Pfurtscheller, G., & Aranibar, A. (1977). Event-related cortical desynchronization detected by power measurements of scalp EEG. *Electroencephalography and Clinical Neurophysiology, 42,* 817–826.

Pfurtscheller, G., & Lopes da Silva (1999). Event-related EEG/EMG synchronization and desynchronization: Basic principles. *Clinical Neurophysiology, 110,* 1842–1857.

Posner, M. I., & Mitchell, R. F. (1967). Chronometric analysis of classification. *Psychological Review, 74,* 392–409.

Prabhakaran, V., Smith, J. A. L., Desmond, J. E., Glover, H., & Gabrieli, J. D. E. (1997). Neural substrates of fluid reasoning: An fMRI study of neocortical activation during performance of the Raven's Progressive Matrices Test. *Cognitive Psychology, 33,* 43–63.

Raven, J. C. (1958). *Advanced Progressive Matrices.* London: Lewis.

Reed, T. E., & Jensen, A. R. (1991). Arm nerve conduction velocity (NCV), brain NCV, reaction time, and intelligence. *Intelligence, 15,* 33–48.

Reed, T. E., & Jensen, A. R. (1992). Conduction velocity in a brain nerve pathway of normal adults correlates with intelligence level. *Intelligence, 16,* 259–272.

Smith, E. E., & Jonides, J. (1999). Storage and executive processes in the frontal lobes. *Science, 283,* 1657–1661.

Stankov, L. (2000). Complexity, metacognition, and intelligence. *Intelligence, 28,* 121–143.

Stankov, L., & Crawford, J. D. (1993). Ingredients of complexity in fluid intelligence. *Learning and Individual Differences, 5,* 73–111.

Stankov, L., & Raykov (1995). Modeling complexity and difficulty in measures of fluid intelligence. *Structural Equation Modeling, 2,* 335–366.

Stankov, L., & Roberts, D. R. (1997). Mental speed is not the "basic" process of intelligence. *Personality and Individual Differences, 22,* 69–84.

Sternberg, S. (1966). High-speed scanning in human memory. *Science, 153,* 652–654.

Sternberg, S. (1969). Memory-scanning: Mental processes revealed by reaction time experiments. *American Scientist, 57,* 421–457.

Sternberg, R. J., & Kaufman, J. C. (1998). Human abilities. *Annual Review of Psychology, 49,* 479–502.

Vernon, P. A. (1990). An overview of chronometric measures of intelligence. *School Psychology Review, 19,* 399–410.

Vernon, P. A. (1993). Intelligence and neural efficiency. In D. K. Detterman (Ed.), *Current topics in human intelligence* (Vol. 3, pp. 171–187). Norwood, NJ: Ablex.

Vernon, P. A., & Mori, M. (1992). Intelligence, reaction times, and peripheral nerve conduction velocity. *Intelligence, 16,* 273–288.

Vickers, D., Nettelbeck, T., & Wilson, R. J. (1972). Perceptual indices of performance, the measurement of "inspection time" and "noise" in the visual system. *Perception, 1,* 263–295.

Vitouch, O., Bauer, H., Gittler, G., Leodolter, M., & Leodolter, U. (1997). Cortical activity of good and poor spatial test performers during spatial and verbal processing studied with slow potential topography. *International Journal of Psychophysiology, 27,* 183–199.

Wickett, J. C., & Vernon, P. A. (1994). Peripheral nerve conduction velocity, reaction time, and intelligence – An attempt to replicate Vernon and Mori (1992). *Intelligence, 18,* 127–131.

5

The Neural Bases of Intelligence

A Perspective Based on Functional Neuroimaging

Sharlene D. Newman and Marcel Adam Just

INTRODUCTION

The study of intelligence has provided two major and enduring contributions to the understanding of human thought: a comprehensive characterization of human intelligence and a method to measure the variation in intelligence among individuals. These contributions have been based almost exclusively on behavioral measures of intelligence, using primarily paper-and-pencil tests. The development of brain imaging technology at the end of the twentieth century provided the ability to measure brain activity in individuals during the performance of tasks like those that compose intelligence tests. These brain imaging measures have the potential of providing a new and possibly more comprehensive view of intelligence as well as providing insight into the basis of individual differences. In this chapter, we sketch the very beginnings of this approach to intelligence that may provide a new comprehensive characterization of intelligence enriched by insights from recent brain imaging findings. This novel approach may also provide suggestions of methods to measure individual differences.

Intelligence is difficult to define, and in fact, there is little consensus among scientific researchers as to what is meant by intelligence (Jensen, 1998). A general definition provided by Sternberg and Salter (1982) that we will use is "goal-directed adaptive behavior." Intelligent behavior is adaptive in that it changes to confront and effectively meet challenges. Because it is not enough for intelligent behavior to simply be adaptive, it is also thought to be goal-directed, or purposeful. However, it is the adaptive nature of intelligence that will be the primary focus of this chapter.

Spearman situated g at the apex of a hierarchy of abilities. g represents an individual's general problem-solving skill, accounts for a person's performing well on a variety of cognitive tasks, and is sometimes referred to as fluid intelligence or g_f. According to Spearman, one of the factors that determines g is "mental energy," which "enters into the measurement of ability of all kinds, and is thought to be constant for any individual, although varying greatly for different individuals" (Spearman, 1927, p. 411; Jensen, 1998). Because very little was known about brain function in the 1920s, Spearman was unable to elaborate further as to what corresponded to mental energy. However, our proposal below implicitly includes an energy facet.

The conventional psychometric study of behavioral performance has been accompanied by attempts to correlate individual differences in intelligence with biological measures. In some sense these attempts have been in search of a definition of mental energy. For example, for over a hundred years researchers have been examining the correlation between head circumference (a proxy for brain size) and intelligence measures, generally suggesting that the larger the brain, the more intelligent the individual. Although many studies have found a modest correlation, these studies have been quite controversial (for a review see Van Valen, 1974; Jensen & Sinha, 1992) and have not provided insights into either the nature of intelligence or the measurement of individual differences.

In the 1980s, Jensen hypothesized that it was not necessarily the size of the brain but the speed of processing that was central to intelligence, showing a relationship between reaction time and intelligence (Brody, 1992, p. 56; Vernon, 1992). This relationship suggested that the characteristics of the nervous system determine reaction time, and that individuals whose nervous systems function more effectively and rapidly develop more complex intellectual skills. Electrophysiological recordings (ERP) of electrical activity measured on the scalp have also shown a relationship between neural processing characteristics and intelligence. Studies using ERP have revealed consistent correlations with intelligence (Jensen, 1998; Jensen & Sinha, 1992) and have been used to measure individual differences both in the normal population (McGarry-Roberts, Stelmack, & Campbell, 1992; King & Kutas, 1995; Vos & Friederici, 2003) and those with psychiatric and neurological dysfunctions (John et al., 1994). The electrophysiological approach attempts to relate the electrical activity of the brain to the ongoing cognitive information processing. For example, this approach has found that individuals who are extreme in their ability (e.g., good vs. poor comprehenders; King & Kutas, 1995) have distinguishable electrical signatures during a reading comprehension task. This approach has been successful in showing that there are electrophysiological differences that are correlated with individual differences in performance, but the electrical measures are indirect and not related to a comprehensive theory of intelligence.

In this chapter we present a theory of neural processing that is derived from the use of functional neuroimaging, particularly functional MRI (fMRI). Magnetic resonance imaging, primarily fMRI and possibly diffusion tensor imaging (DTI) in the future, has the potential to provide a clearer characterization of the neural bases of intelligence. A key contribution of fMRI is its ability to provide information about several important properties of the large-scale neural networks that underlie cognition. These properties include the specification of the set of brain regions that are involved in a given task; the temporal profile of the activation, or a reflection of the neural processing time course; and the degree of synchronization between pairs of activated regions, which reflects the functional connectivity between regions.

The theory presented in this chapter provides an initial account for g_f, or fluid intelligence. Intelligence is born out of networks of cortical areas; therefore, the investigation of the behavior of these large-scale cortical networks may lead to an explanation of individual differences in ability. The major proposal of this chapter is that how well the neural system can adapt to changes in the environment will affect the quality and efficiency of its processing, thereby constituting a major source of individual differences. The theory is composed of a set of operating principles for cortical computation put forth by Just and Varma (2003):

1. Energy is consumed during the performance of cognitive tasks and each cortical area has a limited resource capacity. This principle has direct implications for individual differences in intelligence. First it suggests that the amount of resources available or the resource capacity within the neural system may vary across individuals. Second, the amount of resources required to perform a task may differ across individuals due to variations in efficiency.
2. The topology (cortical composition) of neurocognitive networks associated with a given task changes dynamically, adapting itself to the demands of a given task. Therefore, the efficiency with which this topological change occurs may contribute to individual differences in task performance.
3. Cortical regions function collaboratively to perform tasks. Variation in the degree of synchronization or efficiency of the communication between regions may contribute to individual differences in task performance.
4. The quality of the white matter tracts connecting cortical areas may also affect processing speed. The variation in the degree or quality of the anatomical connections between processing regions may contribute to individual differences in task performance.

These principles suggest possible sources of individual differences in intelligence. The remainder of this chapter further explores these properties and provides citations of supporting experimental data.

PROCESSING CAPACITY

Thinking is biological work that requires resources and is thus constrained by their availability. In any biological system, there is an upper limit on resource availability. Certainly there are upper bounds on thinking, such that one can do only so much thinking per unit time. It turns out to be helpful to consider such limitations as resource availability. Tasks that attempt to impose a load greater than the maximum that the resources permit will produce performance that is errorful, slow, or incapable of meeting some task requirement – deteriorations consistent with decreased resources. This phenomenon is evident in the differences in cognition observed as a function of individual differences in working memory capacity (Just & Carpenter, 1992).

Recent neuroimaging research has provided extensive support for the resource consumption perspective. The amount of cortical activation within a given region increases with the computational demands that are placed on the region, as demonstrated in several types of cognitive tasks, including sentence comprehension (Just et al., 1996; Keller, Carpenter, & Just, 2001; Röder et al., 2002), working memory (Braver et al., 1997; Rypma et al., 1999), and mental rotation tasks (Carpenter et al., 1999; Just et al., 2001). For example, in language comprehension, the volume of fMRI-measured cortical activation in both Broca's area and Wernicke's area has been shown to increase with linguistic complexity of the sentence being comprehended (Just et al., 1996). These findings indicate that as a task places additional computational demands on a cortical region, it consumes more resources, eliciting greater fMRI-measured activation.

One of the implications of the resource consumption approach is that individuals may differ in resource availability and/or efficiency. In other words, those with above-average performance may either have a greater computational capacity or use the available resources more efficiently or both. Evidence lends support to the efficiency hypothesis: several PET studies have reported negative correlations between psychometrically measured abilities and the volume of cortical activation produced by tasks that draw upon these abilities (Just, Carpenter, & Miyake, 2003; Haier et al., 1988; Parks et al., 1988, 1989; Newman et al., 2003). Reichle, Carpenter, and Just (2000) conducted a fMRI study that tested this hypothesis. The study examined the relation between individual differences in cognitive ability (verbal or spatial ability) and the amount of cortical activation engendered by two strategies (linguistic vs. visual-spatial) in a sentence–picture verification task. The study showed that the fMRI-measured activation was correlated with behaviorally assessed cognitive abilities in the two processing domains. The direction of the correlation is consistent with the idea that higher ability individuals use their resources more efficiently: higher ability individuals showed less fMRI-measured activation than did less

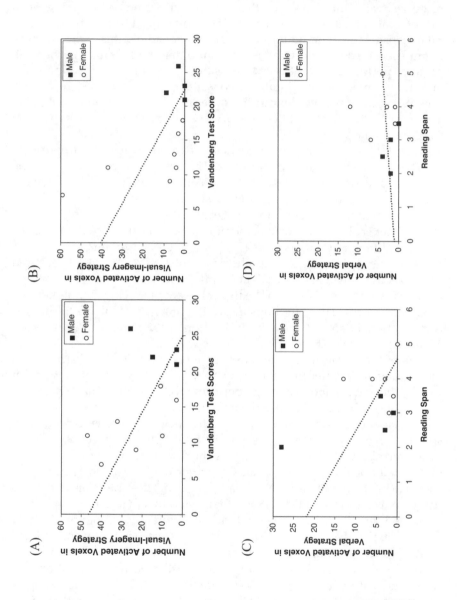

proficient individuals. Specifically, individuals with better verbal proficiency (as measured by the reading span test) had less activation in Broca's area when they used the verbal strategy, while individuals with better visual-spatial proficiency (as measured by the Vandenberg, 1971, mental rotation test) had less activation in the left parietal cortex when they used the visual-spatial strategy (see Fig. 1).

While several studies have shown that high ability individuals tend to exhibit less neural activation than less proficient individuals, two recent studies have revealed the opposite trend in areas associated with the control of attention (Osaka et al., 2003; Gray, Chabris, & Braver, 2003). In both studies, high ability individuals (defined in terms of either a higher listening span score or greater g) performing attention-demanding tasks revealed more activation in the anterior cingulate cortex than did less proficient individuals. In the Gray et al. (2003) study, a positive correlation was found between general fluid intelligence, g_f, and the activation levels within three *a priori* regions thought to be associated with attention (lateral prefrontal cortex, dorsal anterior cingulate, and lateral cerebellum). However, negative correlations between activation levels and g_f were still found in regions outside the *a priori* search space.

To summarize, these studies demonstrate the adaptation of individual brains to the magnitude of the computational load. Many studies show that the amount of cortical resources consumed, as measured by fMRI, increases as a function of task demand, regardless of ability level. A second set of studies cited indicate less activation (i.e., resource consumption) among high ability individuals, suggesting that highly proficient individuals use their resources more efficiently than do less proficient individuals in doing the central cognitive computations. Finally, the two studies discussed that were particularly attention-demanding indicate that the lower resource consumption in higher performing individuals is not a global difference. Instead, there may be attentional control mechanisms that are more active in higher performing individuals. Together, these results show that

---

FIGURE 1. The relation between visual-spatial skill (as measured by the Vandenberg, 1971, mental rotation task) and the volume of cortical activation generated in the left (Panel A) and right (Panel B) parietal regions of interest (ROIs), as a function of gender. The best-fitting regression lines indicate that visual-spatial skill was negatively correlated with activation volume in both the left ($r = -.74$) and right ($r = -.61$) hemispheres. Panels C and D show the relation between individual differences in verbal skill (as measured by the Daneman & Carpenter, 1980, reading span task) and the volume of cortical activation generated in the left (Panel C) and right (Panel D) inferior frontal ROIs, as a function of gender. As the best-fitting regression lines indicate, verbal skill was negatively correlated with activation volume in the left hemisphere ($r = -.49$), but not the right ($r = .16$). (Adapted from Reichle, Carpenter, & Just, 2000.)

the resource consumption rate is related to the individual differences in ability.

MALLEABILITY OF PROCESSING NETWORKS

Intelligent responding at the cortical level must include the ability to arbitrarily map inputs and outputs (Garlick, 2002). At the large-scale cortical network level, this suggests that the network of cortical areas activated in a given task – its composition and topological pattern of collaboration – is neither structurally fixed nor static. Rather, it varies dynamically during task performance. The previous conception of the neural basis of intelligence was that some fixed volume of brain tissue in a fixed set of brain areas (i.e., a fixed hardware infrastructure) is used to perform a particular task, like mental rotation or reasoning. According to the dynamic view we advocate, the "underlying hardware" is a moving target, changing not only from one type of stimulus item to another, but also from moment to moment during the processing of a given item.

At least two circumstances may necessitate a dynamic change in the neural underpinnings of a cognitive task: 1) changes in the availability of cortical resources and 2) fluctuations in the computational demands of a task. As the resource pool of an area with a given set of specializations is exhausted, some overflow of its functions migrates from a more specialized area to less specialized areas. Although there is a typical set of areas activated in a given type of task, additional areas can become activated if the task is made significantly more demanding. For example, when a sentence comprehension task is made progressively more difficult by increasing the structural complexity of the sentences, activation in the right hemisphere homolog of Wernicke's area (left posterior superior temporal gyrus) systematically increases from a negligible level to a substantial level (Just et al., 1996). One of the sources of individual differences in cognition may be the flexibility with which additional regions are recruited.

The second situation that may necessitate dynamic self-assembly of a large-scale cortical network is a fluctuation in the computational demands of a given task. The dynamic assembly of neurocognitive networks is incremental or continuous, not all-or-none. This provides for just-in-time, as-needed, neural support for cognitive processing. This principle is demonstrated in a study of verbal reasoning conducted by Newman, Just, and Carpenter (2002). There, two conditions were presented that varied the location of the maximal reasoning load within a sentence. In the first (early/low load) condition, the reasoning load occurred early in the sentence; in the second (late/high load) condition, the maximal reasoning load occurred late in the sentence (see Table 1). The time of occurrence of the maximal activation of prefrontal cortex varied as a function of the location of the maximal reasoning load in the expected direction

TABLE 1. *Early versus Late Imposition of Computational Load*

Early/Low Load	Late/High Load
The first month after April is the month before my favorite month. What is my favorite month? June, July, Other	The day before my favorite day is the first day after Monday. What is my favorite day? Thursday, Friday, Other

(see Fig. 2). This difference in the time course of activation supports the idea that cortical regions are recruited as needed. The ability to dynamically recruit additional resources may very well be a source of individual differences.

Dynamic self-assembly may be the physiological manifestation of the adaptive nature of thought. When a task becomes too difficult for the current strategy, a new one is "devised." The ability to switch strategies and

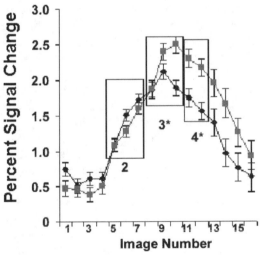

FIGURE 2. The blue curve depicts the time course observed in the left dorsolateral prefrontal cortex during the early/low load condition and the pink curve the late/high load condition. Box 2 encompasses images related to the first phrase of the problem (e.g., the first month after April), box 3 encompasses images related to the second phrase (e.g., is the month before my favorite month), and box 4 encompasses images related to the response interval. As shown, the early/low load condition engenders more activation during the early phase of the problem compared to the late/high load condition, while the late/high load condition induces more activation later in the problem. The delay in peak activation for the late/high load condition corresponds to the increased recruitment of dorsolateral prefrontal cortex (DLPFC) processing later in this problem type. (Adapted from Newman et al., 2002.)

dynamically change the cortical landscape related to a given task may contribute to individual differences. In fact, Garlick (2002) showed that an artificial neural network which was better able to adapt its connections to the environment learned to read faster, accommodated information from the environment better, and scored higher on fluid intelligence tests. Each of these properties are characteristic of people with higher *g*.

FUNCTIONAL CONNECTIVITY

A number of cortical regions are involved in performing any cognitive task. These regions must be coordinated, possibly by passing information back and forth. Evidence of such intercommunication pathways between cortical areas in humans performing a cognitive task comes from two sources. The first is the existence of anatomical pathways between areas (discussed in the next section). The corpus callosum is a prime example of an anatomical pathway between potentially collaborating cortical areas. In addition, many other cortico–cortico pathways are known from primate neuroanatomical studies (see Mesulam, 2000) as well as from more recent diffusion tensor imaging studies of white matter tracts in humans that are related to cognitive function (Klingberg et al., 2000). Furthermore, many additional anatomical links exist between cortical areas via subcortical regions, such as the thalamus.

The second source of evidence for coordination among the activated areas during cognitive activity is found in functional neuroimaging. The activation in a set of cortical areas is highly synchronized, indicating collaboration among areas. An increasingly used technique measures the correlation of the activation levels in two activated areas over some time period, and generally shows systematic synchronization between areas, modulated by a number of variables. The synchronization is taken as evidence of *functional connectivity* (or *effective connectivity*; Friston, 1994; Horwitz, Rumsey, & Donohue, 1998). Functional connectivity in the context of brain imaging refers to indirect evidence of communication or collaboration between various brain areas. The general assumption is that the functioning of voxels whose activation levels rise and fall together is coordinated.

A consistent finding is that more demanding conditions tend to produce higher functional connectivity than qualitatively similar but less demanding conditions (Diwadkar, Carpenter, & Just, 2000; Hampson et al., 2002). For example, in the domain of language there is a demonstrable functional connectivity between Broca's and Wernicke's areas both when participants are listening to texts and when they are at rest; the connectivity is substantially higher when they are listening to texts (Hampson et al., 2002). Another example of this increased functional connectivity with increased demand was observed when an object recognition task was made more

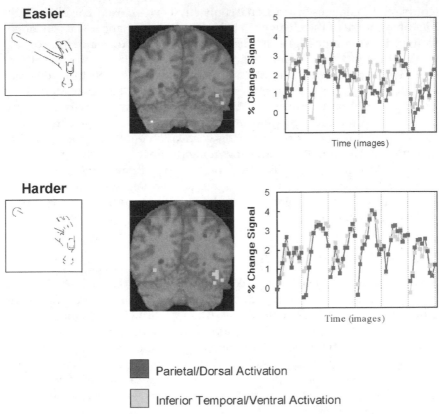

FIGURE 3. Increase in functional connectivity with workload in an object recognition task, where workload was increased by deleting more of the object contour. (From Diwadkar et al., 2003.)

demanding by deleting more of the object contour (Diwadkar, Carpenter, & Just, 2003). In this case, the degree of synchronization between the inferior temporal (ventral) area and the parietal (dorsal) area increased with difficulty, as shown in Figure 3.

Recent studies have shown a direct relationship between ability and functional connectivity measures (Osaka et al., 2003; Kondo et al., 2004). Kondo et al. (2004), for example, found that individuals with a high reading span revealed greater functional connectivity between anterior cingulate and Broca's area than did low span individuals. There is also evidence that functional connectivity increases with learning (Buchel et al., 1999). In that study fMRI was used to examine the neural basis of associative learning of visual objects and their locations. The study found an increase in the functional connectivity between cortical regions associated with spatial and object processing with learning in the task. In addition, the time course of the changes in functional connectivity was closely correlated with the time course of the changes in behavioral performance. The functional connectivity became higher at those times when performance improved.

All three of these adaptations (the increase in functional connectivity with task difficulty, with ability, and with learning) support the idea that a system-wide attribute of brain function may be a key characteristic of intelligence. In particular, the increase in functional connectivity with ability is one of the first such indicators of a system-wide characteristic of intelligence. Like any correlation, this correlation between functional connectivity and an ability measure does not indicate the underlying causality. Nevertheless, this technique allows for the exploration of the level of coordination between cortical regions across individuals, which may provide further insights into the biological underpinnings of individual differences in task performance.

ANATOMICAL CONNECTIVITY

Recently, a novel MRI technique (diffusion tensor imaging or DTI) has been developed that can potentially provide information regarding the microstructure of white matter *in vivo* (Basser, Mattiello, & LeBihan, 1994). DTI has been used to examine anatomical connectivity, or the physical neuronal connections between regions. The anatomical connections between cortical regions are essential to inter-region communication. In fact, research suggests that the quality of these connections directly affects processing speed. For example, recent developmental research has shown that the neural changes that take place during the first two years of life include a dramatic increase in the number of synaptic connections and an increase in the thickness of the myelin sheath that envelops nerve cell axons (Siegler, 1998; Anderson, 2000). These two changes are important because they both affect conduction speed, which is thought to, in turn, affect processing speed. Combined with fMRI, information about white matter tracts has the potential to reveal important information about neurocognitive networks, which may help to elucidate the neural basis of individual differences.

Given that DTI is such a new technique, very few studies have used it. One of the first studies, that of Klingberg and colleagues (2000), compared the white matter tracts within the temporo-parietal region of poor and normal readers. There, Klingberg et al. found significant group differences in the myelination of the white matter in both the left and right hemispheres. In addition, they found a high positive correlation between the DTI measure of the left hemisphere and reading ability, as measured by the Word Identification test (Woodcock, 1987). Their results show not only the importance of the temporo-parietal region in language processing, but also that differences in the white matter tracts contribute significantly to individual differences observed in reading. It will be interesting to learn from future

DTI studies whether the properties of white matter tracts are related to individual differences in cognitive abilities or to conventional measures of intelligence. As this technique is further developed, it promises to shed further light onto the neurological basis of intelligence.

IS INTELLIGENCE LOCALIZED IN THE BRAIN?

Both g and the frontal lobe have often been linked to executive functions such as control processing, strategy formulation, planning, and monitoring the contents of working memory (Luria, 1966; Norman & Shallice, 1980; Snow, 1981; Duncan et al., 1996). Support for this idea comes from both behavioral studies of normal and patient populations (Duncan, Emslie, & Williams, 1996) and a recent neuroimaging study (Duncan et al., 2000). For example, in the neuroimaging study, Duncan and colleagues attempted to determine the cortical area that underpins g. In that study, two variables were manipulated, the g loading (low or high) and test type (verbal or spatial) (an example problem is shown in Fig. 4). Duncan et al. found that in both the verbal and spatial conditions, the frontal cortex revealed greater activation for the high-g condition compared to the low-g condition, supporting the idea that g reflects functions of the frontal lobe. Further support for the importance of the frontal lobe in intelligence was found in a recent review of the neuroimaging literature. Frontal activation similar to that observed during the high-g condition was also elicited by such processing demands as novelty, response competition, working memory load, and perceptual difficulty (Duncan & Owen, 2000).

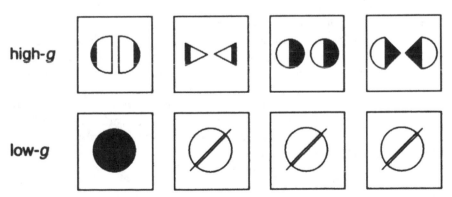

FIGURE 4. Materials from the high-g and low-g spatial task. Display elements were four panels, each containing one or more shapes, symbols, or drawings. One panel differed in some respect from the others. Compared to the low-g problems, the high-g problems required extensive problem solving to identify the "different" panel. (From Duncan et al., 2000.)

We do not dispute that the frontal lobes play an important role in problem solving and intelligence, but suggest instead that the biological basis of intelligence extends beyond the frontal lobe. In fact, intact frontal functions are somewhat unrelated to intelligence, as measured by psychometric tests (Teuber, 1972). IQ scores are rarely affected by damage to that region. We argue here that intelligence does not lie in any particular brain region, but is instead a function of a more distributed, dynamically configured set of areas. According to this theory, the commonality or generality of processing that *g* represents refers to the ability of the neural system to adapt and be flexible. More specifically, *g* may represent the neural system's ability to adapt to dynamic changes in the quantity and quality of changing computation demands. A study conducted by Duncan et al. (1996) found that the frontal processes most central to *g* were goal neglect and goal activation. This finding is in agreement with our dynamic processing account because in order to adapt to changes in strategy, there must be efficient goal switching. Therefore, the theory presented in this chapter suggests that intelligence cannot be localized to any particular brain region. It arises, instead, from the coordination and collaboration of several neural components.

SUMMARY

Although many research approaches have attempted to localize differences in intelligence to an elementary cognitive process (Kane, 2003; Jensen, 1993; Kyllonen & Christal, 1990), we suggest a different approach in this chapter by examining the properties of the neural system that underlies intelligence. According to the principles described here, fluid intelligence may be the product of an adaptive, flexible neural system. More specifically, fluid intelligence may represent the neural system's ability to adapt to dynamic changes in a complex cognitive process.

The principles outlined here are not considered to be exhaustive, but are meant to be a springboard from which new studies and theories of individual differences can emerge. We now have the technological capability to explore the human brain in its active state with the use of fMRI and soon will be able to investigate the integrity of its white matter tracts *in vivo* with DTI. With the combination of new imaging techniques and computational modeling, it becomes possible to address new central questions regarding the neural basis of intelligence.

References

Anderson, J. R. (2000). *Cognitive psychology and its implications*. New York: Worth.
Basser, P. J., Mattiello, J., & LeBihan, D. (1994). Estimation of the effective self-diffusion tensor from the NMR spin echo. *Journal of Magnetic Resonance, B103*, 247–254.

Braver, T., Cohen, J. D., Jonides, J., Smith, E. E., & Noll, D. C. (1997). A parametric study of prefrontal cortex involvement in human working memory. *NeuroImage, 5,* 49–62.

Brody, N. (1992). *Intelligence.* San Diego: Academic Press.

Buchel, C., Coull, J. T., & Friston, K. J. (1999). The predictive value of changes in effective connectivity for human learning. *Science, 283,* 1538–1540.

Carpenter, P. A., Just, M. A., Keller, T., Eddy, W. F., & Thulborn, K. R. (1999). Graded functional activation in the visuospatial system with the amount of task demand. *Journal of Cognitive Neuroscience, 11,* 9–24.

Daneman, M., & Carpenter, P. A. (1980). Individual differences in working memory and reading. *Journal of Verbal Learning and Verbal Behavior, 19,* 450–466.

Diwadkar, V. A., Carpenter, P. A., & Just, M. A. (2000). Collaborative activity between parietal and dorso-lateral prefrontal cortex in dynamic spatial working memory revealed by fMRI. *NeuroImage, 12,* 85–99.

Diwadkar, V. A., Carpenter, P. A., & Just, M. A. (2003). Collaborative activation in ventral and dorsal regions during visual object recognition: fMRI evidence. *Center for Cognitive Brain Imaging Technical Report.*

Duncan, H., Emslie, H., & Williams, P. (1996). Intelligence and the frontal lobe: The organization of goal-directed behavior. *Cognitive Psychology, 30,* 257–303.

Duncan, J., & Owen, A. M. (2000). Common regions of the human frontal lobe recruited by diverse cognitive demands. *Trends in Neurosciences, 23,* 475–483.

Duncan, J., Seitz, R. J., Kolodny, J., Bor, D., Herzog, H., Ahmed, A., Newell, F. N., & Emslie, H. (2000). A neural basis for general intelligence. *Science, 289:* 457–460.

Friston, K. J. (1994). Functional and effective connectivity: A synthesis. *Human Brain Mapping, 2,* 56–78.

Garlick, D. (2002). Understanding the nature of the general factor of intelligence: The role of individual differences in neural plasticity as an explanatory mechanism. *Psychological Review, 109,* 116–136.

Gray, J. R., Chabris, C. F., & Braver, T. S. (2003). Neural mechanisms of general fluid intelligence. *Nature Neuroscience, 6,* 316–322.

Haier, R. J., Siegel, B. V., Neuchterlein, K. H., Hazlett, E., Wu, J. C., Paek, J., Browning, H. L., & Buchsbaum, M. S. (1988). Cortical glucose metabolic rate correlates of abstract reasoning and attention studied with positron emission tomography. *Intelligence, 12,* 199–217.

Hampson, M., Peterson, B. S., Skudlarski, P., Gatenby, J. C., & Gore, J. C. (2002). Detection of functional connectivity using temporal correlations in MR images. *Human Brain Mapping, 15,* 247–262.

Horwitz, B., Rumsey J. M., & Donohue, B. C. (1998). Functional connectivity of the angular gyrus in normal reading and dyslexia. *Proceedings of the National Academy of Sciences USA, 95,* 8939–8944.

Jensen, A. R., & Sinha, S. N. (1992). Physical correlates of human intelligence. In P. A. Vernon (Ed.), *Biological approaches to human intelligence.* Norwood, NJ: Ablex.

Jensen, A. R. (1993). Why is reaction time correlated with psychometric *g*? *Current Directions in Psychological Science, 2,* 53–56.

Jensen, A. R. (1998). *The g factor: The science of mental ability.* Westport, CT: Praeger.

John, E. R., Prichep, L. S., Alper, K. R., Mas, F. G., Cancro, R., Easton, P., Sverdlov, L. (1994). Quantitative electrophysiological characteristics and subtyping of schizophrenia. *Biological Psychiatry, 36,* 801–826.

Just, M. A., & Varma, S. (2003). The organization of thinking: What functional brain imaging reveals about the neuroarchitecture of cognition. *Center for Cognitive Brain Imaging Technical Report.*

Just, M. A., Carpenter, P. A., & Miyake, A. (2003). Neuroindices of cognitive workload: Neuroimaging, pupillometric, and event-related potential studies of brain work. *Theoretical Issues in Ergonomics, 4,* 56–88. Special Edition.

Just, M. A., & Carpenter, P. A. (1992). A capacity theory of comprehension: Individual differences in working memory. *Psychological Review, 99,* 122–149.

Just, M. A., Carpenter, P. A., Keller, T. A., Eddy, W. F., & Thulborn, K. R. (1996). Brain activation modulated by sentence comprehension. *Science, 274,* 114–116.

Just, M. A., Carpenter, P. A., Maguire, M., Diwadkar, V., & McMains, S. (2001). Mental rotation of objects retrieved from memory: An fMRI study of spatial processing. *Journal of Experimental Psychology: General, 130,* 493–504.

Kane, M. J. (2003). The intelligent brain in conflict. *Trends in Cognitive Sciences, 7,* 375–377.

Keller, T. A., Carpenter, P. A., & Just, M. A. (2001). The neural bases of sentence comprehension: An fMRI examination of syntactic and lexical processing. *Cerebral Cortex, 11,* 223–237.

Kyllonen, P. C., & Christal, R. E. (1990). Reasoning ability is (little more than) working-memory capacity?! *Intelligence, 14,* 389–433.

King, J. W., & Kutas, M. (1995). Who did what and when? Using word – and clause – level ERPs to monitor working memory usage in reading. *Journal of Cognitive Neuroscience, 7,* 376–395.

Klingberg, T., Hedehus, M., Temple, E., Saltz, T., Gabrieli, J. D. E., Moseley, M. E., & Poldrack, R. A. (2000). Microstructure of temporo-parietal white matter as a basis for reading ability: Evidence from diffusion tensor imaging. *Neuron, 25,* 493–500.

Kondo, H., Morishita, M., Osaka, N., Osaka, M., Fukuyama, H., & Shibasaki, H. (2004). Functional roles of the cingulo-frontal network in performance on working memory. *NeuroImage, 21,* 2–14.

Luria, A. R. (1966). *Higher cortical functions in man.* London: Tavistock.

McGarry-Roberts, P. A., Stelmack, R. M., & Campbell, K. B. (1992). Intelligence, reaction time, and event-related potentials. *Intelligence, 16,* 289–313.

Mesulam, M.-M. (2000). Behavioral neuroanatomy: Large-scale networks, association cortex, frontal syndromes, the limbic system, and hemispheric specializations. In M.-M. Mesulam (Ed.), *Principles of behavioral and cognitive neurology,* Second ed. (pp. 1–120). New York: Oxford University Press.

Newman, S. D., Just, M. A., & Carpenter, P. A. (2002). Synchronization of the human cortical working memory network. *NeuroImage, 15,* 810–822.

Newman, S. D., Carpenter, P. A., Varma, S., & Just, M. A. (2003). Frontal and parietal participation in problem solving in the Tower of London: fMRI and computational modeling of planning and high-level perception. *Neuropsychologia, 41,* 1668–1682.

Norman, D. A., & Shallice, T. (1980*). Attention to action: Willed and automatic control of behavior* (Report No. 8006). San Diego: University of California, Center for Human Information Processing.

Osaka, M., Osaka, N., Kondo, H., Morishita, M., Fukuyama, H., Aso, T., & Shibasaki, H. (2003). The neural basis of individual differences in working memory capacity: An fMRI study. *NeuroImage, 18,* 789–797.

Parks, R. W., Lowenstein, D. A., Dodrill, K. L., Barker, W. W., Yoshii, F., Chang, J. Y., Emran, A., Apicella, A., Sheramata, W. A., & Duara, R. (1988). Cerebral metabolic effects of a verbal fluency test: A PET scan study. *Journal of Clinical and Experimental Neuropsychology, 10,* 565–575.

Parks, R. W., Crockett, D. J., Tuokko, H., Beattie, B. L., Ashford, J. W., Coburn, K. L., Zec, R. F., Becker, R. E., McGeer, P. L., & McGeer, E. G. (1989). Neuropsychological "systems efficiency" and positron emission tomography. *Journal of Neuropsychiatry, 1,* 269–282.

Reichle, E. D., Carpenter, P. A., & Just, M. A. (2000). The neural basis of strategy and skill in sentence–picture verification. *Cognitive Psychology, 40,* 261–295.

Röder, B., Stock, O., Neville, H., Bien, S., & Rosler, F. (2002). Brain activation modulated by the comprehension of normal and pseudo-word sentences of different processing demands: A functional magnetic resonance imaging study. *NeuroImage, 15,* 1003–1014.

Rypma, B., Prabhakaran, V., Desmond, J. E., Glover, G. H., & Gabrieli, J. D. E. (1999). Load-dependent roles of frontal brain regions in the maintenance of working memory. *NeuroImage, 9,* 216–226.

Siegler, R. S. (1998). *Children's thinking.* Upper Saddle River, NJ: Prentice-Hall.

Snow, R. E. (1981). Toward a theory of aptitude for learning. I. Fluid and crystallized abilities and their correlates. In M. P. Friedman, J. P. Das, & N. O'Connor (Eds.), *Intelligence and learning* (pp. 345–362). New York: Macmillan.

Spearman, C. (1927). *The abilities of man: Their nature and measurement.* New York: Macmillan.

Sternberg, R. J., & Salter, W. (1982). Conceptions of intelligence. In R. J. Sternberg (Ed.), *Handbook of human intelligence* (pp. 3–28). Cambridge, UK: Cambridge University Press.

Teuber, H.-L. (1972). Unity and diversity of frontal lobe functions. *Acta Neurobiologiae Experimentalis, 32,* 615–656.

Van Valen, L. (1974). Brain size and intelligence in man. *American Journal of Physical Anthropology, 40,* 417–424.

Vandenberg, S. G. (1971). *Mental rotation test.* Boulder, CO: University of Colorado.

Vernon, P. A. (Ed.) (1992). *Biological approaches to the study of human intelligence.* Norwood, NJ: Ablex.

Vos, S. H., & Friederici, A. D. (2003). Intersentential syntactic context effects on comprehension: The role of working memory. *Cognitive Brain Research, 16,* 111–122.

Woodcock, R. W. (1987). *The Woodcock reading mastery test–Revised.* Circle Pines, MN: American Guidance Service.

6

The Role of Working Memory in Higher-Level Cognition

Domain-Specific versus Domain-General Perspectives

David Z. Hambrick, Michael J. Kane,
and Randall W. Engle

INTRODUCTION

The idea that short-term memory is an important component of intelligence is not new. For example, over a century ago James (1890) wrote, "All the intellectual value for us of a state of mind depends on our after memory of it. Only then is it combined in a system and knowingly made to contribute to a result. Only then does it *count* for us." Around the same time, Binet (1905) included a test of short-term memory in a test battery designed to identify learning disabled children in the Paris school system. And more recently, short-term memory has been conceptualized as a fundamental component of human cognition. For example, Miller (1956) famously proposed that the capacity of short-term memory is limited to 7 ± 2 bits of information. Later, Atkinson and Shiffrin (1968) incorporated this idea of a central bottleneck in information processing into their "modal" model of memory.

Nevertheless, the extent to which short-term memory plays an important role in higher-level cognition – intelligence manifested in complex cognitive activities like reasoning and learning – has been a topic of considerable debate in cognitive psychology. Consider, for example, the results of a series of experiments by Baddeley and Hitch (1974). The surprising finding in these experiments was that a secondary task designed to tax short-term memory had little or no effect on a variety of reasoning, comprehension, and memory primary tasks. In one such experiment, subjects performed a task in which the goal was to verify sentences purporting to describe the relationship between two letters (e.g., A precedes B – BA) while maintaining a memory load. The secondary task had little effect on subjects' success in the task – a finding logically inconsistent with the assumption of short-term memory as a central bottleneck in information processing.

Baddeley and Hitch (1974) therefore proposed that short-term memory – the passive storage of information – is but one part of a memory system in which a limited capacity "workspace" can be divided between processing and storage functions. This concept provided a tidy explanation for their findings. Subjects were able to divide this limited capacity workspace between the primary task and the secondary task, as long as the latter did not overtax the system. Following this initial work, Baddeley and his colleagues proposed a working memory model consisting of three major components: two "slave" systems – the *phonological loop* and *visuospatial sketchpad* – devoted to temporary storage and maintenance of information and a *central executive* responsible for planning and control processes involved in higher-level cognition (e.g., Baddeley, 1986). Understanding the nature of this latter component of the system and its involvement in higher-level cognition has since been a major focus of research in cognitive psychology.

AN INDIVIDUAL-DIFFERENCES PERSPECTIVE ON WORKING MEMORY

In the early 1980s, research on individual differences in working memory (WM) took off with the development of a procedure for measuring the construct – the Daneman and Carpenter (1980) reading span task. Consistent with Baddeley and Hitch's (1974) conception of the central executive, Daneman and Carpenter designed this task to include both a processing component – reading sentences – and a storage component – remembering the final word of each sentence for later recall. For example, given the sentences *When at last his eyes opened, there was no gleam of triumph, no shade of anger* and *The taxi turned up Michigan Avenue where they had a clear view of the lake*, the task would be to report *anger* and *lake*. Daneman and Carpenter discovered that *reading span* – the number of sentences a subject could read while maintaining perfect recall of the sentence-final words – correlated with global measures of language comprehension (e.g., verbal SAT score) as well as with specific measures (e.g., resolving pronominal ambiguity). Moreover, reading span was a better predictor of comprehension than was a measure of short-term memory (word span).

A variety of WM tasks modeled after reading span have been introduced since Daneman and Carpenter's (1980) study. Like reading span, each of these tasks is a dual task in the sense that it involves alternating between interleaved processing and storage subtasks. To illustrate, in *operation span* (Turner & Engle, 1989), the goal is to solve a series of simple math problems while remembering a word following each problem, whereas in *counting span*, the goal is to count the number of target objects in a series of displays (e.g., light blue circles among dark blue circles and light blue triangles) while remembering the count from each display. Nonverbal WM tasks have been developed as well. For example, Shah and Miyake (1996) introduced a task called *spatial span* in which subjects decide whether each of a series of rotated letters is normal or mirror-imaged while remembering the orientation of each letter.

Two observations can be made from the hundreds of independent studies in which WM tasks have been administered. The first observation is that WM tasks are reliable; that is, these tasks measure accurately *whatever it is that they measure*. For example, with approximately two months between test intervals, Klein and Fiss (1999) reported a test–retest reliability coefficient of .88 for the operation span task. Moreover, internal consistency estimates (e.g., coefficient alphas) for WM tasks are typically in the range from .70 to .90. This evidence can be understood in terms of classical test theory (e.g., Novick, 1966; Spearmen, 1927). The basic assumption of classical test theory is that a single test score consists of a *true score* – which reflects stable characteristics of the attribute one is trying to measure – and *error*. Within this framework, reliability is interpreted as an index of the proportion of variance in test scores (*total variance*) that is caused by variability in true scores (*true-score variance*). Because reliability coefficients of WM tasks are seldom lower than .70, and are often much higher, it therefore appears that scores on these tasks are more attributable to stable characteristics of subjects – to true scores – than to error.

The second observation is that individual differences in WM span correlate with measures of many aspects of higher-level cognition, including reading comprehension (e.g., Daneman & Carpenter, 1980), abstract reasoning (e.g., Kyllonen & Christal, 1990), problem solving (e.g., Welsh, Satterlee-Cartmell, & Stine, 1999), and complex learning (e.g., Kyllonen & Stephens, 1990). Nevertheless, on the basis of the available evidence, it remains unclear *what* various measures of WM reflect and *why* they correlate with higher-level cognition. In other words, although it is evident that WM tasks accurately measure *some* capability that seems to be important for higher-level cognition, what is the nature of this capability? At least two major hypotheses concerning this question have been advanced.

The premise of the first hypothesis is that WM tasks capture factors that are applicable to only a particular task or class of tasks. For example, according to this domain-specific hypothesis, reading span correlates with reading comprehension simply because reading span itself involves reading comprehension. In line with this hypothesis, Daneman and Carpenter (1980) proposed that by virtue of their greater efficiency in the processing component of the reading span task – reading sentences – the high-span individuals in their study had more residual capacity to devote to memorization of the sentence-final words than did the low-spans. Similarly, MacDonald and Christiansen (2002) claimed that "the distinction commonly drawn between language-processing tasks and linguistic WM tasks is an artificial one, and ... all of these tasks are simply different measures of language processing skill" (p. 36) (see also Ericsson & Kintsch, 1995).

In contrast, the second hypothesis proposes that, in addition to any domain-specific factors, WM tasks capture factors that are involved in a wide range of cognitive tasks. In particular, this domain-general hypothesis assumes that there is nothing special about a particular WM task like reading span or operation span. Rather, all WM tasks, regardless of their specific requirements, tap domain-general factors that play a role in many different cognitive tasks. For example, consistent with this hypothesis, we have argued that one domain-general factor captured by WM tasks is the capability for attention control, which we believe underlies the ability to maintain goals and other task-relevant information in a highly activated and accessible state, particularly under conditions of interference or distraction (Engle, Kane, & Tuholski, 1999a; Engle, Tuholski et al., 1999b). As another example, Hasher and Zacks (1988) proposed that individual differences in WM span arise from the efficiency and effectiveness of a number of inhibitory processes that regulate the contents of conscious thought. Although the theoretical mechanisms of these theories differ – ours emphasizes maintenance of task-relevant information whereas theirs emphasizes inhibition of task-irrelevant information – the theories are similar in that both assume that domain-general factors underlie individual differences in WM and its involvement in higher-level cognition.

Which Hypothesis Is Correct?

Domain-specific factors almost certainly account for some of the true-score variance in WM tasks because, as Spearman (1927) observed, we must assume that performance on any test of mental ability is influenced by factors unique to that test, in addition to any factors that operate across different tests. Stated differently, no task is "process-pure" in the sense that it captures only the task-independent construct of interest. For example, skill in math may contribute to the total variance in operation span, whereas skill in reading may contribute to the total variance in reading span. In fact, dozens of factors may contribute to the total variance in WM span as measured by a particular task. At the same time, evidence suggests that a sizeable proportion of the true-score variance in WM tasks is accounted for by domain-general factors, above and beyond the contribution of any domain-specific factors. For example, in a study by Engle et al. (1999b), subjects completed a battery of WM tasks that included reading span, operation span, and counting span. Even though the requirements of these tasks were quite different, the average inter-task correlation was .43, indicating that an average of 18% of the variance in one task was accounted for by factors operating in the other tasks (i.e., $.43^2 = .184$). Of course, another way to interpret this observation is that 82% of the variance in these tasks was accounted for by factors *not* operating in the other tasks. However, the central claim of the domain-general hypothesis is not that the total variance in WM span is accounted for entirely by domain-general factors – or even mostly – but rather that these factors explain the correlation of WM span with higher-level cognition, with little or no contribution from domain-specific factors. In other words, if the true-score variance in WM span can be decomposed into two types – domain-specific and domain-general – then the prediction is that the latter drives correlations of WM span with higher-level cognition. Evidence from studies that have followed two quite different research approaches supports this conclusion.

Microanalytic Research

The first approach is *microanalytic* because the goal is to investigate how WM span relates to performance in what might be considered "elementary" attention tasks; that is, tasks designed to capture basic information processes underlying higher-level cognition. This research has revealed that individual differences in these elementary tasks are strongly related to individual differences in a variety of WM tasks, suggesting that the capability for attention control may lie at the heart of individual differences in WM span.

Consider the results of a study by Kane et al. (2001). Subjects classified as either low or high in WM span (*low-span* or *high-span*) performed a version of the so-called antisaccade task. The procedure was simple: In the *prosaccade* condition, a flashing cue appeared in the same location on the screen as an upcoming stimulus – the letter B, P, or R – and the task was to press a key corresponding to the stimulus. By contrast, in the *antisaccade* condition, the target always appeared in the location opposite to that of the cue. The results were straightforward: the advantage of high-spans over low-spans in both reaction time and accuracy was larger in the antisaccade condition than in the prosaccade condition. Moreover, in a follow-up experiment, Kane et al. monitored eye movements and found that this was because low-spans made more reflexive eye movements toward the flashing cue in the antisaccade condition than did high-spans. Similarly, in a study by Schrock and Engle (in preparation), in which the subject simply had to look at a box on the opposite side of the screen from a flashing cue, low-spans were much more likely than high-spans to make their first saccade an erroneous movement to the flashing cue. In fact, even when low-spans were correct in their first saccade, they were slower than high-spans to begin the eye movement.

We believe that the results of these studies provide especially strong support for a domain-general hypothesis of WM because there are no apparent domain-specific factors to which span-related differences in the antisaccade task can be attributed. Results of other studies from our labs are consistent with this hypothesis as well. For example, Kane and Engle (2000) used a three-trial serial recall task in which subjects were presented with three 10-word lists, each of which was followed by a 30-second rehearsal preventative task before recall. As predicted, there was greater buildup of proactive interference in low-spans than in high-spans. One interpretation of this finding is that, after the first trial, high-spans were better able to maintain the words in an activated state than were low-spans and were hence less likely to confuse these words with those from the previous trial or trials. To test this hypothesis, in a second experiment, subjects performed the task as before or while performing a continuous, attention-demanding secondary task. If attention control was responsible for the span-related difference in proactive interference observed in the first experiment, then the secondary task should have produced more of an increase in proactive interference for high-spans than for low-spans. This is what happened; indeed, in the divided-attention condition, the performance of low-spans and high-spans was indistinguishable.

In another microanalytic study, Kane and Engle (2003) used the Stroop task to investigate the possibility that WM span is related to a phenomenon Duncan (1990) termed "goal neglect." The basic idea of goal neglect is that attention failures occur when goal-relevant information is lost from the active portion of memory because the environment lacks external cues for appropriate action. In a series of experiments, Kane and Engle set up this type of situation by manipulating percentages of congruent and incongruent trials in the Stroop task. In the 0% congruent conditions, almost all of the trials were incongruent (e.g., BLUE displayed in red), and so the task context reinforced the goal, to ignore the word, on virtually every trial. By contrast, in the 75% congruent conditions, subjects could neglect the task goal on a majority of trials with no negative consequences. However, accurate responding on the rare incongruent trials here required that subjects maintain access to the *ignore-the-word* goal. Taken together, the results revealed that low-spans were much more error-prone than high-spans in the 75% conditions but not in the 0% conditions. Thus, low-spans were at a disadvantage when the task placed a premium on actively maintaining the goal of ignoring words in a task environment that lacked external prompts to action.

As a final example, Conway, Cowan, and Bunting (2001) found that WM span is related to a phenomenon first reported by Moray (1959). In a series of experiments by Cherry (1953), subjects were instructed to repeat a message presented in one ear and to ignore a message presented in the other ear. Subjects had little difficulty performing this task, and thus theorists such as Broadbent (1958) proposed that attention acts as an all-or-none filter, letting relevant information into short-term memory but blocking out irrelevant information. Nevertheless, Moray demonstrated that content from an unattended message is not rejected completely. In particular, a substantial number of subjects (33%) heard their name when it was presented in the unattended message. By contrast, very few participants could recall a word that was repeated 35 times in the unattended ear. Why, though, did 100% of Moray's subjects not hear their own names? Conway et al. reasoned that if what WM tasks capture is related to the ability to control attention – to direct it toward relevant information and away from irrelevant information – then high-spans would be *less* likely to notice their names in an unattended message than low-spans. Thus, Conway et al. replicated Moray's experiment, but with low-span and high-span subjects. The results were striking: 65% of low-spans heard their names in the unattended message, whereas only 20% of high-spans did so.

The Role of Strategies?

We believe that the evidence considered thus far supports the hypothesis that individual differences in various span tasks reflect differences in the capability for attention control, and elsewhere we have argued that this individual-difference characteristic is a relatively stable aspect of cognition (e.g., Engle et al., 1999a). Nevertheless, an alternative hypothesis – and one that is particularly appealing because it implies that deficits in WM can be ameliorated through instruction – posits that these differences stem not from differences in any fixed information processing capacity, but rather from differences in the *strategies* that low-spans and high-spans use to perform the tasks.

Using the reading span task, McNamara and Scott (2001) investigated this possibility by training subjects in the use of a mnemonic technique called "chaining" that involves memorizing words by generating sentences to connect them. McNamara and Scott found that training improved reading span performance by 41% and 53% in two experiments. Moreover, these improvements did not come at the expense of poorer performance in the comprehension component of the reading span task, as comprehension actually improved from pretest to post-test in both experiments. McNamara and Scott concluded that strategy training enhanced subjects' efficiency in performing the reading span task, thereby freeing up resources for use in the comprehension component of the task.

The McNamara and Scott (2001) study convincingly suggests that strategies can influence performance in WM tasks; in addition, this study is important because it highlights the importance of taking into account the possibility of strategy use when assessing WM. Nevertheless, McNamara and Scott's finding is not surprising because many studies have demonstrated beneficial effects of strategy instruction on cognitive performance. For example, a number of researchers have reported that strategy training enhances performance on a task that is regarded as a relatively pure indicator of general intelligence – Raven's Progressive Matrices (e.g., Blieszner, Willis, & Baltes, 1981; Klauer, Willmes, & Phye, 2002; Denney & Heidrich, 1990). There simply is no reason to expect that strategy training would not also enhance WM span. Furthermore, McNamara and Scott did not address the important question of whether differential strategy use by low-spans and high-spans accounts for the correlation of WM span with higher-level cognition.

To answer this question, Turley-Ames and Whitfield (2003) conducted an impressive, large-scale study ($N = 360$) to investigate effects of different types of strategies on the correlation between operation span and reading comprehension. After taking a pretest of operation span, subjects were assigned to a control condition or to a condition in which they were instructed in use of a strategy for the operation span task involving rote rehearsal, visual imagery, or forming semantic associations. Subjects then completed another version of operation span. Consistent with McNamara and Scott's (2001) finding, strategy training enhanced WM performance. However, strategy training did not reduce – much less eliminate – the correlation between operation span and reading comprehension. In fact, at post-test, operation span correlated *more* positively with reading comprehension in each strategy condition – rehearsal ($r = .56$), imagery ($r = .32$), and semantic ($r = .47$) – than in the control condition ($r = .30$).

Therefore, the results of the Turley-Ames and Whitfield (2003) study suggest that differential strategy use by low-spans and high-spans may *suppress* rather than account for the relationship between WM span and higher-level cognition. Results of an earlier study by Engle, Cantor, and Carullo (1992) provide additional support for this conclusion. In this study, using a "moving-window" technique in which elements of either operation span or reading span were presented sequentially rather than simultaneously, Engle et al. measured the amount of time subjects spent on the processing component of the task. They then interpreted this measure as an estimate of the extent to which subjects strategically traded off time on the processing component for time on the storage component. In agreement with Turley-Ames and Whitfield's (2003) finding, for both operation span and reading span, there was no evidence for a decrease in the correlation between WM span and reading comprehension after controlling for this estimate; that is, the correlation increased slightly for operation span ($.34 \rightarrow .40$) and was unchanged for reading span ($.40 \rightarrow .40$).

To sum up, based on the available evidence, it appears that the main effect of strategy use may be on the total variance in WM performance. That is, as both McNamara and Scott (2001) and Turley-Ames and Whitfield (2003) demonstrated, it seems clear that strategy use can influence scores in WM tasks. At the same time, the available evidence does not support the hypothesis that differential strategy use by low-spans and high-spans accounts for the relationship between WM span and higher-level cognition. To the contrary, if anything, differential strategy use appears to suppress the true magnitude of this relationship. Additional research like that by Turley-Ames and Whitfield will be critical to understanding why this is so.

Macroanalytic Research

An advantage of microanalytic research on WM is that it is potentially informative about the precise nature of basic information processing mechanisms underlying individual differences in WM. That is, if WM span correlates with individual differences in some experimental task, then the implication is that a common mechanism is operating in both tasks. To reiterate, based on results of the microanalytic studies just reviewed, we argue that WM reflects the capacity for attention control, which is critical for tasks that demand maintenance of task-relevant information. However, a potential disadvantage of this approach is a consequence of a basic psychometric principle alluded to earlier: no single task can be expected to provide a process-pure measure of the construct it is hypothesized to measure. For this reason, although a factor like attention control may indeed play an important role in the experimental tasks we have investigated in our research, we must assume that a number of other factors contribute to true scores in the tasks. Furthermore, on the basis of evidence from microanalytic studies alone, the possibility that these factors contribute to the correlation of scores in the task with WM span cannot be unequivocally rejected.

With this in mind, a second approach that we have used in research on the nature of individual differences in WM is *macroanalytic* in that the goal is to investigate the relationship between WM and individual differences in broad, psychometrically established constructs. In particular, this research has focused on the link between WM and the aspect of cognition that Cattell (1943) first termed *fluid intelligence* (g_f) – the ability to solve novel problems and adapt to new situations. Summarized, evidence from macroanalytic research suggests that WM may be an important component of g_f. For example, at the latent-variable level, Kyllonen and Christal (1990) found a strong positive correlation (.90) between WM and g_f. Furthermore, Kyllonen (1996) also reported high positive correlations between g_f and latent variables representing WM in three content areas: verbal (.94), spatial (.96), and numerical (.95). Kyllonen summarized his research as follows:

We have observed in study after study, under a variety of operationalizations, using a diverse set of criteria, that working memory capacity is more highly related to performance on other cognitive tests, and is more highly related to learning, both short-term and long-term, than is any other cognitive factor. This finding of the centrality of the working memory capacity factor leads to the conclusion that working memory capacity may indeed be essentially Spearman's g. (p. 73)

Engle et al. (1999b) further investigated the relationship between WM and g_f. WM was measured with span tasks similar to those described earlier, while short-term memory (STM) was measured with simple memory span tasks (e.g., word span); g_f was measured with two nonverbal tests of abstract reasoning ability. Engle et al. predicted that latent variables representing WM and STM would correlate, given that some of the same domain-specific skills and procedures were captured by both. For example, skill in encoding information into long-term memory could contribute to performance in both the reading span and word span tasks. However, they also predicted that once this correlation was taken into account, the WM residual variance would reflect individual differences in attention control and would correlate positively with g_f, whereas the STM residual would not. The data were consistent with this prediction: the WM residual correlated significantly with g_f (.49) whereas the STM residual did not (.12).

Verbal versus Spatial WM?

Recently, we have focused more directly on the question of whether WM is domain-specific or domain-general. Given that verbal WM tasks predict both g_f and low-level attention control, it is quite likely that WM tasks measure a general cognitive capability. However, other work suggests that verbal and spatial WM tasks may measure different constructs. For example, Shah and Miyake (1996) observed the correlations between scores in verbal and spatial WM tasks (reading span and spatial span) and independent estimates of verbal ability and spatial ability. The major finding of this study was that spatial span correlated with spatial ability (.66), but not with verbal ability (.07), whereas the reading span measure correlated with verbal ability (.45), but not with spatial ability (.12). In addition, the correlation between the two WM tasks was weak (.23). Shah and Miyake (1999) therefore concluded that "the predictive powers of the two complex memory span tasks seem to be domain specific" (p. 11).

Nevertheless, a limitation of the Shah and Miyake (1996) study is that the subjects were college students from two relatively selective universities. Therefore, as Shah and Miyake themselves acknowledged, it is possible that variability in the span scores due to a domain-general WM factor was restricted compared to what might be expected within a more heterogeneous sample. With this in mind, we recently conducted a study in which over 200 subjects, recruited from university subject pools and from the general population, completed both verbal and spatial WM and STM tasks; in addition, subjects completed tests of verbal reasoning and spatial reasoning, as well as "decontextualized" reasoning (e.g., Raven's Progressive Matrices). As described before, each WM task included a processing component and a storage component, while each STM task included only a storage component.

As expected, there were moderate positive correlations among all of the memory tasks. However, the patterns of intercorrelations differed for STM and WM. The mean correlation among domain-matching WM measures was .64, compared to a mean of .56 among domain-mismatching measures. By contrast, the mean correlation among domain-matching STM measures

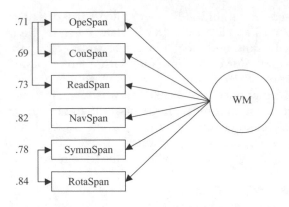

1-Factor Model

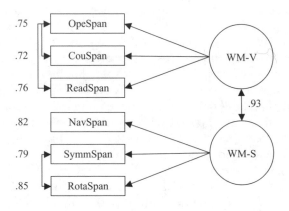

2-Factor Model

FIGURE 1. Domain-general model (top panel); domain-specific model (bottom panel).

was .68, compared to a mean of .47 among domain-mismatching measures. Thus, the domain-matching versus domain-mismatching difference was greater for the STM measures (.21) than for the WM measures (.08). In line with other research (e.g., Park et al., 2002; Swanson & Howell, 2001), these results suggest that the verbal and spatial STM span tasks measured more distinct constructs than did the verbal and spatial WM span tasks.

To further investigate the possibility that WM is domain-general, we conducted both exploratory and confirmatory factor analyses on the WM measures. In an exploratory factor analysis, the first factor accounted for a large proportion of the variance (65.9%), and it was the only factor that met the criterion for extraction (i.e., eigenvalue greater than one), suggesting that the WM measures tapped a single construct. To perform a more rigorous test, we also conducted confirmatory factor analyses to compare 1-factor and 2-factor models, with the latter model consisting of separate but correlated verbal and spatial factors (WM-V and WM-S). The results, illustrated in Figure 1, were as follows: In the 1-factor model, each of the WM measures had a strong positive loading on the common factor. In addition, while the 2-factor model provided a slightly better fit to the data than did the 1-factor model, the improvement was not statistically significant, and the verbal and spatial factors correlated near one (.93). The data clearly do not lead us to reject the parsimonious view that WM capacity reflects a domain-general construct.

We conducted two additional analyses to examine the involvement of a domain-general WM in g_f. In the first analysis, the "predictor-side" model was a 1-factor WM model, whereas the "criterion-side" model was a 3-factor reasoning model with a g_f factor, onto which all of the reasoning measures loaded, plus domain-specific verbal and spatial factors, onto which the verbal and spatial measures loaded (REA-V and REA-S). This "nested" model of the reasoning tasks allowed us to isolate the variance shared among all the reasoning tasks (g_f), as well as the residual variance that was uniquely shared among the verbal tasks and among the spatial tasks. As shown in Figure 2, WM predicted about 35% of the variance in g_f, a value consistent with estimates from prior studies (Conway et al., 2002; Engle et al., 1999b). In addition, WM had weaker, but still significant, effects on domain-specific aspects of both verbal and spatial reasoning (.27 and .30, respectively). Thus, the variance shared by verbal and spatial WM tasks, reflecting domain-general WM, predicted both general and specific reasoning abilities.

In the second analysis, we added the STM measures to the structural equation model shown in Figure 2. In this model, all of the memory measures loaded onto a factor that we hypothesized to represent the central factor underlying individual differences in WM: executive attention (EA). In addition, the six verbal memory measures simultaneously loaded onto a verbal factor, whereas the six spatial memory measures loaded onto a spatial factor. We interpreted these domain-specific factors (STORAGE-V and STORAGE-S) as reflecting storage or coding processes specific to verbal or spatial stimuli and independent of domain-general executive attention. The logic guiding specification of this model was that no WM or STM task is purely domain-general or domain-specific. Instead, WM measures capture a domain-general factor primarily but also domain-specific factors, whereas STM tasks capture domain-specific factors primarily but also a domain-general factor. Therefore, from each measure, we extracted domain-general variance and domain-specific variance.

Consistent with the model in Figure 2, EA had a strong effect on g_f (.57) and weaker effects on REA-V (.26) and REA-S (.33). These correlations

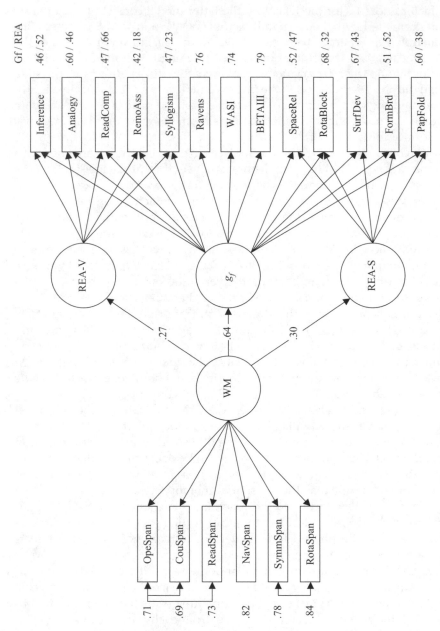

FIGURE 2. Structural equation modeling relating WM and g_f.

almost perfectly matched the ones we found when we modeled "executive attention" with only the WM span tasks (cf. Fig. 2). In addition, STORAGE-V had a positive effect on REA-V (.42) but a nonsignificant effect on g_f. As prior studies have found (e.g., Engle et al., 1999b), verbal storage and rehearsal processes account for unique variance in verbal ability over and beyond that accounted for by WM. However, the same is not true for g_f, where only WM accounts for unique variance. Lastly, STORAGE-S showed a quite different pattern of relations to reasoning, with strong effects on both REA-S (.39) and g_f (.51). Thus, not only did spatial-storage processes account for aspects of spatial reasoning that are independent of g_f, but they also accounted for a sizeable proportion of g_f variance that is not shared with EA. Consistent with other research (e.g., Miyake et al., 2001; Oberauer, 1993), this finding suggests that spatial storage may be more closely tied to executive functioning than is verbal storage. A possible interpretation of this finding is that verbal storage is supported by well-learned coding and storage processes (e.g., rehearsal), whereas spatial storage, due to its novelty, must rely more on attention control ability. This is an intriguing hypothesis as it suggests that executive attention can be measured in span tasks without dual-task requirements, but it must await further investigation.

Toward a Broader Perspective on the Role of WM in Higher-Level Cognition

To sum up, evidence from two types of research is consistent with a domain-general hypothesis of individual differences in WM. First, microanalytic research suggests that an important factor underlying individual differences in WM is the capacity for attention control. That is, WM span correlates with performance in elementary attention tasks like antisaccade. Once again, we believe that this evidence is compelling because there are no apparent domain-specific factors to which span-related differences can be attributed in these tasks. Second, macroanalytic research suggests that WM plays an important role in the broad aspect of cognition referred to as g_f. That is, WM span predicts g_f even after the contribution of domain-specific factors has been taken into account.

But how important is WM for real-world tasks in which many other factors might be expected to play a role? For example, does WM contribute to success in tasks like choosing a move in a chess game, or even in more mundane tasks like financial planning? We have begun to explore this sort of question. The general approach in this research is to create a laboratory simulation of some real-world task and then to determine whether, and to what extent, WM contributes to performance above and beyond the influence of other possible predictors. For example, in a recent study by Hambrick and Engle (2002), subjects performed a task that involved listening to, and then answering questions about, simulated radio broadcasts of baseball games. The subjects were 181 adults with wide ranges of WM and knowledge about baseball, and the radio broadcasts were recorded by a baseball announcer for a local radio station.

Not surprisingly, baseball knowledge was a strong predictor of memory for information from the baseball games, including changes in which bases were occupied after each turn at bat and information about the players (e.g., batting averages). In fact, baseball knowledge accounted for over half of the variance. However, there was evidence that WM enhanced the effect of domain knowledge on memory performance. That is, for information that was judged directly relevant to the games (e.g., players' batting averages), the effect of domain knowledge on memory performance was greater for high-spans than for low-spans. Based on this finding, we suggested that WM may serve as a "bottom-up" constraint on knowledge use in cognitive performance. In particular, we suggested that to the extent that integrating new information with preexisting knowledge depends on maintaining that information in an activated state for some period of time, high-spans should benefit more from preexisting knowledge than low-spans.

Additional evidence concerning the interplay between domain knowledge and WM was reported by Wittmann and Süß (1999), who investigated the effects of domain knowledge and WM on performance in work simulations. For example, in one task, the goal was to control the energy output of a coal-fired power plant by manipulating a number of variables (e.g., coal input); another task involved managing the production of a garment manufacturing company. A consistent finding from this research was that task-specific knowledge (i.e., knowledge acquired during the simulations) was a strong predictor of final performance. However, Wittmann and Süß also reported that WM was a significant predictor of performance above and beyond knowledge. Thus, there is reason to believe that effects of WM on higher-level cognition are not limited to simple laboratory tasks. Rather, WM may be an important contributor to success in complex task environments in which many other factors might also be expected to play a role.

SUMMARY AND CONCLUSIONS

Working memory has now been a topic of intensive research in cognitive psychology for more than 25 years. What has this research revealed about the nature of this construct and its involvement in higher-level cognition? At least two conclusions seem warranted. First, the work from two complementary perspectives – microanalytic and macroanalytic – converges on the conclusion that individual differences in WM span reflect something more general than factors tied to particular domains. For example, WM span correlates with individual differences in elementary attention tasks and in tests of general intelligence. Second, it now seems clear that these domain-general factors may be responsible for the correlation of WM span with higher-level cognition. Important goals for future research are to refine understanding of the nature of these factors and to study their involvement in complex, real-world activities.

References

Atkinson, R. C., & Shiffrin, R. M. (1968). Human memory: A proposed system and its control processes. In K. W. Spence & J. T. Spence (Eds.), *Advances in the psychology of learning and motivation research and theory* (Vol. 2, pp. 89–195). New York: Academic Press.

Baddeley, A. D. (1986). *Working memory*. London/New York: Oxford University Press.

Baddeley, A. D., & Hitch, G. (1974). Working memory. In G. A. Bower (Ed.), *The psychology of learning and motivation* (Vol. 8, pp. 47–89). New York: Academic Press.

Broadbent, D. (1958). *Perception and communication*. Oxford: Permagon.

Binet, A. (1905). New methods for the diagnosis of the intellectual level of sub-normals. *L'Année Psychologique, 12*, 191–244.

Blieszner, R., Willis, S. L., & Baltes, P. B. (1981). Training research in aging on the fluid ability of inductive reasoning. *Journal of Applied Developmental Psychology, 2*, 247–265.

Cattell, R. B. (1943). The measurement of adult intelligence. *Psychological Bulletin, 40*, 153–193.

Cherry, C. E. (1953). Some experiments on the recognition of speech, with one and with two ears. *Journal of the Acoustical Society of America, 25*, 975–979.

Conway, A. R. A., Cowan, N., & Bunting, M. F. (2001). The cocktail party phenomenon revisited: The importance of working memory capacity. *Psychonomic Bulletin and Review, 8*, 331–335.

Conway, A. R. A., Cowan, N., Bunting, M. F., Therriault, D., & Minkoff, S. (2002). A latent variable analysis of working memory capacity, short term memory capacity, processing speed, and general fluid intelligence. *Intelligence, 30*, 163–183.

Daneman, M., & Carpenter, P. A. (1980). Individual differences in working memory and reading. *Journal of Verbal Learning & Verbal Behavior, 19*, 450–466.

Denney, N. W., & Heidrich, S. M. (1990). Training effects on Raven's Progressive Matrices in young, middle-aged, and elderly adults. *Psychology and Aging, 5*, 144–145.

Duncan, J. (1990). Goal weighting and the choice of behavior in a complex world. *Ergonomics, 33*, 1265–1279.

Engle, R. W., Cantor, J., & Carullo, J. J. (1992). Individual differences in working memory and comprehension: A test of four hypotheses. *Journal of Experimental Psychology: Learning, Memory, & Cognition, 18*, 972–992.

Engle, R. W., Kane, M. J., & Tuholski, S. W. (1999a). Individual differences in working memory capacity and what they tell us about controlled attention, general fluid intelligence, and functions of the prefrontal cortex. In A. Miyake & P. Shah (Eds.),

Models of working memory: Mechanisms of active maintenance and executive control (pp. 102–134). New York: Cambridge University Press.

Engle, R. W., Tuholski, S. W., Laughlin, J. E., & Conway, A. R. A. (1999b). Working memory, short-term memory, and general fluid intelligence: A latent-variable approach. *Journal of Experimental Psychology: General, 128*, 309–331.

Ericsson, K. A., & Kintsch, W. (1995). Long-term working memory. *Psychological Review, 102*, 211–245.

Hambrick, D. Z., & Engle, R. W. (2002). Effects of domain knowledge, working memory capacity, and age on cognitive performance: An investigation of the knowledge-is-power hypothesis. *Cognitive Psychology, 44*, 339–384.

Hasher, L., & Zacks, R. T. (1988). Working memory, comprehension, and aging: A review and a new view. In G. Bower (Ed.), *The psychology of learning and motivation* (Vol. 22, pp. 193–225). New York: Academic Press.

James, W. (1890). *Principles of psychology*. New York: Holt.

Kane, M. J., & Engle, R. W. (2003). Working memory capacity and the control of attention: The contributions of goal neglect, response competition, and task set to Stroop interference. *Journal of Experimental Psychology: General, 132*, 47–70.

Kane, M. J., & Engle, R. W. (2000). Working memory capacity, proactive interference, and divided attention: Limits on long-term memory retrieval. *Journal of Experimental Psychology: Learning, Memory, and Cognition, 26*, 333–358.

Kane, M. J., Bleckley, M. K., Conway, A. R. A., & Engle, R. W. (2001). A controlled-attention view of working-memory capacity. *Journal of Experimental Psychology: General, 130*, 169–183.

Klauer, K. J., Willmes, K., & Phye, G. D. (2002). Inducing inductive reasoning: Does it transfer to fluid intelligence? *Contemporary Educational Psychology, 27*, 1–25.

Klein, K., & Fiss, W. H. (1999). The reliability and stability of the Turner and Engle working memory task. *Behavior Research Methods, Instruments and Computers, 31*, 429–432.

Kyllonen, P. C. (1996). Is working memory capacity Spearman's *g*? In I. Dennis & P. Tapsfield (Eds.), *Human abilities: Their nature and measurement* (pp. 49–75). Mahwah, NJ: Erlbaum.

Kyllonen, P. C., & Christal, R. E. (1990). Reasoning ability is (little more than) working-memory capacity? *Intelligence, 14*, 389–433.

Kyllonen, P. C., & Stephens, D. L. (1990). Cognitive abilities as determinants of success in acquiring logic skill. *Learning and Individual Differences, 2*, 129–160.

MacDonald, M. C., & Christiansen, M. H. (2002). Reassessing working memory: Comment on Just and Carpenter (1992) and Waters and Caplan (1996). *Psychological Review, 109*, 35–54.

McNamara, D. S., & Scott, J. L. (2001). Working memory capacity and strategy use. *Memory and Cognition, 29*, 10–17.

Miller, G. A. (1956). The magical number seven, plus or minus two: Some limits on our capacity for processing information. *Psychological Review, 63*, 81–97.

Miyake, A., Friedman, N. P., Rettinger, D. A., Shah, P., & Hegarty, M. (2001). How are visuospatial working memory, executive functioning, and spatial abilities related? A latent-variable analysis. *Journal of Experimental Psychology: General, 130*, 621–640.

Moray, N. (1959). Attention in dichotic listening: Affective cues and the influence of instructions. *Quarterly Journal of Experimental Psychology, 11*, 56–60.

Novick, M. R. (1966). The axioms and principal results of classical test theory. *Journal of Mathematical Psychology, 3*, 1–18.

Oberauer, K. (1993). Die Koordination kognitiver Operationen. Eine Studie zum Zusammenhang von 'working memory' und Intelligenz [The coordination of cognitive operations. A study of the relationship of working memory and intelligence]. *Zeitschrift für Psychologie, 201*, 57–84.

Park, D. C., Lautenschlager, G., Hedden, T., Davidson, N., Smith, A. D., & Smith, P. K. (2002). Models of visuospatial and verbal memory across the adult lifespan. *Psychology and Aging, 17*, 299–320.

Schrock, C., & Engle, R. W. (in preparation). Working memory capacity and behavioral inhibition.

Shah, P., & Miyake, A. (1996). The separability of working memory resources for spatial thinking and language processing: An individual differences approach. *Journal of Experimental Psychology: General, 125*, 4–27.

Shah, P., & Miyake, A. (1999). Models of working memory: An introduction. In A. Miyake & P. Shah (Eds.), *Models of working memory: Mechanisms of active maintenance and executive control* (pp. 1–27). Cambridge, UK: Cambridge University Press.

Spearman, C. (1927). *The abilities of man*. London: MacMillan.

Swanson, H. L., & Howell, M. (2001). Working memory, short-term memory, and speech rate as predictors of children's reading performance at different ages. *Journal of Educational Psychology, 93*, 720–734.

Turley-Ames, K. J., & Whitfield, M. M. (2003). Strategy training and working memory task performance. *Journal of Memory and Language, 49*, 446–468.

Turner, M. L., & Engle, R. W. (1989). Is working memory capacity task dependent? *Journal of Memory and Language, 28*, 127–154.

Welsh, M. C., Satterlee-Cartmell, T., & Stine, M. (1999). Towers of Hanoi and London: Contribution of working memory and inhibition to performance. *Brain & Cognition, 41*, 231–242.

Wittmann, W. W., & Süß, H. (1999). Investigating the paths between working memory, intelligence, and complex problem-solving performances via Brunswik Symmetry. In P. L. Ackerman, P. C. Kyllonen, & R. D. Roberts (Eds.), *Learning and individual differences* (pp. 77–110). Washington, DC: American Psychological Association.

7

Higher-Order Cognition and Intelligence

Edward Nęcka and Jarosław Orzechowski

INTRODUCTION

We define higher-order cognition as information processing phenomena in which the metacognitive factors of monitoring and control play the fundamental role. This term is practically synonymous with complex cognition, because compound problems rely on the processes of monitoring and control to much greater extent than simple problems do. In this chapter, we review the literature on the relationships between human intelligence and complex, higher-order information processing. First, we will discuss the criteria of complexity of cognitive tasks. Then, we will provide a selection of empirical data concerning intelligence and problem solving. A section will be devoted to the studies that directly address the problem of the role of metacognition in intelligence. The chapter ends with the discussion of basic methodological problems involved in the study of relationships between higher-order cognition and intelligence.

INTELLIGENCE AND COGNITIVE COMPLEXITY

Intelligence is frequently defined as the ability to solve complex problems (Sternberg & Detterman, 1986). According to Carlstedt, Gustafsson, & Ullstadius (2000), who commented on the results of the survey conducted by Linda Gottfredson (1997), two aspects of human intelligence appear essential: quick adaptation to new situations and efficient solution of complex cognitive tasks. Hence, to determine who is intelligent we need to work out the criteria based on either novelty or complexity. In practice, the complexity criterion is more frequently applied, at least in measurement, because novel tasks and situations are hard to arrange in controlled conditions of

Preparation of this chapter has been supported by the grant No. 2 H01F 056 22 from the Polish Scientific Research Committee (KBN) to Edward Nęcka.

psychological assessment. Intelligence tests are thus typically constructed as sets of items that require the solution of a series of complex problems, usually inductive reasoning problems, like analogies, series completions, and classifications (Lohman, 2000; Primi, 2002).

It is not an easy job to define the complexity of cognitive tasks (Marshalek, Lohman, & Snow, 1983; Primi, 2002). The simplest criterion applies to the time needed to complete a certain task. If an average person needs less than one second to respond, a task is judged as simple, although even in that case some differences in the level of complexity are discernable (Deary, 2000; Larson, 1990). Tasks that need more than one hour to be solved are usually complex. We start to doubt the chronometric criterion when we switch to tasks that require several seconds or a couple of minutes to respond. Are they complex enough to serve as an indication of human intelligence? Another criterion refers to the complication of the information processing model that represents the problem-solving process. For instance, flow charts that represent analogical reasoning (Sternberg, 1977) are much more complicated than flow charts referring to sentence verification (Clark & Chase, 1972) and other elementary cognitive tasks. This criterion may be questionable on the basis of the obvious fact that flow charts are just theoretical constructs created at any level of abstraction, either low or high, depending on the hypothetical goal they are supposed to serve. It is therefore quite possible to represent complex tasks with simple models or vice versa.

A third possible criterion of complexity pertains to the number of factors influencing human performance or the number of variables used to manipulate the task's structure (Primi, 2002). The majority of elementary cognitive tasks (ECTs) used in intelligence research, such as simple and choice reaction time tasks, the Hick paradigm, or the sentence–picture verification task (SPVT), are not complex at all (Carlson & Widaman, 1987). On the other hand, there exists an increasing category of tasks that simulate certain real-life situations, such as the fire brigade's work, factory management, or consumers' behavior. These microworlds are becoming more and more popular in intelligence research, because their measures of performance tend to show reasonable correlations with standard intelligence tests (Rigas, Carling, & Brehmer, 2002). The fourth criterion of complexity pertains to the control and monitoring processes involved in the completion of a task. If certain tasks require such metacognitive factors in order to be properly tackled, they are probably complex enough; otherwise they are judged to be simple. However, the use of metacognitive tools may depend on one's capabilities, preferences, or styles of thinking rather than on the requirements inherent in the task's structure.

As we can see, the criteria of complexity are dubious and overlapping. We therefore suggest that the term "complexity" be used as a marker of the specific approach to the study of human intelligence rather than the precise

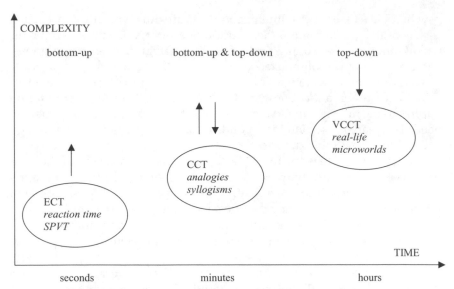

FIGURE 1. Levels of complexity of cognitive tasks, estimated time needed for their solution, and the hypothesized direction of causation in the intelligence/performance relationship (ECT = elementary cognitive tasks, CTT = complex cognitive tasks, VCCT = very complex cognitive tasks).

defining criterion for categorization of cognitive tasks. According to these criteria, tasks that are commonly applied in psychological experiments have one of three levels of complexity that correspond to respective time periods. We realize that the temporal criterion is rather imperfect because there exist tasks that require a lot of time and still are quite simple in nature, like multiplication of two 10-digit numbers by hand. However, the dimension of time as a criterion of complexity should work in most cases. So, at the lowest level, there are various elementary cognitive tasks (e.g., simple and choice reaction time or sentence–picture verification), which are normally performed in not more than several seconds (Fig. 1). At the intermediate level, there are reasoning problems, including analogies and syllogisms. Their solution time is articulated in minutes rather than seconds. The third level involves real-life or simulated problems that need at least several hours to complete. The data prove that people who differ in the standard psychometric measures of intelligence deal with both simple (Deary, 2000) and complex (Lohman, 2000) tasks in a different way. We do not know, however, whether intelligence is a causal factor determining the way people tackle various problems or just the result of some specific mode of solving them.

Although it is not always possible to resolve this problem on empirical grounds, it seems worthy of consideration on a theoretical level of analysis. We speculate that, in the case of simple tasks, intelligence is probably a result rather than the cause (the bottom-up hypothesis). According to this line of reasoning, intelligence is viewed as a complex mental ability consisting of elementary cognitive processes, which in turn depend on the neural efficiency (speedy or flawless transmission of signals in the CNS). An efficient brain causes effective processing of information at the elementary level of analysis, and such efficacy renders high levels of intellectual abilities. In the case of complex tasks, intelligence is regarded to be a causal factor (the top-down hypothesis). According to this supposition, intelligence is something like the general mental capacity that allows people to cope effectively with complex tasks. If the mental capacity is general enough, it should help to solve a broad category of tasks, especially the complex ones. It is why the concept of g (general factor of human intelligence) is attractive as a means to account for the fact that smart people do better in a variety of tasks (Jensen, 1998). As to the intermediate level of complexity, we hypothesize both directions of determination.

PROBLEM SOLVING AND INTELLIGENCE

Extensive psychological literature on the subject of problem solving is mostly focused on general issues, such as the rules of reasoning (e.g., Newell & Simon, 1972), strategies and heuristics used to work out a tenable solution (e.g., Thomas, 1974), the role of mental representation of the task (e.g., Hayes, 1989), and factors hindering the accomplishment of good solutions (e.g., Duncker, 1945). There is a category of problem-solving studies, though, which is motivated by the search for mechanisms of human intelligence. These studies focus on two questions: (1) What is the structure and composition of "intelligent" cognitive processes? and (2) Are there any relationships between psychometrically assessed abilities and problem-solving efficiency? These questions refer to different research paradigms adopted in the field.

The Processual Approach

In the processual approach, researchers aim at discovering the structure of cognitive processes that are judged as intelligent on the basis of intuition, consensus, or comprehensive theoretical considerations. For instance, it is widely believed that inductive reasoning tasks, mostly analogies, are diagnostic of one's general cognitive competence (Primi, 2002). This conviction comes from Spearman's (1923) theory of intelligence as an ability to carry on abstract rules of thinking, which he called eduction of relations and eduction of correlates. Having defined the cognitive ability as proficiency in drawing inductive conclusions, psychologists started to produce various assessment tools, many of which consist of the analogical reasoning or series completion tasks. From this point of view, it is not worth asking whether intelligent people perform better than less intelligent ones in numerous inductive reasoning tasks, because such tasks are practically synonymous with many intelligence tests. What is worth doing, though, is the investigation of cognitive processes underlying inductive inference. Decomposition of the cognitive processes responsible for test taking, reasoning, and other intellectual tasks became the landmark of the cognitive revolution in the study of human intelligence, symbolized by the works of Carroll (1976), Hunt (1980), and Sternberg (1977). This kind of approach has been also adopted by the authors who aimed at describing certain tests, like Raven's matrices (Carpenter, Just, & Shell, 1990) or Kohs block designs (Rozencwajg & Corroyer, 2002), in terms of underlying cognitive processes.

Sternberg's (1977, 1985) componential analysis is particularly interesting from this point of view. Having established the number and sequence of components of a chosen intellectual process, he was able to assess their duration and relative importance in the machinery of intelligence. For instance, he demonstrated the indispensability of mapping as a component in analogical reasoning processes as well as in metaphorical thinking. Although this approach was not primarily motivated by the attempt to account for individual differences, it allowed detection of some important sources of such differences. It revealed, for instance, that people characterized by high levels of reasoning skills used more time for the initial component of encoding at the expense of the final component of response execution. Such findings were not only counterintuitive at first sight but also highly informative concerning the structure of intellectual processes and the cognitive sources of mental abilities.

Apart from the decomposition of intellectual processes, the processual approach stimulated a new wave of research on how intelligence is related to thinking and knowledge. Ontologically, thinking is a fluid cognitive process whereas intelligence is a solid structure, that is, an ability or set of abilities. How can we investigate the relationships between such different phenomena? The relation of thinking to intelligence became much easier to explore thanks to the realization that intelligence is also a process or set of processes, namely, the processes hidden behind the solution of psychometric tests. Such conceptualization allowed the formulation of the theory of intelligent thinking (Frensch & Sternberg, 1989), which was supposed to link the domains of expertise, thinking, and intelligence. According to the authors, "skilled problem solving can be viewed as a special case of intelligent thinking, and intelligent thinking refers to the activation of intelligence in a particular problem solving situation" (p. 180). Thus, intelligent people may think in a stupid way if they cannot invest their abilities properly. As much as their investments are appropriately located into some complex domain, intelligent people act as experts. Otherwise, they act as typical underachievers, being able to obtain high IQ scores without an ability to use their resources properly.

Theories of intelligence do not have to be differential in nature. Psychologists are not obliged to regard the existence of huge differences among people concerning their cognitive skills as an empirical fact worthy of explanation. Developmental theories, like Piaget's (1972) or Vygotsky's (1978), are particularly ignorant of individual differences, focusing on age differences instead. The field of artificial intelligence also prefers a general rather than a differential approach (Schank, 1980). As long as such theories are able to account for the structure, composition, and peculiarities of intellectual processes, they do not need to bother with individual differences. However, the existence of such differences was historically the most important factor underlying the construction of theoretical models and assessment tools of intelligence. The next section demonstrates that the situation has not changed very much.

The Individual-Differences Approach

In this approach, researchers concentrate on differences between people characterized by high versus low levels of cognitive abilities regarding their efficiency in solving complex problems. The abilities are normally assessed by psychometric tools, although some studies have adopted more realistic criteria.

Empirical evidence concerning the hypothesized supremacy of high IQ people in many popular problem-solving tasks is surprisingly scarce. This is paradoxical because intelligence is by definition the ability to solve problems. For instance, performance on tasks like the Tower of Hanoi, or missionaries and cannibals, seems not to depend on the individual level of intelligence, although these tasks are widely used in cognitive psychology (Eysenck & Keane, 1995); moreover, they have been adopted by neuropsychologists as tools to investigate the so-called executive functions (Robbins et al., 1998). Performance on syllogistic reasoning tasks is also less dependent on IQ than might be expected (e.g., Rychlicka & Nęcka, 1990). Does it mean that the definition of intelligence as problem-solving efficiency is not valid or that problems like the Tower of Hanoi or syllogistic inference do not need much intelligence? To answer this question we have to realize that many experimental tasks are puzzles rather than problems (Eysenck & Keane, 1995), that is, they usually involve some kind of trap. The ability to disclose hidden traps may be a prerequisite of human intelligence, but probably not the most important one. Additionally, many experimental tasks, especially syllogisms, are presented in the abstract form which precludes low IQ people from the process of solution. The very essence of deductive reasoning as reaching conclusions exclusively on the basis of the content of the premises, while ignoring other sources of information (e.g., common sense), is probably not clear for the majority of people. If less intelligent persons cannot tackle such problems, research samples are usually restricted in range concerning the distribution of IQ, so the relationships between intelligence and problem-solving efficiency must be concealed. Finally, traditional IQ tests consist of rather specific and homogeneous items, mostly relying on inductive reasoning processes. So, their being weakly correlated with problem-solving effectiveness may result from specificity of IQ tests, specificity of typical problem-solving tasks, or both.

On the other hand, the use of more complex and real-life problems brings about interesting results concerning the role of psychometric intelligence. For instance, Wittmann and Süß (1999) employed three computerized simulation tasks that required management of a power station, a textile manufacturer, and a high-tech company. These tasks involved from four to more than one hundred variables to control, so their complexity was overwhelming compared to the puzzles widely used in laboratory experiments. The researchers obtained correlation coefficients of about $r = .4$ between psychometric measures of the reasoning ability and performance on the simulation tasks. The aggregated index of joint performance on three simulation tasks correlated with the reasoning factor at the level of $r = .567$. Other factors (e.g., speed, memory, or creativity) appeared less important as predictors of simulation task performance. Similar results have been obtained in other studies employing complex simulation tasks (e.g., Tucker & Warr, 1996; Rigas et al., 2002). As we can see, using problems rather than puzzles is a means of examining the actual relationship between intelligence and problem-solving efficiency.

But sometimes even puzzles can work, provided that they form a long series of thoroughly elaborated items. In the study reported by Janet Davidson (1995), participants solved a series of insight problems. Such problems are much less complex than simulations, and they usually involve overcoming some mental trap. However, participants obtained two booklets, each consisting of up to 24 problems. Moreover, the author deliberately prepared these problems in order to stimulate the processes of selective encoding, comparison, and combination, which are supposedly responsible for insight problem solving. In the cued condition the information vital to a proper solution was underlined, whereas in the control condition it was not. The author observed the correlation coefficients between IQ and insight task accuracy at the level of $r = .65$ (uncued condition) and $r = .60$ (cued condition). So, even relatively simple tasks that involve mental traps are able to differentiate high and low IQ people, provided that they are presented in long series. Maybe it is the low reliability of many experimental tasks that is responsible for the lack of significant correlations between IQ and problem-solving efficiency. Increasing the number of items is the simplest possible way to raise reliability indices, and this is a conclusion that we can draw from Davidson's study.

In our own approach (Orzechowski, 1999) we investigated the complex interactive relationships between psychometric intelligence, basic cognitive mechanisms of short-term memory and attention, and the parallel versus sequential organization of information processing (OIP). The paradigm adopted in these studies amounted to the presentation of nonverbal analogies (cf. Sternberg, 1977). Consecutive parts of each task were activated on the screen by the participant in the self-paced procedure. In the "freewheeling" condition, formerly activated portions did not disappear from the screen, whereas in the "forced" condition they did. In this way, the "freewheeling" condition allowed either parallel or sequential organization of information processing, whereas the "forced" condition definitely encouraged the sequential mode. According to our assumptions, this asymmetry should cause quite different consequences for people who differ in their preferred OIP. A person who prefers the parallel mode of processing should lose much more in the "forced" condition than a person who prefers the sequential mode. This is expected because the former person has to operate in conditions that are unfavorable to his or her natural preferences, whereas the latter person does not have to face any incongruity between the task conditions and his or her preferences. Thus, if we compute the reaction time differences between forced and freewheeling conditions, we should be able to know the preferred mode of OIP of a specific person.

Having assessed the natural preferences of participants concerning OIP, we could check how these differences interacted with the general mental ability in determination of performance on the analogical reasoning task. As we can see (Fig. 2), low IQ people committed more errors than high IQ

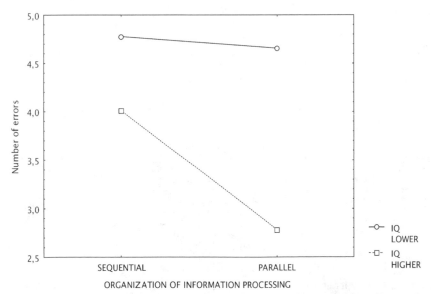

FIGURE 2. The number of errors in an analogical reasoning task depending on intelligence and the parallel versus sequential organization of information processing.

participants and the "parallel group" was more accurate than the "sequential group." But the most efficient problem solving was demonstrated by people of increased intelligence and parallel mode of OIP. Further analysis of this interaction revealed that intelligent people who preferred the parallel mode of OIP were not dependent on structural limitations of the information processing system. Two limitations were taken into account in these studies: capacity of short-term memory and amount of attentional resources. Persons of lower intelligence, as well as the ones of higher intelligence but with sequential OIP, depended on their individual parameters of STM and attention to a great extent. In their case, accuracy of analogical reasoning was determined by the individual capacity of processing resources, like short-term memory and attention. In the case of intelligent persons with parallel OIP, such relationships did not emerge. Hence, we can conclude that the parallel OIP increases one's level of competence in inductive reasoning tasks if it is accompanied by a high level of general cognitive ability.

To account for these findings, we propose the theoretical model included in Figure 3. Efficiency of analogical reasoning is hypothetically determined by processing capacities (efficient working memory, capacious STM, and resourceful attention), by the organization of information processing (parallel rather than sequential), and by intelligence understood here as a set of metacognitive skills. Processing capacities are important to psychometric intelligence, and to some extent they decide on its level of development

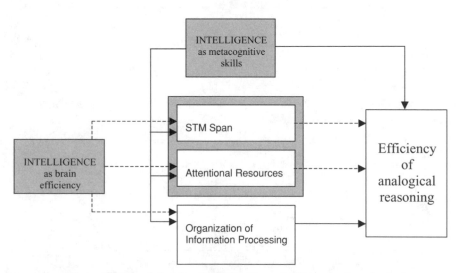

FIGURE 3. Theoretical model of the determination of efficiency of analogical reasoning by processing resources (STM and attention), parallel or sequential organization of information processing, and general intelligence.

(Conway et al., 2002; Hunt & Lansman, 1982). But obviously intelligence is not reducible to working memory, short-term memory, or attentional resources. Otherwise, we would not be able to obtain results showing that resourceful processing capacities sometimes lose their importance in complex cognitive tasks if the parallel mode of organization of information processing is switched on. Moreover, merely talking about people who are resourceful but not intelligent, or intelligent but not resourceful, would be nonsensical. For these reasons, the suggested model refers to three kinds of intelligence (Fig. 3, shadowed areas): one is rooted in the efficiency of neural mechanisms, another is equivalent to the amount of available processing resources, and the third consists of the metacognitive skills of monitoring and cognitive control. Thanks to these skills, parallel OIP is flexibly switched on in order to increase one's accuracy of reasoning as soon as the processes of monitoring suggest doing so.

According to the model, processing capacities are vital for reasoning as long as the level of metacognitive intelligence is low. They are also important if its level is high but accompanied by sequential OIP. These capacities lose their importance, however, as soon as a person starts to process information in the parallel mode. For that, a person needs highly developed metacognitive skills, which constantly monitor cognitive processes and are able to intervene if it is advisable. From this point of view, the joint influence of metacognitive intelligence and OIP is more important than the influence of processing capacities alone because the former may substitute for the latter but not vice versa. In other words, parallel OIP accompanied by a high level of metacognitive intelligence is indispensable as a condition for successful dealing with analogical reasoning tasks (solid lines), whereas resourceful processing capacities are not (dotted lines). The proposed model relies on the distinction between various kinds and sources of intelligence, with particular stress put on the mechanisms of monitoring and cognitive control. The significance of such skills for our understanding of human intelligence is systematically discussed in the next section.

METACOGNITION AND INTELLIGENCE

Cognitive psychologists divide mental phenomena into cognition and metacognition (Brown, 1978; Flavell, 1979). The former term refers to regular information processing, which is directly responsible for the execution of cognitive tasks, whereas the latter involves the processes of monitoring and control, thanks to which regular cognitive processes are executed in the appropriate order and according to some superordinate rules. As long as the mind only "knows" what is going on at the basic level of information processing, we can speak about the bottom-up phenomenon of monitoring. Once it begins to "govern" the basic processes, we refer to the top-down phenomenon of control. Metacognitive functions usually require at least some amount of consciousness (e.g., the feeling of knowing), although there seem to exist processes of monitoring and control of which we are not fully aware (Moses & Baird, 1999). For instance, we can be aware of feedback information that is vital for efficient control of our mental as well as motor actions, although we are usually not able to know any details of the execution of the control processes. Similarly, we sometimes know consciously that a response is unwanted and should be inhibited but we are unable to know how to implement the inhibition processes themselves.

Sternberg's (1985) triarchic theory is probably the best recognized and most influential attempt to link human intelligence with metacognition. The author divided mental processes into the performance components, which are responsible for direct execution of cognitive tasks, the knowledge-acquisition components, responsible for the intake of information, and the metacomponents, responsible for monitoring and control. As many as ten specific functions have been ascribed to metacomponents: (1) problem finding, (2) problem definition, (3) choice of the set of necessary performance components, (4) choice of the optimal strategy of composition of these components, (5) appropriate mental representation of the problem, (6) attention deployment, (7) monitoring of the problem-solving implementation, (8) feedback reception, (9) feedback processing, and (10) practical implementation of feedback information. Sternberg believes that the proper use of metacomponents is responsible for the adequacy with which people tackle complex cognitive tasks, including intelligence tests. He also formulates the hypothesis that the general mental ability (g factor) may be explicable in terms of the general nature of metacomponents, which take part in every mental activity.

Empirical studies of the relationships between metacognition and intelligence belong to two categories, depending on their research paradigm. These are the studies on cognitive strategies and cognitive control.

Cognitive Strategies

Cognitive strategy is a distinctive mode of dealing with a task or class of tasks. People are capable of accomplishing various cognitive tasks using many different tactics of almost equal efficiency. For instance, there are good reasons to talk about pictorial versus verbal strategy for tackling spatial orientation tasks, or about the analytical versus synthetic mode of dealing with block design tasks (Rozencwajg & Corroyer, 2002). Strategies are not abilities because, instead of referring to the "better–worse" dimension of intellectual performance, which is typical of psychometrics, they pertain to the manner in which cognitive tasks are performed. There is usually no reason to treat some strategies as better than others; their choice and use is therefore a matter of preference rather than abilities.

Relationships between intelligence and cognitive strategies have been studied in several ways. First, researchers sought to determine whether intelligent people show any preference concerning the choice of a particular strategy. In the study by Kossowska and Nęcka (1994) participants were presented with a series of analogical reasoning problems. Presentation of consecutive portions of every task was self-paced, so participants could take as much time to read them as they wished. Pieces of information that had been presented earlier did not disappear from the screen; therefore they could be analyzed either one by one in the order of their appearance, or concurrently after the last piece of information had been assimilated. The authors assumed that, if a certain participant paid adequate attention to initial stages of analogical reasoning, he or she should be assigned to the "analytical strategy" group. If somebody tended to speed up the pace of presentation in order to obtain quickly the entire information available, he or she should be assigned to the "holistic strategy" group. The holistic approach amounts to processing simultaneously all the available information, whereas the analytic approach takes advantage of proceeding successively from one piece of information to another. It appeared that high IQ participants preferred the analytical strategy over the holistic one. Using a completely different research paradigm, Rozencwajg and Corroyer (2002) recently demonstrated that what they call to be the "synthetic" strategy of solving a block design task was typical of younger children, whereas older participants preferred the analytical strategy. Does it mean that the analytical strategy is in itself more intelligent than the holistic one? Not necessarily. The analytical strategy is more demanding for working memory because it requires that relevant pieces of information be kept in mind until the end of the reasoning process. Therefore, the preference of intelligent people to this kind of strategy may result from their being endowed with more capacious short-term storage (Conway et al., 2002; Kyllonen & Christal, 1990; Nęcka, 1992). For less endowed persons, preference of the holistic strategy may be much wiser.

The mechanism of proper choice of strategy illustrates the importance of compatibility between ability profiles and the use of strategy. Such compatibility has been demonstrated in a number of studies. Kyllonen, Lohman, and Woltz (1984) presented their participants with a series of geometrical figures which were to be memorized, adjoined to each other, and finally compared with a probe figure. Thus, the task was devised to engage both visual working memory and reasoning ability. Some participants memorized consecutive figures step by step, with an attempt to synthesize them as early as possible (synthesis strategy). Others concentrated on the probe figure and, having it in mind, tried to retrieve from immediate memory the figures that were presented earlier (backward search strategy). Still others applied mixed strategies, relying on either synthesis or backward search. These mixed approaches appeared typically for high IQ participants, which was rather adaptive for them because different items of the experimental procedures might have called for different modes of thinking. It also appeared that people whose various mental abilities remained approximately at the same level of development were more likely to choose one of the mixed strategies. This preference was adaptive, too, because mixed strategies require that various cognitive components be sufficiently developed. The study also demonstrated that people who tended to choose the synthesis strategy were characterized by increased levels of spatial ability and visual working memory span, whereas people who tended to choose the backward search strategy obtained generally low indices in the whole battery of cognitive tests. It can therefore be concluded that there is a kind of compatibility between preferences toward certain cognitive strategies and levels of development of cognitive abilities that may be necessary to use them. Lack of such compatibility probably results in inadequacy of dealing with a task.

It also appears that intelligent persons show plasticity concerning the change of cognitive strategy. MacLeod, Hunt, and Mathews (1978) presented participants with the sentence–picture verification task (Clark & Chase, 1972), where the subject decides whether the content of a sentence corresponds to the content of a picture. In this task, people have two strategies to choose from. Sometimes they start with building up a mental representation of the situation illustrated by the picture and then they proceed to verify whether the sentence is an accurate description of the picture. This strategy is called verbal. In this case the time of verification depends on the grammatical complexity of the sentence. Sometimes people start with building up a mental representation of the meaning of a sentence and afterward they compare this representation with the graphic content of the picture. This strategy is called pictorial. In that case, the time of verification does not depend on the complexity of the sentence because its meaning is represented in the person's mind before the process of verification begins. MacLeod et al. (1978) demonstrated that the majority of participants chose the verbal strategy. They also taught their participants to use one of these strategies, and then they changed the experimental conditions so as to make the opposite strategy more advisable. It appeared that people who scored high on psychometric tests of intelligence demonstrated easiness in switching the cognitive strategy. The authors concluded that intelligence is related to increased plasticity of the use and choice of cognitive strategies (Hunt, 1980; MacLeod et al., 1978).

Furthermore, cognitive strategies sometimes operate as a means of compensation for the lack of abilities. A study by Kossowska (1996) observed complex interactions among strategies, abilities, and personality traits. Openness to experience, measured by the Big Five personality questionnaire, appeared particularly important as a modifier of the strategy/ability relationships. For instance, increased levels of openness complemented with the verbal strategy helped to improve the participants' scores in an intelligence test, as did low levels of openness accompanied by the pictorial strategy. Other combinations of openness and cognitive strategies appeared less adaptive. As we can see, cognitive strategies are not "intelligent" or "stupid" by themselves; rather, they cooperate with other dimensions of individual differences, thus causing the desirable effects. It is also worth mentioning that strategies are able to compensate for the lack of abilities, particularly if complemented by certain personality dimensions, although theoretical meaning of this phenomenon is unclear.

Cognitive Control

Higher-order cognition is closely linked to the processes of cognitive control. These processes are responsible for the supervisory operations, attributed by Allan Baddeley (1986, 1996) to the "central executive" part of the working memory system and by Norman and Shallice (1986) to the "supervisory attentional system" (SAS). The executive functions include attention deployment, attention switching, updating of the content of the short-term store, and inhibition of irrelevant information or unwanted behavioral tendencies (Miyake & Shah, 1999). Cognitive control is believed to be crucially important for execution of the processes that are resourceful, effortful, and not automatic. For that reason, this mechanism is a "natural" candidate for the job of being responsible for the development of human intelligence.

The importance of control processes for individual differences in intelligence has been demonstrated by Susan Embretson (1995). She assumed that general mental ability depends on two factors: working memory capacity and efficiency of control processes. The latter is responsible for the appropriate and orderly utilization of the processing space supplied by the short-term store. A relatively less capacious store may work much better than a sizeable one, provided that a good strategy is employed. Embretson invented 130 new items for what she labeled the Abstract Reasoning Test. These items differed in the number of relations needed to keep in mind in order to solve the certain item. Thus, the items varied in terms of the demand they put on working memory. People differ in their individual capacity of working memory, so, according to Embretson, they should deal with various test items at different levels of accuracy, depending on the complexity of these items. Moreover, the author assumed that if two persons are dealing with items of the same level of complexity, and they still differ in accuracy, these differences probably result from the efficiency of control processes rather than short-term memory capacity. In this way, Embretson was able to assess the extent to which the individual differences in the general mental ability are explainable by working memory capacity or by the processes of cognitive control. It appeared that the former factor explained 48% of variance, the latter factor accounted for 71% of variance, and the joint activity of both factors was able to account for as much as 92% of variance of the intelligence test scores (Embretson, 1995).

In our own approach (Nęcka, 1999; Nęcka, Gruszka, & Orzechowski, 1996) we adopted the interference tasks as a means to measure the strength of cognitive control. Such tasks as the Stroop (1935) or Navon (1977) involve an element of incongruity between various aspects of the stimulus material. For instance, the word "green" may be written with red ink, and the task is to identify the color of the ink instead of reading the word (Stroop, 1935). Or, a person is presented with a capital letter "T" built of small letters "r," and the task is to identify the building letters instead of reading the dominant capital letter. People doing the incongruity tasks have to suppress the prevailing response tendency (e.g., to read the colorful word or to identify the dominant letter) in order to give an unusual and much less automatic response. This is an effortful, slow, and error-prone activity. Efficacy of cognitive control is therefore estimated as a difference score; reaction time in the control condition is subtracted from reaction time in the incongruity condition. If the result is relatively small, the mechanism of cognitive control is judged to be efficient. Hence, if intelligent people are characterized by increased efficiency of cognitive control, we should predict negative correlations between mental ability measures and the indices of the strength of cognitive control.

Such correlations have been obtained, indeed, in two studies reported by Nęcka (1999). Participants performed the Navon task in four consecutive series in which the indices of the strength of cognitive control were computed. Additionally, they completed two ability tests, referring to the fluid and crystallized intelligence (Raven's matrices and verbal analogies, respectively). We observed that correlation coefficients between the indices of the strength of cognitive control and ability measures were always negative and statistically significant (Table 1), although these associations were slightly weaker in the case of the verbal test of intelligence. In an earlier study (Nęcka et al., 1996), a group of 36 gifted adolescents performed both

TABLE 1. *Psychometric Intelligence and the Indices of Strength of Cognitive Control (Nęcka, 1999, p. 171)*

	Raven's Matrices	Verbal Analogies
I-C, series 1	−.28	−.13
I-C, series 2	−.33	−.22
I-C, series 3	−.25	−.24
I-C, series 4	−.21	−.16

Note: I-C is the difference between mean reaction time in the incongruent condition and mean reaction time in the congruent condition.

the Stroop and the Navon tasks. Compared to their nongifted control peers, the gifted participants obtained better indices for the strength of cognitive control only in the Navon task. The absence of similar results in the Stroop task suggests that either the cognitive control is domain-specific rather than general phenomenon or the Stroop task does not allow the precise estimation of the strength of cognitive control. The Navon task draws on verbal material that is highly overlearned and automatically processed, whereas the Stroop task requires the quite "exotic" skill of naming the color of the ink. The increased ability of gifted people to resist interference in the former case may suggest that cognitive control is particularly important in domains that are closer to one's intellectual functioning.

Strength of cognitive control has also been investigated in creativity studies (Groborz & Nęcka, 2003), where people scoring high on divergent thinking tests obtained better indices of cognitive control. Moreover, cognitive control was associated with the originality of one's productions but not with fluency or flexibility. Among many indices of creative abilities, originality is closely linked to the quality of one's productions, although all indices are quantitative in terms of computations needed to obtain them. This study defined fluency as the number of produced ideas, flexibility as the number of categories into which the produced ideas could be included, and originality as the number of ideas that were infrequent or unique in the sample. So, the obtained results suggest that cognitive control may prevent a person from producing many ideas with no apparent value, which is often the case with people scoring high on fluency and flexibility but low on originality. Moreover, we demonstrated that the increased strength of control characterizes people who are able to judge other participants' productions more accurately. For instance, a participant was asked to assess the level of originality of ideas produced by another participant. His or her subjective assessment was subsequently compared to the actual level of originality, based on the distribution of responses observed in the whole sample of participants. In this way, the accuracy of one's assessments could be evaluated and correlated with the indices of strength of cognitive control, with positive results. It may therefore be concluded that efficiency of cognitive control is an important source of individual differences in broadly defined intelligence, including creative thinking skills.

CONCLUDING REMARKS

The review presented in this chapter clearly shows that higher-order cognitive processes are vital for our understanding of human intelligence. The use of complex tasks increases the level of ecological and theoretical validity of psychological experiments. Complex tasks are much more similar than elementary cognitive tasks to what people do in real life. Their usage is also better grounded in theories and definitions of intelligence.

On the other hand, this review demonstrated the weaknesses of the top-down approach to intelligence research. These weaknesses are mostly rooted in methodological problems connected with studying complex mental phenomena. First, we can speak about something like the complexity trap. Many problem-solving tasks are too difficult to be tackled effectively by people of low intelligence. For instance, the syllogistic reasoning tasks may be confronted only by people who understand the essence of logical thinking. Syllogisms are particularly difficult if they are expressed in the abstract form and if the task consists in overcoming "common sense" in order to give way to the "pure" logic. For that reason, only high IQ people can take part in many syllogistic reasoning experiments. Consequently, experimental samples are severely restricted in IQ range; that is, they are homogeneous concerning the distribution of intelligence test scores. Some simulation problems are also quite difficult to understand for an average person. The more complex our experimental tasks are, the more they resemble real-life situations, and the more they are supposed to reflect human intellectual capability. At the same time, we are less and less able to investigate the actual relationship between intelligence and competence with which people tackle such tasks.

Second, we should not ignore the role of motivational factors in people's dealing with complex tasks. Such tasks need a lot of time to be solved; therefore, they may provide a good estimation of one's endurance, patience, or diligence rather than intelligence. Susceptibility to boredom (Zuckerman, 1979) and other personality factors also play a role in human performance on complex tasks. For that reason, usage of complex tasks is risky because we have to control numerous factors which are difficult to control and mostly not intellectual in nature. It is trivial to say that human behavior is determined by many different factors. Experimental cognitive psychologists usually reduce the number of these factors through careful control of variables and simplification of mental tasks people are supposed to do. But how much simplicity can we allow in order to avoid the criticism of oversimplification? It seems that, at least in the field of human intelligence, simple and complex cognition are equally important. Therefore, simple and complex cognitive tasks should be used in our experiments as complementary rather than competing approaches.

References

Baddeley, A. (1986). *Working memory*. Oxford, UK: Clarendon Press.

Baddeley, A. (1996). Exploring the central executive. *The Quarterly Journal of Experimental Psychology, 49A*, 5–28.

Brown, A. L. (1978). Knowing when, where, and how to remember: A problem of metacognition. In R. Glaser (Ed.), *Advances in instructional psychology* (Vol. I, pp. 77–165). Hillsdale, NJ: Erlbaum.

Carlson, J. S., & Widaman, K. F. (1987). Elementary cognitive correlates of *g*: Progress and prospects. In P. A. Vernon (Ed.), *Speed of information processing and intelligence* (pp. 69–100). Norwood, NJ: Ablex.

Carlstedt, B., Gustafsson, J.-E., & Ullstadius, E. (2000). Item sequencing effects on the measurement of fluid intelligence. *Intelligence, 28*, 145–160.

Carpenter, P. A., Just, M. A., & Shell, P. (1990). What one intelligence test measures: A theoretical account of the processing in the Raven Progressive Matrices Test. *Psychological Review, 97*, 404–431.

Carroll, J. B. (1976). Psychometric tests as cognitive tasks: A new "structure of intellect." In L. B. Resnick (Ed.), *The nature of intelligence* (pp. 27–56). Hillsdale, NJ: Erlbaum.

Clark, H. H., & Chase, W. G. (1972). On the process of comparing sentences against pictures. *Cognitive Psychology, 3*, 472–517.

Conway, A. R. A., Cowan, N., Bunting, M. F., Therriault, D. J., & Minkoff, S. R. B. (2002). A latent variable analysis of working memory capacity, short term memory capacity, processing speed, and general fluid intelligence. *Intelligence, 30*, 163–183.

Davidson, J. E. (1995). The suddenness of insight. In R. J. Sternberg & J. Davidson (Eds.), *The nature of insight* (pp. 125–155). Cambridge, MA: MIT Press.

Deary, I. J. (2000). Simple information processing and intelligence. In R. J. Sternberg (Ed.), *Handbook of intelligence* (pp. 267–284). Cambridge, UK: Cambridge University Press.

Duncker, K. (1945). On problem solving. *Psychological Monographs, 58*(270), entire issue.

Embretson, S. E. (1995). The role of working memory capacity and general control processes in intelligence. *Intelligence, 20*(2), 169–189.

Eysenck, M. W., & Keane, M. T. (1995). *Cognitive psychology: A student's handbook.* Hillsdale, NJ: Erlbaum.

Flavell, J. H. (1979). Metacognition and cognitive monitoring: A new area of cognitive-developmental inquiry. *American Psychologist, 34*, 906–911.

Frensch. P. A., & Sternberg, R. J. (1989). Expertise and intelligent thinking: When is it worse to know better? In R. J. Sternberg (Ed.), *Advances in the psychology of human intelligence* (Vol. 5, pp. 157–188). Hillsdale, NJ: Erlbaum.

Gottfredson, L. S. (1997). Mainstream science on intelligence: An editorial with 52 signatories, history, and bibliography. *Intelligence, 24*, 13–23.

Groborz, M., & Nęcka, E. (2003). Creativity and cognitive control: Explorations of generation and evaluation skills. *Creativity Research Journal, 15*(2/3), 183–198.

Hayes, J. R. (1989). The complete problem solver (2nd edition). Hillsdale, NJ, England: Erlbaum.

Hunt, E. B. (1980). Intelligence as an information processing concept. *The British Journal of Psychology, 71*, 449–474.

Hunt, E. B., & Lansman, M. (1982). Individual differences in attention. In R. J. Sternberg (Ed.), *Advances in the psychology of human intelligence* (Vol. 1, pp. 207–254). Hillsdale, NJ: Erlbaum.

Jensen, A. R. (1998). *The g factor: The science of mental ability.* Westport, CT: Praeger.

Kossowska, M. (1996). Związki strategii poznawczych, inteligencji i osobowości [Relationships between cognitive strategies, intelligence, and personality]. Unpublished doctoral dissertation, Jagiellonian University.

Kossowska, M., & Nęcka, E. (1994). Do it your own way: Cognitive strategies, intelligence, and personality. *Personality and Individual Differences, 16,* 33–46.

Kyllonen, P. C., & Christal, R. E. (1990). Reasoning ability is (little more than) working-memory capacity? *Intelligence, 14*(4), 389–433.

Kyllonen, P. C., Lohman, D. F., & Woltz, D. J. (1984). Componential modeling of alternative strategies for performing spatial tasks. *Journal of Educational Psychology, 76,* 1325–1345.

Larson, G. E. (1990). Novelty as "representational complexity": A cognitive interpretation of Sternberg and Gastel (1989). *Intelligence, 14,* 235–238.

Lohman, D. F. (2000). Complex information processing and intelligence. In R. J. Sternberg (Ed.), *Handbook of intelligence* (pp. 285–340). Cambridge, UK: Cambridge University Press.

MacLeod, C. M., Hunt, E., & Mathews, N. N. (1978). Individual differences in the verification of sentence–picture relationships. *Journal of Verbal Learning and Verbal Behavior, 17,* 493–507.

Marshalek, B., Lohman, D. F., & Snow, R. E. (1983). The complexity continuum in the radex and hierarchical models of intelligence. *Intelligence, 7,* 107–127.

Miyake, A., & Shah, P. (1999). *Models of working memory: Mechanisms of active maintenance and executive control.* New York: Cambridge University Press.

Moses, L. J., & Baird, J. A. (1999). Metacognition. In R. A. Wilson & F. C. Keil (Eds.), *The MIT encyclopedia of the cognitive sciences* (pp. 533–535). Cambridge, MA: MIT Press.

Navon, D. (1977). Forest before trees: The precedence of global features in visual perception. *Cognitive Psychology, 9,* 353–383.

Nęcka, E. (1992). Cognitive analysis of intelligence: The significance of working memory processes. *Personality and Individual Differences, 13,* 1031–1046.

Nęcka, E. (1999). Learning, automaticity, and attention: An individual differences approach. In P. L. Ackerman, P. C. Kyllonen, & R. D. Roberts (Eds.), *Learning and individual differences: Process, trait, and content determinants* (pp. 161–181). Washington, DC: American Psychological Association.

Nęcka, E., Gruszka, A., & Orzechowski, J. (1996). Selective attention in gifted children. *Polish Psychological Bulletin, 27,* 39–51.

Newell, A., & Simon, H. A. (1972). *Human problem solving.* Englewood Cliffs, NJ: Prentice-Hall.

Norman, D. A., & Shallice, T. (1986). Attention and action: Willed and automatic control of behavior. In R. J. Davidson, G. E. Schwartz, & D. Shapiro (Eds.), *Consciousness and self-regulation: Advances in research and theory* (Vol. 4, pp. 1–18). New York: Plenum Press.

Orzechowski, J. (1999). *Nieliniowo-równolegly model rozumowania przez analogię a różnice indywidualne w funkcjonowaniu poznawczym człowieka* [Non-linear parallel model of information processing and individual differences in human cognition]. Unpublished doctoral dissertation, Jagiellonian University.

Piaget, J. (1972). *The Psychology of intelligence.* Totowa, NJ: Littlefield Adams.

Primi, R. (2002). Complexity of geometric inductive reasoning tasks: Contribution to the understanding of fluid intelligence. *Intelligence, 30,* 41–70.

Rigas, G., Carling, E., & Brehmer, B. (2002). Reliability and validity of performance measures in microworlds. *Intelligence, 30,* 463–480.

Robbins, T. W., James, M., Owen, A. M., Sahakian, B. J., Lawrence, A. D., McInnes, L., & Rabbitt, P. M. A. (1998). A study of performance on tests from the CANTAB battery sensitive to frontal lobe dysfunction in a large sample of normal volunteers: Implications for theories of executive functioning and cognitive aging. *Journal of the International Neuropsychological Society, 4,* 474–490.

Rozenzwajg, P., & Corroyer, D. (2002). Strategy development in a block design task. *Intelligence, 30,* 1–25.

Rychlicka, A., & Nęcka, E. (1990). Syllogistic reasoning, intelligence, and dogmatism. *Polish Psychological Bulletin, 21,* 3–15.

Schank, R. C. (1980). How much intelligence is there in artificial intelligence? *Intelligence, 4,* 1–14.

Spearman, C. (1923). *The nature of "intelligence" and the principles of cognition.* London: Macmillan.

Sternberg, R. J. (1977). *Intelligence, information processing, and analogical reasoning: The componential analysis of human abilities.* Hillsdale, NJ: Erlbaum.

Sternberg, R. J. (1985). *Beyond IQ: A triarchic theory of human intelligence.* Cambridge, UK: Cambridge University Press.

Sternberg, R. J., & Detterman, D. K. (Ed.) (1986). *What is intelligence? Contemporary viewpoints on its nature and definition.* Norwood, NJ: Ablex.

Stroop, J. R. (1935). Studies of interference in serial verbal reactions. *Journal of Experimental Psychology, 18,* 624–643.

Thomas, J. C. (1974). An analysis of behavior in the hobbits–orcs problem. *Cognitive Psychology, 6,* 257–269.

Tucker, P., & Warr, P. (1996). Intelligence, elementary cognitive components and cognitive styles as predictors of complex task performance. *Personality and Individual Differences, 21,* 91–102.

Vygotsky, L. S. (1978). *Mind in society: The development of higher psychological processes.* Cambridge, MA: Harvard University Press.

Wittmann, W. W., & Süß, H.-M. (1999). Investigating the paths between working memory, intelligence, knowledge, and complex problem solving performances via Brunswik symmetry. In P. L. Ackerman, P. C. Kyllonen, & R. D. Roberts, (Eds.), *Learning and individual differences: Process, trait, and content determinants* (pp. 77–108). Washington, DC: American Psychological Association.

Zuckerman, M. (1979). *Sensation seeking: Beyond the optimal level of arousal.* Hillsdale, NJ: Erlbaum.

8

Ability Determinants of Individual Differences in Skilled Performance

Phillip L. Ackerman

At the most fundamental level, the relationship between intelligence and learning is close and convincing. Indeed, the modern era of intelligence assessment is identified with the critical success of Binet and Simon (1905) in their development of a set of scales that provided valid predictions of school success. These scales, or similar assessments inspired by this approach (such as the Wechsler Intelligence Scale for Children; Wechsler, 1949), continue to represent the best predictors of school success. School success, at least for children and adolescents, is considered by many to be the indicator of learning achievement. While this analysis works quite well for global measures of learning, there is far less utility of omnibus IQ-type measures for predicting individual differences in narrower domains of learning. If we want to predict which students will excel in learning a musical instrument, mastering power tools, or becoming adept at a particular sport, or even which students will become the fastest typists, the relationship between intelligence and learning appears to be much more complicated.

Part of the reason why IQ-type measures are less valid for predicting individual differences in skilled performance has to do with the relative "bandwidth" of the assessment instrument and the breadth of the criterion, or what has been referred to as a lack of Brunswik symmetry (Wittmann & Süß, 1999). That is, IQ tests have high bandwidth – they are typically constructed from as many as a dozen different scales (e.g., memory, reasoning, vocabulary, math, etc.). Measures of academic achievement such as cumulative grade point average are similarly broad – thus the breadth of the predictor measure matches the breadth of the criterion. Measures of skilled performance, such as typing speed and accuracy, are quite narrow in scope. When compared against an IQ predictor, there is a substantial mismatch between the breadths of the predictor and the criterion, which ordinarily yields a much lower validity index. There is, of course, more to the story. The rest of this chapter is devoted to a brief review of the critical theoretical issues and empirical data associated with ability–skilled performance relations.

A BRIEF HISTORICAL REVIEW

Psychologists have long been interested in the nature of skill acquisition and skilled performance. One of the first major studies in this field concerned the acquisition of skilled performance in telegraphy (Bryan & Harter, 1899), a skill which is now long obsolete. Nonetheless, such studies described skills in terms of a hierarchy, such that initial learning focused on small units of learning (such as letters) and only later on larger units (such as words or phrases). Indeed, many skills have similar characteristics, such as the development of skilled reading (e.g., see Frederiksen, Warren, & Roseberry, 1985) or playing chess (e.g., see Ericsson & Lehmann, 1996, for a review). As a general descriptive framework, Fitts and Posner (1967) described skill acquisition as a three-stage process. The first stage (called "cognitive") occurs when the learner first confronts the task. At this stage, the learner must encode rules and develop strategies for task accomplishment. This stage is highly dependent on the kinds of specific abilities that underlie general intellectual abilities (such as memory, reasoning, and particular content abilities, such as verbal, spatial, or numerical abilities, depending on the task content). Performance during this stage of skill acquisition is slow, effortful, and error-prone. The second stage was described by Fitts and Posner as the "associative" stage. That is, once the learner has mastered the general rules for task accomplishment, he/she seeks to make the process of performance more efficient, for example, by eliminating inefficient or unnecessary steps. During this stage of skilled performance, the task is accomplished much more quickly than in the first stage, but there are occasional errors as the learner tries to streamline the procedures for task accomplishment. Effort is still needed to perform the task, and effort is further needed to make additional refinements and improvements to the skill. The third stage of skill acquisition was referred to as the "autonomous" stage. Performance at this stage is fast and characterized by few errors. Learners who reach this stage of skilled performance can frequently perform the task almost or completely effortlessly, even when attention is diverted to other activities.

The task of driving an automobile provides a good example of these stages of skill acquisition. When a learner is first confronted with the vast array of controls and displays, the task of driving can seem almost overwhelming (especially with a manual transmission car). The student has to remember to visually sample the speedometer, the view out of the windshield, and the mirrors for traffic, while trying to control the steering, accelerator, brake, and so on. The idea of trying to change radio stations or talking on the cell phone at the same time one is trying to drive around a parking lot would be rejected as overwhelming by almost all but the most efficacious performers at this stage of learning. However, after perhaps only tens of hours of practice, the learner usually has internalized a strategy for sampling the displays and controlling the vehicle. He or she may both be reasonably competent and feel reasonably confident in driving, even though performance is not entirely smooth, and both planning efficiency and reaction speed are suboptimal. With only a few additional months of practice, however, the student driver can perform the task relatively effortlessly, with a low error rate (even though performance will normally continue to improve over the next several years of practice).

A year after initially trying the task of driving, the learner can effectively operate the vehicle with only limited attention devoted to the operation of the car. Changing radio stations or carrying on a conversation under such circumstances rarely results in losing control of the vehicle. The key to the transition from cognitive, to associative, to autonomous skilled performance is *consistent practice*. That is, the nature of the task is constant, the controls work in the same way from one occasion to the next, and extensive practice leads to substantial improvement in the speed and accuracy of performance, for most learners. This is not to say that every student learner is capable of becoming a world-class racing car driver. The difference between driving to the local grocery store and driving around a track at high speed is partly a function of the speed with which decisions need to be made and implemented and partly because inconsistencies are introduced in the control of vehicles that operate at their physical limits. Under such circumstances, performance is not autonomous but is highly effortful and error-prone, because the tolerances are so much smaller than they are in normal everyday driving. Also, it is important to note two points of which most drivers (and pedestrians) are painfully aware: (a) even though most drivers can adequately perform the task, there exist individual differences in performance of a sizable magnitude, and (b) although driving can frequently be performed with only a limited amount of attention, increased levels of attention result in performance improvements.

THEORY AND CONTROVERSY

Early modern psychologists who proposed that intelligence was the "ability to learn" (e.g., see Thorndike, 1924) were frequently frustrated in obtaining confirmatory evidence for the proposition when considering specific tasks rather than broad measures of academic achievement (e.g., see Woodrow, 1946). There were two major impediments to the evaluation of the relationship between overall intelligence (or more narrow intellectual abilities) and learning. The first impediment was the operationalization of "learning" per se. That is, within traditional learning theory, degree of learning is defined as the *difference* between an initial state of knowledge or skill and a final state of knowledge or skill (typically after some intervention or practice). Unfortunately, difference scores have some relatively undesirable psychometric properties when it comes to evaluating individual differences (e.g., see Cronbach & Furby, 1970). When two measures are substantially correlated (as in a pretest and post-test in skill learning), the reliability of the difference score declines. So, when investigators examined "learning scores" for correlations with intelligence, they frequently found very low correlations – yielding the rather counterintuitive finding that intelligence did not appear to be related to learning (e.g., see Ackerman, 1987, for a review). For most of these studies, though, the finding is, to a nontrivial degree, a statistical artifact that results from the low reliability of difference scores, rather than a specific demonstration that intelligence and learning are orthogonal (i.e., uncorrelated) constructs (e.g., see recent discussion by Lohman, 1999).

The second impediment toward demonstrating a relationship between intelligence and specific-task learning is more subtle than a statistical artifact. This impediment was due to the fact that, with the exception of relatively rare tasks (such as concept attainment or simple conditioning; see Zeaman & House, 1967), there are substantial individual differences in task performance, *even on the first task trial*. A brief example illustrates this problem. In a standard skill learning paradigm, the learners are presented with a series of instructions on how to perform the task. Frequently, the learners are presented with a few, unscored "practice trials" just to familiarize them with what is required in the task. After the instructions and practice trials, the learner is presented with the main task trials, and then a series of practice trials, leading up to the final practice or criterion performance assessment. Even on the first scored task trial, there are large individual differences in levels of performance. In fact, the initial task trials often have higher variability in performance than post-practice task performance (see Ackerman, 1988; Ackerman & Woltz, 1994; Adams, 1957, for several examples of declining inter-individual variance with consistent task practice; also see Ackerman, 1987, for a review and re-analysis of 24 early studies of individual differences in skill learning).

One way to characterize this phenomenon is to consider that some individuals either benefit from transfer of prior learning (e.g., see Ferguson, 1956), are simply more adept at understanding the instructions, or are more able to develop effective strategies for task performance even prior to actually engaging in the task. All of these possibilities suggest that, ceteris paribus (i.e., other things being equal), individuals with either greater relevant prior learning or higher levels of memory, reasoning, and other intellectual abilities, will perform better on the first task trial than those individuals with less prior learning or lower abilities. This hypothesis is clearly supported by the large corpus of data accumulated since the 1930s.

At the other side of the learning curve, however, there are typically physical system or psychomotor constraints that limit the speed of performance (e.g., see Card, Moran, & Newell, 1983). Such constraints effectively limit the range of inter-individual differences for expert levels of skilled performance. That is, while one may frequently find reliable differences in performance for highly skilled performers, the magnitude of differences between expert performers is much smaller than the magnitude of differences among novice performers. These kinds of effects are notable in sports-related skills – where the differences between the scores of professional golfers or batting averages of professional baseball players are quite small in comparison to the variability of scores among novice golfers or novice baseball players.

Putting the two phenomena together yields another conceptual difficulty. That is, if there is a relative physical limit to skilled performance (such as the speed of neural response time to a signal, or the physical speed of moving the fingers from one computer keyboard key to another) and if individuals start practice with vastly different levels of performance, then those individuals who start off with the best performance have the smallest amount of "learning" that can be acquired, and those individuals who start off with the worst performance have the largest potential for learning "improvement." Even if a group of individuals shows consistent rank ordering in performance from initial to final practice, it is the worst initial performers who show the greatest improvement, relatively speaking. If initial performance (as discussed earlier) is positively related to intellectual abilities, then it is possible (and quite frequently found) that intelligence is *negatively* related to the difference between initial and final task performance, *even though final task performance may also be positively correlated with intellectual abilities.*

These two impediments (the statistical artifacts associated with simple difference scores and the problems associated with substantial individual differences in initial task performance) have suggested to many researchers that it is not particularly informative to ask the question of whether intelligence predicts learning in cases where learning is operationalized as the difference between initial and final task performance (see Cronbach & Furby, 1970). Instead, the question of the association between intelligence (or intellectual abilities) and learning is conceptualized as an issue about changes in the degree of association between abilities and performance, from an initial task trial to performance after some amount of task practice (Ackerman, 1987; Fleishman, 1972).

Three Theoretical Orientations

When it comes to describing or predicting the relationship between abilities on the one hand, and individual differences in performance during and after skill acquisition on the other hand, researchers follow two fundamentally different theoretical orientations: a universal theory and two conditional theories.

Universally Declining Associations

The first orientation, articulated by Fleishman and his colleagues (e.g., Fleishman & Hempel, 1956), claims that intellectual abilities are substantially correlated with performance during early practice – that is, when the learner first confronts the task. However, with each additional practice trial, intellectual abilities become less well correlated with task performance. At high levels of skill, according to Fleishman, it is essentially impossible to predict task performance from measures that were administered prior to task practice. (Adams, 1987, referred to this as a "doctrine of despair" in that it holds that it is impossible to predict individual differences in skilled performance – see Adams, 1987, for a discussion.) Fleishman suggested that rather than conventionally defined intellectual abilities, only measures of the task itself, after practice, could predict future skilled performance – which he referred to as a "task-specific factor" (see Fleishman & Hempel, 1955).

Although Fleishman's purported demonstration of the declining validity for ability measures and the rise in the influence of a task-specific factor proved to be the result of an artifact of the methods of analysis he performed (see Ackerman, 1987), this theory has been remarkably attractive to researchers. The universal declining validity coefficient theory was resurrected by Hulin and his students (e.g., Henry & Hulin, 1987; Hulin, Henry, & Noon, 1990), though their evidence was largely based on logical and empirical flaws. The empirical flaws had to do with their equating initial task performance with "ability" and failing to actually assess ability (see Ackerman, 1989; Barrett, Alexander, & Doverspike, 1992). The logical flaw is that the existence of any single experiment that reliably shows no attenuating correlations, such as the data reported in Humphreys and Taber (1973) or later results from Ackerman (1988, 1990, 1992), invalidate the universal claim (i.e., a proposition that "all swans are white" is invalidated if a single non-white swan is found).

Ackerman's Three-Phase Theory

A conditional theory relating abilities to individual differences in task performance during skill acquisition was offered by Ackerman (1988). The theory specifies that under some conditions (such as when the task continues to require attentional effort and is resistant to the development of automaticity), the correlations between intellectual abilities and performance will remain stable. However, the theory also specifies that for many tasks, the abilities that are most highly associated with task performance will depend on the stage of skill acquisition under consideration. When

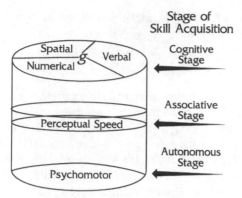

Stage of
Skill Acquisition

FIGURE 1. Depiction of the Ackerman (1988) theory of ability determinants of individual differences in performance on skill learning tasks. As skills develop from the cognitive, to the associative, and then to the autonomous stages, abilities associated with performance will transition from general and broad content (verbal, spatial, numerical) to perceptual speed, and then psychomotor abilities, respectively. Tasks with substantial requirements for inconsistent or novel information processing remain associated with the initial, or cognitive stage of skill acquisition (and thus show static correlations with general and broad content abilities). $g =$ general intellectual ability. Adapted from Ackerman (1988), Figure 1 (p. 291).

tasks are consistent and are within the capabilities of most or all learners, correlations between general intelligence and individual differences in task performance are predicted to decline as the learners transition from the cognitive stage of skill acquisition to the associative and autonomous stages of skill acquisition. For such tasks and for general intellectual ability, Ackerman's theory and the Fleishman/Hulin theory make similar predictions of declining correlations with increasing practice. In contrast, Ackerman's theory suggests that at the two later stages of skill acquisition, other abilities increase in predictive validity.

Specifically, the Ackerman three-phase theory proposes that there is a correspondence between Fitts and Posner's (1967) three phases of skill acquisition and three classes of ability determinants of individual differences in performance with each stage of skill acquisition (see Fig. 1). General cognitive/intellectual abilities (such as IQ measures) are associated with the cognitive stage of skill acquisition; the performance at the associative stage of skill acquisition is aligned with perceptual speed abilities; and performance at the autonomous stage of skill acquisition is associated with psychomotor abilities (see Ackerman, 1988, for details). Tasks that do not show this pattern of progression from cognitive, to associative, and then autonomous stage of skill acquisition are predicted to be relatively static in their ability–performance associations. Thus, tasks that involve substantial demands for processing of novel or inconsistent information (where the learner must make different responses to the same stimuli from one trial to the next) are predicted by the Ackerman theory to have stable correlations with broad cognitive/intellectual abilities.

The main thrust of the Ackerman theory is to address the predictability of individual differences in task performance after extensive task practice. That is, consistent with Adams (1957), the underlying belief is that it is possible to predict individual differences in skilled performance from measures that are administered prior to task practice. The ultimate goal of this approach is to find the constructs related to asymptotic performance levels, and then adapt or design new measures to aid in the prediction of such performance. To date, many new or revised measures of perceptual speed and psychomotor abilities have been developed for this purpose, with substantial success. Some examples of these investigations are presented later in this chapter.

The Four-Source Framework

Largely complementary to the Ackerman (1988) theory is the proposal of Kyllonen and Christal (1989) that individual differences in skilled performance during and after learning trials are associated with four sources of influence: "(1) breadth of declarative knowledge, (2) breadth of procedural skills, (3) capacity of the working memory, and (4) speed of processing (encoding information into working memory, retrieving knowledge from the long term memories, and executing a motor response)" (Ackerman & Kyllonen, 1991, p. 213). The breadth of declarative knowledge and capacity of working memory are analogous to Ackerman's Phase 1 (general and content abilities), while the breadth of procedural skills encompasses some of Ackerman's Phase 2 (perceptual speed abilities). The speed of processing is not entirely analogous to Ackerman's Phase 3 (psychomotor abilities); however, the four-source framework focuses on tasks that are more dependent on cognitive processes, even after extended practice. The four-source framework may represent a more accurate approach for such tasks, while the Ackerman approach may be more suitable for tasks that are amenable to automatized performance, once substantial levels of skill are acquired.

This framework is not inherently dynamic, in that it does not spell out changes in associations with individual differences in performance across the three stages of skill development. However, the authors suggest that there are differences in the magnitude of association between these four sources of abilities and skills and criterion task performance, as a function of two factors: (1) the characteristics of the task (e.g., whether it requires speeded responding or prior knowledge to perform the task) and (2) the amount of practice accorded to the task.

INFORMATION PROCESSING APPROACHES

The two conditional theories of ability determinants of individual differences in skilled performance (namely Ackerman, 1988; and Kyllonen &

Christal, 1989) should be viewed in the context of the zeitgeist in which they were developed. This zeitgeist started with initial attempts to link concepts of intelligence and abilities on the one hand to information processing tasks on the other hand (e.g., see Hunt, Frost, & Lunneborg, 1973; Sternberg, 1977). From the late 1970s until approximately the mid-1990s, various investigators attempted to "find" intelligence among information processing tasks as basic as simple reaction time, and proceeding up the scale of complexity to such tasks as mental rotation, numerical computation, and semantic processing (e.g., see Carroll, 1980, for an early review; see also Sternberg, 1985). Perhaps hundreds of articles were published during that period, as various investigators sought to establish reliable and meaningful associations between individual differences in basic information process tasks and both broad and specific measures of intellectual ability.

Although substantial controversy exists about the success of these research programs (especially in terms of the significance of individual differences in choice reaction time tasks, see Jensen, 1998; and the significance of individual differences in the inspection time task, see Deary & Stough, 1996, for a review), most of these investigations failed to demonstrate that basic information processing tasks (such as the S. Sternberg memory scanning task or the Posner letter matching task) had more than the most minimal correlations with broad measures of intellectual ability or with individual differences in skilled performance, at least in normal populations. With respect to the correlations between information processing and extant ability measures, these results largely corroborate the Wittmann and Süß (1999) proposition of Brunswik symmetry – that is, validity is impaired when there is a mismatch between the breadth of the predictor and the breadth of the criterion, that is, when narrow (information processing task) predictors are correlated with broad (ability) criteria. When information processing task measures are correlated with measures of skilled performance, the results typically reflect a similar situation – as skill tasks become more complex, the basic information processing tasks show decreased correlations. Simple skill tasks occasionally show larger correlations with performance on information processing tasks, but this usually occurs in the context of shared method variance (e.g., when the same computer display and input device are used for both the predictor and criterion skill measures).

EXTANT DATA AND EVALUATION OF THEORY

Numerous studies were reported during the 1980s and 1990s concerning the ability determinants of individual differences in skilled performance. They range from small one-shot studies (frequently fewer than 30 participants) to large-scale investigations (with several hundred participants). However, no studies were designed to contrast the different theories of ability–skill relations. Research that supported some or all of the four-source framework of Kyllonen and Christal (1989) included experiments concerned with the acquisition of programming skills (Pena & Tirre, 1992), solution of short-term logic skills (similar to electronics troubleshooting; Kyllonen & Stephens, 1990; Kyllonen & Woltz, 1989), sequential numerical computation skills (Woltz et al., 1996), an associative learning task (Kyllonen, Tirre, & Christal, 1991), and aspects of reading skills (Tirre, 1992). Research that supported some or all of the three components of the Ackerman (1988) theory included experiments on a relatively simple air traffic controller task (e.g., Ackerman, 1990; Ackerman & Cianciolo, 1999; Kanfer & Ackerman, 1989), an associative learning task (Ackerman & Woltz, 1994), and a more complex air traffic control simulation task (Ackerman, 1992; Ackerman & Cianciolo, 2000; Ackerman, Kanfer, & Goff, 1995).

The four-source framework does not make specific predictions in terms of either magnitude of association or the nature of changes in ability–performance relations over practice; rather it asserts that the four sources may be relevant in different proportions to different tasks or different levels of practice. Thus, evidence reported to date is largely confirmatory – that is, demonstrations that one or more of the sources significantly predict individual differences in skilled performance. In contrast, both the Fleishman/Hulin "universally declining correlations" theory and the Ackerman (1988) three-phase theory make predictions that are more readily testable. Both approaches yield concordant predictions for a declining trend in correlations between broad intellectual abilities and performance as consistent task skills are acquired. For most tasks in this class that have been examined, the predicted pattern is obtained (though there are a few notable exceptions, such as when suboptimal learning strategies are adopted by some learners – see Ackerman & Woltz, 1994).

However, the Ackerman theory predicts stable correlations between intelligence and performance on skill learning tasks that have strong demands on handling novel or inconsistent information. One task that exemplifies these requirements is the complex air traffic controller task called TRACON (an acronym for the terminal radar approach control simulation task). In three separate studies of this task, Ackerman and his colleagues demonstrated stable correlations with measures of broad or general intellectual ability (Ackerman, 1992; Ackerman & Cianciolo, 2000; Ackerman et al., 1995), even over as many as 18 hours of time-on-task practice.

The other aspects of Ackerman's (1988) theory have met with mixed success. Associations between perceptual speed abilities and task performance have proven to be less tractable than previously predicted. That is, sometimes correlations between perceptual speed abilities and performance increase, then correlations with task performance decrease as skills are developed, which is consistent with the theory. In other task situations, the correlations are relatively stable throughout skill acquisition, and in still others, the correlations between perceptual speed and performance decline with increased skill. Initial indications that perceptual speed abilities represent an underlying multidimensionality were first noticed by Ackerman (1990). Only recently have new tests been created and sufficient data been collected to show that in fact, there are at least four broad perceptual speed factors (Ackerman & Cianciolo, 1999, 2000). These different factors appear to differentially predict performance at various stages of skill acquisition; they also appear to be differentially predictive for different skill learning tasks.

The assessment of the association between psychomotor abilities and individual differences in skilled performance has been complicated by the fact that traditional measures of psychomotor abilities have either existed as apparatus tests (which are not conducive to group testing) or paper-and-pencil analogs of the apparatus tests (which generally lack both validity and reliability). Early studies with apparatus-based psychomotor abilities measures have shown them to be highly effective predictors of individual differences in skilled performance (e.g., Melton, 1947; Fleishman, 1956). However, since the 1950s, large-scale psychomotor assessment has been infrequently attempted (perhaps with the exception of the two scales of the General Ability Test Battery). Within the last half-dozen years, new computerized methods for psychomotor ability have been developed (e.g., see Ackerman & Cianciolo, 1999, 2000; Chaiken, Kyllonen, & Tirre, 2000). Only a few studies have been conducted with these measures, but so far, tests of psychomotor ability have proven to be relatively effective in predicting skilled performance.

Results from one recent study illustrate both the stability (or increase) in correlations between general intellectual abilities and task performance during practice in complex, inconsistent tasks and the changes in ability determinants of performance on consistent skill acquisition tasks (see Fig. 2). In this study (Ackerman & Cianciolo, 2000), multiple measures of broad content abilities (numerical, verbal, and spatial abilities), perceptual speed (PS) abilities (representing factors of PS-Complex, PS-Memory, PS-Pattern Recognition, and PS-Scanning), and psychomotor abilities (mirror tracing, pursuit, serial reaction time, maze tracing, and choice/simple reaction time) were administered to 98 participants. The participants were allowed to practice the complex TRACON simulation (which has repeatedly been shown to have substantial and continuous processing demands across practice trials) and the consistent Kanfer–Ackerman Air Traffic Controller task (which has been shown to have attenuated general ability requirements with practice, and increased associations with perceptual speed and psychomotor abilities). A single LISREL model of the abilities and task performance variables early and late in practice was derived. As can be seen from the figure, initial performance on both tasks was substantially associated with general intellectual abilities, consistent with all of the

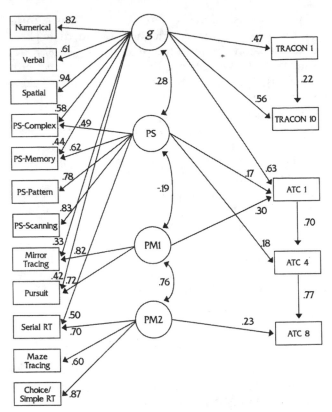

FIGURE 2. A LISREL model for ability determinants of individual differences in performance for two tasks: a high-fidelity complex air traffic control simulation (TRACON) and a consistent, less complex air traffic control task (the Kanfer–Ackerman ATC task). PS = Perceptual Speed, PM = Psychomotor, *g* = general intellectual ability; ATC = Kanfer-Ackerman ATC task. Lines indicate significant path coefficients. PM1 = (composite of mirror tracing and pursuit tests); PM2 = (composite of choice reaction time, serial reaction time, and maze tracing tests). TRACON 1 = First 30-minute task trial; TRACON 10 = tenth 30-minute task trial. ATC 1 = average of first four 10-minute task trials; ATC 4 = average of trials 13–16; ATC 8 = average of trials 29–32. Figure 12 (p. 286) from Ackerman and Cianciolo (2000), reprinted by permission.

previously discussed theories of ability–performance relations. However, in the TRACON task, increased levels of practice showed stable correlations with general intelligence – disconfirming the Fleishman/Hulin theory. Note also that perceptual speed and psychomotor abilities do not significantly add to the prediction of performance with TRACON either initially or after practice.

In contrast, the ATC task (which can become automatized within 5 or 6 hours of task practice) only had a significant path from general intelligence at the initial practice session. Perceptual speed was significantly associated with initial practice performance and intermediate practiced performance, but did not contribute to the prediction of final practiced performance. Some of the psychomotor abilities were associated with initial performance on the ATC task (disconfirming one part of the Ackerman theory), but other psychomotor abilities were significantly related to post-practice ATC performance, which is consistent with the theory.

Thus, all three classes of abilities (general/content, perceptual speed, and psychomotor) were significantly related to performance on the ATC task. While Ackerman's theory specifies that these three classes of abilities will be related to performance across skill acquisition trials, the specific timing of the significant correlations for perceptual speed and psychomotor abilities was not concordant with the theory. Because there has been so little research on the underlying representation of both perceptual speed and psychomotor abilities, it is perhaps early to discount the efficacy of the theory. Rather, the theory may need to be modified in light of the fact that extant measures of both perceptual speed and psychomotor abilities are themselves complex – including influences from each other and from more general abilities.

SUMMARY, CONCLUSIONS, AND FUTURE DIRECTIONS

Early intelligence theorists considered intelligence and the ability to learn to be virtually identical constructs. Subsequent failures to demonstrate substantial correlations between intelligence measures and "learning" scores for specific tasks were quite unsettling to some researchers (e.g., Woodrow, 1946), but they spurred on many investigators to attempt to understand the reasons underlying these surprising findings. Over the course of the past five decades, several facets of the problem have been illuminated, especially in terms of statistical artifacts and conceptual errors in associating learning with the difference between initial performance and performance after practice or training. More recent analyses (Wittmann & Süß, 1999) have also focused on the deleterious effects of a mismatch between the breadth of the predictor space (ability measures) and breadth of the criterion space (specific task performance). By reframing the consideration of the ability determinants of skills in terms of predicting performance at various stages of task practice or learning, rather than "amount of learning" per se, it has been possible to address the more fundamental question of whether intelligence is related to skill learning.

Three theories have been offered to predict patterns of correlations between ability measures and performance measures during task practice or training. The Fleishman/Hulin theory states that correlations between abilities and performance decline with increasing time-on-task, regardless of the nature of the task. The Ackerman theory states that the pattern of correlations is dependent on, among other things, the consistency of the task to be learned. For consistent tasks, initial performance is most highly related to general and broad-content intellectual abilities; performance at an intermediate stage of skill is most highly related to perceptual speed; and performance at the final, autonomous stage of skill acquisition is most highly related to psychomotor abilities. The Kyllonen and Christal four-source framework states that performance on tasks is determined to a greater or lesser degree by four broad sources of information processing capabilities: breadth of declarative knowledge, breadth of procedural knowledge, working memory capacity, and processing speed.

The Kyllonen and Christal four-source framework does not make specific predictions, and therefore it cannot be falsified. However, it does offer insight into four domains of abilities that can be expected to be related to individual differences in task performance during skill acquisition. The Fleishman/Hulin and Ackerman theories are more specifically testable, and as with all testable scientific theories, are certainly wrong. On the positive side, from a scientific perspective, the Fleishman/Hulin theory has the most desirable characteristics (at least from a Popperian perspective; see Popper, 1963), because the universal specification it makes of the reduction in correlations between ability and performance prediction is the most easily refuted. On the negative side, the Fleishman/Hulin theory has the least scientific verisimilitude (truth-likeness), because several studies have shown the prediction to be false.

The Ackerman theory makes risky relative predictions of the dynamic changes in ability–performance relations during skill acquisition. However, there is substantial slippage in the original theory (e.g., because the task "consistency" is somewhat arbitrarily defined). Several studies have demonstrated, however, that some of the predictions made by the Ackerman theory are certainly false. The theory has been modified, in terms of spelling out the heterogeneity of perceptual speed and psychomotor abilities, but in some sense, such modifications run the risk of making the approach ad hoc (see Lakatos, 1978, for a discussion of the philosophy of science approach to research programs).

If all of these theories are either untestable or wrong, where does that leave the researcher in search of an answer to whether abilities are related to skills? At this point, three general conclusions can be stated:

1. For consistent skill learning tasks, general cognitive abilities most frequently show declines in correlations with task performance as skills develop.
2. For many skill learning tasks, substantial correlations are found between perceptual speed abilities, psychomotor abilities, and performance across stages of skill acquisition. The exact pattern of correlations, however, appears to depend on task factors and

the choice of particular ability measures that are not yet well understood.
3. For inconsistent tasks, stable relations between abilities and performance are often found.

Research and theory up to the middle of the last century indicated that intelligence and specific task learning were largely unrelated to one another. In contrast, current theory and empirical data clearly demonstrate that intelligence (or intellectual abilities) is related to performance on skill learning tasks. Consistent with some views about the underlying properties of intelligence, IQ-type measures are most highly related to aspects of task performance that have the highest dependence on memory, reasoning, and strategy development (i.e., the cognitive stage of skill acquisition). However, once the vast majority of learners reach a point where they understand how to perform the task, the role of broad intellectual abilities in determining performance begins to attenuate. As learners become quite skilled (i.e., the autonomous stage of skill acquisition), individual differences in other abilities (such as perceptual speed and psychomotor abilities) appear to be increasingly important predictors of individual differences in performance. To return to the automobile driving example, it seems that our thought experiment is largely consistent with this view. Individuals of average intellectual ability, or even somewhat below average ability, are as capable of operating an automobile safely after extensive practice, compared with individuals of above average intelligence. The same can be said about myriad other skill learning tasks in the real world. The fastest skilled typists may not have the highest levels of general intelligence (but rather may have superior levels of perceptual speed and psychomotor abilities). Intelligence determines the ease with which an individual conceptualizes the task requirements, but does not guarantee the best performance in the long run. Performance at high levels of skill, however, does appear to be predictable from abilities other than general intelligence. It remains to be seen how influential these abilities are, in comparison to other personal characteristics that relate to long-term investment of effort toward maximizing performance, such as personality and motivation. Continuing investigations into these issues are needed, especially where both ability and non-ability predictors of skilled performance are evaluated simultaneously, rather than in piecemeal fashion (e.g., see Ackerman et al., 1995, for one example of such an experiment).

References

Ackerman, P. L. (1987). Individual differences in skill learning: An integration of psychometric and information processing perspectives. *Psychological Bulletin*, *102*, 3–27.

Ackerman, P. L. (1988). Determinants of individual differences during skill acquisition: Cognitive abilities and information processing. *Journal of Experimental Psychology: General, 117*, 288–318.

Ackerman, P. L. (1989). Within-task intercorrelations of skilled performance: Implications for predicting individual differences? *Journal of Applied Psychology, 74*, 360–364.

Ackerman, P. L. (1990). A correlational analysis of skill specificity: Learning, abilities, and individual differences. *Journal of Experimental Psychology: Learning, Memory, and Cognition, 16*, 883–901.

Ackerman, P. L. (1992). Predicting individual differences in complex skill acquisition: Dynamics of ability determinants. *Journal of Applied Psychology, 77*, 598–614.

Ackerman, P. L., & Cianciolo, A. T. (1999). Psychomotor abilities via touchpanel testing: Measurement innovations, construct, and criterion validity. *Human Performance, 12*, 231–273.

Ackerman, P. L., & Cianciolo, A. T. (2000). Cognitive, perceptual speed, and psychomotor determinants of individual differences during skill acquisition. *Journal of Experimental Psychology: Applied, 6*, 259–290.

Ackerman, P. L., Kanfer, R., & Goff, M. (1995). Cognitive and noncognitive determinants and consequences of complex skill acquisition. *Journal of Experimental Psychology: Applied, 1*, 270–304.

Ackerman, P. L., & Kyllonen, P. C. (1991). Trainee characteristics. In J. E. Morrison (Ed.), *Training for performance: Principles of applied human learning* (pp. 193–229). West Sussex, UK: Wiley.

Ackerman, P. L., & Woltz, D. J. (1994). Determinants of learning and performance in an associative memory/substitution task: Task constraints, individual differences, and volition. *Journal of Educational Psychology, 86*, 487–515.

Adams, J. A. (1957). The relationship between certain measures of ability and acquisition of a psychomotor response. *Journal of General Psychology, 56*, 121–134.

Adams, J. A. (1987). Historical review and appraisal of research on the learning, retention and transfer of human motor skills. *Psychological Bulletin, 101*, 41–74.

Barrett, G. V., Alexander, R. A., & Doverspike, D. (1992). The implications for personnel selection of apparent declines in predictive validities over time: A critique of Hulin, Henry, and Noon. *Personnel Psychology, 45*, 601–617.

Binet, A., & Simon, T. (1905). New methods for the diagnosis of the intellectual level of subnormals. *L'Année Psychologique, 11*, 191–244. Translated by Elizabeth S. Kite and reprinted in J. J. Jenkins & D. G. Paterson (Eds.), *Studies of individual differences: The search for intelligence* (pp. 90–96). New York: Appleton-Century-Crofts.

Bryan, W. L., & Harter, N. (1899). Studies on the telegraphic language: The acquisition of a hierarchy of habits. *Psychological Review, 6*, 345–375.

Card, S. K., Moran, T. P., & Newell, A. (1983). *The psychology of human–computer interaction*. Hillsdale, NJ: Erlbaum.

Carroll, J. B. (1980). *Individual difference relations in psychometric and experimental cognitive tasks*. (Tech. Rep. No. 163). Chapel Hill: University of North Carolina, The L. L. Thurstone Psychometric Laboratory. (Also NTIS document AD-A 086057 and ERIC Doc. ED-191–891.)

Chaiken, S. R., Kyllonen, P. C., & Tirre, W. C. (2000). Organization and components of psychomotor ability. *Cognitive Psychology, 40*, 198–226.

Cronbach, L. J., & Furby, L. (1970). How we should measure "change" – or should we? *Psychological Bulletin, 74*, 68–80.

Deary, I. J., & Stough, C. (1996). Intelligence and inspection time: Achievements, prospects, and problems. *American Psychologist, 51*, 599–608.

Ericsson, K. A., & Lehmann, A. C. (1996). Expert and exceptional performance: Evidence of maximal adaptation to task constraints. *Annual Review of Psychology, 47*, 273–305.

Ferguson, G. A. (1956). On transfer and the abilities of man. *Canadian Journal of Psychology, 10*, 121–131.

Fitts, P., & Posner, M. I. (1967). *Human performance*. Belmont, CA: Brooks/Cole.

Fleishman, E. A. (1956). Psychomotor selection tests: Research and application in the U.S. Air Force. *Personnel Psychology, 9*, 449–467.

Fleishman, E. A. (1972). On the relation between abilities, learning, and human performance. *American Psychologist, 27*, 1017–1032.

Fleishman, E. A., & Hempel, W. E., Jr. (1955). The relation between abilities and improvement with practice in a visual discrimination reaction task. *Journal of Experimental Psychology, 49*, 301–316.

Fleishman E. A., & Hempel, W. E., Jr. (1956). Factorial analysis of complex psychomotor performance and related skills. *Journal of Applied Psychology, 40*, 96–104.

Frederiksen, J. R., Warren, B. M., & Rosebery, A. S. (1985). A componential approach to training reading skills: Part 1. Perceptual units training. *Cognition and Instruction, 2*, 91–130.

Henry, R. A., & Hulin, C. L. (1987). Stability of skilled performance across time: Some generalizations and limitations on utilities. *Journal of Applied Psychology, 72*, 457–462.

Hulin, C. L., Henry, R. A., & Noon, S. L. (1990). Adding a dimension: Time as a factor in the generalizability of predictive relationships. *Psychological Bulletin, 107*, 1–13.

Humphreys, L. G., & Taber, T. (1973). Postdiction study of the graduate record examination and eight semesters of college grades. *Journal of Educational Measurement, 10*, 179–184.

Hunt, E., Frost, N., & Lunneborg, C. (1973). Individual differences in cognition: A new approach to intelligence. In G. Bower (Ed.), *Advances in learning and motivation* (Vol. 7, pp. 87–122). New York: Academic Press.

Jensen, A. R. (1998). *The g factor: The science of mental ability*. Westport, CT: Praeger.

Kanfer, R., & Ackerman, P. L. (1989). Motivation and cognitive abilities: An integrative/aptitude-treatment interaction approach to skill acquisition. *Journal of Applied Psychology – Monograph, 74*, 657–690.

Kyllonen, P. C., & Christal, R. E. (1989). Cognitive modeling of learning abilities: A status report of LAMP. In R. Dillon and J. W. Pellegrino (Eds.), *Testing: Theoretical and applied issues*. San Francisco: Freeman.

Kyllonen, P. C., & Stephens, D. L. (1990). Cognitive abilities as determinants of success in acquiring logic skill. *Learning and Individual Differences, 2*, 129–160.

Kyllonen, P. C., Tirre, W. C., & Christal, R. E. (1991). Knowledge and processing speed as determinants of associative learning. *Journal of Experimental Psychology: General, 120*(1), 57–79.

Kyllonen, P. C., & Woltz, D. J. (1989). Role of cognitive factors in the acquisition of cognitive skill. In R. Kanfer, P. L. Ackerman, & R. Cudeck (Eds.), *Abilities, motivation, and methodology: The Minnesota symposium on learning and individual differences* (pp. 239–280). Hillsdale, NJ: Erlbaum.

Lakatos, I. (Ed.) (1978). *The methodology of scientific research programmes: Philosophical papers* (Vol. 1). Cambridge, UK: Cambridge University Press.

Lohman, D. F. (1999). Minding our p's and q's: On finding relationships between learning and intelligence. In P. L. Ackerman, P. C. Kyllonen, & R. D. Roberts (Eds.), *Learning and individual differences: Process, trait, and content determinants* (pp. 55–76). Washington, DC: American Psychological Association.

Melton, A. W. (Ed.) (1947). *Army Air Forces Aviation Psychology Program Research Reports: Apparatus Tests*. Report No. 4. Washington, DC: U.S. Government Printing Office.

Pena, C. M., & Tirre, W. C. (1992). Cognitive factors involved in the first stage of programming skill acquisition. *Learning and Individual Differences, 4*, 311–334.

Popper, K. R. (1963). *Conjectures and refutations*. New York: Harper & Row.

Sternberg, R. J. (1977). *Intelligence, information processing, and analogical reasoning: The componential analysis of human abilities*. Hillsdale, NJ: Erlbaum.

Sternberg, R. J. (1985). *Human abilities: An information-processing approach*. New York: Freeman.

Thorndike, E. L. (1924). Measurement of intelligence. *Psychological Review, 31*, 219–252.

Tirre, W. C. (1992). Can reading ability be measured with tests of memory and processing speed. *Journal of General Psychology, 119*, 141–160.

Wechsler, D. (1949). *Wechsler Intelligence Scale for Children*. NY: Psychological Corporation.

Wittmann, W. W., & Süß, H.-M. (1999). Investigating the paths between working memory, intelligence, knowledge, and complex problem-solving performances via Brunswik symmetry. In P. L. Ackerman, P. C. Kyllonen, & R. D. Roberts (Eds.), *Learning and Individual Differences: Process, Trait, and Content Determinants* (pp. 77–108). Washington, DC: American Psychological Association.

Woltz, D. J., Bell, B. G., Kyllonen, P. C., & Gardner, M. K. (1996). Memory for order of operations in the acquisition and transfer of sequential cognitive skills. *Journal of Experimental Psychology: Learning, Memory, and Cognition, 22*, 438–457.

Woodrow, H. (1946). The ability to learn. *Psychological Review, 53*, 147–158.

Zeaman, D., & House, B. J. (1967). The relation of IQ and learning. In R. M. Gagné (Ed.), *Learning and individual differences* (pp. 192–212). Columbus, OH: Charles Merrill.

9

Complex Problem Solving and Intelligence

Empirical Relation and Causal Direction

Dorit Wenke, Peter A. Frensch,
and Joachim Funke

INTRODUCTION

The breadth of human problem solving is truly striking. On the one hand, human problem solving makes possible the most wondrous achievements, such as "an 800-seat airliner with wings that blend smoothly into the fuselage instead of protruding from its sides that is scheduled to be in the air by 2006" (AP news from February 9, 2001). Yet, on the other hand, errors in problem solving can lead to catastrophic and near-catastrophic disasters, such as, for instance, the nuclear reactor accident at Three Mile Island, Pennsylvania, in 1979. Whatever "problem solving" is, and scientists disagree vehemently on the proper meaning of the term, there can be little doubt that it has shaped human culture to an extent that is almost unrivaled by any other human ability.

From the inception of the concept of "intelligence," the ability to solve problems has featured prominently in virtually every definition of human intelligence (e.g., Sternberg & Berg, 1986). In addition, intelligence has often been viewed as one of the best predictors of problem-solving ability (e.g., Putz-Osterloh, 1981; Putz-Osterloh & Lüer, 1981). Thus, whatever the causal relation between the two concepts, prevailing theoretical positions strongly suggest that intelligence and problem solving are related. In this chapter we concentrate on complex rather than on simple problem solving. Our main goal is to review the extent to which the ability to solve complex problems is indeed tied, empirically, to intelligence and to discuss which causal direction holds between the two concepts. More specifically, we discuss the extent to which individual differences in complex problem-solving competence can be tied, both theoretically and empirically, to individual differences in global intelligence and/or to individual differences in specific intelligence components.

The chapter is divided into three main sections. In the first section, we briefly describe the history of the mainly European complex problem-solving research and offer a definition of "complex problem solving." In the second and third sections, we review much of the existing empirical work that relates complex problem-solving competence to intelligence. We distinguish two forms of complex problem solving. In the second section, we focus on explicit complex problem solving, that is, problem solving that is controlled by a problem solver's intentions. In the third section our focus is on implicit, that is, automatic or nonconscious, complex problem solving.

Our main argument throughout the chapter will be that no convincing empirical evidence exists to support a relation between complex, implicit or explicit, problem-solving competence on the one hand, and global intelligence on the other hand. We are aware that arguing the null hypothesis is difficult at best and dangerous at worst. Thus, we do not deny the possibility that a relation between complex problem-solving competence and global intelligence might exist in reality; we argue only that there is no convincing empirical evidence at the present time that supports such a conclusion. On the other hand, however, we believe that a considerable amount of empirical data does suggest that specific components of intelligence, such as processing capacity, might be related to specific components of explicit complex problem solving. On the whole, therefore, we argue that the available evidence suggests that the global concepts of intelligence and problem solving are not related, but that specific subcomponents of intelligence and explicit problem solving might share variance. The existing empirical evidence does not allow us, however, to draw any conclusion on the causal relation between subcomponents of intelligence and subcomponents of problem solving.

DEFINITIONS AND CLARIFICATIONS

As pointed out by Frensch and Funke (1995), researchers in the area of human problem solving have often been quite inconsistent in their use of terms such as "problem," "problem solving," and "intelligence." Although perhaps understandable, different uses of the same term seriously undermine scientific progress. Because the definition of a term affects the choice of experimental tasks and methods, and thus, ultimately affects the conclusions to be drawn (Frensch & Funke, 1995), we make an attempt in this section to delineate what exactly we mean when we talk about "problems" in general and "complex problems" in particular. First, however, we give a brief historical overview of complex problem-solving research.

Simple and Complex Problems

Beginning with the early experimental work of the Gestaltists in Germany (e.g., Duncker, 1935), and continuing through the 1960s and early 1970s, research on problem solving was typically conducted with relatively simple laboratory tasks (e.g., Duncker's "X-ray" problem; Ewert & Lambert's "disk" problem, 1932, later known as "Tower of Hanoi") that were novel to research participants (e.g., Mayer, 1992). Simple novel tasks were used for a variety of reasons; they had clearly defined optimal solutions, they were solvable within a relatively short time frame, research participants' problem-solving steps could be traced, and so on. The underlying assumption was, of course, that simple tasks, such as the Tower of Hanoi, capture the main properties of real-life problems, and that the cognitive processes underlying participants' solution attempts on simple problems were representative of the processes engaged in when solving real problems. Thus, simple problems were used for reasons of convenience, and generalizations to more complex problems were thought possible. Perhaps the best known and most impressive example of this line of research is the work by Newell and Simon (1972).

However, beginning in the 1970s researchers became increasingly convinced that empirical findings and theoretical concepts derived from simple laboratory tasks were not generalizable to more complex, real-life problems. Even worse, it appeared that the processes underlying complex problem solving (CPS) in different domains were different from each other (Sternberg, 1995). These realizations have led to rather different responses in North America and Europe.

In North America, initiated by the work of Herbert Simon on learning by doing in semantically rich domains (e.g., Anzai & Simon, 1979; Bhaskar & Simon, 1977), researchers began to investigate problem solving separately in different natural knowledge domains (e.g., physics, writing, chess playing), thus abandoning their attempts to extract a global theory of problem solving (e.g., Sternberg & Frensch, 1991). Instead, these researchers frequently focused on the development of problem solving within a certain domain, that is, on the development of expertise (e.g., Anderson, Boyle, & Reiser, 1985; Chase & Simon, 1973; Chi, Feltovich, & Glaser, 1981). Areas that have attracted rather intensive attention in North America include such diverse fields as reading, writing, calculation, political decision making, managerial problem solving, lawyers' reasoning, mechanical problem solving, problem solving in electronics, computer skills, game playing, and even personal problem solving.

In Europe, two main approaches have surfaced, one initiated by Donald Broadbent (1977; see Berry & Broadbent, 1995) in Great Britain and the other by Dietrich Dörner (1975, 1980; see also Dörner & Wearing, 1995) in Germany. The two approaches have in common an emphasis on relatively complex, semantically rich, computerized laboratory tasks that are constructed to be similar to real-life problems. The approaches differ somewhat in their theoretical goals and methodology (see Buchner, 1995, for a more detailed comparison). The tradition initiated by Broadbent emphasizes the distinction between cognitive problem-solving processes that operate under awareness versus those operating outside of awareness, and typically employs mathematically well-defined computerized systems. The tradition initiated by Dörner, on the other hand, is interested in the interplay of cognitive, motivational, and social components of problem solving, and utilizes very complex computerized scenarios that contain up to 2,000 highly interconnected variables (e.g., the Dörner et al., 1983, Lohhausen project).

With these considerations in mind, it is not surprising that there exists a wide variety of definitions of the term "complex problem solving" that have little in common (e.g., Frensch & Funke, 1995). Any general conclusion regarding complex problem solving, however, and any theoretical model of complex problem solving can only be meaningful if all agree on what constitutes a problem and what constitutes complex problem solving. For the remainder of this chapter we define complex problem solving as follows:

Complex problem solving occurs to overcome barriers between a given state and a desired goal state by means of behavioral and/or cognitive, multi-step activities. The given state, goal state, and barriers between given state and goal state are complex, change dynamically during problem solving, and are intransparent. The exact properties of the given state, goal state, and barriers are unknown to the solver at the outset. Complex problem solving implies the efficient interaction between a solver and the situational requirements of the task, and involves a solver's cognitive, emotional, personal, and social abilities and knowledge. (Frensch & Funke, 1995, p. 18)

There are at least two reasons for why we focus, in this chapter, on the relation between intelligence and complex, rather than simple, kinds of problem solving. First several reviews already exist of the relation between intelligence and simple problem-solving competence as displayed when typical laboratory problems are solved (e.g., Sternberg, 1982). The conclusion from these reviews appears to be that if indeed a relation exists between intelligence and problem-solving competence, then it is probably quite modest in size (i.e., correlations around .30). By comparison, the potential relation between intelligence and complex problem-solving competence has been rarely discussed and reviewed in detail (for exceptions, see Kluwe, Misiak, & Haider, 1991a; Kluwe, Schilde, et al., 1991b).

Second, and perhaps more importantly, the external validity of the artificial laboratory tasks typically used to study the relation between intelligence and problem-solving competence is highly questionable. The tasks have little resemblance to the problem-solving situations typically encountered by humans.

As will become apparent later in the chapter, we distinguish between complex problem solving that is dependent upon the intended actions of a problem solver (i.e., explicit problem solving) and problem solving that occurs, more or less, outside the realm of intention (i.e., implicit problem solving). For both types of problem solving, we will ask to what extent individual differences in CPS competence might be tied to individual differences in intelligence.

Evaluation Criteria

We strongly believe that any theoretical and/or empirical approach arguing for a relation between problem-solving competence and intelligence must meet a number of criteria in order to be taken seriously. We use three criteria to assess and evaluate the research considered:

Criterion 1. Problem-solving competence and intelligence need to be explicitly defined and must not overlap at theoretical and/or operational levels. At a theoretical level, this criterion implies that both intelligence and problem-solving competence need to be defined explicitly and, more importantly, independently of each other. If the latter is not the case, then any attempt to relate problem-solving competence to intelligence is necessarily circular and redundant – one would find what is a priori true (Greve, 2001). At the operational level, Criterion 1 implies that independent and reliable measures need to be used to assess the respective constructs. When overlapping measures (e.g., items that appear on a questionnaire used to measure intelligence also appear on a questionnaire used to measure problem-solving competence) are used, then empirically observed correlations may reflect methodological artifacts rather than theoretically relevant relations.

Criterion 2. The presumed relation between intelligence and problem-solving competence must have a theoretical explanation. This criterion demands that some theory or model exists that specifies the proposed relation between CPS competence and intelligence. In principle, there appear to be at least three main possibilities regarding the relation between complex problem solving and intelligence. First, individual differences in intelligence may cause individual differences in CPS ability. Second, the causal relation might work the other way around; that is, individual differences in CPS ability may cause individual differences in intelligence. Third, individual differences on the two concepts might be not only correlated but also causally related to a third variable. Without an understanding of the direction of the causal link between the two concepts, that is, without a theoretical foundation linking the two concepts, there exists no explanation.

Criterion 3. The direction of the presumed causality must be demonstrated empirically. Whatever the theoretically proposed direction of causality, it needs to be demonstrated empirically. Because a direct experimental manipulation of degree of intelligence is not feasible, indirect assessments of the direction of causality are required. Acceptable approaches might be to (a) use longitudinal research designs or (b) experimentally manipulate the use of intelligence by varying either instructions or task properties, which requires (c) control of potential third variables that possibly modulate empirically observed relations.

In the next section, we discuss theoretical ideas and empirical research that are relevant to exploring the relation between intelligence and explicit, intention-driven, problem-solving competence for complex problems. In the third section, we focus on the relation between intelligence and implicit, that is, nonintentional problem solving.

INDIVIDUAL DIFFERENCES IN COMPLEX EXPLICIT PROBLEM SOLVING

In this section, we review first some of the research on the relation between complex explicit problem solving (CEPS) and intelligence as assessed by traditional intelligence tests or specific subtests thereof. The assumption underlying this approach is that a person's IQ score reflects some global and relatively stable intellectual ability that might potentially be associated with CEPS. With few exceptions, the tasks used to assess CEPS competence consist of dynamic scenarios presented on a computer, with the number of (independent exogenous and interconnected endogenous) variables ranging from 3 to about 2000. The scenarios are described to research participants with the more or less clearly specified goal to optimize some aspects of the scenario's output (for a review, see Funke, 1995).

Perhaps surprisingly, empirical support for a relation between intelligence and problem-solving ability is poor. Typically, the reported correlations are low or even zero, at least when the problem situation is nontransparent and/or the goal to be achieved is poorly specified (for detailed reviews, see Kluwe et al., 1991a, b; Beckmann & Guthke, 1995). The probably best-known study producing zero correlations was conducted by Dörner and colleagues (Dörner et al., 1983) using the Lohhausen system. Participants' task was to take care of the future prosperity of a small town called Lohhausen over a simulated 10-year period. About 2,000 variables were involved in this system (e.g., number of inhabitants, earnings of the industry, etc.). Participants interacted with the system through an experimenter. Problem-solving competence on this task did not correlate with Raven's Advanced Progressive Matrices (APM; Raven, Court, & Raven, 1980) scores, nor did it correlate with scores on the Culture Fair Intelligence Test (CFT; Cattell & Weiss, 1980).

Results such as these have been interpreted and discussed quite controversially by different groups of researchers. One group of researchers (e.g., Dörner & Kreuzig, 1983; Putz-Osterloh, 1981) has argued that zero correlations between problem-solving competence and general intelligence reflect the fact that traditional IQ measures tend to be ecologically less valid than CEPS measures. More specifically, these researchers claim that in dynamic scenarios (a) the goals are often ill specified, (b) information needs to be actively sought after, and (c) semantic/contextual embeddedness (i.e., a meaningful cover story) is almost always present, and that traditional intelligence tests do not measure the intellectual abilities (such as the so-called operative intelligence; Dörner, 1986) required for successful problem-solving performance in highly complex and ecologically valid environments.

According to a second group of researchers (e.g., Funke, 1983, 1984; Kluwe et al., 1991b), low correlations between IQ and CEPS are due to methodological and conceptual shortcomings. Kluwe et al. (1991a, b) have pointed out, for instance, that it is impossible to derive valid indicators of problem-solving performance for tasks that are not formally tractable and thus do not possess a mathematically optimal solution. Indeed, when different dependent measures are used in studies with the same scenario (i.e., Tailorshop; e.g., Funke, 1983; Putz-Osterloh, 1981; Süß, Kersting, & Oberauer, 1991), then the empirical findings frequently differ for different dependent variables.

Second, the reliability of the performance indices is often low (e.g., Funke, 1983, 1984; Kluwe et al., 1991b), ranging between .2 and .7, depending on the dependent variable used (see, e.g., Müller, 1993; Putz-Osterloh & Haupts, 1989; Strohschneider, 1986). Other quite serious methodological criticisms concern the narrow sampling of IQ in most of the studies just mentioned (e.g., Funke, 1991) and the ecological validity of the scenarios.

However, the empirical picture is far more complicated and less clear than might have been suggested thus far. Although zero correlations between test intelligence and complex problem-solving competence are frequently obtained, this is not always the case. For example, Putz-Osterloh (1981; Putz-Osterloh & Lüer, 1981) has argued that the relation between global intelligence and complex problem-solving competence is mediated by the transparency of the problem-solving task. Like Dörner et al. (1983), Putz-Osterloh (1981) failed to find significant correlations between problem-solving competence and Raven's APM in a nontransparent experimental condition with the Tailorshop scenario, a scenario simulating a small company in which shirt production and sales are controlled by purchasing raw materials and modifying the production capacity in terms of the number of workers and machines. The participant's goal in the study was to maximize the company's profit, either in a transparent condition, in which they had access to a diagram depicting the relations between the system variables, or in a nontransparent condition in which no diagram was shown.

Putz-Osterloh (1981, see also Putz-Osterloh & Lüer, 1981; Hörmann & Thomas, 1989) found a statistically reliable relation ($Tau = .22$) between IQ and problem-solving competence (operationalized by the number of months with increasing capital assets) in the transparent experimental condition (but see Funke, 1983, for different results).

A different moderator variable affecting the link between global intelligence and complex problem-solving competence has been suggested by Strohschneider (1991). The author, using the Moro system in which participants are asked to improve the living conditions of nomads in the Sahel zone, manipulated the specificity of the to-be-attained goals. In the specific-goal condition, participants were asked to reach specified values on critical variables (e.g., number of cattle, number of inhabitants, etc.). In the unspecific-goal condition, the participants' task was to take actions that guaranteed long-term improvements of the Moro living conditions.

In the unspecific-goal condition, problem-solving performance did not correlate with general intelligence as measured by the Berlin Intelligence Structure (BIS) test (Jäger, 1982; Jäger, Süß, & Beauducel, 1997); however, substantial correlations (up to $r = -.59$) were found in the specific-goal condition.

Yet another variable affecting the relation between global intelligence and complex problem-solving ability may be the semantic context of a problem-solving task. Hesse (1982) investigated the impact of the semantic embeddedness of the problem-solving task on the relation between IQ and CEPS. In the semantic condition, participants were asked to solve the Dori problem, a computerized system involving ecological variables and relations. In the semantic-free condition, a system with an isomorphic problem structure but without the cover story and without meaningful variable names was presented to the participants. In addition, transparency was manipulated in the same way as had been done in the Putz-Osterloh (1981) experiment described earlier. Hesse (1982) obtained moderate correlations between problem-solving performance and APM scores only in the semantic-free condition ($r = .38$ and $r = .46$ for the transparent and the nontransparent condition, respectively).

On the whole, these empirical findings do not support a strong link between global intelligence and complex problem-solving competence when goal specificity and transparency are low and when the semantic content is rich; the link appears to be somewhat stronger when the intelligence-testing conditions more closely resemble the problem-solving testing conditions. We agree with Kluwe et al. (1991a, b) that on the basis of these results, it cannot be determined whether low correlations are due to invalid intelligence testing (i.e., their failure to assess real-world intellectual abilities necessary for dealing with complexity) or are due to a lack of reliability of the CEPS measures. The heterogeneity of the scenarios and IQ tests used further complicates the interpretation of the existing results.

Evaluation of Approach

Criterion 1. Problem-solving competence and intelligence need to be explicitly defined and must not overlap at theoretical and/or operational levels. Because independent tasks are typically used to assess problem-solving competence and intelligence, the measures used in the described research do not overlap at an operational level. However, the fact that significant correlations between complex problem-solving competence and IQ are obtained when goal specificity is high and/or semantic embeddedness is missing suggests an overlap at the level of task requirements.

Criterion 2. The presumed relation between intellectual ability and problem-solving competence must have a theoretical explanation. Apart from general statements, it is not obvious how exactly intelligence should contribute to CEPS. This is so because (a) to date researchers have not agreed on the nature of intelligence (see, for example, Kray & Frensch, 2001, for an overview of different accounts of the nature of g), and (b) no models exist that theoretically link intelligence to (specific aspects of) complex problem-solving behavior. The latter problem may partly be due to the difficulty to define an objective problem space for mathematically intractable scenarios. For that reason, some researchers recommend the use of formally tractable scenarios like finite-state automata or linear structural equation systems (see Buchner, 1999; Funke, 2001).

Criterion 3. The direction of the presumed causality must be demonstrated empirically. To our knowledge, no longitudinal or training designs have been used to assess the direction of causality. Some empirical studies have manipulated task properties such as transparency, but only Funke (1983) used a between-group design (sampling from the extremes of the IQ distribution). Furthermore, it is questionable whether potential moderator variables have been adequately controlled for. For instance, when both semantic embeddedness and transparency are varied, as in the study by Hesse (1982), then transparency does not affect problem-solving performance in the semantic-free condition. Hence, the direction of causality (if any exists) remains unclear.

To summarize, correlating global IQ scores with complex problem-solving performance does not seem to be particularly useful when the goal is to understand the potential link between intelligence and complex problem-solving competence. Our main concern with this approach relates to a lack of theoretical explanation. In the next part, we review research that goes beyond correlating global IQ with CEPS performance by singling out individual components of intelligence that may affect problem-solving competence.

CEPS and Specific Intelligence Components

In the research reviewed next, IQ subtests such as those inherent in the BIS or learning-test scores were correlated with complex problem-solving performance. For example, Süß et al. (1991, 1993; see also Hussy, 1991) had problem solvers work on a nontransparent version of the Tailorshop.

The authors hypothesized that to successfully control this system, problem solvers needed to infer the relations among critical variables and to deduce meaningful goals and actions. Therefore, reasoning ability, as assessed by the BIS K-factor (processing capacity, capturing the ability to recognize relations and rules and to form logical inferences in figure series, number series, and verbal analogies) was predicted to be the single most predictive ability of problem-solving ability. This is indeed what the authors found. Overall problem-solving performance correlated substantially with K ($r = .47$). In addition, *knowledge* (specific system knowledge as well as general economic knowledge) was found to be a predictor of problem solving (see also Putz-Osterloh, 1993).

Similar findings have been reported by Hörmann and Thomas (1989), who administered the Tailorshop under two different transparency conditions. When problem solvers' system knowledge, as assessed by a questionnaire, was high, then the K-factor ($r = .72$) and the G-factor (indicating memory performance, $r = .54$) correlated with CEPS performance in the nontransparent condition, whereas the B-factor (processing speed) was the best predictor in the transparent condition. However, when system knowledge was not considered, then significant correlations only emerged in the transparent condition.

Hussy (1989), on the other hand, found the K-factor to be the single most predictive operative factor, regardless of transparency condition and system knowledge. The scenario used by Hussy was the Lunar Lander, a mathematically well-defined system with only six variables and a very specific goal, which makes it difficult to compare this study directly to those using the Tailorshop. Nevertheless, it is interesting to note that Hussy (1989) also found the G-factor (memory) to be significantly correlated with problem-solving performance in the nontransparent condition. This finding is similar to Hörmann and Thomas's result (1989) and points to the possibility that nontransparent problems may pose particularly high memory demands when problem solvers attempt to develop internal models of the task (cf. Buchner, 1995).

In general, these results appear to be inconsistent with Strohschneider's (1991, see previous section) finding of high correlations between almost all BIS operative factors and problem-solving performance in the specific-goal condition of the Moro system. But then again, Strohschneider's study differs substantially in terms of task demands, such as system complexity and operationalization of goal specificity, from these studies, making direct comparisons difficult.

A different "componential" approach has been taken by Beckmann (1995; for a comprehensive overview see Beckmann & Guthke, 1995). Beckmann and colleagues argue that successful problem-solving performance involves the ability to learn from success and failure. The authors therefore use learning tests (e.g., Guthke, 1992) that assess problem solvers' learning potential, in addition to the reasoning subtests of traditional intelligence tests (Intelligence Structure Test, IST; Amthauer, Brocke, Liepmann, & Beauducel, 1973; and Learning Test Battery "Reasoning," LTS 3; Guthke, Jäger, & Schmidt, 1983) to predict problem-solving performance and knowledge acquisition. Diagrams for which the relevant relations need to be filled in assess the latter. The authors' six-variable system is based on a linear equation system and was administered in either an abstract Machine version or in a semantically meaningful version (Cherrytree, for which water supply, warmth, etc., had to be manipulated in order to control the growth of cherries, leaves, and beetles).

In the abstract Machine version, problem solvers acquired substantial system knowledge, and learning-test scores correlated substantially with the system knowledge measure as well as with problem-solving performance measures, whereas traditional intelligence subtest scores only correlated (albeit to a smaller degree) with problem-solving performance. In contrast, in the Cherrytree version, problem solvers did not demonstrate system knowledge nor did test scores (regardless of type) correlate with problem-solving performance (see also Hesse, 1982). Interestingly, the two experimental groups (i.e., Machine vs. Cherrytree) did not differ in terms of the quality of their CEPS performance, that is, in their control of the system. This and similar results have led several researchers (e.g., Berry & Broadbent, 1984) to propose different modes of learning and of problem solving; we return to this issue in the third section when we discuss implicit problem solving.

To summarize, when specific intelligence components are correlated with problem-solving performance in complex systems and when the problem-solving goals are clearly specified, then moderate to substantial correlations are obtained, even under nontransparent task conditions. The most important intelligence components predicting problem-solving competence appear to be processing capacity/reasoning ability and learning potential. Semantic content appears to be an important mediator of the relation between abilities and CEPS (e.g., Hesse, 1982), implying that the content may activate prior knowledge and affect the problem representation. Furthermore, inconsistent results have been obtained regarding the relation between system knowledge (i.e., knowledge about the relations among variables) and problem-solving performance.

Evaluation of Approach

Criterion 1. Problem-solving competence and intelligence need to be explicitly defined and must not overlap at theoretical and/or operational levels. Regarding operational overlap, much the same can be said as in the previous section. There is little reason to expect much overlap at the operational level although task requirements may overlap to some extent. Concerning theoretical overlap, the situation is even more satisfying. Learning and reasoning are better defined than is global intelligence, and the overlap between the theoretical concepts appears to be low.

Criterion 2. The presumed relation between intellectual ability and problem-solving competence must have a theoretical explanation. Although interesting with regard to hypothesis generation, the approach just discussed suffers from a lack of theoretical explanation. Demonstrating that a person's reasoning ability is related to problem-solving competence, for instance, does not tell us much about the specific reasoning processes and representations that may be required for successful problem solving. Thus, the theoretical foundation of the link between the proposed ability and problem-solving performance remains rather unclear at the level of mechanisms. A closer task analysis (plus the use of mathematically tractable tasks) as well as a more systematic variation of task properties may be needed to better understand how specific intelligence components might be related to complex problem-solving competence.

Criterion 3. The direction of the presumed causality must be demonstrated empirically. Largely the same conclusions can be drawn regarding this criterion as in the first part of the present section. In our view, a causal link between intellectual ability and specific intelligence components has not been demonstrated within this line of research.

On the whole, the approach of correlating specific intelligence components with CEPS performance is theoretically much more interesting than correlating CEPS performance with global IQ. However, to theoretically understand CEPS in terms of the underlying intellectual abilities, three things are needed: (1) more detailed models of knowledge acquisition processes in CEPS situations, (2) more detailed theoretical accounts of the links between the proposed abilities and CEPS performance, as well as (3) research designs that allow inferences about the direction of causality.

Expertise and Intelligence

Instead of assessing complex problem-solving competence with the aid of computerized systems, researchers have also explored the relation between intelligence and problem-solving competence in a more natural context, namely by correlating global intelligence with expertise. Arguably the best-known work in this regard has been performed by Ceci and his colleagues (e.g., Ceci & Liker, 1986a, b; Ceci & Ruiz, 1992, 1993), who claim that expertise is unrelated to global IQ. Ceci and Liker (1986a, b), for instance, compared experts and novices in terms of their ability to handicap races and in the cognitive complexity underlying their handicapping performance. Furthermore, the relation between expertise and IQ, as measured by the WAIS, as well as between cognitive complexity and IQ was examined.

Experts differed from novices in terms of their ability to correctly predict post-time odds for the top three horses in ten actual races on the basis of a priori factual information about the horses although the two groups were comparable in terms of their factual knowledge about races (as assessed by a screening questionnaire), years of track experience, years of education, and, most importantly, IQ. That is, both groups contained high-IQ as well as low-IQ individuals.

Experts as well as novices subsequently handicapped 50 experimentally contrived races, in which an "experimental" horse had to be compared to a "standard" horse. For the former, values on potentially important variables (such as lifetime speed, claiming price, trace surface condition, etc.) were systematically varied. To model how experts and novices arrived at their odds predictions, Ceci and Liker used multiple-regression analyses.

The results of the study can be summarized as follows. First, the modeling results showed that a simple additive model was not sufficient to predict performance, at least not for experts. Rather, quite complicated interactive terms needed to be included. Second, experts gave more weight to higher-order interactions than did novices, suggesting a higher degree of cognitive complexity in their reasoning. Third, the weight of the higher-order interactions correlated highly with handicapping ability, but did not correlate with IQ. The latter finding is particularly important because it suggests that global intelligence is unrelated to cognitive complexity in real-life complex problem solving such as handicapping races.

Interestingly, similar results have been obtained in very different areas of expertise. For example, in their recent work on practical intelligence (i.e., situational-judgment tests that present work-based problems for participants to solve), Sternberg and colleagues have repeatedly found no correlation between performance and IQ. In their most recent article, Sternberg et al. (2001) describe work done with 85 children between the ages of 12 and 15 in a rural village in western Kenya. The main dependent variable of interest was children's scores on a test of tacit knowledge for natural herbal medicines used to fight illnesses. Sternberg et al. found that scores on the tacit knowledge correlated trivially or even significantly negatively with measures of IQ and achievement, even after controlling for socioeconomic status.

Even if it is true that global intelligence is not related to expertise, it might still be related to the acquisition of expertise. To explore the latter possibility, Ceci and Ruiz (1992, 1993) conducted a follow-up case study in which they investigated the acquisition of expertise on a novel task of two race-handicapping experts with different IQ levels. The new task was constructed such that it had the same underlying "problem structure" as the race-handicapping task. That is, the authors constructed a stock market game that included just as many variables as were included in the handicapping task. In the new task, an experimental stock had to be compared to a standard stock. The two handicapping experts were asked to decide which of the two stocks would yield a better future price/earnings ratio. Experimental trials were constructed such that the equation modeling handicapping performance held for a subset of the stock market variables.

The results of this study showed that the two experts did not spontaneously transfer the "handicapping" rule to the new task before they were informed that the task-relevant variables could be weighed and combined in the same manner as they had done in predicting post-time odds. After receiving this hint, performance increased considerably for both experts. Modeling indicated that the experts had not developed a model as complex as the equation they used for handicapping. Rather, they appeared to work with models containing only lower-order interactions. Consequently, performance never reached impressive levels, although both experts managed to eventually perform above chance. Most importantly, the high and low IQ experts did not differ in their performance nor in terms of the cognitive complexity they brought to bear on the new task.

Ceci and colleagues interpret their results as indicating that (a) intelligence always manifests itself as an interaction between underlying intellectual abilities and experience in particular domains, and is therefore context/content dependent, (b) multiple intelligences exist, and (c) IQ tests measure only a specific type of intelligence, namely one developed in academic settings.

The Ceci studies have not remained without criticism. Detterman and Spry (1988; see also Ceci & Liker, 1988, for a reply), for instance, argued that sampling procedure, sample size, and questionable reliabilities (but see Ceci & Liker, 1988) might have led to an underestimation of the "true" correlations. Ceci and Ruiz (1993) themselves made the point that the difficulty of the novel task might have prevented transfer to occur.

Regardless of the validity of the criticisms, it is important to acknowledge that the Ceci and Liker and Ceci and Ruiz studies are two of the very few studies that have related global intelligence to expertise and to the acquisition of problem-solving competence. The empirical result is both intriguing and consistent with the European research reviewed earlier: IQ does not seem to predict expertise (i.e., CEPS competence), nor does it predict the acquisition of CEPS competence.

Evaluation of Approach

Criterion 1. Problem-solving competence and intelligence need to be explicitly defined and must not overlap at theoretical and/or operational levels. Except for possibly similar task demands, no overlap appears to exist at the operational level. That is, the measures used to assess level of expertise and global intelligence differ. In addition, the reliability of the prediction performance scores may be better than has been pointed out by critics (e.g., Detterman & Spry, 1988).

The argument Ceci and colleagues are pushing is that global intelligence and expert problem-solving competence do not overlap theoretically. As for separately defining expertise and global intelligence, some effort has been made to define critical (cognitive) characteristics of expertise. The problem concerning the nature of g discussed in the first part of the present section remains unsolved, however.

Criterion 2. The presumed relation between intellectual ability and problem-solving competence must have a theoretical explanation. While an overall correlation between global intelligence and expertise was not expected, Ceci and Liker (1986b) state that "each of us possesses innate potentialities for achievement in abstract reasoning, verbal analysis, creative expression, quantification, visual-spatial organization, and so on" (Ceci & Liker, 1986b, p. 139) that are funneled into specific expressions of intelligence according to experience and motivation. Thus, a more stringent test of the existence of independent context-specific manifestations of intelligence would be to correlate prediction performance/complexity with (IQ) subtest scores. For example, it would be interesting to see whether people with different learning test scores differ with respect to learning and transfer on the stock market task.

Criterion 3. The direction of the presumed causality must be demonstrated empirically. Because a number of potential moderator variables, such as age, years of experience, and preexisting knowledge, have been taken into account, the Ceci and Ruiz training study can be considered a first step in demonstrating (the lack of) a causal relation between IQ and the acquisition of complex problem solving. Of course, methodological shortcomings such as small sample size and possible floor effects regarding learning and problem-solving performance demand replication. Moreover, the empirically demonstrated lack of a global IQ effect does not tell us much about (a) whether more specific abilities would have had predictive value and (b) how much overlap in content is required for two "ability measures" to be correlated.

In summary, Ceci and colleagues have undertaken an impressive attempt to demonstrate that expertise, defined as people's ability to reason complexly in one domain (i.e., race handicapping), is independent of general intelligence. Expertise has been relatively clearly defined and an attempt has been made to study the cognitive processes involved in successful performance by careful task analysis. Moreover, the training study is the first attempt at assessing causality. However, as amply discussed earlier, correlating global intelligence with CEPS is not particularly informative as to the exact nature of the intellectual abilities underlying problem solving.

IMPLICIT PROBLEM SOLVING

Some recent findings with artificial grammar-learning, sequence-learning, and complex problem-solving tasks all suggest that people are capable of successfully solving problems even when they are not able to verbally express the knowledge they are utilizing (e.g., Frensch & Rünger, 2003). Such findings have led some researchers (e.g., Berry & Broadbent, 1984, 1987; Nissen & Bullemer, 1987; Reber, 1967, 1969) to propose independent learning systems that might underlie performance in a problem-solving task: an explicit learning system and an implicit learning system. The former is thought to be based on deliberate hypothesis testing, to be selective with respect to what is learned, and to lead to consciously accessible and verbalizable knowledge. Implicit learning, on the other hand, has been characterized as involving "the unselective and passive aggregation of information about the co-occurrence of environmental events and features" (Hayes & Broadbent, 1988, p. 251). Thus, implicit learning is assumed to take place irrespective of the intention to learn, to not rely on hypothesis testing, and to lead to implicit (tacit) knowledge that cannot or can only partially be accessed (Frensch, 1998). Furthermore, it has been argued (Reber, Walkenfield, & Hernstadt, 1991; see also Anderson, 1998) that implicit learning is an evolutionarily older, less variable, and more robust ability, suggesting that problem-solving performance that is based on implicit learning might not be correlated with intelligence.

In this section of the chapter we address whether or not this suggestion is correct. Before we do so, however, we briefly describe the tasks that have been used to demonstrate the existence of implicit problem solving and the arguments that have been exchanged between proponents and opponents of the implicit-learning assumption.

The Tasks Used

The dynamic scenario most often used in the studies reported below consists of a simple linear equation relating one input variable to an output variable, also taking into account the previous output. In addition, in most studies a random component is added on two-thirds of the trials, such that on these trials the system changes to a state one unit above or below the state that would be correct according to the deterministic equation. The system is frequently used in one or both of two semantic versions, the Sugar Factory and the Computer Person. When controlling the Sugar Factory, problem solvers are required to reach and maintain specified levels of sugar output by varying the number of workers employed. In the Computer Person task, problem solvers enter attitude adjectives (e.g., "friendly" or "polite") from a fixed adjective set in order to get the computer person to display a specified behavior (e.g., "very friendly").

A second task that is frequently used is the City Transportation system. This task is similar to the linear equation systems described in the previous section in that two variables (free parking slots and number of people taking the bus) need to be adjusted by varying two exogenous variables (time schedule for buses and parking fee). In the majority of studies, problem solvers are asked to control the system from the beginning (i.e., there is no exploration phase). In addition, instructions and/or system features are varied. After controlling the system for a while, problem solvers are probed for their structural knowledge. This is usually done with the help of multiple-choice questionnaires that require problem solvers to predict outcomes, given a specified previous output and novel input. The experimental approach thus differs from the standard procedure of the studies discussed in the previous section in that (a) the systems are usually less complex in terms of the underlying variables and relations, (b) problem solvers are typically not allowed to explore the system before they are asked to reach specified target values, and (c) problem solvers are usually not probed for their structural knowledge before they have completed the experiment.

Empirical Evidence Supporting the Assumption of an Implicit Learning System

Empirical evidence supporting the existence of an implicit learning system mainly comes from two types of dissociations: (1) dissociations between problem-solving performance and questionnaire answers and (2) differential effects on problem-solving performance when systems are controlled that are assumed to engage different learning systems.

For instance, Berry and Broadbent (1984), using both the Sugar Factory and the Computer Person task, found that problem-solving performance improved with practice (two vs. one block of practice), but that structural knowledge was unaffected. Furthermore, correlations between problem-solving performance and knowledge tended to be negative. In contrast, informing problem solvers about the rules of the system after the first practice block improved structural knowledge but did not affect performance. Again, no positive correlations between problem-solving performance and knowledge emerged.

Berry and Broadbent (1987, 1988) demonstrated that this type of dissociation critically depends on the salience of the relations among variables. In their 1988 study, salience was manipulated by varying feedback delay in the Computer Person task. In the salient version, the output depended on the input of the current trial. In contrast, in the nonsalient version, the output was determined by the problem solver's input on the preceding trial. Berry and Broadbent assumed that nonsalient tasks would induce implicit learning, whereas the easier salient task would be learned explicitly. The authors reported that performance improved with practice for both task versions, although performance on the salient task was generally better than on the nonsalient task. More interestingly, instructions to search for systematic relations between variables improved performance for the group working on the salient task, but impaired performance in the nonsalient group. Moreover, structural knowledge scores were higher in the salient group than in the nonsalient group, and correlations between knowledge and problem-solving performance tended to be somewhat higher in the salient group (yet none of the correlations reached significance).

The nature of the underlying relations also seems to affect the ability to transfer knowledge to novel situations (Berry & Broadbent, 1988; Hayes & Broadbent, 1988). Hayes and Broadbent found that a change in the equation after an initial learning phase impaired problem-solving performance in the nonsalient condition of the Computer Person, but not in the salient condition. More dramatically, however, this pattern of results reversed when problem solvers worked under dual-task conditions (i.e., when they performed a concurrent random letter generation task). That is, when a secondary task had to be performed concurrently, relearning was impaired in the salient but not in the nonsalient condition. Based on these and similar results, Berry and Broadbent concluded that two independent learning systems exist, and that the unselective and unintentional implicit-learning mechanism is particularly well suited to dealing with highly complex situations in which deliberate hypothesis testing has little chance of being successful.

Unfortunately, however, not all researchers have empirically obtained such clear-cut dissociations between problem-solving performance and questionnaire answers supporting the existence of two independent learning systems as have Berry and Broadbent (1987, 1988), nor do all researchers agree with Berry and Broadbent's interpretation. For example, Green and Shanks (1993), in an attempt to replicate the Hayes and Broadbent (1988) study, found that problem solvers in the salient and nonsalient conditions were similarly impaired by an equation reversal (transfer), as well as by an equation change under dual-task conditions. Moreover, under dual-task conditions, initial learning was better in the salient than the nonsalient group. Green and Shanks concluded that feedback delay may simply influence task difficulty and hence the amount of knowledge acquired, instead of tapping into two functionally distinct learning systems. When problem solvers who learned nothing or very little during the initial learning phase were included in the analysis, Green and Shanks found that the performance of nonlearners in the nonsalient/dual-task condition improved after the equation change. However, Berry and Broadbent (1995) re-analyzed the Hayes and Broadbent data and could not confirm this latter pattern in their data analysis. Instead, they raised the possibility that differences in instructions may have contributed to these obviously contradictory results.

Although results such as these have led researchers to doubt the existence of two truly independent and possibly antagonistic learning systems, most researchers (e.g., Berry & Broadbent, 1988; Buchner, Funke, & Berry, 1995; Dienes & Fahey, 1995, 1998; Frensch & Rünger, 2003; Stanley et al., 1989) now seem to at least agree that complete and adequate explicit knowledge is not a necessary condition for successful problem solving in complex systems.

Implicit Learning and Intelligence

If indeed, as argued by Reber et al. (1991), implicit learning is an evolutionarily old, less variable, and more robust ability, then it is conceivable that problem-solving performance that is based on implicit learning might not be correlated with intelligence. Reber et al. (1991) were among the first to empirically explore the relation between implicit learning and intelligence.

Reber et al. compared participants' performance on an explicit letter series completion task (i.e., requiring an explicit search for underlying rules) with implicit learning (i.e., a well-formedness judgment) following an artificial grammar learning task. During the learning phase of the artificial grammar learning task, participants were instructed to memorize letter strings produced by a finite state grammar. They were informed about the existence of rules underlying the strings only after the learning phase had ended, that is, before the test phase took place. During the test phase, participants were asked to judge whether a given string corresponded to the rules (i.e., well-formedness task). In order to ensure a common metric for the series completion task and the well-formedness task, performance on the series completion task was assessed via 2-choice response alternatives. In addition, participants were required to explain their choices.

Reber et al. found relatively small individual differences on the well-formedness task as compared to much larger individual differences on the series completion task. This result could be corroborated by a re-analysis of former studies (e.g., Reber, 1976) in which implicit versus explicit learning was manipulated by varying the instruction for the artificial grammar task.

More to the point and much more interesting was the fact that Reber et al. (1991) could show that participants' WAIS scores correlated only weakly and nonsignificantly with performance on the well-formedness task ($r = .25$). Thus, implicit learning did not correlate significantly with IQ.

Recently, McGeorge, Crawford, and Kelly (1997) replicated and extended the earlier findings from Reber et al. (1991) in interesting ways. First, a factor analysis showed that while the correlation between performance on the implicit task and overall IQ was not significant ($r = .12$), there was a small but statistically reliable correlation between implicit learning and the perceptual organization factor ($r = .19$). Interestingly, this factor is the one most clearly associated with fluid intelligence. Second, there were no differences in performance on the implicit task with increasing age.

Using a somewhat different implicit-learning type task, Zacks, Hasher, and Sanft (1982) reported no difference in frequency encoding for students from a university with median verbal Scholastic Aptitude Test (SAT) scores of 610 and those from a school with median verbal SAT scores of 471.

Furthermore, Maybery, Taylor, and O'Brien-Malone (1995) found that performance on an implicit contingency detection task was not related to IQ ($r = .02$ and $.04$ for children in grades 1–2 and 6–7, respectively). Also, the children in these studies showed no association between their success on the implicit task and actual verbalized knowledge of the contingency tested ($r = .05$ for both groups). Interestingly, the low correlations between implicit learning and IQ seem not to have been due to lack of variation in implicit functioning. That is, there were individual differences in implicit learning, but these were not related to the differences obtained on the IQ measure. Also of interest is the fact that performance on the implicit tasks increased systematically with age.

Unfortunately, in more recent work, Fletcher, Maybery, and Bennett (2000) were not able to replicate their earlier findings. Comparing twenty children with intellectual disability (mean mental age = approximately 5.8 years) with intellectually gifted children (mean mental age = approximately 12.4 years) of similar chronological age (approximately 9.5 years), the authors found that implicit learning varied with intellectual level. It is unclear at present why the earlier and the more recent studies using essentially the same methodology yielded conflicting results.

In a somewhat different and yet related area of research, Ellis and colleagues found that individuals identified as retarded often display intact incidental learning. In the first of their studies, Ellis, Katz, and Williams (1987) found that mildly retarded adolescents, normal children, and normal adults were all equivalent in incidental learning of location. As with the studies discussed before, individual differences were obtained but were unrelated to gross measures of high-level cognitive functioning.

Ellis and Allison (1988) painted a more complex picture. Incidental learning of frequency of occurrence was equivalent for mildly retarded adolescents and college students, but only for visual information. While many individuals with a diagnosis of retardation displayed normal incidental learning of verbal-semantic material, several such individuals did not. The findings suggest that uncontrolled, unintentional learning processes show little age and IQ variation when visual-spatial or noncomplex materials are used, but that individual differences might emerge in processing of verbal or complex materials. Anderson (1998) recently reviewed research into related phenomena, arguing that variation in IQ is associated primarily with variations in mechanisms that are amenable to conscious control and reflection.

On the whole, although the implicit learning tasks used by Reber and colleagues cannot necessarily be considered CPS tasks, the typically obtained null findings are nevertheless interesting because they point to the possibility that implicit and explicit problem-solving competence might rely on different intellectual abilities.

Evaluation of Approach

Criterion 1. Problem-solving competence and intelligence need to be explicitly defined and must not overlap at theoretical and/or operational levels. In most studies using implicit learning tasks, structural knowledge was assessed separately from problem-solving performance. Concerning theoretical independence, the concepts of implicit and explicit learning were defined independently of each other; thus, one may argue that – at least according to the original assumptions – no theoretical overlap exists.

Unfortunately, none of the studies reviewed in the present section reported reliabilities, neither for performance indicators nor for the questionnaires. Given the assumptions regarding the nature of the two learning mechanisms and the evidence regarding changes in learning/knowledge with practice, it would not make much sense to assess retest reliability. There is indirect evidence, however, that parallel-test reliability may not be very high. For example, several researchers (e.g., Stanley et al., 1989) have reported that problem solvers are better at controlling the Computer Person than the Sugar Factory task although the structure of the two tasks is identical. This, again, points to the impact of semantic embedding and of prior knowledge that is brought to the task, which may differ across individuals and domains.

Criterion 2. The presumed relation between intellectual ability and problem-solving competence must have a theoretical explanation. The proposal that an implicit learning mechanism might contribute to complex problem solving and is functionally dissociable from explicit learning is an exciting one because most work on abilities and individual differences has exclusively concentrated on explicit/conscious cognition. Unfortunately, however, convincing evidence for truly independent learning mechanisms does not exist at the present time (Frensch & Rünger, 2003). Rather, recent work suggests that what differs might not be learning per se, but the processing of study episodes. It may well be the case that the processing induced by different task demands correlates with different subtests of traditional intelligence tests and/or learning tests. Clearly, better definitions of critical task-related concepts such as "salience" and more thorough accounts of which processing requirements and abilities are afforded by certain task characteristics are needed in order to gain a better understanding of the abilities underlying implicit complex problem solving.

Criterion 3. The direction of the presumed causality must be demonstrated empirically. Evidence for a causal influence of an implicit learning mechanism on complex problem solving does not exist at the present time. However, some work (e.g., Geddes & Stevenson, 1997; Stanley et al., 1989; Vollmeyer,

Burns, & Holyoak, 1996) suggests that task demands encourage the use of particular strategies, which in turn affect what is being learned (see Wenke & Frensch, 2003, for a more extensive discussion of this argument). Of course, more work including experimental strategy induction as well as training, in combination with between-group designs, is necessary to gain a more complete understanding of strategic abilities. In addition, these study should address the issues of (a) semantic embeddedness and its influence on the mental models problem solvers bring to the task and (b) factors that lead to potential strategy shifts in the course of practice (e.g., chunking), or when working with enlarged solution spaces.

SUMMARY AND CONCLUSIONS

The main goal of the present chapter was to discuss to what extent, if indeed at all, individual differences in complex problem-solving competence are related to individual differences in intelligence. In the first section of the chapter we provided a definition of "complex problem solving." In the second and third sections, we evaluated much of the empirical work that relates complex problem-solving competence to some measure of intelligence with regard to three evaluation criteria. Two forms of problem solving were distinguished. In the second section, we focused on explicit problem solving, which is controlled by a problem solver's intentions. In the third section, our focus was on implicit, that is, automatic or nonconscious, complex problem solving.

Our main conclusions are as follows. First, no convincing empirical evidence exists that would support a relation, let alone a causal relation, between complex explicit or implicit problem-solving competence, on the one hand, and global intelligence on the other hand. It is important to emphasize, again, that this conclusion is one that is based upon a lack of evidence, not necessarily a lack of theoretical relation. That is, we do not deny the theoretical possibility that a relation between global intelligence and CPS competence might exist; we argue only that there exists no convincing empirical evidence to date that would support such a relation. Nevertheless, the evidence reviewed in this chapter is consistent with a wealth of empirical findings on the relation between intelligence and simple problem solving that suggest that even when a relation between intelligence and problem-solving competence is obtained, it is quite modest in size (e.g., Sternberg, 1982).

Second, however, a considerable amount of empirical data suggest that specific components of intelligence, such as processing capacity, might be related to specific components of explicit complex problem solving. To what extent a similar conclusion might be warranted for implicit complex problem solving remains to be seen; the available research has thus far not addressed this specific question.

On the whole then, the available evidence suggests that the global concepts of intelligence and problem solving are not related, but that specific subcomponents of intelligence and explicit problem solving might share variance. The existing empirical evidence does not speak, unfortunately, to the issue of whether subcomponents of intelligence predict subcomponents of problem solving or whether the opposite causal relation holds; the empirical designs used simply cannot answer this question.

The conclusions have two important consequences. First, the intellectual abilities investigated thus far are frequently too coarse, too general, and too abstract to allow a prediction of inter-individual differences in complex problem-solving competence; what is clearly needed in future research is a focus on much more specific and narrower intellectual abilities that more closely capture the cognitive system's architecture and functioning.

Second, from the empirical evidence that is currently available, it appears that the relation between intelligence and complex problem-solving performance might be moderated by a complex interaction between individuals, tasks, and situations. Thus, the future task will not be to find correlations between intelligence and problem solving, but rather to find out when which kind of relation holds. More exact experimental assessments of specific subcomponents of the relevant concepts along with longitudinal designs that assess causal directionality are a sine qua non if we will ever have a chance to find out whether individual differences in intelligence cause individual differences in complex problem-solving ability or whether the opposite is true.

References

Amthauer, R., Brocke, B., Liepmann, D., & Beauducel, A. (1973). *Intelligence Structure Test (IST 70)*. Göttingen: Hogrefe.

Anderson, J. R., Boyle, C. B., & Reiser, B. J. (1985). Intelligent tutoring systems. *Science, 228,* 456–462.

Anderson, M. (1998). Individual differences in intelligence. In K. Kirsner, C. Speelman, M. Maybery, A. O'Brien-Malone, M. Anderson, & C. MacLeod (Eds.), *Implicit and explicit processes* (pp. 171–185). Mahwah, NJ: Erlbaum.

Anzai, K., & Simon, H. A. (1979). The theory of learning by doing. *Psychological Review, 86,* 124–140.

Beckmann. (1995). *Lernen und komplexes Problemlösen. Ein Beitrag zur Validierung von Lerntests [Learning and problem solving. A contribution to validate learning potential tests].* Bonn: Holos.

Beckmann, J. F., & Guthke, J. (1995). Complex problem solving, intelligence, and learning ability. In P. A. Frensch & J. Funke (Eds.), *Complex problem solving. The European perspective* (pp. 3–25). Hillsdale, NJ: Erlbaum.

Berry, D. C., & Broadbent, D. E. (1984). On the relationship between task performance and associated verbalizable knowledge. *Quarterly Journal of Experimental Psychology, 36A,* 209–231.

Berry, D. C., & Broadbent, D. E. (1987). The combination of explicit and implicit learning processes in task control. *Psychological Research, 49*, 7–15.

Berry, D. C., & Broadbent, D. E. (1988). Interactive tasks and the implicit–explicit distinction. *British Journal of Psychology, 79*, 251–272.

Berry, D. C., & Broadbent, D. E. (1995). Implicit learning in the control of complex systems. In P. A. Frensch & J. Funke (Eds.), *Complex problem solving. The European perspective* (pp. 3–25). Hillsdale, NJ: Erlbaum.

Bhaskar, R., & Simon, H. A. (1977). Problem solving in semantically rich domains: An example from engineering thermodynamics. *Cognitive Science, 1*, 193–215.

Broadbent, D. E. (1977). Levels, hierarchies, and the locus of control. *Quarterly Journal of Experimental Psychology, 29*, 181–201.

Buchner, A. (1995). Basic topics and approaches to the study of complex problem solving. In P. A. Frensch & J. Funke (Eds.), *Complex problem solving. The European perspective* (pp. 27–63). Hillsdale, NJ: Erlbaum.

Buchner, A. (1999). Komplexes Problemlösen vor dem Hintergrund der Theorie finiter Automaten [Complex problem solving viewed from the theory of finite state automata]. *Psychologische Rundschau, 50*, 206–212.

Buchner, A., Funke, J., & Berry, D. (1995). Negative correlations between control performance and verbalizable knowledge: Indicators for implicit learning in process control tasks? *Quarterly Journal of Experimental Psychology, 48A*, 166–187.

Cattell, R. B., & Weiss, R. H. (1980). *Culture Fair Intelligence Test, Scale 3 (CFT3)*. Göttingen: Hogrefe.

Ceci, S. J., & Liker, J. K. (1986a). A day at the races: A study of IQ, expertise, and cognitive complexity. *Journal of Experimental Psychology: General, 115*, 255–266.

Ceci, S. J., & Liker, J. K. (1986b). Academic and nonacademic intelligence: An experimental separation. In R. J. Sternberg & R. K. Wagner (Eds.), *Practical intelligence* (pp. 119–142). Cambridge, UK: Cambridge University Press.

Ceci, S. J., & Liker, J. K. (1988). Stalking the IQ–expertise relation: When critics go fishing. *Journal of Experimental Psychology: General, 117*, 96–100.

Ceci, S. J., & Ruiz, A. (1992). The role of general ability in cognitive complexity: A case study of expertise. In R. R. Hoffmann (Ed.), *The psychology of expertise: Cognitive research and empirical AI* (pp. 218–230). New York: Springer.

Ceci, S. J., & Ruiz, A. (1993). Transfer, abstractness, and intelligence. In D. K. Detterman & R. J. Sternberg (Eds.), *Transfer on trial: Intelligence, cognition, and instruction* (pp. 168–191). Norwood, NJ: Ablex.

Chase, W. G., & Simon, H. A. (1973). Perception in chess. *Cognitive Psychology, 4*, 55–81.

Chi, M. T. H., Feltovich, P. J., & Glaser, R. (1981). Categorization and representation of physics problems by experts and novices. *Cognitive Science, 5*, 121–152.

Detterman, D. K., & Spry, K. M. (1988). Is it smart to play the horses? Comment on "A day at the races: A study of IQ, expertise, and cognitive complexity" (Ceci & Liker, 1986). *Journal of Experimental Psychology: General, 117*, 91–95.

Dienes, Z., & Fahey, R. (1995). The role of specific instances in controlling a dynamic system. *Journal of Experimental Psychology: Learning, Memory, & Cognition, 21*, 848–862.

Dienes, Z., & Fahey, R. (1998). The role of implicit memory in controlling a dynamic system. *Quarterly Journal of Experimental Psychology, 51A*, 593–614.

Dörner, D. (1975). Wie Menschen eine Welt verbessern wollten [How people wanted to improve a world]. *Bild der Wissenschaft, 12*, 48–53.

Dörner, D. (1980). On the difficulty people have in dealing with complexity. *Simulation & Games, 11*, 87–106.

Dörner, D. (1986). Diagnostik der operativen Intelligenz [Assessment of operative intelligence]. *Diagnostica, 32*, 290–308.

Dörner, D., & Kreuzig, H. W. (1983). Problemlösefähigkeit und Intelligenz [Problem solving and intelligence]. *Psychologische Rundschau, 34*, 185–192.

Dörner, D., & Wearing, A. (1995). Complex problem solving: Toward a (computer simulated) theory. In P. A. Frensch & J. Funke (Eds.), *Complex problem solving: The European perspective* (pp. 65–99). Hillsdale, NJ: Erlbaum.

Dörner, D., Kreuzig, H. W., Reither, F., & Stäudel, T. (1983). *Lohhausen. Vom Umgang mit Unbestimmtheit und Komplexität [Lohhausen. On dealing with uncertainty and complexity]*. Bern, Switzerland: Hans Huber.

Duncker, K. (1935/1974). *Zur Psychologie des produktiven Denkens* [On productive thinking]. Berlin: Julius Springer.

Ellis, N. R., & Allison, P. (1988). Memory for frequency of occurrence in retarded and nonretarded persons. *Intelligence, 12*, 61–75.

Ellis, N. R., Katz, E., & Williams, J. E. (1987). Developmental aspects of memory for spatial location. *Journal of Experimental Child Psychology, 44*, 401–412.

Ewert, P. H., & Lambert, J. F. (1932). The effect of verbal instructions upon the formation of a concept. *Journal of General Psychology, 6*, 400–413.

Fletcher, J., Maybery, M. T., & Bennett, S. (2000). Implicit learning differences: A question of developmental level? *Journal of Experimental Psychology: Learning, Memory, and Cognition, 26*, 246–252.

Frensch, P. A. (1998). One concept, multiple meanings. On how to define the concept of implicit learning. In M. A. Stadler & P. A. Frensch (Eds.), *Handbook of implicit learning*. Thousand Oaks, CA: Sage.

Frensch, P. A., & Funke, J. (1995). Definitions, traditions, and a general framework for understanding complex problem solving. In P. A. Frensch & J. Funke (Eds.), *Complex problem solving. The European perspective* (pp. 3–25). Hillsdale, NJ: Erlbaum.

Frensch, P. A., & Rünger, D. (2003). Implicit learning. *Current Directions in Psychological Science, 12*, 13–18.

Funke, J. (1983). Einige Bermerkungen zu Problemen der Problemlöseforschung oder: Ist Testintelligenz doch ein Prädiktor [Some remarks on the problems of problem solving research or: Does test intelligence predict control performance?]. *Diagnostica, 29*, 283–302.

Funke, J. (1984). Diagnose der westdeutschen Problemlöseforschung in Form einiger Thesen [Assessment of West German problem solving research]. *Sprache & Kognition, 3*, 159–172.

Funke, J. (1991). Solving complex problems: Exploration and control of complex systems. In R. J. Sternberg & P. A. Frensch (Eds.), *Complex problem solving: Principles and mechanisms* (pp. 185–222). Hillsdale, NJ: Erlbaum.

Funke, J. (1995). Experimental research on complex problem solving. In P. A. Frensch & J. Funke (Eds.), *Complex problem solving: The European perspective* (pp. 243–268). Hillsdale, NJ: Erlbaum.

Funke, J. (2001). Dynamic systems as tools for analysing human judgement. *Thinking and Reasoning, 7*, 69–89.

Geddes, B. W., & Stevenson, R. J. (1997). Explicit learning of a dynamic system with a non-salient pattern. *Quarterly Journal of Experimental Psychology, 50A*, 742–765.

Green, R. E., & Shanks, D. R. (1993). On the existence of independent explicit and implicit learning systems: An examination of some evidence. *Memory & Cognition, 21*, 304–317.

Greve, W. (2001). Traps and gaps in action explanation. Theoretical problems of a psychology of human action. *Psychological Review, 108*, 435–451.

Guthke, J., Jäger, C., & Schmidt, I. (1983). *LTS: Learning Test Battery "Reasoning."* Berlin: Humboldt-Universität zu Berlin, Institut für Psychologie.

Hayes, N. A., & Broadbent, D. E. (1988). Two modes of learning for interactive tasks. *Cognition, 28*, 249–276.

Hesse, F. W. (1982). Effekte des semantischen Kontexts auf die Bearbeitung komplexer Probleme [Effects of semantic context on problem solving]. *Zeitschrift für Experimentelle und Angewandte Psychologie, 29*, 62–91.

Hörmann, J. J., & Thomas, M. (1989). Zum Zusammenhang zwischen Intelligenz und komplesem Problemlösen [On the relationship between intelligence and complex problem solving]. *Sprache & Kognition, 8*, 23–31.

Howe, M. J. (1988). Intelligence as an explanation. *British Journal of Psychology, 79*, 349–360.

Howe, M. J. A. (1996). Concepts of ability. In I. Dennis & P. Tapsfield (Eds.), *Human abilities. Their nature and their measurement* (pp. 39–48). Mahwah, NJ: Erlbaum.

Hussy, W. (1989). Intelligenz und komplexes Problemlösen [Intelligence and complex problem solving]. *Diagnostica, 35*, 1–16.

Hussy, W. (1991). Problemlösen und Verarbeitungskapazität [Complex problem solving and processing capacity]. *Sprache & Kognition, 10*, 208–220.

Jäger, A. O. (1982). Mehrmodale Klassifikation von Intelligenzleistungen [Multimodal classification of intelligent performance]. *Diagnostica, 28*, 195–225.

Jäger, A. O., Süß, H.-M., & Beauducel, A. (1997). *Berliner Intelligenzstrukturtest. BIS-Test, Form 4* [Berlin Intelligence Structure Test, Manual]. Göttingen: Hogrefe.

Kersting, M. (1999). Diagnostik und Personalauswahl mit computergestützten Problemlöseszenarien? Zur Kriteriumsvalidität von Problemlöseszenarien und Intelligenztests [Assessment and personnel selection with computer simulated problem-solving scenarios? On the validity of problem-solving scenarios and intelligence tests]. Göttingen: Hogrefe.

Kersting, M., & Süß, H.-M. (1995). Kontentvalide Wissensdiagnostik und Problemlösen: Zur Entwicklung, testtheoretischen Begründung und empirischen Bewährung eines problemspezifischen Diagnoseverfahrens [Content-validity of knowledge assessment and problem-solving: Development, psychometric foundation, and empirical assessment of a problem-specific assessment instrument]. *Zeitschrift für Pädagogische Psychologie, 9*, 83–93.

Kluwe, R. H., Misiak, C., & Haider, H. (1991a). Systems and performance in intelligence tests. In H. Rowe (Ed.), *Intelligence: Reconceptualization and measurement* (pp. 227–244). Hillsdale, NJ: Erlbaum.

Kluwe, R. H., Schilde, A., Fischer, C., & Oellerer, N. (1991b). Problemlöseleistungen beim Umgang mit komplexen Systemen und Intelligenz [Problem solving performance when interacting with complex systems and intelligence]. *Diagnostica, 37*, 291–313.

Kray, J., & Frensch, P. A. (2001). A view from cognitive psychology: "g" – (G)host in the correlation matrix? In R. J. Sternberg & E. E. Grigorenko (Eds.), *The general factor of intelligence: Fact or fiction?* Hillsdale, NJ: Erlbaum.

Maybery, M., Taylor, M., & O'Brien-Malone, A. (1995). Implicit learning: Sensitive to age but not IQ. *Australian Journal of Psychology, 47,* 8–17.

Mayer, R. E. (1992). *Thinking, problem solving, cognition.* Second ed. New York: Freeman.

McGeorge, P., Crawford, J. R., & Kelly, S. W. (1997). The relationships between psychometric intelligence and learning in an explicit and an implicit task. *Journal of Experimental Psychology: Learning, Memory, & Cognition, 23,* 239–245.

Müller, H. (1993). *Komplexes Problemlösen: Reliabilität und Wissen [Complex problem solving: Reliability and knowledge].* Bonn: Holos.

Newell, A., & Simon, H. A. (1972). *Human information processing.* Englewood Cliffs, NJ: Prentice-Hall.

Nissen, M. J., & Bullemer, P. (1987). Attentional requirements of learning: Evidence from performance measures. *Cognitive Psychology, 19,* 1–32.

Putz-Osterloh, W. (1981). Über die Beziehung zwischen Testintelligenz und Problemlöseerfolg [On the relationship between test intelligence and success in problem solving]. *Zeitschrift für Psychologie, 189,* 79–100.

Putz-Osterloh, W. (1993). Strategies for knowledge acquisition and transfer of knowledge in dynamic tasks. In G. Strube & K. F. Wender (Eds.), *The cognitive psychology of knowledge* (pp. 331–350). Amsterdam: Elsevier.

Putz-Osterloh, W., & Haupts, I. (1989). Zur Reliabilität und Validität computergestützter Diagnostik komplexer Organisations-und Entscheidungsstrategien [On the reliability and validity of computer-based assessment of complex organizational and decision strategies]. *Untersuchungen des Psychologischen Dienstes der Bundeswehr, 24,* 5–48.

Putz-Osterloh, W., & Lüer, G. (1981). Über die Vorhersagbarkeit komplexer Problemlöseleistungen durch Ergebnisse in einem Intelligenztest [On the predictability of complex problem solving performance by intelligence test scores]. *Zeitschrift für Experimentelle und Angewandte Psychologie, 28,* 309–334.

Raven, J. C., Court, J. & Raven, J., Jr. (1980). *Advanced Progressive Matrices (APM).* Weinheim: Beltz.

Reber, A. S. (1967). Implicit learning of artificial grammars. *Journal of Verbal Learning and Verbal Behavior, 77,* 317–327.

Reber, A. S. (1969). Transfer of syntactic structure in synthetic languages. *Journal of Experimental Psychology, 81,* 115–119.

Reber, A. S. (1976). Implicit learning and tacit knowledge. *Journal of Experimental Psychology: Human Learning and Memory, 2,* 88–94.

Reber, A. S., Walkenfield, F. F., & Hernstadt, R. (1991). Implicit and explicit learning: Individual differences and IQ. *Journal of Experimental Psychology. Learning, Memory, and Cognition, 17,* 888–896.

Stanley, W. B., Mathews, R. C., Buss, R. R., & Kotler-Cope, S. (1989). Insight without awareness: On the interaction of verbalization, instruction, and practice in a simulated process control task. *Quarterly Journal of Experimental Psychology, 41A,* 553–577.

Sternberg, R. J. (1982). Reasoning, problem solving, and intelligence. In R. J. Sternberg (Ed.), *Handbook of human intelligence* (pp. 225–307). Cambridge, UK: Cambridge University Press.

Sternberg, R. J. (1995). Expertise in complex problem solving: A comparison of alternative conceptions. In P. A. Frensch & J. Funke (Eds.), *Complex problem solving: The European perspective* (pp. 295–321). Hillsdale, NJ: Erlbaum.

Sternberg, R. J., & Berg, C. A. (1986). Quantitative integration: Definitions of intelligence: A comparison of the 1921 and 1986 symposia. In R. J. Sternberg & D. K. Detterman (Eds.), *What is intelligence? Contemporary viewpoints on its nature and definition* (pp. 155–162). Norwood, NJ: Ablex.

Sternberg, R. J., & Frensch, P. A. (Eds.). (1991). *Complex problem solving: Principles and mechanisms.* Hillsdale, NJ: Erlbaum.

Sternberg, R. J., Nokes, C., Geissler, P. W., Prince, R., Okatcha, F., Bundy, D. A., & Grigorenko, E. L. (2001). The relationship between academic and practical intelligence: A case study in Kenya. *Intelligence, 29,* 401–418.

Strohschneider, S. (1986). Zur Stabilität und Validität von Handeln in komplexen Realitätsbereichen [On the stability and validity of complex problem-solving behavior]. *Sprache & Kognition, 5,* 42–48.

Strohschneider, S. (1991). Problemlösen und Intelligenz: Über die Effekte der Konkretisierung komplexer Probleme [Complex problem solving and intelligence: On the effects of problem concreteness]. *Diagnostica, 37,* 353–371.

Süß, H. M., Kersting, M., & Oberauer, K. (1991). Intelligenz und Wissen als Prädiktoren für Leistungen bei computersimulierten komplexen Problemen [Intelligence and knowledge as predictors of performance in solving complex computer-simulated problems]. *Diagnostica, 37,* 334–352.

Süß, H.-M., Kersting, M., & Oberauer, K. (1993). Zur Vorhersage von Steuerungsleistungen an computersimulierten Systemen durch Wissen und Intelligenz [Predicting control performance in computer-simulated systems by means of knowledge and intelligence]. *Zeitschrift für Differentielle und Diagnostische Psychologie, 14,* 189–203.

Vollmeyer, R., Burns, B. D., & Holyoak, K. J. (1996). The impact of goal specificity on strategy use and the acquisition of problem structure. *Cognitive Science, 20,* 75–100.

Wenke, D., & Frensch, P. A. (2003). Is success or failure at solving complex problems related to intellectual ability? In J. E. Davidson & R. J. Sternberg (Eds.), *The nature of problem solving* (pp. 87–126). New York: Cambridge University Press.

Zacks, R. T., Hasher, L., & Sanft, H. (1982). Automatic encoding of event frequency: Further findings. *Journal of Experimental Psychology: Learning, Memory, & Cognition, 8,* 106–116.

10

Intelligence as Smart Heuristics

Markus Raab and Gerd Gigerenzer

"The great end of life is not knowledge but action."

Thomas H. Huxley (1825–1895)

Humans and other animals differ in the amount of intelligence ascribed to them or that can be tested. Observed behavior reflects the underlying cognitive abilities of the individual that are either thought of as a general device system or a system of more or less independent parts. On this continuum, the view of intelligence as *fast and frugal heuristics* orientates toward a concept that models intelligence as parts (tools) of a larger system (*adaptive toolbox*). This view departs from the notion of intelligence as an assembly of "factors": either one (*g*), a few, or many. The idea that one could model the intelligence of a person by the values of one or several factors became prominent after the invention of factor analysis, a statistical tool, in the early twentieth century. A key problem with this tool-driven metaphor of intelligence is that it does not describe how cognition translates into behavior. The consequence of this missing link is that the usefulness of factor values to predict behavior is quite limited (Sternberg, Grigorenko, & Bundy, 2001). More importantly, the exclusive focus on paper-and-pencil tasks has estranged the notion of intelligence from the abilities and heuristics that are relevant for everyday behavior as well as for solving the problems that experts struggle with.

In this chapter, we propose a radically different view of intelligence that links cognition with behavior in terms of heuristics. A heuristic is a mental device that can solve a class of problems in situations with limited knowledge and time. Unlike an IQ value or a set of values on several intelligence factors, models of heuristics describe mechanisms or processes with which people solve problems. Because there are many classes of problems that confront humans, there are many heuristics, each one adapted to a specific class. However, these heuristics are composed of a smaller number of building blocks, the set of which we call the adaptive toolbox. The relation between heuristics and building blocks is analogous to the relation between chemical elements and subatomic particles: There are many heuristics, just as there are a large number of elements, but they are made of only a few building blocks, such as protons and electrons.

The vision of intelligence as an adaptive toolbox embodies an ecological and social view of rationality, not a logical one. The goal of the research program is (a) to describe the building blocks and heuristics, that is, the content of the adaptive toolbox; (b) to describe the problem structures or environments in which various heuristics can be successful, that is, the ecological rationality of heuristics; and (c) to determine individual differences in the use of heuristics. The program is outlined in Gigerenzer, Todd, and the ABC Research Group (1999) and Gigerenzer and Selten (2001) and has its intellectual roots in the work of Herbert Simon (e.g., 1955, 1956) on bounded rationality. Let us start with three illustrative examples of heuristics.

Recognition Heuristic

Imagine you are a contestant in the show "Who Wants to Be a Millionaire" and face the one-million-dollar question: "Which city has a larger population: San Diego or San Antonio?" If you are as knowledgeable as a group of undergraduates at the University of Chicago, then your chance of winning is not bad: Almost two-thirds of them got the answer right – San Diego. What, however, if you had as little knowledge as a group of German students, who knew scarcely anything about San Diego and had mostly not even heard of San Antonio? When a dozen Germans answered this question, 100% got the answer right (Goldstein & Gigerenzer, 2002). How can it be that people who know less about a subject nevertheless make more correct inferences? The answer is that the Germans used a smart heuristic, the *recognition heuristic*: If you have heard of one city (San Diego) but not the other (San Antonio), infer that the one you recognize by name has the larger population. Note that the Americans could not use this heuristic because they knew too much; they had heard of both cities. The recognition heuristic can be used by people who are partially ignorant, that is, have heard of one but not the other alternative. When British soccer fans want to predict the winner of Manchester United playing Shrewsbury Town, they cannot use the recognition heuristic because they recognize both names, but most Americans know immediately who will win the game. In fact, when Turkish students predicted the outcomes of all the English F.A. Cup third-round soccer games, they followed the recognition heuristic in 95% (627 out of 662) of the cases where they recognized only one of the team's names, and were nearly as accurate as the highly informed British group (Ayton & Önkal, 1997).

Note that the point is not that less knowledge is always better. The point is that we are regularly in situations where we have limited knowledge, and in these situations the recognition heuristic is a smart mind tool for extracting information from ignorance. Note also that the Americans, Germans, British, and Turkish students in these experiments may have a range of IQs, but an IQ does not describe how one solves a problem, nor can the variability in IQs predict the counterintuitive results.

For the general task of inferring which of two objects scores higher on a criterion, the recognition heuristic can be defined as the following: If one of two objects is recognized and the other is not, then infer that the recognized object has the higher value.

The heuristic does not always guarantee the making of good inferences; its success depends on the problem structure, or the structure of the environment. The recognition heuristic is successful when recognition is informative, that is, not random, but positively correlated with the criterion.

The recognition heuristic guides a broad range of behaviors, from selecting brands in the supermarket, buying CDs, and watching movies, to food and habitat choice. People who use the recognition heuristic show two kinds of counterintuitive behavior. First, the recognition heuristic searches only for recognition information, not for recall information, and thus tends to ignore information concerning the recognized object. For instance, Goldstein and Gigerenzer (2002) taught American students a powerful cue for predicting the population of German cities: whether or not a city has a soccer team in the major league. After the training session, the participants (who only learned about soccer teams, whereas the predictive power of name recognition was never mentioned) were tested on critical pairs: one city that they recognized from before the experiment but they had now learned has no soccer team (such as Hanover), and one city that they did not recognize (such as Bielefeld). Participants knew that all cities were among the largest in terms of population. Despite being trained on soccer team information, more than 90% of the participants inferred that the city they recognized had the larger population, thus ignoring the soccer team cue. There is comparative evidence in animals that recognition dominates competing information. For instance, when wild Norway rats choose between two foods, one that they recognize from the breath of a fellow rat and one that they do not recognize, they tend to choose the recognized one, even if the fellow rat is (experimentally made) sick at the time (Galef, 1987; Galef, McQuoid, & Whiskin, 1990).

The second counterintuitive prediction is the *less-is-more effect* (Gigerenzer & Goldstein, 1999). A less-is-more effect occurs when less knowledge leads, with the help of the recognition heuristic, to better inferences than more knowledge would have done. The San Diego question illustrates this effect. Since the recognition heuristic can be easily formalized, one can predict exactly when the less-is-more effect will occur and when it will not. Individual differences in recognition are of utmost importance for these predictions. For instance, when about half of the objects (such as sports teams or stocks) are recognized, then the chances for the less-is-more effect are best.

The recognition heuristic is not the only case where wisdom can emerge from the poorly informed mind. An interesting variant is the situation in which collective wisdom emerges from the poorly informed masses, in honey bees (Seeley & Buhrmann, 2001) as well as in humans. Let us return to "Who Wants to be a Millionaire." You are trying to decide whether Nashville or Knoxville is the capital of Tennessee and you have no idea, but you can appeal to two outside sources for help. You can call the smartest person you know, or you can ask the audience to vote. So whom would you chose: your brainy brother-in-law or a random bunch of loafers who have nothing better to do on a weekday afternoon than sit in a TV studio? The friend gets it right two-thirds of the time, but the audience nine times out of ten. Similarly, when experts predicted that the influx of inexperienced investors would create a situation that the stock market would not be able to absorb, that situation did not happen. The market is smart even when the people within it are dumb.

Gaze Heuristic

Imagine you want to build a robot that can catch balls to play baseball, for instance. (It's a thought experiment – no such robots yet exist.) If you follow a classical artificial intelligence (AI) approach, you will aim to give your robot a complete representation of its environment and the most sophisticated computational machinery. First, you might feed your robot the family of parabolas (because thrown balls have parabolic trajectories). In order to choose the right parabola, the robot needs instruments that can measure the ball's initial distance, its initial velocity, and its projection angle. But in the real world, balls do not fly in true parabolas because of air resistance and wind. Thus, the robot would need additional instruments to measure the wind speed and direction at each point on the ball's flight and compute the resulting path. A true challenge. And there is more: spin and myriad other factors that the robot would have to measure and incorporate into a complete representation.

There is, however, an alternative strategy that does not aim at complete information and representation, but rather at smart heuristics. One method to discover such heuristics is to study actual players. McLeod and Dienes (1996) discovered that experienced players use a simple heuristic, which is the *gaze heuristic*. When a ball comes in high, the player fixates on the ball and starts running. The heuristic is to adjust the running speed so that the angle of gaze, that is, the angle between the eye and the ball, remains constant (or within a certain range). In our thought experiment, a robot that uses this heuristic does not need to measure wind, air resistance, spin, or the other causal variables. It can get away with ignoring this information. All the relevant information is contained in one variable: the angle of gaze. Attending to this one variable alone and ignoring all causal relevant variables is an example of a class of decision rules that are known as one-reason decision making.

Note that the gaze heuristic achieves its goal by transforming the relationship between the eyes of the player and the relevant part of the environment, the moving ball, into a linear line. Like all heuristics, the gaze heuristic is domain-specific, because it can only be used when balls come in high and therefore an angle of gaze exists. Imagine catching a ball as a baseball catcher. Unlike the outfielder, who can use the angle of gaze to catch the flying ball, the catcher is frontally approached by the ball. However, he can use the *time-to-contact heuristic* that looks for retinal image information (search rule) to estimate the time to collision between ball and hand (Hubbard & Seng, 1954). And indeed people mainly use the change in size of the approaching baseball (stopping rule; no further information such as background information is used) to estimate the time when the ball will collide (e.g., Savelsbergh, Whiting, & Bootsma, 1991). Therefore, players preplan their movement (decision rule) on one information source. Pigeons also use this type of information, although not to collide but to avoid collision in the air. This time-to-contact information can be tracked down to the level of neurons (Wang & Frost, 1992), and serves as a prototype example of how mechanisms for even more complex behavior can be described on a low level. Just like the recognition heuristic, the gaze heuristic and the time-to-contact heuristic search only for one piece of information and ignore the rest.

Tit-for-Tat Heuristic

Let us now turn to social intelligence. Two people play a game: Each has two behavioral options, to cooperate with the other, or to "defect." If one cooperates and the other defects, the first is exploited by the second, a situation that can be represented in monetary terms, for example, by stating that the first loses $1 whereas the second gains $3. If neither cooperates, nobody loses and nobody gains anything. If both cooperate, each gains $2. Such a situation is known as the prisoner's dilemma. Standard rational choice theory says that the optimal behavior is for both sides to defect, because whatever the other person does, it is always an advantage to defect. There is, however, a fast and frugal heuristic called *tit-for-tat* that can outperform the "optimal" strategy. In the first round, tit-for-tat always cooperates, that is, it trusts the partner. Thereafter it searches in memory for the partner's response (search rule), memorizes only the last move of the partner (stopping rule), and reciprocates, that is, imitates the partner's behavior (decision rule). In a famous tournament, Axelrod (1984) showed that tit-for-tat outperformed highly sophisticated strategies that analyzed more information about the partner's moves and based their behavior on heavy computational machinery.

Tit-for-tat is a social exchange heuristic that can perform well in environments where other tit-for-tat players exist. It illustrates how simplicity and transparency can lead to highly efficient social behaviors. Together with other social heuristics, such as searching for information that could detect cheaters in social contracts (Cosmides & Tooby, 1992), the view of social intelligence as part of the adaptive toolbox provides, in our opinion, a better basis for understanding the nature of social intelligence than the current program of quantifying social and emotional intelligence by questionnaires and factor values (Gigerenzer, 2000).

THE ADAPTIVE TOOLBOX

These three heuristics and their building blocks illustrate some of the mental tools that underlie intelligent behavior, both social and nonsocial. The adaptive toolbox is, in two respects, a Darwinian metaphor for intelligence. First, evolution does not follow a grand plan, but results in a patchwork of solutions for specific problems. The same holds true for the toolbox: Its heuristics are domain-specific, not general. Second, the heuristics in the adaptive toolbox are not intrinsically good or bad, rational or irrational, but only relative to an environment, just as adaptations are context-bound. In these two restrictions lies their potential: Heuristics can perform astonishingly well when used in a suitable environment. The rationality of the adaptive toolbox is not logical, but rather ecological. In the context of the toolbox, "adaptive" refers to the cognitive abilities that allow us to perform well in our particular (past) environments.

Ecological Rationality

Herbert Simon once compared bounded rationality, that is, intelligent behavior under conditions of limited time and knowledge, to a pair of scissors. One blade is cognition, the other the environment. If one looks at just a single blade, one will not understand how human intelligence works. A football coach who constantly ignores the opponents' line-up when defining the strategy of his own team's attacks will sooner or later be fired. In other words, the structure of the environment and the cognitive heuristics have to match. Putting two knives together, however, does not make a pair of scissors; a heuristic such as *divide and conquer* can only solve complicated problems if they can be decomposed. Fast and frugal heuristics are domain-specific; they succeed in one environment but may fail in another. Computer simulations and mathematical proofs have given us a better understanding of the environmental structures in which specific heuristics operate (Gigerenzer et al., 1999; Martignon & Hoffrage, 2002; Payne, Bettman, & Johnson, 1993). This work has shown that many fast and frugal heuristics, like tit-for-tat, can match or even outperform more complex statistical models in situations ranging from medical decision making to investment choice.

Intelligent behavior needs to satisfy important constraints other than finding the best behavior, including being able to act fast and on the basis of incomplete information. A cartoon illustrates this point. An early Homo sapiens is standing in front of a cave, facing a lion. Our ancestor is calculating the trajectory of the jump and the magnitude of the impulse a lion will have in order to decide what to do. The last picture shows a sated, happy lion. The cartoon makes us smile because its message conflicts with our superego of rational decision making, which demands: Search through all the available information, deduce all the possible consequences, and compute the optimal decision. Intelligent decision making, from this point of view, is based on the ideals of omniscience and optimization. An organism aiming for these heavenly ideals, however, might not survive on Earth. Nevertheless, the majority of rational decision making models in the social, behavioral, and cognitive sciences, as well as in economics, rely on some version of this doctrine. Even when empirical studies show that real human beings cannot live up to it, the doctrine is not abandoned as other models would be, but is instead retained and declared a norm, that is, how we *should* reason. The concept of ecological rationality, however, clarifies that intelligent behavior can be achieved by smart heuristics applied to the proper situations, and that it does not need the fiction of a superintelligence.

Building Blocks

Heuristics, such as the recognition, gaze, and tit-for-tat heuristic, are composed of building blocks. The most important ones are search rules, stopping rules, and decision rules.

Search Rules

There are two kinds of search that intelligent behavior requires: search for alternatives and search for cues. In game shows such as Millionaire, the alternatives are fixed, and one has to search for cues to decide what the correct answer is. Mere name recognition is a minimal cue. When both alternatives are recognized, then the search for cues in memory or in external sources, such as the Internet or a good friend, can be guided by a number of search rules. *Search randomly* is the most simple rule; *try the cues with the highest validity first* is a more promising one (Gigerenzer & Goldstein, 1999). When the alternatives are not known or not fixed a priori, then intelligent behavior has to employ search rules for alternatives. When searching for houses or potential spouses, search can again be more or less random, that is, one happens to encounter possible objects or persons without taking measures that the better options tend to come first, or it can be structured, as in traditional societies where parents, matchmakers, or horoscopes guide the search.

Stopping Rules
Search for cues or alternatives must be stopped at some point. Classical models of optimal search assume that there is a way to compute the optimal stopping point, that is, where the costs of further search exceed its benefits. In the real world, however, such cost–benefit trade-offs are rarely knowable and predictable. Heuristics employ search rules that stop search without explicit cost–benefit computations. For instance, the recognition heuristic stops the search when it has recognized one alternative but not the other. It does not proceed and look up information about the recognized object. In Simon's satisfying heuristic, the search for alternatives (e.g., houses or potential spouses) is stopped when the first alternative that meets a specific aspiration level is encountered (Simon, 1955). If search takes too long, for instance, because the aspiration level of a person is too high, then the aspiration level itself can be lowered (Selten, 2001). More effectively than cognitive rules, emotions such as love can also stop the search, enabling commitment to the loved one.

Decision Rules
A decision rule describes how a decision is made after the search has been stopped. Decision rules define how the information searched and found is used to make a decision. Psychology has a tradition of assuming that intelligent behavior implies weighting and combining cues (e.g., multiple linear regression models), but the research on fast and frugal heuristics has shown that less is often more. The recognition heuristic, the gaze heuristic, and tit-for-tat all employ one-reason decision making, because they rely on only one cue to make the decision and ignore all others.

Domain-Specificity of Heuristics

The heuristics in the adaptive toolbox are domain-specific cognitive abilities. As mentioned before, the domain-specificity of the heuristics is more expressed than that of their building blocks, just as chemical elements are quite distinct and show different processes, yet, as far as we know, consist of the same particles. Thus, domain-specificity must be discussed relative to the level of analysis. The domain definition seems very crucial to determining the specificity of the tools in the toolbox. For instance, eyes may be domain-specific in the sense that they process visual but not acoustic information. On the other hand, we do not have different eyes for different perceptual abilities, such as for locating objects in space or detecting features of objects. However, we know from different locations within the visual cortex that they are specialized to detect the color, shape, or direction of a moving object. Similarly, the same heuristic may be used in different environments. The process that activates the use of one heuristic over another is not well understood today.

At least four arguments favor a domain-specific intelligence that works with fast and frugal heuristics. First, much of intelligence involves going beyond the information given, that is, to make reasonable inferences. Although there are powerful statistical tools for induction, no single statistical method works in every environment (Gigerenzer et al., 1989). In addition, our own intuition tells us that we are often capable of producing smart solutions in one domain but quite stupid ones in another. Second, a general purpose mechanism would run into the well-known problem of computational explosion; that is, even if it were known, it could not work. Even for well-defined problems such as chess, there is no optimal algorithm known, and experts, just like Deep Blue, have to rely on heuristics. This indicates that general purpose notions such as the g factor for intelligence (Jensen, 1998) are doomed to fail in the face of computational complexity. Third, the lesson artificial intelligence designers had to learn when they actually tried to build robots was similar: A general inference machine was not feasible, and designers opted for a number of modules that practiced and orchestrated division of labor, as do the organs in our bodies or a symphony orchestra. The more general an intelligence is, the slower it becomes. Fourth, human intelligence has to achieve more than correct answers to a test, as is obvious when we come to social or emotional intelligence. Domain-specific intelligence can be modeled by modularity of the tools in the adaptive toolbox. The term modular or module has multiple meanings, from Fodor's (1987) ideas that modules consist of the senses plus language, to the evolutionary-based idea that a module is an array of sensory, cognitive, and emotional tools designed to solve important adaptive tasks such as raising children, finding food, and avoiding predators (e.g., Cosmides & Tooby, 1992). The example of catching a ball makes it plausible to argue for sensory intelligence *and* motor modules (see Hossner, 1995; Keele, Jennings, et al., 1995). The modularity hypothesis of social intelligence postulates that modules draw on a number of heuristics as tools and are hierarchically organized (see Gigerenzer, 2000, for a detailed argumentation). In addition, it is plausible to assume that cognitive modules have less hard-wired properties than sensory and motor modules. For instance, the distinction between different sensors and different effectors is easily defined, and concepts such as equilibrium sense can be tracked down to modular entities because of this specific neuronal architecture. Even with the new power of techniques in neuroscience, however, precisely locating the specific networks that are active for cognitive or social problems still seems far away. Due to the less restricted array of modules for cognitive abilities, the modularization is even more interwoven with the environmental system that humans confront.

Social Intelligence

Homo sapiens is one of the few species where genetically unrelated members cooperate in certain tasks. Social intelligence, that is, the ability to handle interactions with others intelligently, has consequently been proposed as the hallmark of human intelligence and one of the defining features of Homo sapiens, together with profound tool use and language. Nevertheless, it is far from clear exactly what entails social intelligence – or Machiavellian intelligence, its exploitive sibling. Again, we argue that the way to find out about social intelligence is to discover and model the actual mechanisms, that is, the heuristics people use when dealing with others. We believe that this is far superior to asking people to answer a questionnaire and to giving them values on "factors" of social intelligence, or a quotient of emotional intelligence. With these numbers, just as with standard intelligence tests, one will never discover what people do when they try to handle others.

The framework of the adaptive toolbox can be applied to unravel social intelligence (Gigerenzer, 1997; Miller & Todd, 1998). This provides precise models and a modular perspective that has different degrees of generality: The building blocks of social intelligence will be fewer but more general than the social heuristics themselves. Table 1 lists examples of social and nonsocial heuristics, their building blocks, and applications.

Tit-for-tat , which we discussed earlier, is a fast and frugal social heuristic. It can handle social exchange situations, such as asking someone for help and offering something in return. There are numerous candidates for social heuristics and building blocks, but they are typically not as clearly defined as tit-for-tat. These include forms of social imitation, known as *follow the crowd* (Boyd & Richerson, 2001; Marsh, 2002). The advantage of such imitation behavior is well understood in animals, for example, in schools of fish (Laland, 2001; Williams, 1996). Growing evidence from a variety of other human imitation behaviors, from childhood to panic behaviors, shows how social imitation can be defined in each context in a variety of domains (Noble & Todd, 2002). Social categorization heuristics, such as judgments about others that either are within the same group (ingroup) or from another group (outgroup), seem to be the rule rather than the exception. The heuristic that a person from the same group is a "good person," and that their information or judgments are accurate, enables fast decisions about a topic based on other persons' information or judgments.

TABLE 1. *Examples of Social and Nonsocial Heuristics, Their Building Blocks, and Applications*

Heuristic	Building Blocks	Applications
Recognition Heuristic	*Search rule:* Look for recognition information *Stopping rule:* If you recognize one option and not the other, stop search *Decision rule:* Infer that the option you recognize has the higher value on the criterion	Answering general knowledge questions; predicting outcomes of sports games (Goldstein & Gigerenzer, 2002); investment decisions; stock picking (Borges et al., 1999)
Gaze Heuristic	Fixate the ball and start running, thereafter: *Search rule:* Look for information concerning the angle of gaze *Stopping rule:* Use the angle of gaze only *Decision rule:* When the angle changes, adjust speed so that the angle remains constant	Catching balls that come in high, as in baseball and cricket (McLeod & Dienes, 1996); avoiding collision in flight; avoiding collisions in sailing
Tit-for-Tat Heuristic	Trust first, thereafter: *Search rule:* Recall information concerning the behavior (cooperation or defection) of your partner *Stopping rule:* Ignore everything except the last behavior of your partner *Decision rule:* Imitate the behavior of your partner	Exchange of goods; international politics; social behavior and trust in dyadic relations (Kollock, 1994; Messick & Liebrand, 1995)
Take-the-First Heuristic	*Search rule:* Generate options in the order of validity *Stopping rule:* Stop after the first option is generated that can be implemented, ignore all the rest *Decision rule:* Take this option	Chess playing (Klein et al., 1995); allocation decisions in ball games
Take-the-Best Heuristic	*Search rule:* First try the recognition heuristic; if both objects are recognized, look up cues in order of their validity *Stopping rule:* Stop search when the first cue is found that has a positive value for one alternative, but not for the other *Decision rule:* Infer that the alternative with the positive cue value has the higher criterion value	Hindsight bias (Hoffrage, Hertwig, & Gigerenzer, 2000); attractiveness judgments of famous men or women; predicting high school dropout rates; homelessness rates; (Czerlinski, Gigerenzer, & Goldstein, 1999)

Again, the specific description of this ingroup–outgroup heuristic is lacking. Is the information from ingroup members just weighted higher than the information from outgroup members, or does it dominate the other information, just as recognition information dominates competing information? We do not know these details, but it seems possible to experimentally test the different ways of how such social heuristics work, once they are precisely formulated. From our standpoint, the starting point is set; that is, we do not expect to find only one general purpose tool, but rather several heuristics for social intelligence. This also has methodological and practical consequences. For instance, if no such general social intelligence exists, there is no point in developing and measuring with a one-dimensional social intelligence test or using a single observation, scale, or another method to detect social intelligence. On the other hand, the modular perspective needs to define a research agenda of how to find proposed heuristics of social intelligence, and how to define environments in which specific heuristics do and do not work, and we are just starting this adventure. We do have proposals: modules for social contracts, threats, precautions, as well as cheating mechanisms (Cosmides, 1989; Gigerenzer & Hug, 1992; Kummer et al., 1997).

Nonsocial Intelligence

Imagine that you are attending a conference and wish to buy a new laser pointer in your free time. The first shop you encounter has two special offers near the entrance. The recognition heuristics would assume that if you recognize one company label (e.g., Sony) and not the other, the Sony laser pointer will be chosen. However, if it happens that both are from Sony, you may continue searching for more information such as the price or size, until you find a difference that favors one laser pointer over the other. A fast and frugal heuristic *take-the-best* can describe this behavior (Gigerenzer & Goldstein, 1999). The heuristic is called take-the-best because it takes the option based on the first cue that favors one option over the other and ignores all other available information. Take-the-best consists of three buildings blocks: rules for searching, stopping, and making a decision. Search for cues is in the order of cue validities (search rule). These validities, which are based on the relative frequency with which a cue predicts the criterion, can be acquired by individual or social learning, or, in the case of some animal species, such as female guppies with regard to mate choice, seem to be genetically coded (Dugatkin, 1996). Search is stopped when the first cue is found on which the two alternatives differ (stopping rule). The alternative with the positive cue value (e.g., lower price, smaller size of the laser pointer) is chosen (decision rule). In experiments conducted by Newell et al. (2004), the searching, stopping, and decision rules of take-the-best are followed in 75% to 92% of all cases (see also Bröder, 2000, 2003; Newell & Shanks, 2003).

In this chapter, we have seen evidence that less information can result in better performance. Whereas the recognition heuristic and the take-the-best heuristic describe how to choose between given alternatives, the *take-the-first* heuristic describes how people generate alternatives from their memory. For instance, in chess it is known that experts can generate a large number of options, but that the first ones generated are often the best options (Klein et al., 1995). Take-the-first describes how options are generated from the memory (Johnson & Raab, 2003). The options are generated by order of their appropriateness in a specific situation. Like take-the-best (where cues are searched for in order of cue validity), take-the-first looks up alternative options by option validity (search rule). In familiar, yet ill-defined tasks, take-the-first chooses one of the initial options, once a goal and strategy have been defined. When generating options in sports, experts generate only a few options (stopping rule) and decide predominantly on the first option that can be implemented (decision rule). Limited search and quick stopping can be beneficial: Experts are not only faster but also more accurate with this fast heuristic, compared to making the choice after generating and giving due consideration to all possible alternatives. For instance, Johnson and Raab (2003) showed experienced handball players a 10-second video sequence from a game, then froze the video and asked the players what option they would take, such as pass right, pass left, or throw at the goal. The results indicated that these players searched for options in order of their appropriateness, generated only a few options, and picked mostly one of the first that was generated. In contrast, when they were asked to generate all possible options and then, after reflection, to pick the one that seemed best, their choices were no longer as appropriate as when they spontaneously picked the first good one that came to mind.

Ecological Rationality

Domain-specific heuristics are designed to work in specific environments. Therefore it is natural that they may not work equally well in another environment. Table 2 gives examples of heuristics and specific environments in which these heuristics fail or succeed. For instance, the recognition heuristic can only be used in situations with partial ignorance, that is, when one object is recognized and the other is not. Using this heuristic is ecologically rational to the degree that recognition is correlated with the criterion; when such a correlation does not exist, it is no longer a promising strategy (although it may not hurt). For instance, although brand-name recognition is typically correlated with quality, firms that invest their money in advertisement that does not give information about the product, but is only intended to increase name recognition, can exploit people's reliance on the

TABLE 2. *Fast and Frugal Heuristics and Examples for Environmental Structures that Enable Good or Poor Performance*

Heuristics	Environments that Enable Good Performance	Environments that Enable Poor Performance
Recognition Heuristic	Positive correlation between recognition and criterion	Zero correlation between recognition and criterion
Gaze Heuristic	Intersection of moving objects for which the angle of gaze changes (relative to a fixed observer)	Intersection of moving objects for which the angle of gaze is constant (relative to a fixed observer)
Tit-for-Tat Heuristic	Mostly tit-for-tat players present; the possibility to exclude noncooperative players by custom or law (Dawkins, 1989; Boyd & Lorberbaum, 1987)	Only defectors present
Take-the-First Heuristic	An environment in which the person is highly trained by feedback, that is, options are automatically generated from memory in the order of validity	An environment in which the person is a novice, that is, options are not generated in the order of validity
Take-the-Best Heuristic	Noncompensatory environments, in which higher-ranking cues cannot be compensated by combinations of lower-ranking cues (Martignon & Hoffrage, 1999)	Compensatory environments, in which higher-ranking cues can be compensated by combinations of lower-ranking cues

recognition heuristic. In an international study of stock picking, the recognition heuristic – based on laypeople's name recognition – outperformed the level of major mutual funds and the market (Borges et al., 1999). The take-the-first heuristic works quite well for experts (e.g., chess masters). However, on the assumption that novices do not have the experience to generate options automatically in order of their appropriateness, take-the-first would not be advantageous at this low level of knowledge.

RELATION TO OTHER APPROACHES

The view of intelligence as an adaptive toolbox with smart heuristics is not a minor variation of the existing theories of intelligence, but represents a radical break with several entrenched ideas. First and most important, all theories that try to capture the nature of intelligence in terms of factor values – one, a few, or many – follow an entirely different conception of intelligence. If one thinks of intelligence as an interaction between the mind and the world, then one needs to model exactly this, and this is what models of heuristics are all about. Factor values are mute about the mechanisms of this interaction. Second, all theories – differential approaches, information processing approaches, and componential approaches (see Sternberg & Kaufman, 2002) – that look at only one blade of Simon's pair of scissors (the cognitive abilities), at the price of ignoring the other blade (the structure of the environment), are hardly compatible with the present approach. Third, approaches that incorporate cognitive abilities and the environment but ignore the domain-specificity (e.g., the person–situation interaction theory of Snow, 1994) can be distinguished from our approach. Fourth, many approaches ignore the evolutionary perspective on intelligence (for examples, see Sternberg, 1999).

Frames of Mind and Multiple Intelligences

Gardner (1983) argues that the notion of relative autonomous cognitive abilities ("multiple intelligences" in his concept) is relevant to understanding the specialized performance of humans in many domains. This domain-specificity is similar to the view of intelligence as smart cognitive heuristics, but with two important differences. First, Gardner's multiple intelligences (e.g., linguistic, spatial, or musical intelligence) are, like most approaches, still partly based on psychometric data. Specifically, the absence of correlations such as those between spatial and verbal abilities (Gardner, Kornhuber, & Wake, 1996) as well as studies from specific populations (e.g., brain-damaged patients, low IQ savants) supports his view of multiple independent intelligences. According to this view, a person can be ascribed high or low musical intelligence, but the heuristics that people actually use when making music, such as how to practice, how to overcome a block or stage fright, how to perform and electrify the audience, and where to find inspiration for composing are not explicated. Second, an evolutionary view on domain-specificity results in important adaptive tasks (e.g., handling social contracts), although not in domains such as Gardner's musical or mathematical intelligences, which seem to be more motivated by university curricula.

The Mind as a Swiss Army Knife

A conception that is a close relative of the view of intelligence as an adaptive toolbox is the modular perspective of intelligence by Cosmides and Tooby (2002). The authors separate dedicated intelligence (systems or programs that are designed for solving a target set of adaptive computational problems) from improvisational intelligence (components that are designed to exploit transient or novel local conditions to achieve adaptive outcomes). The image of the mind as a Swiss Army knife stresses the idea that the mind holds domain-specific rather than general purpose tools. Like the adaptive toolbox, the Swiss Army knife view of intelligence is not based on the factor analysis analogy of mind, but on the actual processes needed to solve important adaptive problems and their modern equivalent. More so than the Swiss Army knife analogy, the concept of the adaptive toolbox brings the possibility for novel combinations of building blocks and nesting heuristics into the foreground. Most important, however, are the models of heuristics and building blocks (Gigerenzer & Selten, 2001; Gigerenzer et al., 1999) that can flesh out the nature of the "Darwinian algorithms" and allow new and sometimes counterintuitive predictions to be deduced.

PROGRAM REVIEW AND FUTURE

To learn more about the view outlined in this chapter, we recommend Gigerenzer, Todd, and the ABC Research Group (1999). Briefly stated, the research program starts with computational models of heuristic candidates in a specific domain, analyzes the environmental structure of this domain, tests the heuristics in real-world environments by means of simulation, and tests whether and when people use these heuristics by means of experiment. This procedure can be varied to the specific problem on hand. Individual differences in the use of heuristics have been documented in a number of situations (e.g., Goldstein & Gigerenzer, 2002; Rieskamp & Hoffrage, 1999).

We would now like to highlight two routes into the future of the program. First, in the beginning of this chapter we extended the notion of cognitive modules to lower-level systems, such as the sensory and motor domains. This extension draws attention to the biological underpinnings of the candidate tools in a toolbox (Duchaine, Cosmides, & Tooby, 2001). An example of this, as demonstrated in this chapter, is the ecological rationality perspective, in which evolutionary accounts may help us find the roots of the intelligent behavior observed nowadays.

Second, neuropsychological evidence may provide further insights into possible instantiations of proposed cognitive heuristics. At a minimum, neuropsychological evidence can help us understand whether different heuristics are biologically alike or different, both qualitatively and quantitatively. For quantitative differences we would expect activation quantity only in the same neuronal circuit, whereas for qualitative differences we would assume to see activation of different neuronal circuits. In addition, the arguments about the amount and kind of domain-specificity versus arguments about domain-generality can also be tested by comparing shared versus nonshared activation in different tasks of nested and nonnested heuristics.

As with every perspective on intelligence, the adaptive toolbox will have its limits. Shepard (2001) speculated that fast and frugal heuristics reflect the nature of ordinary human intelligence, that is, the conscious and sometimes unconscious forms of reasoning and decision making in everyday life. Shepard believes that heuristics cannot do two things: describe the lower cognitive processes, such as those involved in perception, and describe those at the high-level end, the creative processes of scientific discovery. We do not know to what degree Shepard is right; we know of heuristics that work at the lower end, for example, the gaze heuristic and the time-to-contact heuristics. But many evolutionary hard-wired processes seem to need different kinds of models, such as the processes of face perception. The creative processes of artists and scientists are also mostly out of reach for modeling by fast and frugal heuristics, although one might add that they are out of reach of any theory. However, substantial evidence exists for a heuristic that describes the discovery of new theories in the cognitive sciences, the tools-to-theories heuristic (Gigerenzer, 2000).

The adaptive toolbox provides a research agenda of how to study cognitive abilities in terms of smart heuristics. At the same time, it provides an alternative to the notion of human intelligence driven by factor analysis, which bypasses the actual mechanisms with which humans make intelligent or less intelligent decisions.

References

Axelrod, R. M. (1984). *The evolution of cooperation.* New York: Basic Books.

Ayton, P., & Önkal, D. (1997). *Forecasting football fixtures: Confidence and judged proportion correct.* Unpublished manuscript.

Borges, B., Goldstein, D. G., Ortmann, A., & Gigerenzer, G. (1999). Can ignorance beat the stock market? In G. Gigerenzer, P. Todd, & the ABC Research Group (Eds.), *Simple heuristics that make us smart* (pp. 59–74). New York: Oxford University Press.

Boyd, R., & Lorberbaum, J. P. (1987). No pure strategy is evolutionary stable in the repeated prisoner's dilemma game. *Nature, 327,* 58–59.

Boyd, R., & Richerson, P. J. (2001). Norms and bounded rationality. In G. Gigerenzer & R. Selten (Eds.), *Bounded rationality: The adaptive toolbox* (pp. 281–296). Cambridge, MA: MIT Press.

Bröder, A. (2000). Assessing the empirical validity of the "Take-the-Best" heuristic as a model of human probabilistic inference. *Journal of Experimental Psychology: Learning, Memory, and Cognition, 26,* 1332–1346.

Bröder, A. (2003). *Decision making with the adaptive toolbox: Influence of environmental structure, intelligence, and working memory load. Journal of Experimental Psychology: Learning, Memory, and Cognition, 29,* 611–625.

Cosmides, C. (1989). The logic of social exchange: Has natural selection shaped how humans reason? Studies with the Wason selection task. *Cognition, 31,* 187–276.

Cosmides, C., & Tooby, J. (1992). Cognitive adaptations for social exchange. In J. Barkow, L. Cosmides, & J. Tooby (Eds.), *The adapted mind: Evolutionary psychology and the generation of culture* (pp. 163–228). New York: Oxford University Press.

Cosmides, C., & Tooby, J. (2002). Unraveling the enigma of human intelligence: Evolutionary psychology and the multimodular mind. In R. J. Sternberg & J. C. Kaufman (Eds.), *The evolution of intelligence* (pp. 145–198). Mahwah, NJ: Erlbaum.

Czerlinski, J., Gigerenzer, G., & Goldstein, D. G. (1999). How good are simple heuristics? In G. Gigerenzer, P. Todd, & ABC Research Group (Eds.), *Simple heuristics that make us smart* (pp. 97–118). New York: Oxford University Press.

Dawkins, R. (1989). *The selfish gene*. Oxford, UK: Oxford University Press.

Duchaine, B., Cosmides, L., & Tooby, J. (2001). Evolutionary psychology and the brain. *Current Opinion in Neurobiology, 11*, 225–230.

Dugatkin, L. A. (1996). Interface between culturally based preferences and genetic preferences: Female mate choice in Poecilia Reticulata. *Proceedings of the National Academy of Sciences, 93*, 2770–2773.

Fodor, J. A. (1987). Modules, frames, frigeons, sleeping dogs, and the music of spheres. In J. R. Garfield (Ed.), *Modularity in knowledge and representation and natural-language understanding* (pp. 25–36). Cambridge, MA: MIT Press.

Galef, B. G., Jr. (1987). Social influences on the identification of toxic foods by Norway rats. *Animal Learning & Behavior, 15*, 327–332.

Galef, B. G., Jr., McQuoid, L. M., & Whiskin, E. E. (1990). Further evidence that Norway rats do not socially transmit learned aversions to toxic baits. *Animal Learning & Behavior, 18*, 199–205.

Gardner, H. (1983). *Frames of mind: The theory of multiple intelligences*. New York: Basic Books.

Gardner, H., Kornhuber, M. L., & Wake, W. K. (1996). *Intelligence: Multiple perspectives*. Fort Worth, TX: Harcourt Brace.

Gigerenzer, G. (1997). The modularity of social intelligence. In A. Whiten & R. W. Byrne (Eds.), *Machiavellian intelligence II* (pp. 264–288). Cambridge, UK: Cambridge University Press.

Gigerenzer, G. (2000). *Adaptive thinking: Rationality in the real world*. Oxford, UK: Oxford University Press.

Gigerenzer, G., & Goldstein, D. G. (1999). Betting on one good reason: The Take The Best heuristic. In G. Gigerenzer, P. M. Todd, & ABC Research Group (Eds.), *Simple heuristics that make us smart* (pp. 75–95). New York: Oxford University Press.

Gigerenzer, G., & Hug, K. (1992). Domain-specific reasoning: Social contracts, cheating, and perspective change. *Cognition, 43*, 127–171.

Gigerenzer, G., & Selten, R. (2001). Rethinking rationality. In G. Gigerenzer & R. Selten (Eds.), *Bounded rationality: The adaptive toolbox* (pp. 1–12). Cambridge, MA: MIT Press.

Gigerenzer, G., Swijtink, Z., Porter, T., Daston, L., Beatty, J., & Krüger, L. (1989). *The empire of chance. How probability changed science and everyday life*. Cambridge, UK: Cambridge University Press.

Gigerenzer, G., Todd, P., & ABC Research Group (1999). *Simple heuristics that make us smart*. New York: Oxford University Press.

Goldstein, D. G., & Gigerenzer, G. (2002). Models of ecological rationality: The recognition heuristic. *Psychological Review, 109*, 75–90.

Hoffrage, U., Hertwig, R., & Gigerenzer, G. (2000). Hindsight bias: A by-product of knowledge updating? *Journal of Experimental Psychology: Learning, Memory, and Cognition, 26*, 566–581.

Hossner, E. J. (1995). *Module der Motorik* [Motor Modules]. Schorndorf, Germany: Hofmann.

Hubbard, A. W., & Seng, S. N. (1954). Visual movements of batters. *Research Quarterly of American Association of Health and Physical Education, 25*, 42–57.

Jensen, A. R. (1998). *The g factor*. Westport, CT: Praeger.

Johnson, J., & Raab, M. (2003). Take the first: Option generation and resulting choices. *Organizational Behavior and Human Decision Processes, 91*, 215–229.

Keele, S. W., Jennings, P., Jones, S., Caulton, D., & Cohen, A. (1995). On the modularity of sequence representation. *Journal of Motor Behavior, 27*, 17–30.

Klein, G., Wolf, S., Militello, L., & Zsambok, C. (1995). Characteristics of skilled option generation in chess. *Organizational Behavior and Human Decision Processes, 62*, 63–69.

Kollock, P. (1994). The emergence of exchange structures: An experimental study of uncertainty, commitment, and trust. *American Journal of Sociology, 100*, 313–345.

Kummer, H., Daston, L., Gigerenzer, G., & Silk, J. B. (1997). The social intelligence hypothesis. In P. Weingarten, S. D. Mitchell, P. J. Richardson, & S. Maasen (Eds.), *Human by nature: Between biology and the social sciences* (pp. 157–179). Mahwah, NJ: Erlbaum.

Laland, K. N. (2001). Imitation, social learning, and preparedness as mechanisms of bounded rationality. In G. Gigerenzer & R. Selten (Eds.), *Bounded rationality: The adaptive toolbox* (pp. 233–247). Cambridge, MA: MIT Press.

Marsh, B. (2002). Heuristics as social tools. *New Ideas in Psychology, 20*, 49–57.

Martignon, L., & Hoffrage, U. (1999). Why does one-reason decision making work? A case study in ecological rationality. In G. Gigerenzer, P. Todd, & the ABC Research Group, *Simple heuristics that make us smart* (pp. 119–140). New York: Oxford University Press.

Martignon, L., & Hoffrage, U. (2002). Fast, frugal, and fit: Simple heuristics for paired comparisons. *Theory and Decision, 52*, 29–71.

McLeod, P., & Dienes, Z. (1996). Do fielders know where to go to catch the ball or only how to get there? *Journal of Experimental Psychology: Human Perception and Performance, 22*, 531–543.

Messick, D. M., & Liebrand, W. B. G. (1995). Individual heuristics and the dynamics of cooperation in large groups. *Psychological Review, 102*, 131–145.

Miller, G. F., & Todd, P. M. (1998). Mate choice turns cognitive. *Trends in Cognitive Sciences, 2*, 190–198.

Newell, B., & Shanks, D. R. (2003). Take-the-best or look at the rest? Factors influencing "one-reason" decision making. *Journal of Experimental Psychology: Learning, Memory, and Cognition, 29*, 53–65.

Newell, B., Rakow, T., Weston, N. J., & Shanks, D. R. (2004). Search strategies in decision-making: The success of "success." *Journal of Behavioral Decision Making, 17*, 117–137.

Noble, J., & Todd, P. M. (2002). Imitation or something simpler? Modelling simple mechanisms for social information processing. In K. Dautenhahn & C. Nehaniv (Eds.), *Imitation in animals and artifacts* (pp. 423–440). Cambridge, MA: MIT Press.

Payne, J. W., Bettman, J. R., & Johnson, E. J. (1993). *The adaptive decision maker*. New York: Cambridge University Press.

Rieskamp, J., & Hoffrage, U. (1999). When do people use simple heuristics and how can we tell? In G. Gigerenzer, P. Todd, & the ABC Research Group (Eds.), *Simple heuristics that make us smart* (pp. 141–167). New York: Oxford University Press.

Savelsbergh, G. J. P., Whiting, H. T. A., & Bootsma, R. J. (1991). Grasping tau. *Journal of Experimental Psychology: Human Perception and Performance, 17*, 315–322.

Seeley, T. D., & Buhrmann, S. C. (2001). Nest-site selection in honey bees: How well do swarms implement the "best-of-N" decision rule? *Behavioral Ecology and Sociobiology, 49*, 416–427.

Selten, R. (2001). What is bounded rationality? In G. Gigerenzer & R. Selten (Eds.), *Bounded rationality* (pp. 13–36). Cambridge, MA: MIT Press.

Shephard, R. N. (2001). On the possibility of universal mental laws: A reply to my critics. *Behavioral and Brain Sciences, 24*, 712–748.

Simon, H. A. (1955). A behavioral model of rational choice. *Quarterly Journal of Economics, 69*, 99–118.

Simon, H. A. (1956). Rational choice and the structure of environments. *Psychological Review, 63*, 129–138.

Snow, R. E. (1994). A person–situation interaction theory of intelligence in outline. In A. Demetriou & A. Efklides (Eds.), *Intelligence, mind, and reasoning: Structure and development* (pp. 11–28). Amsterdam: North-Holland.

Sternberg, R. J. (1999). Intelligence as developing expertise. *Contemporary Educational Psychology, 24*, 359–375.

Sternberg, R. J., & Kaufman, J. C. (Eds.). (2002). *The evolution of intelligence*. Mahwah, NJ: Erlbaum.

Sternberg, R. J., Grigorenko, E. L., & Bundy, D. A. (2001). The predictive value of IQ. *Merrill-Palmer Quarterly, 47*, 1–41.

Wang, Y., & Frost, B. J. (1992). Time to collision is signaled by neurons in the nucleus rotundus of pigeons. *Nature, 356*, 236–238.

Williams, G. C. (1996). *Adaptation and natural selection*. Princeton, NJ: Princeton University Press.

11

The Role of Transferable Knowledge
in Intelligence

Susan M. Barnett and Stephen J. Ceci

A prerequisite for cognitively complex behavior in a given realm is the possession of a well differentiated yet integrated knowledge base that gets operated on by efficient cognitive processes.

(Ceci, 1996, p. 22)

The transferability of learning is of prime importance in evaluating these educational claims ... the transferability of skills is key: If the skills developed by such [educational and training] efforts do not transfer beyond the training context, much of the investment may be considered wasted.

(Barnett & Ceci, 2002)

In the past decade, a new approach to understanding development has been put forward that describes a specific form of interaction between biology and environment, called the "bioecological model" (Ceci, 1996; Bronfenbrenner & Ceci, 1993, 1994). The goal of this chapter is to describe how a bioecological approach informs the study of intellectual development. In doing this, we shall focus on the evidence for the tenet of bioecological theory that is most relevant to intellectual functioning, namely, the knowledge-dependent nature of information processing. Following a description of the evidence for this tenet, we will segue into a discussion of the role of the transferability of knowledge in intellectual competence.

The bioecological approach to development posits a close interplay between knowledge and processing efficiency. What this means in the realm of intellectual competence is that, except for the most basic and dedicated processes (e.g., feature detection), processing efficiency is a function of interaction between genetic potentials for processing and the richness of the knowledge base on which the processes operate. This claim of interactivity is in contrast to the traditional assumption of main effects for processing and knowledge. Take a cognitive process such as inductive reasoning and observe it across a range of contexts. You will likely discover that it works unevenly – better in some contexts than in others (Johnson-Laird 1983). Ceci and Liker (1986a, b) provided a graphic demonstration of this when they showed that complex reasoning at the racetrack (appreciation of multiple interactive effects, nonlinearity) was not related to complex reasoning outside the racetrack. Even the complexity of other forms of gambling was not predictable from the complexity exhibited by their subjects at the racetrack. But not all individuals at the racetrack exhibited such complexity in their thinking; only the most knowledgeable did. A certain level of knowledge was prerequisite for complex reasoning. Granted that knowledge alone was not enough to guarantee complex thinking; some highly knowledgeable individuals reasoned simplistically. But no complex thinker at the racetrack was without high levels of knowledge. Their knowledge was organized or formatted in a way that rendered it very useful for making calculations about a horse's speed.

Yet when the most complex thinkers at the racetrack were placed in an isomorphic context having to do with stock market analysis rather than horse racing, their level of complexity dropped dramatically (Ceci & Ruiz, 1992). Even though these individuals clearly possessed the cognitive "hard wiring" to engage in complex thinking, they failed to do so when their domain knowledge was impoverished. We shall have more to say later about the conditions that impede or foster transfer of learning. But for now, the message is that the existence of genetic potentials for processing efficiency will not preordain the outcome unless the individual's knowledge base is sufficiently developed for the processes to be maximized.

KNOWLEDGE

The concept of *knowledge* is broadly construed to refer not only to the accumulation of factual information, but also to the accretion of heuristic rules and strategies (including such things as shortcuts, rules of inference, etc.). Knowledge can be created by an individual – through inferences and concatenations of previously acquired information and thinking about this information in new ways. Measures of aptitude for using cognitive processes in situations where knowledge either is of minimal importance or is so basic that it is thought to be shared by everyone are ill-wrought because it is illusory to imagine that performance on even microlevel cognitive tasks, like the encoding of alpha-numeric stimuli, is devoid of knowledge.

For example, Ceci (1993) showed that the encoding speed of simple alphanumeric stimuli was a function of the knowledge one possessed about these simple stimuli. The time needed to encode the numeral "9," for instance, was related to how much one knew about this number: Those who knew only its ordinal properties (e.g., less than 10 but greater than 8) were slower encoding it than their peers who appreciated cardinality, root properties, etc. On a more global level, chefs' memories for culinary terms were greater than nonchefs', despite having no greater memories for nonculinary terms. And 10-year-old chess experts remembered more chess pieces on an unfinished chess game than graduate students who were not chess experts, despite having no greater memory for nonchess stimuli (Chi, 1978). In a different domain, Spilich et al. (1979) found better memory for a baseball story by those who were more knowledgeable about baseball. Finally, a really intriguing example of the effects of knowledge on microlevel cognitive processes such as memory was provided by Logie and Wright (1992), who asked subjects to remember information that would be important to a house burglar. In addition to a group of "normal" adults, Logie and Wright asked another group to remember this information "from the perspective of the burglar." If you think their results indicate the superiority of the "burglar perspective" condition, you are wrong: Both groups remembered the information equally well (or poorly.) But Wright and Logie also recruited a third group of subjects, a group of men who had been convicted of being house burglars. Although an ordinary convict would probably not be expected to excel on memory or any other cognitive task, these house burglars certainly did. They recalled more significant details from the scene than did the two nonoffender groups. Similar effects for "experts" remembering more about things relevant to their expertise occur throughout the literature (Coltheart and Walsh, 1988).

So, knowledge is important for even microlevel encoding and memory performances. That tests claiming to predict intelligence based on reaction time and other supposedly basic processes are not immune to knowledge effects carries important implications, as we describe later. For now, the point is simply that if knowledge effects can be found even on the most microlevel tasks, then they should be abundantly apparent on higher-order thinking and reasoning tasks. And the literature bears out this expectation. For example, Johnson-Laird, Legrenzi, and Legrenzi (1972) studied answers to the Wason (1968) selection task in which subjects were presented with four cards showing, for example, "A," "M," "6," and "3." In the original version of the task, subjects were told that all cards have a letter on one side and a number on the other side, and that if a card has a vowel on one side it must have an even number on the other side. Next, they are invited to pick which cards need to be turned over to test this rule. Subjects often made the mistake of choosing "A" and "6" or only "A," when the correct answer was "A" and "3." Crucially, Johnson-Laird et al. found that performance changed if the logically identical rule was phrased to tap into existing knowledge. For example, if the researchers used envelopes instead of cards, they could bring into play subjects' knowledge of postal rules. They gave different subjects two versions of the rule: one meaningful and content-based, and the other arbitrary and content-free. The meaningful/content-based version was couched in terms of whether or not the letter was sealed (on the back) and the denomination of stamp that was on the envelope (on the front), a rule that actually existed in the British postal service at the time of the experiment. The arbitrary/content-free version was couched in terms of letters and numbers. Most subjects selected the correct envelopes to turn over in the meaningful condition, whereas in the arbitrary condition most selected the wrong envelopes to turn over. Thus knowing something about the subject matter affected subjects' performance on a problem that otherwise appeared to be a straightforward logical reasoning task.

Again, the same conclusion reached with the microlevel examples is warranted in these cases: Observation of subjects in a limited range of contexts leads to underestimating their macrolevel reasoning skills. Such skills are dependent on a rich knowledge to be actualized.

Similar sensitivity to the specifics of the situation has been found with other macrolevel reasoning processes comparing human performance to formal statistical models. For example, Gigerenzer and his colleagues (Gigerenzer, Hell, & Blank, 1988) investigated the use of base rate information, which Kahneman and Tversky (1973) had shown to be almost completely ignored by most subjects in a task requiring category judgments based on personality and other information. Gigerenzer et al. found that the use of base rate information depends on the problem context and associated differences in subject knowledge. As just one of many examples, Gigerenzer et al. demonstrated that subjects performed Kahneman and Tversky's engineer–lawyer problem according to the rules of statistics, if they knew for sure that the rules applied because they themselves witnessed the randomness of the sampling. If they did not, that is, if they were merely told that the sampling was performed randomly, they showed the same base-rate neglect as Kahneman and Tversky's subjects. Also, in a related study using a task with the same formal structure as the earlier task, but requiring prediction of the outcome of a soccer match, subjects did use base rates. In fact, their performance was indistinguishable from that dictated by Bayes' theorem. Gigerenzer et al. attribute this difference to the subjects' existing knowledge and ways of thinking about soccer matches. Finally, in a recent series of studies, with a wide range of subjects, Gigerenzer and his colleagues demonstrated the knowledge-dependent nature of Bayesian reasoning; when problems are framed in terms of absolute frequencies instead of relative probabilities, subjects are able to recruit their own knowledge to solve them (see Gigerenzer, 2002). Thus, again, knowing something about the subject matter affects subjects' reasoning performance in a context-specific manner.

In addition to the influence of knowledge on encoding, memory, and reasoning tasks, even the detection of perceptual patterns (e.g., an optimization rule for determining which partially filled cases of milk bottles should be used by dairy assemblers) cannot be estimated without reference to the elaborateness of one's knowledge base. As Scribner (1986) concluded from her analysis of everyday problem solving, the ability to solve problems is intimately tied to the amount and quality of relevant knowledge one possesses: "From earlier assumptions that problem-solving can be understood in terms of 'pure process,' a consensus has arisen that problem-solving procedures are bound up with amount and organization of subject matter knowledge" (p. 29). In sum, if one wishes to locate the most complex thinkers in a given domain, the soundest advice is to begin by testing for depth and thorougness of knowledge about that domain.

Elsewhere, one of us has described examples of complex reasoning engaged in by famous scientists and mathematicians, such as von Neumann, Turing, and Ramanujan (Ceci, 1996). These examples reveal that high levels of complexity almost always co-occur with high levels of declarative and procedural knowledge. Complex cognitive processing and elegantly structured knowledge are in symbiosis. It is fascinating to speculate as to how these men's knowledge of numbers was organized. For example, the mathematician Ramanujan was purportedly able to identify underlying features for almost all numbers, a feat that must have seemed arcane even to other mathematicians. For example, he was able to almost instantly specify that the number 1,729 was the "smallest sum of two cubes in two ways." This feat reveals an extremely differentiated, yet integrated knowledge structure. It is difficult to imagine such processing in the absence of a rich knowledge representation.

An implication of the foregoing is that something difficult for one individual may be simple for another individual possessing a more extensive knowledge structure – even if these individuals possess similar processing efficiency when the "playing field is leveled," so to speak. A similar view has led Nisbett and his colleagues to remark that "even quite young children readily reject invalid arguments when they have world knowledge that is helpful, whereas even adults accept invalid arguments when their world knowledge encourages it" (Nisbett et al., 1988, p. 5). Thus, there is no objective measure of processing efficiency or reasoning complexity that can be estimated exclusive of knowledge (given that the definition of the latter includes such things as strategies, shortcuts, factual information, skills, heuristics, and the like). Many years ago, the philosophers Block and Dworkin (1976) made a similar argument: "Individuals probably differ in the knowledge and skills they demonstrate on IQ tests simply because they probably differ in knowledge and skills" (p. 450).

For these reasons, we view it as unsatisfactory to speak of cognitive complexity or processing efficiency as the *sine qua non* of intelligence in one breath and equate IQ with intelligence in the next, in view of the crucial role played by prior knowledge (broadly defined) in the performance of both.[1]

Findings from studies such as the racetrack one are hard to explain from either the traditional psychometric or information processing viewpoints. Highly knowledgeable individuals with low IQs sometimes developed more cognitively complex models of these tasks than did high IQ individuals who were less knowledgeable, even when both groups were equated on experience and motivation. Of course, one can argue that such instances of complex thinking by low IQ persons are extreme aberrations, and that higher IQ persons usually outperform them. But this still requires a causal explanation: How do they do it? How does their expertise develop, if not through more highly efficient cognitive processing?

An implication of this approach is that the domain-specificity/generality of performance on intellectual tasks depends on the specificity/generality of knowledge and of the objects about which one has knowledge. For example, knowing a lot about, and having extensive familiarity with, numbers may yield enhanced comfort in working on all tasks involving numbers. Having a really in-depth knowledge of the benefits and methods of checking one's own work may improve performance on a wide range of tasks for which that skill has bearing. Thus the claim that knowledge is key to intelligent performance does not imply that all determinants of intelligent performance apply only to a narrow range of domains or situations. Breadth of applicability depends on the particular item of knowledge in question.

In traditional cognitive psychology, processes are assumed to be "transdomainal," that is, equally applicable across all content knowledge domains. It is assumed that these processes are transdomainal from the time of their acquisition or very soon thereafter. In the bioecological approach, however, processes are initially tied to a particular domain of knowledge and operate on information only within that domain.[2] With development, these processes gradually become powerful general algorithms capable of

---

[1] This view has been around for a long time:

> What is it to think without knowledge? If we ignore, for now, specific factual knowledge: are not rules for problem solving knowledge – knowledge developed by education and experience? Again, strategies for even the simplest tasks may surely be gained from the environment and by education, such as the skill of concentrating on the test, being confident and yet self-critical – and guessing what kind of answers are needed ... If education did not have such effects, it would be useless ... So, the claim that IQ tests can be freed of education and other biases by suitable choice of tasks seems ill-founded. It is indeed deeply misconceived, for intelligence requires and surely is in large part effective deployment of knowledge. (Gregory, 1981, p. 304)

[2] For example, when a 3-year-old is asked "If I cut an apple in half, how many pieces will I have?," they correctly reply, "two." Same with other tangible, concrete edible objects, such as oranges. But when asked about rugs, they often reply, "How big is the rug?" or "It depends

being applied to information across domains. We explore this in greater detail in our discussion of the conditions necessary for transfer of knowledge and generalization.

At any given time, some domains are likely to be more elaborately developed than others. This is an important feature because various cognitive operations, as already mentioned, must access or "operate on" knowledge, and if the knowledge is insufficient in some sense (e.g., either lacking in quantity or not organized efficiently for a given task), optimal cognitive processing (in the sense of its biologically constrained potential) can be impeded.

According to bioecological theory, some assessment of the elaborateness of knowledge within a given domain is necessary in order to make inferences about the causes of individual differences in cognitive processing. Thus, within bioecological theory it is possible for an individual to appear to lack a certain cognitive potential (e.g., the ability to deduce relationships) when the real problem may be a mismatch between the task at hand and the subject's relevant content knowledge required to actualize this potential. By exploring a variety of contexts and materials, it may be possible to demonstrate the existence of a cognitive potential even in the face of deficits in its operation on a particular task due to the lack of elaborateness of that particular content domain.

An implication of the foregoing argument is that rather than trying to assess an individual's biological capacity for intelligent behavior with a stripped-down, supposedly knowledge-free task, as an IQ test was originally hoped to be, one needs a knowledge-rich task.[3] Otherwise the result will be a measure of knowledge about the specific kinds of things on IQ tests, as suggested by the earlier quote from Block and Dworkin (1976), which is obviously not what is intended by a test of general intelligence. But what kind of knowledge-rich task is most meaningful? As one alternative, intelligence, in this sense, could be viewed as the maximum realized capability to engage in cognitively complex tasks. To assess such an ability, performance must be evaluated in whatever context is most supportive of complex performance for that individual, one in which he or she

on the size of the rug." In other words, they do not initially possess a halving rule, but a more restricted one that operates within a tightly constructed domain.

[3] The opposite approach is to try to create a stripped-down task that is unrelated to any preexisting knowledge, on which all individuals can therefore be assessed equally, independent of their past experience – a more extreme realization of the philosophy behind the IQ test. Unfortunately, as we have discussed earlier, the influence of prior knowledge can extend to such basic cognitive building blocks as recognition of alphanumeric symbols and visual memory. With this pervasive influence of past experience, no task is stripped down enough to be totally unrelated to any preexisting knowledge (except perhaps one conducted in the womb, early in pregnancy, before the auditory system has developed sufficiently to perceive differential exposure to parents' voices and Beethoven symphonies).

possesses the most knowledge possible: Chess masters could be assessed playing chess in a quiet room, drug dealers while dealing drugs on a street corner, and an avid racetrack gambler might be assessed while gambling at the racetrack. This tailored approach ensures that the knowledge base necessary for complex performance is available, so that the individual's capabilities are maximized. Of course, comparison across individuals would necessitate comparison across tasks, rendering standardized scoring impossible for practical purposes.

Another alternative is to give up on the notion of maximum capability and instead investigate realized performance on a set of standardized tasks seen to be particularly representative or important for everyday life and about which everyone can be assumed to possess at least some of the relevant knowledge base. Approaches invoking practical intelligence (Sternberg et al., 1995, 2000; Wagner & Sternberg, 1985; Williams et al., 2002) and wisdom (Baltes & Staudinger, 1993; Sternberg, 2001) could be viewed in this tradition.[4]

But what qualifies as cognitively complex performance in any given situation? What kind of task should be used? Would mindlessly reproducing a rote procedure from memory constitute complex reasoning, if the procedures themselves were complex enough? Surely not, if the notion of intelligence is flexible not rigid knowledge, being able to create one's own argument, not just being able to copy someone else's. Intelligent individuals should be able to apply their knowledge to a novel situation and still behave intelligently. Thus we seek a situation that is materially different from past experience, so as to present a novel challenge, but that nevertheless is framed in terms of or builds on existing knowledge. This, of course, raises definitional issues, such as the meaning of "materially different" and "novel". This brings us squarely to the question of transfer.

TRANSFER

Those studying transfer of learning have long struggled with these questions (see Barnett & Ceci, 2002). They have engaged in a century-long debate about whether significant transfer occurs (see, e.g., Detterman & Sternberg, 1993; Judd, 1908; Thorndike & Woodworth, 1901a, b, c; Barnett & Ceci, 2002), with some arguing that it does (e.g., Halpern, 1998), and

---

[4] Both these knowledge-rich alternatives have the disadvantage of assessing a form of crystallized intelligence. A third alternative is to view intelligence as the ability to learn from a given situation, an ability which, at least superficially, seems more fluid. With this approach more intelligent individuals are seen as those who learn how to perform some new task quickest, given a standard amount of training (see, e.g., Gettinger, 1984; Grigorenko & Sternberg, 1998). However, measures of performance change are just as likely to be subject to the effects of prior learning as measures of static performance, rendering this approach just as subject to the effects of knowledge as the static approaches.

others arguing that it does not and that what is claimed to be transfer is really merely regurgitation of learned facts (e.g., Detterman, 1993). The concept of near versus far transfer has been developed to capture the notion of how different a test or "transfer" situation is from the conditions of original training and thus how novel a challenge it presents. The example of the racetrack gambler can be used to illustrate this concept. Consider two hypothetical gamblers, with equivalent experience and extensive knowledge of how to predict odds of winning, given information about track conditions and so on. Both individuals are highly skilled at estimating odds while betting at their home track, for a stable of familiar horses, and for races at other venues in the same genre (e.g., standardbred racing). However, one of these individuals, when provided with relevant background information, is capable of transferring that knowledge to the sport of thoroughbred racing or perhaps even steeplechasing, both entirely different subsets of the horse racing world from standardbred racing (including the social context, with steeplechasing in America being associated with "high-society" charity fund-raising and social status, whereas standardbred racing is a male working-class pastime), while the other individual is not, despite the fact that both initially had equal ignorance of the world of steeplechasing. If such were true, then the latter individual has shown evidence of only near transfer whereas the former has shown evidence of far transfer. Hence, according to the argument being put forward here, the former's behavior would be considered more intelligent because it could be extended further from its origins.

Our recent work codified this dimension of near versus far transfer more systematically in a taxonomy of far transfer (Barnett & Ceci, 2002), in which we described six relevant dimensions of context: knowledge domain, physical context, temporal context, functional context, social context, and modality. Evidence that many of these dimensions may affect transfer success, in addition to the domain of knowledge, suggests that the broader context in which behavior occurs must be taken into account when evaluating the sophistication of that behavior and the implied intelligence of the individual.

The examples discussed earlier clearly show the importance of knowledge to intelligent performance. These could be seen as demonstrating the sensitivity of performance on such tasks to changes in context, where the dimension of context under investigation is the domain of knowledge. There is also more limited evidence that the other dimensions of context described in the taxonomy of transfer may influence performance on these kinds of tasks. One such dimension is the physical context in which the initial learning and the test or transfer takes place. Evidence for the impact of physical context comes from work from a variety of orientations and with a wide range of ages. For example, Spencer and Weisberg's (1986) work with college students solving Duncker's radiation problem (Duncker,

1945) found that changing a small detail of the physical context (the experimenter) between training and transfer phases had a negative impact on transfer success. Further evidence comes from Rovee-Collier's (1993) work with infants' memories for the association between kicking their feet and the movement of a mobile hung over their cribs. Each infant's foot was connected by a string to a mobile hanging over their crib. The infants then learned that they could move the mobile by moving their leg. When the infants were tested at a later date, minor changes in physical context, such as the change from a yellow crib liner with green squares to a yellow liner with green circles, were found to completely disrupt the transfer. Similarly, in an experiment with older children playing a video game, learning only transferred to a new task if the exact same physical context was used for the training and testing phases (Ceci, 1996).

Ceci and Bronfenbrenner (1985) reported the results of a developmental study in which children of various ages were asked to remember to do things in the future, such as remove cupcakes from the oven in 30 minutes or disconnect a battery charger from a motorcycle battery in 30 minutes. While waiting to do these things, the children were invited to play a popular video game. The data of interest concern children's clock-checking behavior while waiting for the 30 minutes to elapse. Children behaved differently as a function of the setting in which they were studied. When observed in the familiar context of their own homes and in the company of their siblings, children appeared to "calibrate" their psychological clocks through a process of early and frequent clock checking. These early checks permitted the children to synchronize their psychological clocks with the passage of actual clock time. For example, children might begin the waiting period by making several confirmatory checks to ensure that the amount of time that had already transpired was close to their subjective estimate. After several such confirmatory checks, children gained the confidence to allow their psychological clocks to "run" (unchecked) until nearly the end of the 30-minute period, whereupon last-minute incessant clock checking occurred.

The advantage of using a calibration strategy is that it permits children to engage effectively in other activities (e.g., playing video games), unencumbered by the need to look constantly at the clock. It also allows a maximum degree of precision with a minimum amount of effort. Thus, the use of the calibration strategy does not result in a loss of punctuality. None of the children who gave evidence of employing this strategy burned the cupcakes or overheated the motorcycle battery. Support for the assumption that children were indeed synchronizing their psychological clocks with a nearby wall clock was provided by showing subjects were able to adjust their subjective estimations of the passage of clock time, and once this adjustment was achieved, they were successful at gauging the remainder of the waiting period with only a minimal amount of glancing at the clock.

In the laboratory, however, children displayed no evidence of using a calibration strategy. They, too, rarely burned the cupcakes, but they required nearly a third more effort (i.e., clock checks), with the result being a lessened ability to engage effectively in video game activities during the waiting period. With the exception of older boys who were asked to engage in a traditionally female sex-typed task (baking cupcakes), there was no evidence of calibration in the laboratory setting. These data point to the influence of context on strategy use. Here, context is conceived as not only the physical setting in which the task unfolds (laboratory or home), but the sociocultural features as well (e.g., the sex-role expectations of the task, the age-appropriateness of the task, the presence or absence of familiar persons, etc.). Unlike the traditional information processing conceptualization of context as something adjunctive to cognition (i.e., a social/physical address where cognitive tasks are performed), these findings suggest that context should be viewed as a constituent of the cognitive task, influencing the manner in which the task is perceived and the choice of strategies for its completion. Had the investigators assessed children's competence only in the laboratory setting, they would have been led to underestimate the sophistication of their strategies. Conversely, had they observed children's clock checking only in the children's homes, they would have missed the significance of many of the ecological contrasts that the laboratory comparison afforded. A number of other studies by experimental psychologists show similar contextual effects on cognitive strategy use (e.g., Acredolo, 1979).

We have also argued (Barnett & Ceci, 2002) that other dimensions of context may disrupt transfer, though evidence for some of these hypothesized dimensions is less compelling. For example, the modality match between the training and transfer contexts may affect transfer success. This was suggested by a study in which broadly applicable cognitive skills, such as classification and critical use of language, were taught to a large sample of Venezuelan seventh graders (Herrnstein et al., 1986). The researchers tested transfer using multiple choice tests and tests in other modalities, such as verbal questions and open-ended written questions, as well as a practical design task and an oral argumentation task. Although training improved performance on most of these measures, the size of the improvement varied between tests, with the largest benefits generally being found on tests closest in modality to the original training.

Other dimensions that we have proposed as moderators of transfer success include the temporal, social, and functional contexts (Barnett & Ceci, 2002). Memory studies and common knowledge have long shown that the time between training and testing affects retrieval (see, e.g., Bahrick, Bahrick, & Wittlinger, 1975; Squire & Slater, 1975). As retrieval of learned information is a necessary component of transfer, temporal context would also be expected to affect transfer and thus demonstrations of intelligent behavior on cognitively complex tasks. Indeed, even differences in training-transfer time interval that might be expected to be trivial can make a difference to transfer success. For example, Spencer and Weisberg's (1986) study, mentioned in our earlier discussion of physical context, found a difference between results of transfer tests conducted after 45 seconds and after a 6-minute delay.

We do not have direct evidence of the effects of social context on transfer, although many consider learning itself to be a social activity (Reder & Klatzky, 1994), which might therefore be expected to influence transfer success. Similarly, we do not have direct evidence for the effect of functional context on transfer success. Conceptually, we base our expectation of an effect of functional context on the notion of functional fixedness (Duncker, 1945) which suggests that the use of "tools" – for which we substitute any learned skill, knowledge, or problem-solving approach – is tied to their original purpose.

The mechanism for these context effects is poorly understood in many cases, but evidence suggests that it is related to the structure and elaboration of the knowledge base. In a recent series of experiments, Ceci, Brainerd, Williams, and Fitneva (2002) demonstrated that the ability to monitor one's memory, to determine if something has been encoded, depends critically on the richness of the knowledge representation. For example, if a child is to correctly realize that she previously saw a given object, then her ability to do so requires that she richly encoded it in the first place. If she did not, then it is frequently the case that she will claim not to recognize previously presented objects, yet still correctly "guess" their colors, locations, temporal orders, etc. These experiments drive home the point that knowledge representation constrains cognitive processing.

A limited amount of research has been conducted to investigate the question of how to teach in a manner that somehow optimizes the encoded representation to maximize its transfer to novel contexts. Many studies suggest that training that results in deep, theoretical understanding of the material yields greater transfer. This deep understanding is achieved by structuring the training task so as to encourage trainees to work with the materials at a deep theoretical level, for example, by asking them to compare multiple examples that differ superficially but share deep, structural features (Catrambone & Holyoak, 1989), by asking them to explain rather than memorize material (Needham & Begg, 1991), using distant analogies which may require more effortful processing (Halpern, Hansen, & Riefer, 1990), and by using a task requiring concrete and effortful processing (Reed & Saavedra, 1986). Work by Barnett and Koslowski (2002) investigated this in a study of more real-world problem-solving expertise in business. The study compared the behavior of real-life experts and novices on a problem-solving task about running a restaurant. On this task, which required the participants to think through a problem scenario and recommend solution for the imaginary protagonist to pursue, use of theoretical knowledge about business was a powerful predictor of success. The circumstances in which knowledge transfers from one situation to another were investigated by comparing two different kinds of experts. One group of experts had very specific, closely related knowledge, derived from actually managing restaurants. The other group of experts had general experience in business, but knew nothing about restaurants in particular. The experience of the latter group transferred more readily to the situation under investigation. The authors hypothesized that this was due to the breadth of their prior experience and to the group problem-solving situation in which they built their knowledge. This study suggests that the most closely related knowledge is not necessarily the most useful in a transfer situation where novel challenges are faced.

In addition to the empirical work described here, this knowledge-based approach was also instrumental in the development of our taxonomy for far transfer, part of which we alluded to earlier in our discussion of dimensions of context. The framework describes nine relevant dimensions, six for context and three for content. The context dimensions were described earlier – knowledge context, physical context, temporal context, functional context, social context, and modality. The content dimensions involve the nature of the learned skill, the performance change measured, and the memory demands of the transfer test (see Barnett & Ceci, 2002, for a more complete exposition). This theoretical effort has proved useful in provoking and structuring debate concerning issues transfer of learning (see, e.g., Mestre, 2002), particularly the question of whether and when transfer of learning occurs between situations that differ considerably – far transfer (as opposed to near transfer, which is the transfer of learning between situations that differ only slightly). It has forced researchers to pay attention to the comparability of studies used to draw conclusions about this topic, an area of research in which comparisons of "apples and oranges" have frequently been made and in which many aspects of context have habitually been ignored.

Knowledge is important for cognitively complex, intelligent behavior. Furthermore, the context in which that behavior is being demonstrated – that is, the context to which the intelligent behavior is being transferred – also affects the actualization of that behavior. Thus a *theory of context* is required to assess intelligence and to understand how to maximize intelligent performance in a variety of contexts. Our taxonomy of transfer is one component of such a theory. Future research can profitably pursue two directions: (1) investigating the effects of some of the dimensions of context described in the aforementioned transfer taxonomy and (2) conducting studies to explore how transferable knowledge can best be taught and how training interacts with context to affect transferability. If and when such research yields a more complete understanding of the contextual constraints on transfer and how these can best be mitigated, it will allow us to better understand how knowledge can be used to tackle cognitively complex tasks in novel situations – a hallmark of intelligent behavior.

References

Acredolo, L. P. (1979). Laboratory versus home: The effect of environment on the 9-month-old infant's choice of spatial reference system. *Developmental Psychology, 15*(6), 666–667.

Bahrick, H. P., Bahrick, P. O., & Wittlinger, R. P. (1975). Fifty years of memory for names and faces. *Journal of Experimental Psychology: General, 1*, 54–75.

Baltes, P. B., & Staudinger, U. M. (1993). The search for a psychology of wisdom. *Current Directions in Psychological Science, 2*(3), 75–80.

Barnett, S. M., & Ceci, S. J. (2002). When and where do we apply what we learn?: A taxonomy for far transfer. *Psychological Bulletin, 128*(4), 612–637.

Barnett, S. M., & Koslowski, B. (2002). Adaptive expertise: Effects of type of experience and the level of theoretical understanding it generates. *Thinking and Reasoning, 8*, 237–267.

Block, N. J., & Dworkin, G. (1976). *The IQ controversy: Critical readings.* New York: Pantheon Books.

Bronfenbrenner, U., & Ceci, S. J. (1993). Heredity, environment, and the question "how." In R. Plomin & G. McClearn (Eds.), *Nature nurture & psychology* (pp. 313–324). Washington, DC: APA.

Bronfenbrenner, U., & Ceci, S. J. (1994). Nature–nurture in developmental perspective: A bioecological theory. *Psychological Review, 101*, 568–586.

Catrambone, R., & Holyoak, K. J. (1989). Overcoming contextual limitations on problem-solving transfer. *Journal of Experimental Psychology: Learning, Memory, and Cognition, 15*(6), 1147–1156.

Ceci, S. J. (1993). Some contextual trends in intellectual development. *Developmental Review, 13*, 403–435.

Ceci, S. J. (1996). *On intelligence: A bioecological treatise on intellectual development* (Expanded ed.). Cambridge, MA: Harvard University Press.

Ceci, S. J., & Bronfenbrenner, U. (1985). "Don't forget to take the cupcakes out of the oven": Prospective memory, strategic time-monitoring, and context. *Child Development, 56*(1), 152–164.

Ceci, S. J., Brainerd, C. J., Fitneva, S. A., & Williams, W. M. (2002). *Forgetting you remember: representational constraints on monitoring.* Unpublished manuscript, Cornell University.

Ceci, S. J., & Liker, J. (1986a). A day at the races: IQ, expertise, and cognitive complexity. *Journal of Experimental Psychology: General, 115*, 255–266.

Ceci, S. J., & Liker, J. (1986b). Academic versus non-academic intelligence: An experimental separation. In R. J. Sternberg & R. K. Wagner (Eds.), *Practical intelligence: Nature and origins of competence in the everyday world* (pp. 119–142). New York: Cambridge University Press.

Ceci, S. J., & Ruiz, A. (1992). The role of general intelligence in transfer: A case study. In R. Hoffman (Ed.), *The psychology of expertise* (pp. 218–230). NY: Springer-Verlag.

Charlesworth, W. (1976). Human intelligence as adaptation: An ethological approach. In L. Resnick (Ed.), *The nature of intelligence* (pp. 147–168). Hillsdale, NJ: Erlbaum.

Charlesworth, W. (1979). An ethological approach to studying intelligence. *Human Development, 22,* 212–216.

Chi, M. T. H. (1978). Knowledge structures and memory development. In Siegler, Robert S. (Ed.). *Children's thinking: What develops?* (pp. 73–96). Upper Saddle River, NJ: Prentice Hall.

Chi, M. T. H., & Ceci, S. J. (1987). Content knowledge: Its restructuring with memory development. *Advances in Child Development and Behavior, 20,* 91–146.

Coltheart, V., & Walsh, P. (1988). Expert Knowledge and Semantic Memory. In M. M. Gruneberg, P. Morris, & P. Sykes (Eds.), *Practical Aspects of Memory, Vol. 2.* London: Wiley.

Deary, I., J. (1993). Inspection time and WAIS-R IQ subtypes: A confirmatory factor analysis study. *Intelligence, 17,* 223–236.

Deary, I., J. (1995). Auditory inspection time and intelligence: What is the causal direction? *Developmental Psychology, 31,* 237–250.

Deary, I., J., Caryl, P., Egan, V., & Wight, D. (1989). Visual and auditory inspection time: Their interrelationship and correlation with IQ in high ability subjects. *Personality and Individual Differences, 10,* 525–533.

Detterman, D. K. (1993). The case for the prosecution: Transfer as an epiphenomenon. In D. K. Detterman & R. J. Sternberg (Eds.), *Transfer on trial: Intelligence, cognition, and instruction* (pp. 1–24). Norwood, NJ: Ablex.

Detterman, D. K., & Sternberg, R. J. (1993). *Transfer on trial: Intelligence, cognition, and instruction.* Norwood, NJ: Ablex.

Dickens, W. T., & Flynn, J. R. (2001). Heritability estimates versus large environmental effects: The IQ paradox resolved. *Psychological Review, 108*(2), 346–69.

Duncker, K. (1945). On problem-solving. *Psychological Monographs, 58*(5), 113.

Galton, F. (1883). *Inquiries into human faculty.* London: Dent.

Gettinger, M. (1984). Individual differences in time needed for learning: A review of literature. *Educational Psychologist, 19*(1), 15–29.

Gigerenzer, G. (2002). *Calculated risks.* New York: Simon & Schuster.

Gigerenzer, G., Hell, W., & Blank, H. (1988). Presentation and content: The use of base rates as a continuous variable. *Journal of Experimental Psychology: Human Perception and Performance, 14*(3), 513–525.

Grigorenko, E. L., & Sternberg, R. J. (1998). Dynamic testing. *Psychological Bulletin, 124*(1), 75–111.

Halpern, D. F. (1998). Teaching critical thinking for transfer across domains. *American Psychologist, 53*(4), 449–455.

Halpern, D. F., Hansen, C., & Riefer, D. (1990). Analogies as an aid to understanding and memory. *Journal of Educational Psychology, 82*(2), 298–305.

Herrnstein, R. J., Nickerson, R. S., de Sanchez, M., & Swets, J. A. (1986). Teaching thinking skills. *American Psychologist, 41*(11), 1279–1289.

Johnson-Laird, P. N. (1983). *Mental models: Toward a cognitive science of language, inference, and consciousness.* Cambridge, MA: Harvard University Press.

Johnson Laird, P. N., Legrenzi, P., & Legrenzi, M. S. (1972). Reasoning and a sense of reality. *British Journal of Psychology, 63*(3), 395–400.

Judd, C. H. (1908). The relation of special training to general intelligence. *Educational Review, 36*, 28–42.

Kahneman, D., & Tversky, A. (1973). On the psychology of prediction. *Psychological Review, 80*(4), 237–251.

Keil, F. (1984). Mechanisms in cognitive development and the structure of knowledge. In R. J. Sternberg (Ed.), *Mechanisms in cognitive development* (pp. 81–100). New York: W. H. Freeman.

Keil, F. (1985). On the structure-dependent nature of stages of cognitive development. In S. Strauss & I. Levine (Eds.), *Stage and structure in children's development* (pp. 144–163). New York: Ablex.

Logie, R., Wright, R., & Decker, S. (1992). Recognition memory performance and residential burglary. *Applied Cognitive Psychology, 6*(2), 109–123.

Marini, Z., & Case, R. (1989). Parallels in the development of preschoolers' knowledge about their physical and social worlds. *Merrill Palmer Quarterly, 35*, 63–88.

Mestre, J. (2002). Transfer of learning: Issues and research agenda. Report of a workshop held March 21–22, 2002, at the National Science Foundation, Washington, DC.

Needham, D. R., & Begg, I. M. (1991). Problem-oriented training promotes spontaneous analogical transfer: Memory-oriented training promotes memory for training. *Memory and Cognition, 19*(6), 543–557.

Nisbett, R., Fong, G., Lehman, D., & Cheng, P. (1988). *Teaching Reasoning.* Unpublished manuscript. University of Michigan, Ann Arbor.

Peterson, L. R., Hillner, K., & Saltzman, D. (1962). Time between pairings and short-term retention. *Journal of Experimental Psychology, 64*, 550–551.

Reder, L. M., & Klatzky, R. L. (1994). Transfer: Training for performance. In D. Druckman & R. A. Bjork (Eds.), *Learning, remembering, believing: Enhancing human performance* (pp. 25–56). Washington, DC: National Academy Press.

Reed, S. K., & Saavedra, N. C. (1986). A comparison of computation, discovery, and graph procedures for improving students' conception of average speed. *Cognition and Instruction, 3*(1), 31–62.

Rohrer, D., & Wixted, J. T. (1994). An analysis of latency and interresponse time in free recall. *Memory & Cognition, 22*, 511–524.

Rovee-Collier, C. (1993). The capacity for long-term memory in infancy. *Current Directions in Psychological Science, 2*(4), 130–135.

Scribner, S. (1986). Thinking in action: Some characteristics of practical thought. In R. J. Sternberg & R. K. Wagner (Eds.), *Practical intelligence: Nature and origins of competence in the everyday world.* New York: Cambridge University Press.

Spencer, R. M., & Weisberg, R. W. (1986). Context-dependent effects on analogical transfer. *Memory and Cognition, 14*(5), 442–449.

Spilich, G. J., Vesonder, G. T., Chiesi, H. L., & Voss, J. F. (1979). Text processing of domain-related information for individuals with high and low domain knowledge. *Journal of Verbal Learning and Verbal Behavior, 18*(3), 275–290.

Squire, L. R., & Slater, P. C. (1975). Forgetting in very long term memory as assessed by an improved questionnaire technique. *Journal of Experimental Psychology: Human Learning and Memory, 1*, 50–54.

Sternberg, R. J. (2001). Why schools should teach for wisdom: The balance theory of wisdom in educational settings. *Educational Psychologist, 36*(4), 227–245.

Sternberg, R. J., Wagner, R. K., Williams, W. M., & Horvath, J. A. (1995). Testing common sense. *American Psychologist, 50*(11), 912–927.

Sternberg, R. J., Forsythe, G. B., Hedlund, J., Horvath, J. A., Wagner, R. K., Williams, W. M., Snook, S. A., & Grigorenko, E. L. (2000). *Practical intelligence in everyday life*. New York: Cambridge University Press.

Thorndike, E. L., & Woodworth, R. S. (1901a). The influence of improvement in one mental function upon the efficiency of other functions. I. *Psychological Review, 8*(3), 247–261.

Thorndike, E. L., & Woodworth, R. S. (1901b). The influence of improvement in one mental function upon the efficiency of other functions. II. The estimation of magnitudes. *Psychological Review, 8*(4), 384–395.

Thorndike, E. L., & Woodworth, R. S. (1901c). The influence of improvement in one mental function upon the efficiency of other functions. III. Functions involving attention, observation and discrimination. *Psychological Review, 8*(6), 553–564.

Wagner, R. K., & Sternberg, R. J. (1985). Practical intelligence in real-world pursuits: The role of tacit knowledge. *Journal of Personality and Social Psychology, 49*(2), 436–458.

Wason, P. C. (1968). Reasoning about a rule. *Quarterly Journal of Experimental Psychology, 20*(3), 273–281.

Williams, W. M., Blythe, T., White, N., Li, J., Gardner, H., & Sternberg, R. J. (2002). Practical intelligence for school: Developing metacognitive sources of achievement in adolescence. *Developmental Review, 22*(2), 162–210.

12

Reasoning Abilities[1]

David F. Lohman

The topic of human intelligence exceeds the span of any one discipline or method of inquiry. Different aspects of intelligence are best understood from disciplines as diverse as evolutionary biology, neuropsychology, cognitive psychology, anthropology, and education. At its core, however, intelligence is defined by differences between individuals or species. To say that one individual is more intelligent than another is to make a value judgment. Theories of human intelligence must therefore be able to explain those behaviors or accomplishments that societies value as indicants of intelligence (Sternberg, 1985). Such explanations may, at one extreme, invoke the action of neural mechanisms (Garlick, 2002) or, at the other extreme, the importance of social processes (Vygotsky, 1978). Ultimately, however, the theory must explain individual differences in those complex human behaviors that are most commonly understood as indicants of intelligence. Thus, the central facts to be explained by a theory of intelligence must go beyond faster or more efficient processing of elementary tasks, for example, or the efficiency of biological processes and inherited structures, or the influence of schools, environments, or even cultures. Rather, a theory of intelligence must explain the writing of novels, the solving of complex mathematical problems, the designing of skyscrapers and microchips, and the myriad other forms of complex cognition valued by society. In short, an understanding of how individuals solve complex tasks and an explanation of why they differ so markedly in their ability to do so are central facts for any theory of intelligence.

---

[1] Portions of this chapter appear in Lohman, D. F. (2002), Complex information processing and intelligence. In R. J. Sternberg (Ed.), *Handbook of intelligence* (pp. 285–340). Cambridge, UK: Cambridge University Press.

COGNITIVE TESTS AS COGNITIVE TASKS

But which tasks should we study? There are many thousands of complex tasks, each of which might be considered an indicant of intelligence. Correlational studies of human abilities offer a reasonable starting place, since they (a) identify dimensions of individual differences that cut across tasks; (b) show which of these individual-differences constructs best predict performance in nontest situations, such as success school (Brody, 1992) or work (Hunter & Schmidt, 1996); and (c) identify tasks that repeatedly emerge as good measures of particular constructs. Estes (1974) was one of the first to suggest that careful examination of the processes test-takers use when solving items on ability tests might give an initial purchase on a process model of intelligence. Although such tasks commonly lack authenticity, efficient measures of ability constructs tend to make plain the critical cognitive processes that are typically less transparent in more authentic, everyday tasks. To be sure, something is lost, but something is also gained.

In addition to identifying tasks that define ability constructs that predict valued nontest performances, correlational studies also show how ability factors are related to one another. This is useful because it helps investigators know how the ability construct they are studying relates to other ability constructs. There is now broad consensus that these relations can be represented hierarchically (Carroll, 1993; Gustafsson & Undheim, 1996). Even more suggestive for the present discussion, however, was the demonstration that hierarchical factor models are conformable with a radex model. The radex is produced by treating test intercorrelations as distances, which are then scaled in two or three dimensions using nonmetric, multi-dimensional scaling. The resultant scalings show three important features (see Snow, Kyllonen, & Marshalek, 1984). First, tests cluster by content, which typically appear as verbal, spatial, and symbolic/quantitative slices of a two-dimensional radex pie. Second, tests and test clusters that define broad factors tend to fall near the center of the radex plot. More specific primaries fall near the periphery. Indeed, in a well-balanced battery of tests, those that define g fall near the center of the plot. Third, task complexity is roughly related to distance from the center (or g). This suggests that one key to a theory of g, then, may be an understanding of the complexity gradients that emanate like spokes from g to more peripheral or specific abilities.

In this chapter, I briefly survey research on testlike tasks modeled after item types commonly used in intelligence tests. I focus especially on measures of reasoning, particularly inductive reasoning, in part because reasoning tests have been studied extensively and in part because inductive reasoning is the primary ability most commonly associated with g. Gustafsson (1988) claims, for example, that general mental ability (g) can be equated with general fluid ability (g_f), which in turn can be equated with inductive reasoning (I). Sternberg (1986) makes a similar point:

An interesting finding that emerges from the literature attempting to relate cognitive task performance to psychometrically measured intelligence is that the correlation of task performance and IQ seems to be a direct function of the amount of reasoning involved in a given task, independent of the paradigm or label given to the paradigm.... Thus, reasoning ability appears to be central to intelligence. (pp. 309–310)

Even though there is more to intelligence than reasoning, reasoning is a crucial aspect of any understanding of human intelligence.

Measures of Reasoning and Their Uses

Although many different tasks have been used to measure reasoning, a few are used much more commonly than others: analogies, matrix problems, series completions, and classification tasks. Some test batteries also measure verbal reasoning through sentence completion tests, sentence comprehension tests, and even vocabulary. Others include more specific spatial tasks, such as form boards or paper-folding tests. And others use quantitative tests that require examinees to make relational judgments (such as greater than or less than) between quantitative concepts, or to determine how numbers and mathematical operators can be combined to generate a product.

Reasoning tests have important uses in many applied fields, particularly education. When administered to children, the main uses of such tests are (a) to provide an estimate of the student's general cognitive development, which usefully supplements measures of achievement and teacher observations; (b) to provide an alternative frame of reference for interpreting academic achievement; and (c) to guide efforts to adapt instruction. Each of these uses is discussed in considerable detail elsewhere (Lohman & Hagen, 2001a, b; 2002).

Although tests of reasoning abilities have important uses, they are widely misunderstood – both by their critics and their supporters. An all-too-common misunderstanding is that a good ability test of any sort measures (or ought to measure) something like the innate potential or capacity of the examinee. A less common but equally extreme view is that reasoning is nothing more than knowledge, and knowledge is nothing more than experience. As in other domains, such personal theories are often difficult to change. An analogy to physical skills can be helpful. Cognitive skills have much in common with physical skills. Indeed, some models for the acquisition of cognitive skills are taken directly from earlier models of physical skills. My analogy begins with the commonplace distinction between cognitive abilities that are clearly tied to education and experience and those that are less obviously tied to specific experiences. In the domain of reasoning, the former are sometimes called general crystallized abilities and the latter general fluid abilities. Crystallized abilities are like knowledge and skill in playing different sports. These skills are developed through years of practice and training. Athletes show different levels of competence across sports just as students show different levels of competence in various school subjects. But athletes also differ in their levels of physical fitness. Physical fitness is aptitude for acquiring skill in any sport. Athletes who have higher levels of physical fitness or conditioning will generally have an easier time learning new skills and will perform those that they do learn at a higher level. But physical fitness is also an outcome of participation in physically demanding activities. Further, some sports – such as swimming – are more physically demanding than other sports and result in higher increments in physical conditioning for those who participate in them. In a similar manner, reasoning abilities are both an input to as well as an outcome of good schooling (Snow, 1996; Martinez, 2000). Indeed, expecting a measure of reasoning abilities to be independent of education, experience, and culture is like expecting a measure of physical fitness to be uninfluenced by the sports and physical activities in which a person has participated.

THE ROLE OF KNOWLEDGE IN REASONING

Reasoning well in domains of nontrivial complexity depends importantly on knowledge. Expertise is rooted in knowledge, and experts reason differently about problems than do novices. Because of this, some have erroneously assumed that good reasoning is nothing more than good knowledge. This does not take into account the importance of good reasoning in the acquisition of a well-ordered knowledge base. Nonetheless, an increasingly sophisticated knowledge base supports increasingly sophisticated forms of reasoning. For example, experts form problem representations that are more abstract than those of novices. Markman and Genter (2001) argue that the formation of moderately abstract conceptual relations may be a precursor to the detection of coherent patterns. Furthermore, moderately abstract, principle-based concepts are easier to retain and manipulate in working memory, thereby freeing attentional resources for higher-level processes. There is thus an important synergy between good knowledge and good reasoning.

Studies of tasks modeled after item types on intelligence tests often ignore these contributions of knowledge – particularly domain-specific knowledge – to reasoning. The loss is probably most obvious in the domain of verbal reasoning. The verbal reasoning skills of lawyers or scientists go well beyond the sort of decontextualized reasoning abilities assessed on most mental tests. A rich understanding of a domain and of the conventions of argumentation in that domain are needed to identify relevant rather than irrelevant information when understanding the problem, to decide which alternatives are most plausible and need to be considered, and then to decide how best to marshal evidence in support of a position. Strong warrants for an argument are considered highly plausible by those evaluating it. Plausibility judgments reflect both the beliefs of listeners and their assessment of the logical consistency of the argument. Standards for evaluating arguments are thus necessarily somewhat subjective. Nevertheless, some types of arguments are widely recognized as logically unsound. Toulmin, Rieke, and Janik (1984) classify these as (1) missing grounds (e.g., begging the question), (2) irrelevant grounds (e.g., red herring), (3) defective grounds (e.g., hasty generalization), (4) unwarranted assumptions, and (5) ambiguities.

Careful studies of reasoning in knowledge-rich contexts also show processes that generalize across domains. Newell and Simon's (1972) distinction between strong and weak methods of reasoning is especially helpful here. *Strong methods* of reasoning rely heavily on knowledge whereas *weak methods* depend less on content and context. Weak (or domain-general) methods describe what people do when they do not know what to do. Strong (or domain-specific) methods describe what they do when they know what to do. Therefore, children and novices are more likely to use domain-general methods. Furthermore, as Markman and Gentner (2001) observe, many instances of domain-specific thinking result from domain-general processes operating on domain-specific representations. They also note that an exclusive focus on domain-specific thinking can result in a psychology of "particularistic descriptions" (p. 225) rather than of general processes and underlying dimensions. For example, domain-general structural alignment and mapping processes describe how people reason analogically in particular domains. Everyday reasoning depends heavily on the efficacy of past reasoning processes (stored as knowledge) as well as the efficacy of present reasoning processes. Indeed, the ability to adopt a decontextualized reasoning style is considered by some to be the sine qua non of good reasoning (Stanovich, 1999). Such thinking is often quite deliberate and open to introspection. Contextualized reasoning processes, however, often operate outside the realm of conscious awareness.

TACIT AND EXPLICIT PROCESSES

Human reasoning occurs at several different levels. Most cognitive scientists distinguish between tacit and intentional reasoning processes (Evans & Over, 1996; Stanovich, 1999). *Tacit processes* that facilitate reasoning occur without conscious intervention and outside of awareness. They typically do not require attention. Such thinking is sometimes described as associative because it depends on the network of ideas and associations in memory. Tacit processes are typically used when we make a decision in a quick or intuitive way because it feels right, rather than because we have a clearly articulated set of reasons. We are aware of the outcome of these tacit processes but not of the processes themselves. Tacit processes are particularly important in focusing attention and in building a mental model of a problem. Effective problem solvers typically attend to different features of the problem than do less-effective problem solvers. Effective problem solvers know what to look for and what to ignore. In part this is due to greater experience and in part to better use of past experiences. Others describe this automatic attention as the extent to which the person is attuned to certain aspects of a situation and not to others. By temperament or training, some people are more attuned to the distress of others, to the beauty in a painting, to the mathematical properties of objects, or to the alliteration in a poem.

Tacit processes are also importantly linked to feelings that seem essential for solving ill-structured problems that have no single answer. This runs counter to the belief that emotion interferes with reasoning. Yet without ready access to the affective associates of memories, problem solvers seem to drown in a sea of equally plausible but equally bland alternatives (Damasio, 1994).

Intentional reasoning processes, on the other hand, occur within the sphere of conscious awareness. Individuals are aware not only of the outcome of their thinking, as with tacit processes, but also of the processes themselves. It is this type of reasoning that is most distinctly human. Such thinking is often described as strategic or rule based. It typically requires effort. It allows one to bypass the relatively slow accumulation of experiences that underlie tacit learning. We can thereby transfer principles (e.g., one should always capitalize the first letter of the first word in a sentence) rather than an accumulation of varied experiences (e.g., I have seen many sentences, and it feels like it is probably okay to capitalize the first word). Put differently, tacit processes are generally fast, but limited to the range of contexts repeatedly experienced. Intentional reasoning processes, on the other hand, are slow and effortful, but extremely flexible.

Thus, reasoning involves both conscious (explicit) and unconscious (tacit) processes. Although some psychologists refer to both explicit and tacit reasoning processes, others argue that situations elicit reasoning only to the extent that they require conscious application of particular mental processes (Elshout, 1985; Sternberg, 1986). In this chapter, I speak of unconscious processes that facilitate reasoning but reserve the term *reasoning* for certain types of conscious, attention-demanding, nonautomatic thinking.

REASONING AND WORKING MEMORY

One of the more important controversies about reasoning abilities is the extent to which individual differences in reasoning abilities overlap with individual differences in working memory capacity. Kyllonen and Christal

(1990) sparked the controversy with their finding that latent variables for working memory and reasoning factors correlated $r = .80$ to $.88$ in four large studies with U.S. Air Force recruits. Other researchers also found large path coefficients between measures of working memory and measures of fluid reasoning abilities (Süß et al., 2002; Conway et al., 2002). However, critics complained that some tasks used to estimate working memory in these studies were indistinguishable from tasks used to estimate reasoning. For example, the ABC Numerical Assignment test requires examinees to solve for C in problems such as the following: $A = C + 3$, $C = B/3$, and $B = 9$. The task is thought to measure working memory because only one equation is visible at a time and the computations are relatively simple. But it is certainly possible that at least some individuals must use reasoning abilities to solve such tasks. Other critics (e.g., Fry & Hale, 1996) argued that processing speed accounts for most of the relationship between the reasoning and working memory constructs in these studies. Ackerman, Beier, and Boyle (2002) noted that processing speed is itself a multidimensional construct. They concluded that, although there is little doubt that measures of working memory are significantly associated with measures of general intelligence, the two are not synonymous. Indeed, raw correlations between measures of the different construct are typically in the range of $r = .2$ to $.4$.

In part, this is a problem of words. *Working memory* connotes too small a construct; *reasoning* connotes too large a construct – especially given the way each is typically measured. Consider first the reasoning construct. In the best of these studies, reasoning is estimated by performance on a series of short, puzzlelike tasks. More commonly, it is estimated by a single test such as the Raven Progressive Matrices (Raven, Court, & Raven, 1977) that uses a single item format. As Ackerman et al. (2002) noted, "if the Raven is not an exemplary measure of general intelligence (or even g_f), any corroborations between experimental measures (such as [working memory]) and Raven . . . are apt to miss important variance . . . and result in distortion of construct validity" (p. 586). Indeed, figural reasoning tests such as the Raven are typically much poorer predictors of both real-world learning and academic achievement than measures of verbal and quantitative reasoning. Whether measured by one task or several short tasks, the reasoning construct is underrepresented.

On the other hand, the construct measured by the series of "working memory" tests is much more complex than its label suggests. These tasks generally require participants to understand and follow a sometimes complex set of directions, assemble and then revise a strategy for performing a difficult, attention-demanding task, maintain a high level of effort across a substantial number of trials, and then repeat the process for a new task with a new set of directions. By design, many working memory tasks require individuals to process simultaneously one set of ideas while remembering another set. These processes, while generally thought to be easy, are certainly not trivial, especially when performed under memory load. Verbal working memory tasks commonly require reading comprehension, mathematical tasks require computation, and spatial tasks require transformations such as mental rotation. Tasks are also designed to elicit executive functions such as the monitoring of processes, controlling their rate and sequence of operation, inhibiting inappropriate response processes, coordinating information from different domains, and integrating ideas into a coherent mental model.

Therefore, another way to express the conclusion that individual differences in working memory and reasoning overlap would be the following:

A substantial portion of the individual-differences variation in the limited and somewhat artificial set of reasoning tasks included in our study can be accounted for by individual differences in the ability to assemble a strategy for the simultaneous storage and transformation of ideas, to monitor the success of this strategy and change it as needed, to coordinate information from different sources, to inhibit some mental operations and to activate others, to sequence these mental operations, and to integrate ideas into a coherent mental structure or model.

Reasoning Tests as Cognitive Tasks

There is now an extensive body of literature that examines how individuals solve items on reasoning tests, particularly analogy, seriation, and classification tasks. For reviews, see Sternberg (1985), Snow and Lohman (1989), and Lohman (2000). However, constructs such as reasoning ability are defined not by particular tasks, but by the common covariation in several tasks. Put differently, understanding individual differences in solving matrix problems, letter-series problems, or analogy problems is not the same as understanding individual differences in reasoning ability. Every well-constructed test measures something that it shares with other tests designed to measure the same construct and something unique to the particular test. There are no exceptions. The main sources of uniqueness are the idiosyncrasies of the particular sample of items contained in the test and the format in which they are administered. This is shown clearly in factor analyses of wide-ranging test batteries. The loading of a test on the factor it helps define is often only slightly greater than its loading on a test-specific factor. A well-grounded theory of reasoning ability, then, must look beyond the sources of individual differences in particular reasoning tasks to those that are shared by several reasoning tasks.

There are two aspects of constructs to be considered, which are nicely captured in Embretson's (1983) distinction between construct representation and nomothetic span. Construct representation refers to the identification of psychological constructs (e.g., component processes, strategies, structures) that are involved in responding to items on tests. Processes of most interest are those that are common across families of tests that collectively define individual-differences constructs such as inductive reasoning ability.

Nomothetic span, on the other hand, concerns the correlates of individual differences on a test. Of the many processes that are involved in performance on a particular task, only some will be shared with other tasks, and of these common processes, an even smaller subset will be responsible for individual differences that are common across tasks. In other words, even processes and structures that are common to all tests in a family of reasoning tasks may contribute little or not at all to individual differences in reasoning ability.

CONSTRUCT REPRESENTATION OF REASONING TESTS

With these caveats in mind, then, I briefly summarize investigations of the processes test-takers use when solving items on reasoning tests (for a more detailed summary, see Lohman, 2000). In the subsequent section, I summarize hypotheses about which processes are most responsible for generating observed individual differences in reasoning abilities.

Pellegrino (1985; see also Goldman & Pellegrino, 1984) argues that inductive reasoning tasks such as analogies, series completions, and classifications all require four types of processes: encoding or attribute discovery, inference or attribute comparison, relation or rule evaluation, and decision and response processes.

Encoding processes create mental representations of stimuli on which various inference or attribute-comparison processes operate. The nature of these processes differs across tasks. In an analogy [A is to B as C is to D], the inference process must determine how various terms are related to each other. In classification problems [Given the set *apple, pear, banana*, which word belongs: *orange* or *pea*?], the inference process must identify a rule or category that is shared by all the terms. In series problems [Given *3, 4, 6, 9, 13*, what comes next?], the inference process must identify the pattern in a sequence of letters or numbers. Inference processes are usually not sufficient for problem solution, however. One must also determine relationships among two or more first-order relationships in the problem. In an analogy, for example, the relationship between A and B must be identical to the relationship between C and D. In a matrix problem, the relationship among elements in one row must be the same in the other two rows. Pellegrino (1985) argues that one of the most important aspects of inductive reasoning is the ability to create complex relationship structures in memory and to determine their consistency. Errors occur when working memory resources are exceeded.

Sternberg (1986) claims that there are three kinds of reasoning processes, any one of which define a task as a reasoning task. The three processes are (1) selective encoding (distinguishing relevant from irrelevant information), (2) selective comparison (deciding what mentally stored information is relevant for solving a problem), and (3) selective combination (combining selectively encoded or compared information in working memory). Furthermore, the three processes define a reasoning situation only to the extent that they are executed in a controlled rather than in an automatic fashion. This implies that the extent to which a task measures reasoning depends on the relative novelty of the task for the individual.

These processes are implemented by various sorts of inferential rules. Procedural rules include operations called performance components in earlier theories (Sternberg, 1977; Sternberg & Gardner, 1983). Declarative rules vary by problem content and specify the type of semantic relations allowed in a problem. (For verbal analogy problems, for example, the set of possible semantic relations includes equality, set-subset, set-superset, static properties, and functional properties). Not all rules are rules of reasoning; reasoning rules are those that serve the functions of selective encoding, selective comparison, and selective combination. Thus, mnemonic strategies and computation algorithms are not reasoning rules.

The theory also claims that the probability that particular inferential rules will be used in the solution of a reasoning problem is influenced by mediating variables, such as the individual's subjective estimate of the likelihood of the occurrence of a rule, the individual's prior knowledge, working memory capacity, and ability to represent certain types of information (e.g., spatial versus linguistic).

Sternberg claims that the major difference between inductive and deductive reasoning is that the difficulty of the former derives mainly from the selective encoding and comparison processes, whereas the difficulty of the latter derives mainly from the selective combination process. Thus, for verbal analogies, the primary difficulty is determining which of the many features of the A term are relevant to the B term as well. For example, in the analogy paper : tree :: plastic:?, one must decide which of the many attributes of the word "paper" (that we write on it, that it sometimes comes in tablets, that printers use it, that it is a short form of the word "newspaper," that it is made from wood, etc.) also overlap with what one knows about the word "tree." In contrast, figural analogies tend to emphasize selective encoding. A key difficulty of such problems is deciding which features of the stimuli to attend to in the first place.

Series completion problems not only require many of the same processes as analogies (Greeno, 1978; Pellegrino & Glaser, 1980; Sternberg & Gardner, 1983), but also emphasize selective comparison. In a typical series problem, many possible relations could be obtained between successive pairs of numbers or letters. For example, in the series 1, 3, 6, 10, ..., the relation between the first two digits could be plus 2, times 3, next odd number, etc. The relation between 3 and 6 could be plus 3, times 2, etc. Problem difficulty is highly related to the obscurity of the rule. However, when multiple rules account for a series, the "best" rule is typically the most specific rule. A similar set of arguments applies to the analysis of classification problems.

For deductive reasoning tasks such as categorical syllogisms, however, the main source of difficulty lies not in encoding the terms or even in selectively comparing relations among them, but rather in keeping track of the ways in which terms can be combined. Consider, for example, a categorical syllogism such as "Some A are B. All B are C." Is the conclusion "Some A are C" valid? Information processing models of syllogistic reasoning all share four stages of information processing, which Sternberg (1986) calls encoding, combination, comparison, and response. In the encoding stage, the individual must create a mental representation of each premise that is amenable to mental transformation. The large number of combinations between representations of premises taxes processing resources. For example, the problem "Some B are C. Some A are B." involves 16 combinations (four for each of the two premises). Furthermore, the exact inferential rule used also appears to be a major source of difficulty, although there is controversy as to exactly what these rules are. More important, however, has been the recurring finding that many other factors (what Sternberg calls mediators) influence performance as categorical syllogisms. For example, subjects show flagrant biases in solving such problems as a function of the emotionality of the premises, subjects' agreement with the content of the premises, abstractness of the content, and even the form in which the problems are presented. Some strategies simply facilitate performance; others completely bypass the reasoning process (e.g., Yang & Johnson-Laird, 2001). This suggests that although such problems may be interesting candidates for research, they are probably not good candidates for assessments of individual differences in reasoning abilities.

Another type of deductive reasoning task that has been extensively studied is the linear syllogism. These are problems of the sort "Bill is taller than Mary. Mary is taller than Sue. Who's tallest?" Problems of this sort have anywhere from two to four terms, with the most typical number being three. As in other deductive reasoning problems, the major source of difficulty is not in encoding the terms or in comparing them (for example, to know that "short" is the opposite of "tall"), but rather to combine the information in the premises into a single mental model. Unlike linear syllogisms, however, there are fewer content-induced biases to cloud performance. Indeed, the most likely bias occurs when the premise contradicts one's personal knowledge, such as when one knows that Mary is shorter than Sue, whereas the problem asks one to envision the opposite. Such contrafactual reasoning can be deliberately introduced into problems (e.g., "imagine that mice are larger than elephants," etc.). For an introduction to recent investigations of this type of deductive reasoning, see Johnson-Laird (1999).

Johnson-Laird (1999) argues that mental models are useful for predicting performance on these types of tasks. Although models often give rise to images, they are distinct from images because models can contain abstract elements, such as negation, that cannot be visualized. Yang and Johnson-Laird (2001) showed how the theory of mental models could explain some sources of difficulty on the logical reasoning problems from the Analytic subtest of the Graduate Record Examination. They identified three sources of difficulty: the nature of the task (it is easier to identify which conclusion a text implies rather than a missing premise), the nature of the foils (it is easier to reject foils that are inconsistent with the text than foils that are consistent with it), and the nature of the conclusions (it is easier to accept a conclusion that is consistent with the text than one that is inconsistent with it). The second and third sources of difficulty stem from the principle of truth: Individuals minimize the load on working memory by tending to construct mental models that represent explicitly only what is true, and not what is false (Johnson-Laird, 1999). Given the truth of the premises, the probability of a conclusion depends on the proportion of models in which it holds. It is considered possible if it holds in at least one model of the premises and necessary if it holds in all models.

NOMOTHETIC SPAN OF REASONING TESTS

Understanding the common processing demands of tasks is one way to understand the construct they help define. The emphasis is on explaining what makes tasks difficult. Another route is to examine those features of tasks that seem to moderate their relationships with the target construct – here g_f or g. One of the primary uses of visual models of test correlations (such as a two-dimensional radex) is to make these general themes more apparent. Tests that load heavily on g or g_f typically fall near the center of the radex, whereas seemingly simpler tasks are distributed around the periphery.

Several hypotheses have been advanced to explain how processing complexity increases along the various spokes that run from the periphery to g: (1) an increase in the number of component processes; (2) an accumulation of differences in speed of component processing; (3) increasing involvement of one or more critically important performance components, such as the inference process; (4) an increase in demands on limited working memory or attention; and (5) an increase in demands on adaptive functions, including assembly, control, and monitor functions. Clearly these explanations are not independent. For example, it is impossible to get an accumulation of speed differences over components (Hypothesis 2) without also increasing the number of component processes required (Hypothesis 1).

In spite of this overlap, these hypotheses provide a useful way to organize the discussion.

More Component Processes

Even the most superficial examination of tasks that fall along one of the spokes of the radex reveals that more central or g-loaded tasks require subjects to do more than required by the more peripheral tests. Many years ago, Zimmerman (1954) demonstrated that a form-board test could be made to load more on perceptual speed, spatial relations, visualization, and reasoning factors, in that order, by increasing the complexity of the items. Snow et al.'s (1984) re-analyses of old learning-task and ability-test correlation matrices showed similar continua. Spilsbury (1992) argues that the crucial manipulation here is an increase in the factorial complexity of a task. However, increases in the number or difficulty of task steps beyond a certain point can decrease the correlation with g (Crawford, 1988; Raaheim, 1988; Swiney, 1985). Thus, one does not automatically increase the relationship with g simply by making problems harder, or even by increasing the factorial complexity of a task. Indeed, many hard problems (e.g., memorizing lists of randomly chosen numbers or words) are not particularly good measures of g. Furthermore, even for problems that do require the type of processing that causes the test to measure g, problems must be of the appropriate level of difficulty for the subjects.

Speed or Efficiency of Elementary Processing

This hypothesis has taken several forms. In its strongest form, the assertion has been that individuals differ in the general speed or efficiency with which they process information (Jensen, 1998). In principle, processing speed could be estimated on any elementary cognitive task that minimizes the import of learning, motivation, strategy, and other confounding variables. Although disattenuated correlations between RT and g can be substantial when samples vary widely in ability (even, for example, including mentally retarded participants), samples more typical of those used in other research on abilities yield correlations between RT and g in the $r = -.1$ to $r = -.4$ range (Jensen, 1982; Roberts & Stankov, 1999; Sternberg, 1985; Deary & Stough, 1996). Furthermore, response latencies on many tasks show a pattern of increasing and then decreasing correlations with an external estimate of g as task complexity increases. In other words, response latencies for moderately complex tasks typically show higher correlations with g than do response latencies for more complex tasks. But this is unsurprising. The more complex the task, the more room there is for subjects to use different strategies or even to be inconsistent in the execution of different components.

In its weak form, the hypothesis has been that although speed of processing on any one task may be only weakly correlated with more complex performances, such small differences cumulate over time and tasks. Thus, Hunt, Frost, and Lunneborg (1973) noted that although latency differences in the retrieval of overlearned name codes correlated only $r = .3$ with verbal ability, such small differences on individual words cumulate to substantial differences in the course of a more extended activity. Detterman (1986) emphasized the cumulation across different component processes rather than across time. He showed that although individual component processes were only weakly correlated with g, their combined effect was more substantial.

Although individual differences in speed of processing are an important aspect of g, g is more than rapid or efficient information processing. Furthermore, the strength of the relationship between speed of processing and g varies considerably across domains, being strongest ($r \approx -.4$) in verbal domain and weakest ($r \approx -.2$) in the spatial domain. Indeed, for complex spatial tasks, the speed with which individuals perform different spatial operations is usually much less predictive of overall performance than the richness or quality of the mental representations they create (Lohman, 1988; Salthouse et al., 1990).

More Involvement of Central Components

If g is not simply a reflection of more or faster processing, might it be the case that g really reflects the action of particular mental processes? Spearman (1927) was one of the first to argue for this alternative. For him, the essential processes were the "eduction of relations," which Sternberg calls *inference*, and the "eduction of correlates," which Sternberg calls *mapping* and *application*. Evidence favoring this hypothesis is substantial. A common characteristic of tests that are good measures of g_f – such as the matrices, letter/number series, analogies, classification, and various quantitative reasoning tests – is that they are all measures of reasoning, particularly inductive reasoning. Many school learning tasks, particularly in science and mathematics, bear formal similarity to g_f tests. Greeno (1978) refered to such tasks, collectively, as problems of inducing structure. Indeed, the problem of inducing structure in instruction is probably why reasoning tests correlate with achievement tests (Snow, 1980). But to describe the overlap in this way is not to explain it.

Evidence supporting the hypothesis that particular component processes are central to g has been surprisingly difficult to obtain. Sternberg's (1977) investigations of analogical reasoning found little generalizability across tasks of scores for the inference component and at best inconsistent correlations of these scores with reference reasoning tests. Rather, it was the intercept (or "wastebasket" parameter) that showed more consistent correlations with reference abilities. We now know that this is in large measure an inevitable consequence of the way component scores are estimated (Lohman, 1994). Individual differences that are consistent across items that require different amounts of particular component processes will appear in the intercept rather than in the component scores. Therefore, low or inconsistent correlations between scores for particular component processes and other variables do not provide much evidence against the hypothesis that these processes are important.

A second line of evidence on the centrality of particular component processes comes from demonstrations that certain types of task manipulations are more likely than others to increase the g_f loading of a task (Pellegrino, 1985; Sternberg, 1986). Sternberg (1986) calls these *selective encoding*, i.e., the requirement to attend selectively to information and to encode only that subset that is likely to be needed for solving a problem; *selective comparison*, i.e., to retrieve only information that is relevant to a problem, especially when the set of potentially relevant information in memory is vast; and *selective combination*, i.e., to assemble in working memory information already selected as relevant. Selective encoding depends heavily on the individual's store of prior knowledge (schema) and its attunement to the affordances of the situation. It also means the ability to resist the distractions of salient but irrelevant information, or, when solving items on mental tests, looking ahead to the alternatives before studying the stem (Bethell-Fox, Lohman, & Snow, 1984). Selective comparison depends heavily not only on the store of knowledge, but also on its organization and accessibility, especially the ability to search rapidly through memory for intersections between two concepts. This is the essential feature of inference or abstraction problems: finding ways in which concepts A and B are not merely associated with each other, but rather finding the rules or relations that most specifically characterize their association. Problems in inductive reasoning emphasize selective encoding and comparison. Problems in deductive reasoning, on the other hand, emphasize selective combination. For example, syllogistic reasoning problems are difficult not because it is difficult to discern the relevant information in statements such as "all A are B" or in the understanding of the relations between words such as "all" and "some" (although this is a source of confusion for some), rather, the main difficulty in keeping track of all the ways in which the premises can be combined. This taxes both working memory and the ability to manipulate symbols. Thus, although certain processes may be central to intelligent thinking, individual differences in those processes may be in part due to other system limitations – such as working memory resources.

Attention and Working Memory Capacity

All information processing models of memory and cognition posit the existence of a limited-capacity, short-term or working memory that functions not only as a central processor but also as a bottleneck in the system. Some see this in terms of structure or capacity limitations; others

view it in terms of attentional resources, and others in terms of differences in knowledge or experience (see Miyake & Shah, 1999). Hunt and
Lansman (1982) and Ackerman (1988) argue that tasks that show higher
correlations with g require more attentional resources. Attempts to manipulate the attentional demands of tasks often use a dual-task paradigm.
Here, participants are required to do two things simultaneously, such as
searching for a particular stimulus in a visual display while simultaneously listening for a specified auditory stimulus. Although the effect is
often not observed, differences between more and less able subjects are
typically greater in the dual-task than in the single-task condition. However, interpretation of this finding is problematic. For example, in one
study, Stankov (1988) found that correlations with both g_c and g_f,
but especially g_f, were higher for dual tasks than for single tasks. However, high levels of performance in the dual-task situation were due to a
strategy of momentarily ignoring one task while attending to the other.
Thus, what on the surface seemed to implicate attentional resources on
closer inspection implicated self-monitoring and the shifting of attentional
resources.

Attentional requirements of tasks vary according to an individual's familiarity with the task and to the susceptibility of the task to automatiza-
tion. Tasks – or task components – in which there is a consistent mapping
between stimulus and response can be automatized in this way. Individuals who recognize the consistencies thus automatize task components
more rapidly than those who are not so attuned. Put differently, knowledge guides attention and thus constrains the number of features that must
be considered in understanding the problem.

The explanation of differences in reasoning as reflecting differences in
working memory capacity parallels the attentional explanation. Many researchers have claimed that a major source of individual differences on
reasoning tasks lies in how much information one must maintain in working memory, especially while effecting some transformation of that information (Holzman, Pellegrino, & Glaser, 1982). Some argue that the critical
factor is the ability to maintain a representation in the face of interference
from automatically activated but distracting representations (Engle et al.,
1999). Controlling attention in this way is a critical aspect both of selective
encoding and goal management (Primi, 2001). Furthermore, as Kyllonen
and Christal (1990) noted, most of the performance processes (such as encoding and inference) and executive processes (such as goal setting, goal
management, and monitoring) required for problem solution are presumed
to occur in working memory. Thus, even though, say, the inference process may be effective, it must be performed within the limits of the working
memory system. Therefore, although many different processes may be executed in the solution of a task, individual differences in them may primarily
reflect *individual differences* in working memory resources.

Adaptive Processing

While acknowledging that individual differences in *g* reflect differences in all of these levels – in the speed and efficacy of elementary processes, in attentional or working memory resources, and in the action of processes responsible for inference and abstraction (which includes knowledge, skill, and attunement to affordances in the task situation) – several theorists have argued that more is needed. Sternberg (1985) argued that intelligent action requires the application of metacomponents – i.e., control processes that decide what the problem is, select lower-order components and organize them into a strategy, select a mode for representing or organizing information, allocate attentional resources, monitor the solution process, and attend to external feedback. Marshalek, Lohman, and Snow (1983), on the other hand, focused on assembly and control processes. They hypothesized that "more complex tasks may require more involvement of executive assembly and control processes that structure and analyze the problem, assemble a strategy of attack on it, monitor the performance process, and adapt these strategies as performance proceeds, within as well as between items in a task, and between tasks" (p. 124). The Carpenter, Just, and Shell (1990) analysis of the Raven test supports this hypothesis. In their simulation, the crucial executive functions were (a) the ability to decompose a complex problem into simpler problems and (b) the ability to manage the hierarchy of goals and subgoals generated by this decomposition.

In general, assembly processes are reflected in activities in which an individual must organize a series of overt acts or covert cognitive processes into a sequence. They are thus essential for all high-level thinking. These processes are greatly facilitated by the ability to envision future states (i.e., goals) that differ from present states (i.e., what is currently in mind or in view). This is an especially important activity when attempting novel or ill-structured tasks. Control processes are more diverse, although all involve the ability to monitor the effects of one's cognitions and actions, and adjust them according to feedback from the environment or one's body. Both types of processing depend heavily on the ability to maintain ideas or images in an active state in working memory, especially when several ideas must be considered simultaneously or when goal images differ from images activated by perceptions.

More able problem solvers are not always more strategic or flexible or reflective in their problem solving (cf. Alderton & Larson, 1994). Indeed, subjects who are most able often show little evidence of shifting strategies across items on a test. For example, in the Kyllonen, Lohman, and Woltz (1984) study of a spatial synthesis task, subjects very high in spatial ability (but low in verbal ability) were best described by a model that said that they always mentally synthesized stimuli. These subjects probably did not have to resort to other strategies. Rather, the subjects who had less extreme profiles but relatively high scores on g showed the most strategy shifting.

Several investigators have attempted to manipulate the extent to which items require flexible adaptation and thereby alter their relationship with g. For example, Swiney (1985) sought to test the hypothesis that correlations between performance on geometric analogies and g would increase as more flexible adaptation was required, at least for easy and moderately difficult problems. Correlations with g were expected to decline if task difficulty was too great. Adaptation was manipulated by grouping items in different ways. In the blocked condition, inter-item variation was minimized by grouping items with similar processing requirements (estimated by the number of elements and the number and type of transformations). In the mixed condition, items were grouped to be as dissimilar as possible.

Results showed that low ability subjects were more adversely affected by mixing items than high ability subjects, regardless of treatment order. Relationships between task accuracy and g varied systematically as a function of item difficulty and task requirements. Strongest relationships were observed for identifying (i.e., inferring) and applying difficult rules. Weakest relationships were observed for applying easy rules or discovering difficult rules, especially in the mixed condition. Retrospective reports supported the conclusion that high g subjects were better able to adapt their strategies flexibly to meet changing task demands. Swiney also found that low g subjects overestimated their performance on highly difficult items; they also consistently underestimated the difficulty of problems. This suggests differences in monitoring and evaluation processes.

Chastain (1992) reported three additional studies contrasting blocked versus mixed item presentations. Experiments 1 and 2 used items from the Wonderlic Personnel Test, a 50-item test that samples a broad range of item formats. The third experiment used a figural encoding task and a dynamic spatial task. In all studies, flexible adaptation was estimated by a simple difference score (mixed minus blocked) and by a residual score (regression of mixed on blocked). Correlations between these two scores, reference tests, and performance on a logic-gates learning task were small, but generally in the expected direction.

A study by Carlstedt, Gustafsson, and Ullstadius (2000) challenges this interpretation of the blocked–mixed contrast. Carlstedt et al. administered three kinds of inductive reasoning problems to groups of Swedish military recruits. Unexpectedly, they found that g loadings were higher in the blocked condition than in the mixed condition. They argue that the homogeneous arrangement affords better possibilities for learning and transfer across items. However, items were extremely difficult, and so generalization is difficult.

To summarize, as one moves from periphery to center in a two- or even three-dimensional radex, tasks increase in apparent complexity. Tasks near the center typically require more steps or component processes and emphasize accuracy rather than speed of response. But this does not mean that speed of processing is unimportant or that the addition of any type of process will increase the correlation with *g*. Increasing the demand on certain types of processing, which Sternberg describes as selective encoding, comparison, and combination, also increases the correlation with *g*. Importantly, though, such processes require controlled, effortful processing and place heavy demands on working memory resources. They also require subjects to be more strategic, flexible, or adaptive in their problem solving, or to learn from easy item rules that will be needed in combination to solve hard items.

LIMITATIONS OF THE INFORMATION PROCESSING PARADIGM

The information processing paradigm has enormously enriched our understanding of cognitive tests and the ability constructs they estimate. We have moved from trait labels and vague notions of "process" to detailed models of thinking. However, all paradigms are inadequate in some respects. Two shortcomings of the information processing approach are particularly salient: (1) the neglect of affect and conation and (2) the failure to understand the contextual specificity of abilities.

Affect and Conation

Although theorizing about the influence of affect (or feeling) and conation (or willing) on cognition dates back to the Greek philosophers, it is only recently that investigators have attempted to study the complex and reciprocal influences these two factors have on each other. Many promising leads have been identified (see Snow, Corno, & Jackson, 1996; Boekaerts, 1995). It is clear that persons who do well on ability tests expend effort differently from persons who score poorly. The difference is most striking in comparisons of experts and novices in skill domains such as reading. Experts expend their efforts on high-level processes (that include but go beyond comprehension), whereas novices struggle to identify words and the sentences they comprise. Affect enters not only as anxiety or frustration, which further constricts cognition, but also as interest and surprise, which enhance and direct cognition. In particular, those who adopt a constructive motivational orientation toward a task will tend to exhibit more and better self-regulation than individuals who adopt a less constructive or even defensive orientation. Situations differentially elicit these conative and affective resources. Indeed, understanding the role of affect in cognition seems to demand a mode of theorizing and experimentation that attends not only to persons or to situations, but also to the attunement of particular individuals to particular aspects of situations.

Including Situations and Their Affordances

A theory of *g* must explain individual differences in problem solving not only on tests but also in school and other everyday contexts. Although occasionally nodding to the role of culture, cognitive theories of abilities have not yet found ways to incorporate the fact that cognition is situated. Theories that would explain how abilities facilitate goal attainment need to start with the proposition that such action is always situated. Situations evoke or afford the use of some concepts or ways of thinking, but only for those tuned to perceive them. Some tunings reflect biological adaptations, but most are mediated by experience. In the language of Corno et al. (2002), abilities that are actually elicited in a particular situation function as aptitudes. Aptitudes are any characteristics (including affect and motivation, for example) that aid goal attainment in a particular situation. For example, inductive reasoning abilities may be elicited when situations require the identification of pattern or rule and the person has no ready-made solution. The perception that evokes structure-mapping processes is trivial when someone asks, "What do these situations have in common?" More often, it occurs because the individual is actively engaged in making sense of the world. Making sense means finding commonalities. Thus, as Snow (1994) puts it, aptitudes are reflected in the tuning of particular persons to the particular demands and opportunities of a situation, and thus reside in the union of person in situation, not "in the mind" alone.

Toward a Definition of Reasoning

In his summary of correlational studies of reasoning abilities, Carroll (1993) suggests that the general reasoning factor can be decomposed into three subfactors: sequential reasoning, inductive reasoning, and quantitative reasoning. Sequential reasoning is most commonly measured by tasks that require deductive or logical reasoning. Tasks are often (but not always) verbal. Inductive reasoning is commonly measured by tasks that require identification of a pattern or rule in a stimulus set. Tasks are often (but not always) figural. Quantitative reasoning is measured by tasks that require either inductive or deductive reasoning on quantitative concepts. Setting aside task content, then, the critical reasoning processes are sequential (or deductive) and inferential.

When people reason, they must, in Bruner's (1957) helpful phrase, go "beyond the information given." They do this in one or both of the following ways:

1. They attempt to *infer* (either automatically or deliberately) concepts, patterns, or rules that best (i.e., most uniquely) characterize the relationships or patterns they perceive among all the elements (words, symbols, figures, sounds, movements, etc.) in a stimulus set. Better reasoning is characterized by the use of concepts or rules that simultaneously satisfy the opposing needs for abstraction (or generalization) and specificity. Such concepts or rules tend to be at least moderately abstract yet precisely tuned. Put differently, a poor inference is often vague and captures only a subset of the relationships among the elements in the set. The judgment of what constitutes better reasoning is in part dictated by the shared knowledge and conventions of particular communities of discourse and in part by the precision and generality of the inference.

2. They attempt to *deduce* the consequences or implications of a rule, set of premises, or statements using warrants that are rendered plausible by logic or by information that is either given in the problem or assumed to be true within the community of discourse. They often seem to do this by creating and manipulating mental models of the situation. Such models tend to represent explicitly only what is assumed to be true about the situation. Better reasoning involves providing warrants that are more plausible or consistent with the rules of logic or the conditions embodied in a comprehensive mental model. More advanced deductive reasoning involves providing either multiple (possibly divergent) warrants for a single claim or an increasingly sophisticated chain of logically connected and separately warranted assertions.

Clearly, then, reasoning abilities are not static. They are developed through experience and rendered easier to perform through exercise. Recall that individual differences in reasoning are substantially correlated with the amount of information individuals can hold in working memory while performing some transformation on it. The ability to do this depends in large measure on the attentional resources individuals bring to a task, their familiarity with the to-be-remembered information, and their skill in performing the required transformations. Thus, prior knowledge and skill are critical determiners of the level of reasoning that one can exhibit. The dependence on prior knowledge is most pronounced on tasks that require deductive reasoning with authentic stimulus materials, and is least pronounced on tasks that require inferential reasoning with simple geometric or alphanumeric stimuli. The processes that support sophisticated reasoning in a knowledge-rich domain, however, appear to be largely the same as those that enable the neophyte to infer consistencies or deduce likely consequents.

One of the most important uses of tests of reasoning abilities is as an indicator of readiness to discover what to do in situations in which the person cannot rely on stored routines to solve problems. Reasoning tests have long been used in this way to inform decisions about college admission for students who come from impoverished backgrounds. Indeed, good reasoning tests shows smaller differences between majority and minority students than do good achievement tests (Lohman, 2004). Measures of general reasoning abilities also routinely interact with instructional methods. In particular, they predict academic success better when instructional methods require that students discover concepts and relationships for themselves than when instruction is more didactic (Snow & Lohman, 1989). Because of this, one can improve the likelihood that students with poorly developed reasoning abilities will succeed – by reducing either the need for prior knowledge or the working memory demands of ancillary processes. In other words, understanding why individuals differ in their reasoning abilities allows one to alter the prediction of academic success. For this reason alone, educators should pay more attention to students' current levels of reasoning abilities. Indeed, one would be hard-pressed to think of any ability construct that is better understood or has more practical relevance to education at all levels than reasoning abilities.

References

Ackerman, P. L. (1988). Determinants of individual differences during skill acquisition: A theory of cognitive abilities and information processing. *Journal of Experimental Psychology: General, 117*, 299–329.

Ackerman, P. L., Beier, M., & Boyle, M. O. (2002). Individual differences in working memory within a nomological network of cognitive and perceptual speed abilities. *Journal of Experimental Psychology: General, 131*, 567–589.

Alderton, D. L., & Larson, G. E. (1994). Cross-task consistency in strategy use and the relationship with intelligence. *Intelligence, 18*, 47–76.

Bethell-Fox, C. E., Lohman, D. F., & Snow, R. E. (1984). Adaptive reasoning: Componential and eye movement analysis of geometric analogy performance. *Intelligence, 8*, 205–238.

Boekaerts, M. (1995). The interface between intelligence and personality as determinants of classroom learning. In D. H. Saklofske & M. Zeidner (Eds.), *International handbook of personality and intelligence* (pp. 161–183). New York: Plenum Press.

Brody, N. (1992). *Intelligence*. San Diego: Academic Press.

Bruner, J. (1957). Going beyond the information given. In J. S. Bruner (Ed.), *Contemporary approaches to cognition* (pp. 41–69). Cambridge, MA: Harvard University Press.

Carlstedt, B., Gustafsson, J.-E., & Ullstadius, E. (2000). Item sequencing effects on the measurement of fluid intelligence. *Intelligence, 28*, 145–160.

Carpenter, P. A., Just, M. A., & Schell, P. (1990). What one intelligence test measures: A theoretical account of the processing in the Raven Progressive Matrices test. *Psychological Review, 97*, 404–431.

Carroll, J. B. (1993). *Human cognitive abilities. A survey of factor-analytic studies.* Cambridge, UK: Cambridge University Press.

Chastain, R. L. (1992). Adaptive processing in complex learning and cognitive performance. Unpublished doctoral dissertation, Stanford University, Stanford, CA.

Conway, A. R. A., Cowan, N., Bunting, M. F., Therriault, D. J., & Minkoff, S. R. B. (2002). A latent variable analysis of working memory capacity, short-term memory capacity, processing speed, and general fluid intelligence. *Intelligence, 30,* 163–183.

Corno, L., Cronbach, L. J., Kupermintz, H., Lohman, D. F., Mandinach, E. B., Porteus, A. W., & Talbert, J. E. (2002). *Remaking the concept of aptitude: Extending the legacy of Richard E. Snow.* Mahwah, NJ: Erlbaum.

Crawford, J. (1988). Intelligence, task complexity and tests of sustained attention. Unpublished doctoral dissertation, University of New South Wales, Sydney, Australia.

Damasio, A. (1994). *Descartes' error: Emotion, reason, and the human brain.* New York: Putnam.

Deary, I. J., & Stough, C. (1996). Intelligence and inspection time: Achievements, prospects, and problems. *American Psychologist, 51,* 599–608.

Detterman, D. K. (1986). Human intelligence is a complex system of separate processes. In R. J. Sternberg & D. K. Detterman (Eds.), *What is intelligence?* (pp. 57–61). Norwood, NJ: Ablex.

Elshout, J. J. (1985). *Problem solving and education.* Paper presented at the meeting of the American Educational Research Association, San Francisco, June 1985.

Embretson, S. E. (1983). Construct validity: Construct representation versus nomothetic span. *Psychological Bulletin, 93,* 179–197.

Engle, R. W., Tuholski, S. W., Laughlin, J. E., & Conway, A. R. A. (1999). Working memory, short-term memory, and general fluid intelligence: A latent variable approach. *Journal of Experimental Psychology: General, 128*(3), 309–331.

Estes, W. K. (1974). Learning theory and intelligence. *American Psychologist, 29,* 740–749.

Evans, J. S. B. T., & Over, D. E. (1996). *Rationality and reasoning.* Hove, UK: Psychology Press.

Fry, A. F., & Hale, S. (1996). Processing speed, working memory, and fluid intelligence: Evidence for a developmental cascade. *Psychological Science, 7,* 237–241.

Garlick, D. (2002). Understanding the nature of the general factor of intelligence: The role of individual differences in neural plasticity as an explanatory mechanism. *Psychological Review, 109,* 116–136.

Goldman, S. R., & Pellegrino, J. W. (1984). Deductions about induction: Analyses of developmental and individual differences. In R. J. Sternberg (Ed.), *Advances in the psychology of human intelligence* (Vol. 2, pp. 149–197). Hillsdale, NJ: Erlbaum.

Greeno, J. G. (1978). A study of problem solving. In R. Glaser (Ed.), *Advances in instructional psychology* (Vol. 1, pp. 13–75). Hillsdale, NJ: Erlbaum.

Gustafsson, J.-E. (1988). Hierarchical models of individual differences in cognitive abilities. In R. J. Sternberg (Ed.), *Advances in the psychology of human intelligence* (Vol. 4, pp. 35–71). Hillsdale, NJ: Erlbaum.

Gustafsson, J.-E., & Undheim, J. O. (1996). Individual differences in cognitive functions. In D. C. Berliner & R. C. Calfee (Eds.), *Handbook of educational psychology* (pp. 186–242.) New York: Simon & Schuster Macmillan.

Holzman, T. G., Pellegrino, J. W., & Glaser, R. (1982). Cognitive dimensions of numerical rule induction. *Journal of Educational Psychology, 74*, 360–373.

Hunt, E. B., Frost, N., & Lunneborg, C. (1973). Individual differences in cognition: A new approach to intelligence. In G. Bower (Ed.), *The psychology of learning and motivation* (Vol. 7, pp. 87–122). New York: Academic Press.

Hunt, E., & Lansman, M. (1982). Individual differences in attention. In R. J. Sternberg (Ed.), *Advances in the psychology of human abilities* (Vol. 1, pp. 207–254). Hillsdale, NJ: Erlbaum.

Hunter, J. E., & Schmidt, F. L. (1996). Intelligence and job performance: Economic and social implications. *Psychology, Public Policy, and Law, 3/4*, 447–472.

Jensen, A. R. (1982). The chronometry of intelligence. In R. J. Sternberg (Ed.), *Advances in the psychology of human intelligence* (Vol. 1, pp. 255–310). Hillsdale, NJ: Erlbaum.

Jensen, A. R. (1998). *The g factor: The science of mental ability*. Westport, CT: Praeger.

Johnson-Laird, P. N. (1999). Deductive reasoning. *Annual Review of Psychology, 50*, 109–135.

Kyllonen, P. C., & Christal, R. E. (1990). Reasoning ability is (little more than) working-memory capacity?! *Intelligence, 14*, 389–433.

Kyllonen, P. C., Lohman, D. F., & Woltz, D. J. (1984). Componential modeling of alternative strategies for performing spatial tasks. *Journal of Educational Psychology, 76*, 1325–1345.

Lohman, D. F. (1988). Spatial abilities as traits, processes, and knowledge. In R. J. Sternberg (Ed.), *Advances in the psychology of human intelligence* (Vol. 4, pp. 181–248). Hillsdale, NJ: Erlbaum.

Lohman, D. F. (1994). Component scores as residual variation (or why the intercept correlates best). *Intelligence, 19*, 1–11.

Lohman, D. F. (2000). Complex information processing and intelligence. In R. J. Sternberg (Ed.), *Handbook of intelligence* (pp. 285–340). Cambridge, UK: Cambridge University Press.

Lohman, D. F. (2004). Aptitude for college: The importance of reasoning tests for minority admissions. In R. Zwick (Ed.), *Rethinking the SAT: The future of standardized testing in university admissions* (pp. 41–56). New York: Routledge Falmer. Web site: http://faculty.education.uiowa.edu/dlohman/.

Lohman, D. F., & Hagen, E. (2001a). *Cognitive Abilities Test (Form 6): Interpretive guide for teachers and counselors*. Itasca, IL: Riverside.

Lohman, D. F., & Hagen, E. (2001b). *Cognitive Abilities Test (Form 6): Interpretive guide for school administrators*. Itasca, IL: Riverside.

Lohman, D. F., & Hagen, E. (2002). *Cognitive Abilities Test (Form 6): Research handbook*. Itasca, IL: Riverside.

Markman, A. B., & Genter, D. (2001). Thinking. *Annual Review of Psychology, 52*, 223–247.

Marshalek, B., Lohman, D. F., & Snow, R. E. (1983). The complexity continuum in the radex and hierarchical models of intelligence. *Intelligence, 7*, 107–128.

Martinez, M. E. (2000). *Education as the cultivation of intelligence*. Mahwah, NJ: Erlbaum.

Miyake, A., & Shah, P. (1999). *Models of working memory: Mechanisms of active maintenance and executive control*. Cambridge, UK: Cambridge University Press.

Newell, A., & Simon, H. A. (1972). *Human problem solving*. Englewood Cliffs, NJ: Prentice-Hall.

Pellegrino, J. W. (1985). Inductive reasoning ability. In R. J. Sternberg (Ed.), *Human abilities: An information-processing approach* (pp. 195–225). New York: W.H. Freeman.

Pellegrino, J. W., & Glaser, R. (1980). Components of inductive reasoning. In R. E. Snow, P.-A. Federico, & W. E. Montague (Eds.), *Aptitude, learning, and instruction: Vol. 1. Cognitive process analyses of aptitude* (pp. 177–218). Hillsdale, NJ: Erlbaum.

Primi, R. (2001). Complexity of geometric inductive reasoning tasks contribution to the understanding of fluid intelligence. *Intelligence, 30*, 41–70.

Raaheim, K. (1988). Intelligence and task novelty. In R. J. Sternberg (Ed.), *Advances in the psychology of human intelligence* (Vol. 4, pp. 73–97). Hillsdale, NJ: Erlbaum.

Raven, J. C., Court, J. H., & Raven, J. (1977). *Raven's Progressive Matrices and Vocabulary Scales*. New York: Psychological Corporation.

Roberts, R. D., & Stankov, L. (1999). Individual differences in speed of mental processing and human cognitive abilities: Toward a taxonomic model. *Learning and Individual Differences, 11*, 1–120.

Salthouse, T. A., Babcock, R. L, Mitchell, D. R. D., Palmon, R., & Skovronek, E. (1990). Sources of individual differences in spatial visualization ability. *Intelligence, 14*, 187–230.

Snow, R. E. (1980). Aptitude and achievement. *New Directions for Testing and Measurement, 5*, 39–59.

Snow, R. E. (1994). Abilities in academic tasks. In R. J. Sternberg & R. K. Wagner (Eds.), *Mind in context: Interactionist perspectives on human intelligence* (pp. 3–37). Cambridge, UK: Cambridge University Press.

Snow, R. E. (1996). Aptitude development and education. *Psychology, Public Policy, and Law, 2*, 536–560.

Snow, R. E., & Lohman, D. F. (1989). Implications of cognitive psychology for educational measurement. In R. Linn (Ed.), *Educational measurement* (3rd ed., pp. 263–331). New York: Macmillan.

Snow, R. E., Corno, L., & Jackson, D., III. (1996). Individual differences in affective and conative functions. In D. C. Berliner & R. C. Calfee (Eds.), *Handbook of educational psychology* (pp. 243–310). New York: Simon & Schuster Macmillan.

Snow, R. E., Kyllonen, P. C., & Marshalek, B. (1984). The topography of ability and learning correlations. In R. J. Sternberg (Ed.), *Advances in the psychology of human intelligence* (Vol. 2, pp. 47–104). Hillsdale, NJ: Erlbaum.

Spearman, C. E. (1927). *The abilities of man*. London: Macmillan.

Spilsbury, G. (1992). Complexity as a reflection of the dimensionality of a task. *Intelligence, 16*, 31–45.

Stankov, L. (1988). Single tests, competing tasks and their relationship to broad factors of intelligence. *Personality and Individual Differences, 9*, 25–33.

Stanovich, K. E. (1999). *Who is rational? Studies of individual differences in reasoning*. Mahwah, NJ: Erlbaum.

Sternberg, R. J. (1977). *Intelligence, information processing, and analogical reasoning: The componential analysis of human abilities*. Hillsdale, NJ: Erlbaum.

Sternberg, R. J. (1985). *Beyond IQ: A triarchic theory of human intelligence*. Cambridge, UK: Cambridge University Press.

Sternberg, R. J. (1986). Toward a unified theory of human reasoning. *Intelligence, 10,* 281–314.

Sternberg, R. J., & Gardner, M. K. (1983). Unities in inductive reasoning. *Journal of Experimental Psychology: General, 112,* 80–116.

Süß, H.-M., Oberauer, K., Wittmann, W. W., Wilhelm, O., & Schulze, R. (2002). Working memory capacity explains reasoning ability – and a little bit more. *Intelligence, 30,* 261–288.

Swiney, J. F. (1985). A study of executive processes in intelligence. Unpublished doctoral dissertation, Stanford University, Stanford, CA.

Toulmin, S., Rieke, R., & Janik, A. (1984). *An introduction to reasoning* (2nd ed). New York: Macmillan.

Vygotsky, L. S. (1978). *Mind in society: The development of higher psychological processes.* Cambridge, MA: Harvard University Press.

Yanng, Y., & Johnson-Laird, P. N. (2001). Mental models and logical reasoning problems in the GRE. *Journal of Experimental Psychology: Applied, 7*(4), 308–316.

Zimmerman, W. S. (1954). The influence of item complexity upon the factor composition of a spatial visualization test. *Educational and Psychological Measurement, 14,* 106–119.

13

Measuring Human Intelligence with Artificial Intelligence

Adaptive Item Generation

Susan E. Embretson

INTRODUCTION

Adaptive item generation may be the next innovation in intelligence test-ing. In adaptive item generation, the optimally informative item is *developed anew* for the examinee during the test. Reminiscent of computer versus person chess games, the computer generates the next item based on the previous pattern of the examinee's responses. Adaptive item generation requires the merger of two lines of research, psychometric methods for adaptive testing and a cognitive analysis of items.

Adaptive testing is the current state of the art in intelligence mea-surement. In adaptive testing, items are selected individually for opti-mal information about an examinee's ability during testing. The items are selected interactively by a computer algorithm using calibrated psy-chometric properties. Generally, harder items are selected if the examinee solves items, while easier ones are selected if the examinee does not solve items. Adaptive item selection leads to shorter and more reliable tests. In a sense, optimal item selection for an examinee is measurement by artificial intelligence.

Adaptive item generation is a step beyond adaptive testing. Like adap-tive testing, it estimates the psychometric properties of the optimally infor-mative items for the person. Beyond this, however, the impact of specific stimulus content on an item's psychometric properties must be known. That is, knowledge is required of how stimulus features in specific items impact the ability construct.

This chapter describes a system for measuring ability in which new items are created while the person takes the test. Ability is measured online by a system of artificial intelligence. The items that are created are designed to be optimally informative about the person's ability. The system behind the item generation is the cognitive design system approach (Embretson, 1998).

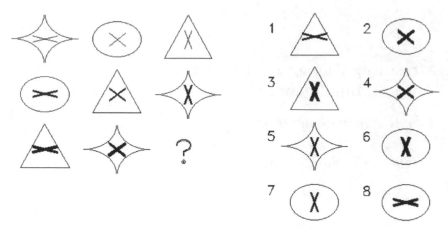

FIGURE 1. A matrix completion item from the Abstract Reasoning Test.

COGNITIVE DESIGN SYSTEM APPROACH TO ADAPTIVE ITEM GENERATION

The cognitive design system approach has been applied, at least partially, to several item types that measure intelligence and aptitude. One of the most extensive applications has been to matrix completion problems, such as shown in Figure 1. Matrix completion problems are found on many intelligence tests, including the Raven Advanced Progressive Matrix Test (Raven, Court, & Raven, 1992), the Naglieri Test of Non-Verbal Intelligence Test, and the Wechsler Intelligence Test for Children. Many scholars regard this item type as central to measuring intelligence (Carroll, 1993; Gustafsson, 1988).

Central to the cognitive design system approach is a cognitive processing model for the item type that measures the construct. However, adaptive item generation also requires several other supporting developments, which include a conceptualization of construct validity that centralizes the role of item design, psychometric models that incorporate design variables, and finally, a computer program that generates items. This section describes the theoretical rationale for cognitive design systems. Then, supporting developments will be elaborated. Finally, the stages involved in applying the cognitive design system to actually generate items will be reviewed.

Theoretical Foundations for Cognitive Design Systems

A cognitive design system is based on an information processing theory of the item type. Such theories originated with cognitive component

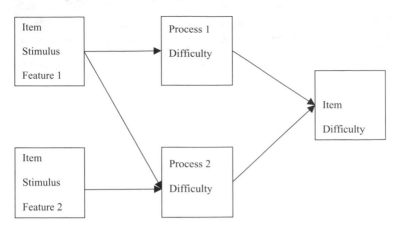

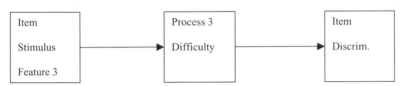

FIGURE 2. Schematic of the cognitive design system variables.

analysis of complex item types for measuring intelligence (Sternberg, 1977) or for other ability items, such as reading (Carroll, 1976). A cognitive theory specifies processes in item solution, the impact of processes on performance, and the impact of stimulus features on processes. To be useful for item generation, a primary dependent measure for performance must be item difficulty (in addition to response time) and, of course, it must be empirically supported.

Figure 2 presents the primary relationship of the cognitive theory to the psychometric properties of items. In Figure 2, the item stimulus properties are related to processing difficulty, which in turn are related to item difficulty and other item properties. Although the primary psychometric property is item difficulty, item discrimination may be influenced by the processes as well. For example, peripheral processes that are not central to the construct that is measured may lower item discrimination.

To illustrate the role of cognitive theory in psychometric tasks, consider again the matrix completion task, as shown on Figure 1. Carpenter, Just, and Shell (1990) postulated and supported two major inference processes involved in performance: goal management and correspondence finding.

TABLE 1. *Stimulus Features to Represent Processing on Matrix Completion Items*

Item	Number of Rules	Abstraction	Object Overlay	Fusion	Distortion
241	1	0	1	0	0
101	1	0	0	1	0
192	1	0	1	1	0
344	2	1	1	0	0
285	2	0	1	1	0
391	2	1	1	0	1
254	3	0	1	0	0
406	4	0	1	0	0
423	4	1	0	0	0

The stimulus features that impacted these processes were the number of rules in the problem and the abstractness of the relationships. In turn, the processes depend on the problem solver's working memory capacity and abstractness capacity. Carpenter et al. (1990) supported their theory with a variety of methods to explicate processing, including a computer simulation of processes, eyetracker studies, and experimental manipulations.

In Figure 1, completing the problem requires identifying three relationships: a change of girth of the X across the rows, a change of boldness of the X down the columns, and a distribution-of-three relationship of the outer shapes, such that each instance appears just once in each row and column. According to the Carpenter et al. (1990) theory, substantial working memory capacity is involved because lower level rules are tried before higher level rules, such as the distribution-of-three relationship. Abstraction capacity is minimized for the item in Figure 1, however, since the figures correspond directly and no entries with null values are given.

Carpenter et al.'s (1990) two major variables, number of rules and abstraction level, represent only inference processing in matrix completion problems. Encoding variables were not part of their model. However, since encoding should be included in any complex processing model, Embretson (1995b; 1998) added some variables to represent the difficulty of encoding the figures in the item. Three perceptual properties – object fusion, object distortion, and object overlay – were added to the inference processing variables for a more complete model.

Table 1 presents scores for these processing variables on some matrix completion items. If these features can be objectively scored, and in turn if they can predict both item response time and item psychometric properties, then a viable cognitive model has been developed for item generation. Although scoring matrices initially required raters, currently all features for generated items can be scored objectively from the item structure specifications (see next section).

Supporting Developments

Construct Validity and Cognitive Design Systems

Cronbach and Meehl's (1955) traditional concept of construct validity has guided ability testing for decades. It provided the conceptual underpinnings for combining diverse data about the quality of the test as a measure of a construct. However, the relevant data could accumulate only after the test was developed. Thus, the data served to elaborate the construct measured by the current test but not to provide guidance for test design.

To incorporate test design into the construct validity concept, two aspects must be distinguished: construct representation and nomothetic span (Embretson, 1983). Construct representation directly concerns the theoretical meaning of test performance. That is, construct representation concerns the processes, strategies, and knowledge that are directly involved in test performance. The research paradigm for construct representation differs sharply from nomothetic span; it involves applying cognitive psychology methods to build information processing models of the measuring task. Typical research involves manipulating the stimulus features of the task to change the relative impact of the postulated processes. This approach has implications for test design because these same features can be manipulated on test items to measure the targeted aspects of processing.

Nomothetic span overlaps substantially with the traditional construct validity concept because it concerns the empirical relationships of test scores. It provides information about the usefulness of the test for measuring individual differences. However, it differs somewhat from the traditional nomological network. That is, relationships should be predictable from construct representation.

Taken together, tests can be designed for both desired construct representation and nomothetic span. In the matrix completion problems, for example, a measure could be designed to require both working memory capacity and abstraction capacity by including matrix items that vary on both number of relationships and abstractness. Or, in contrast, the measure could be designed for only working memory capacity by excluding abstract relationships. Nomothetic span, in turn, will be influenced by these different designs. More limited empirical correlates would be expected if only one capacity was represented, for example.

Psychometric Models for Cognitive Design Systems

Cognitive design systems require psychometric models that can incorporate test design variables. This allows, item properties to be predicted from the cognitive design system variables. The state of the art in psychometric methods is item response theory (IRT). Adaptive testing typically requires IRT models to optimize item selection in measuring ability and to equate measurements between persons who are administered different sets of items. In IRT, the probability of each person's response to each item, $P(\theta)$, is modeled from the person's ability, θ_s, and the properties of items. In the two-parameter logistic model (2PL),

$$P(\theta) = \frac{\exp(\alpha_i(\theta_s - \beta_i))}{1 + \exp(\alpha_i(\theta_s - \beta_i))}. \tag{1}$$

The item properties are item difficulty, β_i, and item discrimination, α_i. A person's ability, θ_s, is estimated in the context of a model, such as in Equation 1. The ability estimate depends not only on the accuracy of the subject's responses, but also on the parameters for the items that were administered. The item parameters are inserted into Equation 1 and ability is estimated to yield the highest likelihood of the observed responses (see Embretson & Reise, 2000, or Hambleton & Swaminathan, 1985, for more information on ability estimation).

The 2PL model, like most standard IRT models, does not include any parameters for the design features behind items. Item difficulties and discriminations are calibrated separately for each item, without regard to their specific design features. However, special IRT models have been developed to estimate the impact of design features on item difficulty (Fischer, 1973; DiBello, Stout, & Roussos, 1995; Adams, Wilson, & Wang, 1997). These models are appropriate if item discriminations do not differ or if they do not relate to design features.

The 2PL-constrained model (Embretson, 1999) was developed to allow design features to influence both item difficulty and item discrimination. Table 1 shows some scored features of matrix items that represent the cognitive model as just described. Scores for each item, q_{ik}, on the k features, define variables that can model item difficulty and discrimination. The 2PL-constrained model replaces calibrated item difficulty and discrimination with a weighted combination of the scored features, q_{ik}, as follows:

$$P(\theta) = \frac{\exp(\Sigma q_{ik}\phi_k(\theta_s - \Sigma q_{ik}\tau_k + \tau_o))}{1 + \exp(\Sigma q_{ik}\phi_k(\theta_s - \Sigma q_{ik}\tau_k + \tau_o))} \tag{2}$$

where τ_k is the parameter for the weight of feature k in item difficulty, ϕ_k is the parameter for the weight of feature k in item slope, and θ_s is the ability of person s. Notice that item difficulty and item discrimination are represented by a weighted combination of the stimulus features, $\Sigma q_{ik}\tau_k$ and $\Sigma q_{ik}\phi_k$, respectively. The weights are estimated in the IRT model to maximize fit to the item response data. Heuristically, however, the weights are roughly equivalent to regression weights in predicting item difficulty and item discrimination.

Once the weights are calibrated to reflect the impact of the stimulus features, item difficulties and discriminations for new items can be predicted directly, without empirical tryout. Obviously, reasonably accurate prediction depends on the fit of the model. An empirical example will be presented below for the matrix problems to show both the calibration of weights and the assessment of model quality.

Computer Programs for Adaptive Item Generation

Adaptive item generation requires two types of computer programs: (1) an item generator program that actually creates the items and (2) an adaptive testing program that can be interfaced with the generator. The item generator program produces items to target levels and sources of cognitive complexity in the cognitive design system approach. Item structures, which are blueprints for the items, are essential for item production. The structures carry the specific sources of cognitive complexity and predicted item difficulty. The nature of the item structures depends on the item type. For nonverbal items, the item structure determines the arrangement and display of objects. Specific objects are randomly selected to fulfill the structure. For verbal items, structures need to specify deep level meanings or logical representations that can be instantiated with different surface features, such as exact vocabulary level and syntax.

Once the item generator is developed, it then must be interfaced with an adaptive testing program. An adaptive testing program not only displays items and records responses, but also interacts with the examinee to estimate ability and to determine the optimal item properties for the next item to be administered. Several adaptive testing programs are available; however, these programs search for existing items in an item bank. To provide adaptive item generation, the testing system must be linked to item structures that produce items of target psychometric properties.

Stages in Applying Cognitive Design Systems

The cognitive design system approach may be applied to new or existing measures of a construct. The stages presented below are most appropriate for existing measures with adequate nomological span. In this case, the usefulness of the test for measuring individual differences is already established. The cognitive design system approach then can be applied to establish the construct representation aspect of construct validity. This provides a basis for designing new items and item generation, as well as possible test redesign. A new measure of construct also could be developed under the cognitive design system approach; in this case, additional studies to establish nomothetic span are needed. Also, for new measures, algorithmic item generation can occur earlier in the process.

Develop Cognitive Model for Existing Items

In the initial stages, the goal is to develop a plausible cognitive processing model for the existing ability test items. Cognitive modeling typically begins with a literature review on underlying processing components and the stimuli that determine their difficulty. Often the literature concerns a related task, rather than the exact item type on an ability test. That is, tasks that are studied in the laboratory are often quite easy and presented in a verification format. Ability test items are much harder and presented in multiple choice format. Thus, a more complex model may need to be postulated to adequately represent processing for solving ability test items. For the matrix completion task, although Carpenter et al. (1990) studied ability test items, their model did not include encoding or decision processing. Thus, a more complete model was developed.

The next step is to empirically support the model. Data on two primary dependent variables on the ability test items must be obtained: item response time and item difficulty. These dependent variables are mathematically modeled from item stimulus features that are postulated to impact processing. Item stimulus features on existing tests often show multicollinearity, which can bias relative importance in the model. Thus, additional studies to unconfound the impact of correlated features are needed. Also, converging operations for supporting the model are needed. For example, eyetracker and simulation studies also provide information about the plausibility of the processing model.

Algorithmic Item Generation and Revised Cognitive Model
The next stage directly concerns test design; that is, can the stimulus features be manipulated separately to impact processing difficulty and item performance? To manipulate item features, a set of item specifications based on the model variables is constructed. Correlated features can be unconfounded by crossing the various levels of the stimulus features. For example, in existing matrix completion problems, the display of objects (e.g., overlay) is correlated with the number of rules. However, in algorithmic item generation, display type can be fully crossed with the number of rules and then items can be constructed to fulfill the various combinations of features.

The newly constructed items are then studied empirically to determine the impact of the stimulus design features on item performance. Although new items can be calibrated in a tryout, the main focus is on calibrating design features. The design features should be sufficiently predictive of item difficulty and other psychometric indicators, as well as response time. Items that represent the same combination of design features should be highly similar empirically.

Item Generation by Artificial Intelligence
As noted before, a computer program must be developed for item generation. Although the programming effort required to develop a mechanism to create and display items is substantial, the development of the item

structures for the particular item type is crucial to success. All items from the same structure carry the same sources and levels of cognitive complexity. Item structures can differ qualitatively between item types; therefore, a new research effort is required to develop structures that are linked to the cognitive model variables. An item generator program, ITEMGEN1, has been developed for six item types that measure nonverbal intelligence, including two types of matrix completion tasks, geometric analogies, geometric series problems, and two types of items for spatial ability (Psychological Data Corp., 2002). The structures for spatial ability items differ qualitatively from the other nonverbal intelligence item structures.

Empirical Tryout of Item Generation

The final stage involves an actual tryout of the generated items. Online testing is essential because continuous data are needed to evaluate the quality of the design principles. This stage has not yet been implemented for the cognitive design system approach.

New psychometric issues arise with adaptive item generation. First, new diagnostic indices are needed to evaluate the effectiveness of the design features, and their various combinations, in yielding items of predicted psychometric quality. Since design features probably will be contained in IRT models, as noted earlier, perhaps current indices for item fit can be extended to assess the design features. Second, further research is needed on how uncertainty in the item parameters (i.e., because they are predicted from design features) impacts ability estimates. Several studies (Bejar et al., 2002; Mislevy, Sheehan, & Wingersky, 1993; Embretson, 1999) have found that measurement error increases modestly when item parameters are predicted rather than calibrated. These studies further suggest that the impact of item uncertainty can be readily countered by administering a few more items. However, in the context of online testing, it may be possible to monitor individual examinees for the impact of item uncertainty. Research on indices to diagnose online problems is also needed.

SUPPORTING DATA FOR COGNITIVE DESIGN SYSTEMS

The cognitive design system approach has been applied to several nonverbal aptitude test items, including matrix completion problems (Embretson, 1998), geometric analogies (Whitely & Schneider, 1981), spatial folding (Embretson, 1994), and spatial object assembly (Embretson, 2000; Embretson & Gorin, 2001). A computer program for item generation has been developed for these item types.

The cognitive design system has also been applied to several other item types, including verbal analogies (Embretson & Schneider, 1989), verbal classifications (Embretson, Schneider, & Roth, 1985), letter series (Butterfield et al., 1985), paragraph comprehension (Embretson & Wetzel, 1987;

Gorin, 2002), and mathematical problem solving (Embretson, 1995a). Although a computer program for generating these items does not yet exist, research is in progress for mathematical problem solving (Embretson, 2002a) and paragraph comprehension (Embretson & Gorin, 2002; Gorin, 2002). However, since all of these item types involve words, some psycholinguistic capabilities will be required for full item generation.

In this section, empirical support for generating matrix completion problems by cognitive design systems will be described. Although research on the object assembly task for measuring spatial ability is somewhat more complete because it includes empirical tryout of AI-generated items (Embretson, 2000), matrix completion problems are often regarded as central to measuring intelligence.

Initial Cognitive Model for Matrix Items

The initial modeling for the matrix items, although conducted early in the studies on matrices, was reported in Embretson (2002b). The Advanced Progressive Matrices (APM, Raven et al., 1992) was selected as the target for an initial cognitive model for the matrix completion task for two reasons. First, Carpenter et al. (1990) had studied APM intensively to develop their theory and they provided scores for many items. Second, APM is widely recognized as a measure of fluid intelligence.

Two mathematical models for the APM were developed to begin the cognitive design system process (see Embretson, 2002b). Model 1 contained Carpenter et al.'s (1990) processing variables for rule induction, the number of rules, and the abstractness of the rules. Three variables to represent encoding difficulty were also included in Model 1. Model 2 contained an alternative measure of rule induction processing, memory load, as well as the encoding variables. The memory load variable operationalized Carpenter et al.'s (1990) postulated processing sequence of rules in matrices. That is, they postulated that examinees attempted to relate matrix entries by higher level rules only after lower level rules failed. Thus, greater amounts of processing and working memory are required for items with higher level rules because lower level rules had to be tried and remembered. Embretson's (2002b) memory load variable operationalized rule induction processing by summing the levels of the rules in each item. Both Model 1 ($R^2 = .79$, $p < .01$) and Model 2 ($R^2 = .81$, $p < .01$) provided adequate prediction of APM item difficulty. Although the encoding variables did increase prediction, the rule induction variables had the strongest impact on item difficulty.

Algorithmic Item Generation and Revised Cognitive Model

The models just identified provided the basis for constructing new items. A bank of 150 items contained five replicates of thirty item structures that

TABLE 2. *Comparisons of Alternative Psychometric Models for 90 Abstract Reasoning Test Items*

Model	−2 Log L	χ^2/df	Parameters	Fit
Null	31,382	–	2	–
LLTM	28,768	522.8**	7	.71[1]
2PL-C, cognitive	28,523	40.8**	12	.74[1]
2PL-C, structural	26,152	49.4**	60	.94
2PL	25,406	6.2**	180	1.00

[1] Comparison to 2PL-constrained structural model.
** $p < .01$.

represented different combinations of cognitive variables (Embretson, 1998). The five replicate items for each structure contained different stimuli. The display type was constant within structures but varied across structures. The relationship between the distractors and the key was also equated within structures, as well as between structures, to the extent possible. The key position was randomly assigned.

An empirical tryout of the items supported the cognitive model for generating items with acceptable and similar psychometric properties (Embretson, 1998). Models 1 and 2 both predicted item difficulties to nearly the same level as for APM items; they also predicted the response times. Also like APM, the encoding variables had much less impact on performance than did the rule induction variables. Thus, the construct representation aspect of construct validity was supported by the strong predictions obtained from the cognitive models.

More recently, Model 1 parameters were estimated for a large sample with three replications of thirty item structures (i.e., ninety items) using the 2PL-constrained model (Embretson, 1999), applied with improved estimators (Embretson & Yang, 2002). Table 2 shows the significance and fit for alternative psychometric models of the data. The null model, in which all items are equally difficult and discriminating, is a comparison standard used in the fit index shown in the far right column (see Embretson, 1997a). The goodness of fit statistic divided by its degrees of freedom, χ^2/df, compares successively more complex models for significance increment in fit. It can be seen that the 2PL-constrained model fits more significantly than the LLTM model, which has equal discriminations for all items. Thus, item discrimination parameters increase fit significantly. The structural model, in which a parameter is estimated for each of the thirty structures, fits significantly better than the cognitive model. These results indicate that the cognitive model does not fully reflect differences in the item structures. Finally, the standard 2PL model, where each of the ninety items has unique difficulty and discrimination parameters, fits significantly better than the 2PL structural model, although the increment in fit is not large. These

TABLE 3. *Estimates and Standard Error for Item Difficulty and Item Discrimination for 2PL-Constrained Model*

Feature	Diff. ϕ	σ_ϕ	Slope τ	σ_τ
#Rules	.715*	.031	−.034	.024
Abstract	.784*	.043	−.033	.041
Fusion	−.748*	.078	−.384*	.047
Distortion	−.373*	.052	−.325*	.057
Overlay	.00	.041	−.504*	.038
Constant	−2.142*	.101	1.379*	.087

* $p < .05$.

results suggest that relatively little variability between the items remains after structure is accounted for. Thus, the replicates of the same structure do not vary substantially.

The estimates for the 2PL-constrained model are shown in Table 3. For item difficulty, both number of rules and abstract correspondence, as well as two perceptual variables, are significant predictors of item difficulty. For item discrimination, only the perceptual variables are significant predictors. The negative weights for the variables indicate that fusion, distortion, and overlay are associated with reduced item discrimination.

The difficulties of new items can be predicted from either the structural model or the cognitive model. The 2PL cognitive model yields the following predictions of item difficulty, β', and item discrimination, α':

$$\beta' = -2.142 + .715(\#\text{Rules}) + .784(\text{Abstract}) - .748(\text{Fusion})$$
$$- .373(\text{Distortion}).$$

$$\alpha' = 1.379 - .034(\text{Rules}) - .033(\text{Abstract}) - .384(\text{Fusion})$$
$$- .325(\text{Distort}) - .504(\text{Overlay}).$$

In the results summarized above, the perceptual variables were not systematically varied within structures. In a recent study, the perceptual variables were varied in an experimental design to examine the strength of their effects (Diehl, 2002; Diehl & Embretson, 2002). Items were generated by crossing eight structures with variations in the perceptual variables. Eight items (with different objects) were created for each structure to observe eight combinations of perceptual features, including display type for multiple cell entries (nested, overlay, adjacent, and platform) and fusion (present versus not present), yielding a total of sixty-four items. Although the perceptual variables had significant impact on item difficulty and response time, again their effect was minor as compared to the rule induction variables. The level of prediction obtained was similar to Embretson (1998), thus yielding further support to the cognitive model.

Item Generation by Artificial Intelligence

Matrix completion items may now be generated from item structures that represent the major cognitive variables, as well as display type. ITEMGEN1 randomly selects stimuli and their attributes to fulfill the structural specifications. All cognitive model variables may be calculated from the structural specifications; hence, item difficulty and discrimination are predictable.

Empirical Tryout of Item Generation

As yet, item generation has not been attempted with the full cognitive approach for the matrix completion items. Further developments to link the generator to a testing system are required, which is expected sometime in 2004.

RELATED APPROACHES TO ITEM DEVELOPMENT

Two other approaches to item development are related to the cognitive design system approach: traditional item development and the item model approach (Bejar et al., 2002; Bejar, 1996). Both of these will be briefly reviewed here.

In the traditional approach, item writing is an art, not a science. Items for intelligence tests are carefully handcrafted by human item writers. Then, the items are submitted for empirical evaluation by calibrating their psychometric properties. Many items do not survive empirical tryout and, consistent with item writing as an art, the reasons for item failure are often unclear. The attrition rate varies substantially for different tests, but rates of 30 to 50% attrition are typical. Surviving items are then calibrated with a psychometric model, particularly IRT models, to be useable for measuring ability. These calibrations are necessary because it is axiomatic to psychometric theory that raw total scores have no meaning because item difficulty levels can vastly influence score levels.

The item model approach (Bejar et al., 2002) is a generative approach, in which existing items are "variablized" to create new items. That is, an item with suitable psychometric qualities serves as a model for new items by allowing one or more of its features to be substituted. For example, an existing mathematics word problem can be variablized by substituting different characters, objects, and settings as well as substituting different numbers. Thus, a family of new items is created. Ability can then be estimated from the new items, without empirical item tryout, as the properties of the item model are assumed inheritable to each new item.

Obviously, the item model approach requires that the item parameters are invariant over the cloned items. Bejar et al. (2002) completed a study of item generation for GRE quantitative items, using the item model approach. The data strongly support the feasibility of the approach. Analysis of item difficulty and response time indicated a high level of isomorphicity across items within models. Furthermore, the ability estimates from generated items with operational GRE scores were as high as test–retest correlations of two operational GRE tests. Thus, the use of newly generated items has minimal impact on ability estimates.

EVALUATION OF APPROACH: ADVANTAGES AND DISADVANTAGES

The cognitive design system approach to adaptive item generation has several advantages over traditional item development methods. First, new items may be readily developed. Traditional item development procedures do not produce enough items to meet the demands of adaptive testing for large numbers of items. Second, items may be developed to target difficulty levels and adequate psychometric quality. With traditional test development methods, item difficulty levels, at best, can be only informally anticipated. Empirical tryouts typically lead to a high percentage of items rejected for poor quality and inappropriate difficulty. Third, given an adequate calibration of the design principles, new items may be placed in the item bank without empirical tryout. The predicted item parameters from the design variables are sufficient to measure ability. Measurement error increases modestly, but may easily be offset by administering a few more items. Fourth, construct validity is available at the item level. That is, the specific sources of cognitive complexity for each item are given by the weights for the model variables. Fifth, tests may be redesigned to represent specifically targeted sources of item difficulty. The impact of some sources of cognitive complexity can be controlled directly when construct validity is available at the item level. For example, perceptual properties would have minimal impact on solving Abstract Reasoning Test (ART) items if fusion and distortion were eliminated in the items.

The cognitive design system approach has some disadvantages. First and foremost, the approach requires substantial initial effort. Developing a reasonably good cognitive model for an item type requires several empirical studies to support the theory and the models. Whether the approach is practical for a particular test depends on how well the initial cost is compensated for by the unlimited number of new items that can be generated. Second, the approach works best for item types that already have been developed. Although the cognitive design system approach can be applied to new item types, establishing usefulness for measuring individual differences would be required early in the process. That is, the nomothetic span aspect of construct validity should be established by studies on the correlates of scores that are derived from the item type. Nothing in the system prevents applications to new item types, however.

FUTURE

Adaptive item generation may become state of the art for ability and achievement measurement relatively soon. Practically, the increasing need for large numbers of new items makes item generation attractive. Large-scale ability and achievement testing is increasing, not decreasing, and there is special emphasis on repeated measurements. In K–12 education, for example, tests are used increasingly to certify achievement at all levels. In lifespan development, increasing interest in cognitive aging requires longitudinal designs with repeated testing of the same abilities. With the increasing number of tests administered, shorter and more reliable tests are highly desirable. Adaptive testing seems to be the obvious solution. However, adaptive testing requires huge item banks to provide efficient measurement at all levels. Furthermore, as testing becomes more frequent and more important, new items become highly desirable to minimize the response bias that results from previous exposure to items. Item generation by artificial intelligence fulfills these practical needs for new items.

Theoretically, item generation by cognitive design systems also has some advantages. New types of interpretations of test scores are possible when construct validity is available at the item level. When the cognitive sources of item complexity are calibrated in an IRT-based model, ability levels may be described by the processing characteristics of the items appropriate for that level (see Embretson & Reise, 2000, for examples). The continuing debate about the nature of intelligence could take a new direction by referring more specifically to the processes that are involved in performance. The many correlates and relationships of intelligence measurements to other variables may be understood more clearly if the characteristic processing at different ability levels can be explicated.

References

Adams, R. A., Wilson, M., & Wang, W. C. (1997). The multidimensional random coefficients multinomial logit model. *Applied Psychological Measurement, 21*, 1–23.

Bejar, I. I. (1996). *Generative response modeling: Leveraging the computer as a test delivery medium* (RR-96-13). Princeton, NJ: Educational Testing Service.

Bejar, I. I., Lawless, R. R., Morley, M. E., Wagner, M. E., Bennett, R. E., & Revuelta, J. (2002). *A feasibility study of on-the-fly item generation in adaptive testing* (GRE Board Research Report 98-12). Princeton, NJ: Educational Testing Service.

Butterfield, E. C., Nielsen, D., Tangen, K. L., & Richardson, M. B. (1985). Theoretically based psychometric measures of inductive reasoning. In S. E. Embretson (Ed.), *Test design: Developments in psychology and psychometrics* (pp. 77–147). New York: Academic Press.

Carpenter, P. A., Just, M. A., & Shell, P. (1990). What one intelligence test measures: A theoretical account of processing in the Raven's Progressive Matrices Test. *Psychological Review, 97*, 404–431.

Carroll, J. B. (1976). Psychometric tasks as cognitive tests: A new structure of intellect. In L. Resnick (Ed.), *The nature of intelligence* (pp. 27–56). Hillsdale, NJ: Erlbaum.

Carroll, J. B. (1993). *Human cognitive abilities: A survey of factor-analytic studies.* Cambridge, UK: Cambridge University Press.

Cronbach, L. J., & Meehl, P. E. (1955). Construct validity in psychological tests. *Psychological Bulletin, 52,* 281–302.

DiBello, L. V., Stout, W. F., & Roussos, L. (1995). Unified cognitive psychometric assessment likelihood-based classification techniques. In P. D. Nichols, S. F. Chipman, & R. L. Brennan (Eds.), *Cognitively diagnostic assessment* (pp. 361–389). Hillsdale, NJ: Erlbaum.

Diehl, K. A. (1998). *Using cognitive theory and item response theory to extract information from wrong responses.* Unpublished Master's thesis, University of Kansas.

Diehl, K. A. (2002). Algorithmic item generation and problem solving strategies in matrix completion problems. Unpublished doctoral dissertation, University of Kansas.

Diehl, K. A., & Embretson, S. E. (2002). Impact of perceptual features on algorithmic item generation for matrix completion problems. Technical Report 02–0100. *Cognitive Measurement Reports.* Lawrence, University of Kansas.

Embretson, S. E. (1983). Construct validity: Construct representation versus nomothetic span. *Psychological Bulletin, 93,* 179–197.

Embretson, S. E. (1994). Applications of cognitive design systems to test development. In C. Reynolds (Ed.), *Advances in cognitive assessment: An interdisciplinary perspective* (pp. 107–135). New York: Plenum.

Embretson, S. (1995a). A measurement model for linking individual change to processes and knowledge: Application to mathematical learning. *Journal of Educational Measurement,* vol. 32(3) 275–294.

Embretson, S. E. (1995b). Working memory capacity versus general central processes in intelligence. *Intelligence, 20,* 169–189.

Embretson, S. E. (1997a). Multicomponent latent trait models. In W. van der Linden & R. Hambleton (Eds.), *Handbook of modern item response theory* (pp. 305–322). New York: Springer-Verlag.

Embretson, S. E. (1998). A cognitive design system approach to generating valid tests: Application to abstract reasoning. *Psychological Methods, 3,* 300–396.

Embretson, S. E. (1999). Generating items during testing: Psychometric issues and models. *Psychometrika, 64,* 407–433.

Embretson, S. E. (2000). Generating assembling objects items from cognitive specifications. HUMRRO Report No. SubPR98-11. Alexandria, VA: Human Resource Research Organisation.

Embretson, S. E. (2002a). Cognitive models for psychometric properties of GRE quantitative items. Report 02-03 to Assessment Design Center. Princeton, NJ: Educational Testing Service.

Embretson, S. E. (2002b). Generating abstract reasoning items with cognitive theory. In S. Irvine & P. Kyllonen (Eds.), *Item generation for test development* (pp. 219–250). Mahwah, NJ: Erlbaum.

Embretson, S. E., & Gorin, J. (2001). Improving construct validity with cognitive psychology principles. *Journal of Educational Measurement,* vol. 38(4), pp. 343–368.

Embretson, S. E., & Reise, S. (2000). *Item response theory for psychologists.* Mahwah, NJ: Erlbaum.

Embretson, S. E., & Schneider, L. M. (1989). Cognitive component models for psychometric analogies: Conceptual driven versus interactive models. *Learning and Individual Differences*, vol. 1(2), 155–178.

Embretson, S. E., & Wetzel, D. (1987). Component latent trait models for paragraph comprehension tests. *Applied Psychological Measurement, 11*, 175–193.

Embretson, S. E., & Yang, X. (2002). Modeling item parameters from cognitive design features using non-linear mixed models. Symposium paper presented at the annual meeting of the American Educational Research Association, New Orleans, LA, April, 2002.

Embretson, S. E., Schneider, L. M., & Roth, D. L. (1985). Multiple processing strategies and the construct validity of verbal reasoning tests. *Journal of Educational Measurement, 23*, 13–32.

Fischer, G. H. (1973). Linear logistic test model as an instrument in educational research. *Acta Psychologica, 37*, 359–374.

Gorin, J. (2002). *Cognitive design principles for paragraph comprehension items.* Unpublished doctoral dissertation, University of Kansas.

Gustafsson, J. E. (1988). Hierarchical models of individual differences in cooperative abilities. In R. J. Sternberg (Ed.), *Advances in the psychology of human intelligence* (Vol. 4, pp. 35–71). Hillsdale, NJ: Erlbaum.

Hambleton, R. K., & Swaminathan, H. (1985). *Item response theory: Principles and applications.* Norwell, MA: Kluwer.

Mislevy, R. J., Sheehan, K. M., & Wingersky, M. (1993). How to equate tests with little or no data. *Journal of Educational Measurement, 30*, 55–76.

Psychological Data Corp. (2002). ITEMGEN1, Item generator for non-verbal intelligence test items. Lawrence, KS: Psychological Data Corporation.

Raven, J. C., Court, J. H., & Raven, J. (1992). *Manual for Raven's Progressive Matrices and Vocabulary Scale.* San Antonio, TX: Psychological Corporation.

Sternberg, R. J. (1977). *Intelligence, information processing, and analogical reasoning: The componential analysis of human abilities.* Hillsdale, NJ: Erlbaum.

Whitely,[1] S. E., & Schneider, L. M. (1981). Information structure on geometric analogies: A test theory approach. *Applied Psychological Measurement, 5*, 383–397.

---

[1] Susan Embretson has also published under the name Susan E. Whitely.

14

Marrying Intelligence and Cognition

A Developmental View

Mike Anderson

I suspect that many of the contributors to this volume are very gung ho about the progress that is being made in the many topics related to intelligence. I would also bet that most are especially optimistic about the marriage advocated by Cronbach (1957) between the two schools of psychology – with a rather cranky (some might say, musty) tradition of individual-differences research finally hitching up, around 1980 or so, with the not-so-blushing bride of cognitive psychology (who is, in fact, the daughter of the experimental psychology that Cronbach so coveted). I am not so gung ho. On a bad day I might even be clinically depressed. Much work has been done and much data have been collected, but in my view we are not much further on than we were in the middle of the last century before cognitive psychology was even thought of. Rather than a happy marriage, what I see is a sham of a relationship marked by a crushing coldness on the part of the once blushing bride (who by contrast flirts outrageously with just about every other intellectual tradition that shows an interest) and a barely restrained anger on the part of a frustrated groom. Before long I think the latter will run off with a new partner (the rather voluptuous and, for some at least, alluring neuroscience). But I see no more hope for the old fellow here. A bit of counseling is in order – maybe the hoped for relationship can be saved? I must declare a vested interest here – I am the mongrel child of this failing relationship (born circa Anderson, 1986) and would dearly love to see the folks get back together and make it work.

More formally, my aim in this chapter is to inspect the current relationship between Cronbach's two psychologies as they manifest themselves in the study of individual differences and the development of intelligence, on the one hand, and the study of cognition, on the other. My central point is that progress in the field depends on a successful marriage of these two traditions but up to now it just has not worked out.

Cronbach's call for the unification of individual-differences and experimental approaches to psychology has been subverted from within the individual-differences school and ignored (to their peril) from within the experimental school. The inability of cognitive psychology to marry individual-differences research has led to two contemporary outcomes that I see as disastrous for Cronbach's agenda. First, there is a capitulation that these really are two different enterprises (Jensen, 1998, 1999). Second, the study of the development of intelligence has represented for the most part a quite independent approach to the study of both cognition and intelligence, which offers a unique opportunity to achieve Cronbach's aim. Finally, as the influence of cognitive psychology wanes in the face of the burgeoning neurosciences, an openly hostile, reductionist agenda is being formulated to entice the future researcher of intelligence. To combat what I regard as a potentially disastrous backward step, I will explain my alternative formulation for a useful and progressive research strategy that might fulfill Cronbach's cherished goal. But first a little bit of history. So, as they say, let us begin at the beginning, which for all intents and purposes has to be with intelligence tests and what they are supposed to measure.

INTELLIGENCE AS "WHAT THE TESTS TEST"

It was Binet who set the mold for modern intelligence tests. He believed that intelligence was to be found in the higher faculties of the mind including knowledge, logic, reasoning, and, particularly, judgment (Binet & Simon, 1905). Binet decided his tests would have to tap these higher mental processes. His genius was to realize that the universally acknowledged increase in intelligence during child development offered the basis of a measurement scale. Using a diverse range of knowledge tests, Binet could identify empirically the difficulty of a test item – given as the chronological age where half of the children could pass the item. Consequently the first intelligence test was based on the central idea that the age at which the average child can succeed at a particular problem is an indication of the difficulty of that problem. In turn, Binet turned this relationship on its head to derive a child's mental age – a radically new concept – from a test score.

A mental age is equivalent to the chronological age for which any test score would represent average performance. Thus a child scoring better than the average child of his or her age would have a higher mental age (MA) than chronological age (CA) and a child scoring lower than average would have a lower mental age than chronological age. It took one short step, by Stern (1912), to derive an index of differences in intelligence within ages. The resulting intelligence quotient, or IQ, was calculated using the classical formula: $IQ = MA/CA \times 100$. The calculation of IQ gave birth to the idea that individual differences in intelligence could be expressed by a single score. Moreover, if many tests of quite different higher (cognitive) faculties are constructed and administered to a random sample from the general population, performance on the tests will covary. This is called the positive manifold of test intercorrelations and provides the empirical bedrock of Spearman's concept of g, or general intelligence (Spearman, 1904). It is the phenomenon of g that provides the justification for taking an average or single IQ score as an indication of anything meaningful.

It was Piaget who realized that errors on intelligence test items might be even more informative than the total test score used in Binet's calculations of mental age. Piaget's approach was to take more interest in the kinds of errors made by children of different ages (subsequently thought of as different stages of cognitive development) as indicators of underlying cognitive structure. So this historical shift in emphasis (mirrored by the conceptual difference between mental age and IQ) led to these two approaches to understanding intelligence – the study of individual differences and the study of developmental change now straddling the two sides of Cronbach's divide (he included developmental under the individual differences, rather than experimental, heading). However, developmental approaches to intelligence, particularly in their modern form, would be classified as part of mainstream or "nomothetic" psychology. Thus, ever since Piaget, the psychometric approach to studying individual differences, founded by Binet, and research in cognitive development unfortunately have had very little to do with each other. Moreover, the psychometric tradition that followed Binet has dominated the study of intelligence, and the analysis of intelligence test scores and their relationships to other variables have been the focus of research.

Many have argued that individual-differences researchers have been locked into a vicious circularity that prevents us from escaping Boring's dictum that "Intelligence is what the tests test" (see for example, Gardner, 1983; Sternberg, 1990). Given that one of the "validity" checks of any new intelligence test is that it should correlate with performance on an older already established test, then it does indeed seem as if we are doomed to follow the yellow brick road to scientific vacuity. However, is it not equally preposterous to suppose that after 100 years of psychometric research that intelligence tests do not measure something that we would like to believe is important for human intelligence? Bear in mind that there has been no end of attempts to produce alternative kinds of tests of intelligence. The overwhelming fact of such attempts is that when anyone has produced a reliable measure of our ability to think, those tests intercorrelate. Clearly a theory of intelligence without g is Hamlet without the Prince. But can cognitive psychology cope with g?

IQ AND KNOWLEDGE

In my view the starting point for any scientific understanding of intelligence – both individual differences and the development of – is that intelligence is a property of knowledge systems. IQ tests work because they test knowledge. They ask us what we know or they ask us to solve problems, evoking cognitive strategies and our capacity to think and reason. Note that, prima facie, this makes the case that a theory of intelligence must be a cognitive theory. Undoubtedly, then, intelligence is a property of knowledge but, as we have seen, 100 years of psychometrics tells us that whatever that property is it must be a general property. Therein lies the rub. Can intelligence-as-knowledge be made compatible with g? Many think not and they eschew the existence of g as nothing more than a statistical artifact, perhaps of test construction, that has been inappropriately reified (Howe, 1988, 1997; Richardson, 1999; Gould, 1996). Indeed, they would go so far as to claim that intelligence is nothing other than knowledge and that its use as an explanatory construct (i.e., someone knows more *because* they are more intelligent) is a confidence trick (Ceci, 1990; Howe, 1990). Jensen (1984) has referred to this view as the specificity doctrine – that the intellectual abilities of individuals are simply the sum total of specific pieces of knowledge that are themselves experientially determined.

The specificity doctrine has two major problems: First, intelligence tests are very good predictors of real-world accomplishments (Hunter, 1986; Herrnstein & Murray, 1994). Second, even within the samples of specific knowledge that sum to generate an intelligence test score, performances on each subsample (subtest) positively correlate. Consistent with this, even performance on different kinds of intelligence tests (individual, group, paper-and-pencil, nonverbal, etc.) positively correlates. This, as we have already seen, is the basis of the calculation of a meaningful IQ score and is the basis of the construct of general intelligence. Thus the very existence of general intelligence refutes the specificity doctrine but then that is why its very existence is the subject of so much dispute.

I have argued elsewhere that the specificity doctrine is demonstrably false (Anderson, 1992a). The essence of this argument follows from the robust empirical observations of the predictive validity of IQ tests and the covariation of abilities as just discussed. The strong version of the specificity doctrine very simply explains both the predictive validity of intelligence tests and the covariation of abilities. Put simply, given the domain specificity of knowledge, an overlap must occur in the contents of intelligence tests and what they predict and among intelligence tests themselves. How can this be if intelligence tests take a tiny sample from what must be an enormously large pool of specific pieces of knowledge? Their predictive validity within this framework must be regarded as nothing short of miraculous. Moreover, it is clear that the best predictors of real-world success are tests of general intelligence rather than specific abilities (Hunter, 1986). Therefore, it is that which is common to all intelligence tests rather than the specific content of individual tests that affords their predictive validity. Moreover, some of the tests of general intelligence that have high predictive validity such as Ravens Progressive Matrices have no content overlap with many of the criteria and no knowledge overlap with many tests of cognitive abilities that are highly correlated with it (e.g., vocabulary tests). Furthermore, over the course of child development, there is strong predictive validity from tests at young ages to tests in early adulthood (in other words, IQ differences are relatively stable) where there is no overlap in knowledge content (Hindley & Owen, 1978). For example, vocabulary scores at five years old predict mathematics scores at sixteen (Yule, Gold, & Busch, 1982). Consequently, a strong version of the specificity doctrine fails to explain both the predictive validity of intelligence tests and the positive intercorrelations among diverse tests.

A weaker version of the specificity doctrine might argue that it is not knowledge overlap per se that affords the predictive validity of intelligence tests and explains the intercorrelations among diverse tests, but rather a more extensive knowledge base aids the learning of new knowledge and so knowledge systems bootstrap themselves. The implication is that it is not the direct transfer of specific pieces of knowledge from one situation to another or between intelligence tests that is crucial (and we have seen that there is to all intents and purposes none anyway), but rather it is task-specific knowledge in one domain that can be abstracted to allow generalization to other different tasks and domains. However, if we look at cognitive analyses of how learning one task aids learning another (transfer of training), what we find no general or abstract knowledge representations that would afford such a transfer. This constitutes what was called in cognitive science the search for the general problem solver. Most experts now agree the enterprise failed. Indeed, one of the best-articulated cognitive theories of learning and transfer, the ACT theory of J. R. Anderson (1983), claims that the only basis of transfer is the number of identical productions (for our purposes each production can be viewed as a specific piece of knowledge) that two tasks or two situations hold in common. So even the weaker version of the specificity doctrine requires common contents among intelligence tests and between intelligence tests and the real-world abilities they predict. But as we have seen, such commonality at this level is simply not there.

So if intelligence is a property of knowledge but cannot be identified with the contents or structure of knowledge, then what kind of property could it be? To answer this we can turn to a distinction that is ubiquitous in the cognitive literature – that between knowledge itself and the information processing mechanisms that process, manipulate, and create knowledge. Indeed, Hunt (1995) claims that there are two kinds of cognitive psychology – that which studies information processing mechanisms and that which studies higher-order problem solving. He is pessimistic that anyone knows how to go from facts of the former to facts of the latter, and clearly it is the latter that most cognitive psychologists would consider the essence of intelligence. Forthwith I will refer to the divide as the low-level and high-level approach respectively. It maps onto the distinction between knowledge itself and its implementation, including the mechanisms that are causally responsible for knowledge acquisition. This divide is where I part company with two other major cognitive approaches to understanding intelligence.

COGNITIVE CORRELATES AND COMPONENTS

In a series of studies Hunt (see Hunt, 1980) and colleagues attempted to use standard cognitive/experimental tasks to measure different facets of information processing in verbal tasks. They then looked to see which processes had the highest correlations with verbal IQ and in this way hoped to identify where in the information processing system the important individual differences lay. To summarize a great deal of research, they claimed that the highest correlations were found in the more complex and higher-order processes (particularly information processing strategies) rather than in the simple and basic information processing mechanisms. Although employing a different experimental strategy, Sternberg (1983) found essentially the same thing. Using techniques of decomposing intelligence test items into their isolable information processing components, Sternberg attempted to determine where in his componential theory of intelligence the greatest individual differences lay. Sternberg, like Hunt, argued that it was not in the performance characteristics of low-level basic information processing mechanisms that the largest sources of IQ-related individual differences lay, but rather they were to be found in the higher-level goal-setting, monitoring, and strategic aspects of information processing. What was radical about both the cognitive correlates and cognitive components approaches was that they constituted the first serious attempts to merge individual differences in intelligence with cognitive psychology. However, what was ultimately disappointing about both of them is that their conclusion offered us nothing new. In essence, both claimed that differences in intelligence are found when people have to behave intelligently, that is, when solving novel problems, reasoning, trying to come up with efficient strategies, and so forth. In retrospect the important claim of this research is a negative one – namely, that differences in intelligence are NOT to be found in very basic and simple operations of the information processing system (and by implication not in some simple neurophysiological correlate of cognition). This claim is interesting because it clashes with an alternative research program and indeed with my own view of what causes differences in general intelligence.

g AND SPEED OF PROCESSING

In the 1970s Jensen began a research program investigating the possibility that psychometric *g* may have its basis in speed of information processing. At first blush the attempt to associate *g* with measures of speed of information processing may look like an attempt to marry individual-differences research with experimental (cognitive) psychology that predates both cognitive correlates and cognitive components. Why it is not so is instructive for one of the main points of this chapter. Rather than adopting a cognitive framework to explore intelligence, this speed of processing research has simply appropriated a "cognitive" measure. Indeed Jensen explicitly claimed that such a measure is knowledge-free and consequently it is not a cognitive measure at all; therefore, he concluded that differences in intelligence are to be found incidentally in knowledge but causally in its neurophysiological underpinnings.

To measure speed of processing Jensen used a very simple decision time procedure where subjects had to respond quickly to the onset of a light. Jensen found that individuals with higher IQs responded faster and were less variable. Jensen claimed that these studies showed that the basis of individual differences in intelligence is to be found in the speed of processing a single bit of information. He conjectured that this may rest on the rate of oscillation of excitatory and inhibitory phases of neuronal firing (Jensen, 1982). Reaction time (RT) tasks have, nevertheless, been criticized as being inadequate measures of cognitive speed. For example, the task confounds number of choices with amount of visual scanning required. Decision time (DT) still contains a motor component, and trade-offs between speed and accuracy may occur (Longstreth, 1984).

The inspection time (IT) task was developed in the hope of overcoming some of these problems. In this task, subjects are presented with a simple visual stimulus and are asked to make a simple decision (e.g., presented with two lines, they must decide whether they are of the same or different lengths; then the stimulus is masked). In this task subjects are not required to respond quickly. Speed of processing is measured as the exposure duration of the stimulus required for an individual to respond at a predetermined level of accuracy. IT has been found to correlate with IQ up to a level of $-.92$ over a wide IQ range; although in IQ groups within the normal range, the correlations have been more modest, generally around $-.50$ (Nettelbeck, 1987).

In sum, it seems that the hypothesis that a biological variable, speed of information processing, might be the basis of general intelligence has received increasing support from RT and IT studies and from some more recent attempts to measure the activity of the nervous system itself (see Deary & Caryl, 1997, for a review). As we shall see later, the speed of processing hypothesis has also been featured in new research on the causal basis of cognitive development.

DEVELOPMENTAL APPROACHES TO INTELLIGENCE

If we now consider developmental approaches to intelligence, we see the same divide between high-level and low-level accounts (in this case of cognitive change rather than cognitive differences). Ever since Piaget, the dominant tradition in developmental psychology has been to attribute cognitive change to qualitative shifts in the structure and organization of knowledge itself. Karmiloff-Smith (1992) presents us with a well-articulated current cognitive theory of developmental processes. Her theory extends Fodor's (1983) distinction between "modular" input systems and central systems. Modules are innate, highly specialized, and efficient information processing devices that offer up representations for scrutiny by central processes of thought. The central systems are domain-neutral and relatively slow, but have the advantage of being flexible rather than hard-wired. Karmiloff-Smith's theory argues, contra Fodor, that modules are not fully specified and operational in infants from birth. Instead, Karmiloff-Smith argues that modules themselves are the result of an ongoing developmental process of modularization, albeit one based on certain innate attentional biases. This ongoing process of modularization takes place over a three-phase cycle of representational redescription (RR). The first phase consists of achieving successful performance on a task at a procedural level. In this phase, the focus is largely on environmental input information. The resulting representation of the stimulus information is essentially modular and implicit. In the second phase, an explicit representation is formed, which is available for central processing. This is much less detailed than the implicit representation, but because it is accessible to central processes, it can now be manipulated and related to other explicit representations within the domain that have been stored previously. The third phase consists of reconciling internal representations with external conditions.

The Karmiloff-Smith position is that the development of intelligence is to be found in the organization of knowledge and the developmental processes of modularization and RR. There is an intermediate position in developmental approaches to intelligence that attributes the causal basis of cognitive change to changing parameters of the implementation of knowledge rather than in the structure of knowledge itself. Nevertheless, this position remains true to the venerable tradition in developmental psychology of relating these parameters to the structure of knowledge. For example, for both Case (1985) and Halford (1987), cognitive "capacity" constrains the development of more complex knowledge systems. For Case, the constraint lessens with development because older cognitive structures become more efficient and less demanding of available capacity, whereas Halford claims that capacity itself increases.

Such developmental models provide ideal examples of profitable ways of trying to use cognitive approaches that usefully combines the two levels of cognition – its structure (high level) and its implementation (low level). But just as in the individual-differences tradition, research on the development of speed of processing has typically divorced the two levels (Kail, 1986, 1991a, 1991b; Hale, 1990), and to some extent so has research on other processes such as inhibition (Bjorklund & Harnishfeger, 1990).

For both individual-differences and developmental approaches to intelligence, there has been a considerable array of cognitive processes hypothesized to be the basis of intelligence. Perhaps this intellectual promiscuity is the very source of the problem for scientific advance in the field? It is time to take stock of the relationship between intelligence and cognition by asking the question – what is the appropriate scientific framework for research in intelligence?

THE SCIENTIFIC UTILITY OF THE CONSTRUCT "INTELLIGENCE"

A fundamental problem for our scientific goal of understanding intelligence is with the meaning of the word "intelligence." Jensen (1998, 1999) has argued that it has been used in so many different senses that it has lost its scientific utility. Indeed, one crucial usage has driven a wedge in the marriage between intelligence and cognition. Cognitive psychologists and cognitive scientists use the word "intelligence" to talk about the property of the entire human cognitive system. So in some sense, it could be argued that cognition and intelligence are synonymous, and that all work in cognitive psychology is about the psychology of intelligence. In this sense I agree with Jensen that it is too broad a use of the term and misses the focus that has interested the traditional researchers of intelligence, namely, the nature of *individual differences* in intelligence. Already we meet the crossroads that was the crux of Cronbach's (1957) APA address. Do these two uses of intelligence refer to the same *thing*? At first look, clearly they do not.

Jensen is quite explicit in distinguishing a study of intelligence that could in principle be done by the study of a single individual – that is, discovering the universal structure of the idealized cognitive mind. This, he argues, is the proper focus of cognitive psychology. There are aspects of intelligence, however, that we can only know about if we have studied a number of different individuals. Of paramount importance is the discovery by individual-differences researchers of general intelligence or g. Thus, g is conceptually and methodologically quite a different object of scientific study. In short, the phenomenon itself is invisible for a study of intelligence from the perspective of a pure cognitive psychologist.

I suspect that many cognitive psychologists would agree with Jensen's analysis, and this may explain why *g* barely rates a mention in books on cognitive psychology. Equally, many individual-differences researchers would think likewise, which would explain why they have looked upon cognitive psychology as a source of alternative measures rather than as a sustaining theoretical framework. In short, Jensen would argue Cronbach was surely wrong in seeking a fundamental reconciliation between the two psychologies. The study of intelligence from an individual-differences perspective should be first and foremost the study of *g* – a phenomenon fundamentally inexplicable within a cognitive framework.

While there are, by definition, methodological differences, I cannot agree that these two approaches represent conceptually distinct scientific enterprises. Not, at least, for the *psychology* of intelligence. What gives *g* its psychological meaning is the role it plays in a theory that relates general intelligence to other aspects of mental functioning. It is this, and this alone, that gives the notion of general intelligence its psychological impact. In other words, while the causal basis of *g* may not be cognitive, it is only useful as a psychological construct if it can be understood as a property of a cognitive mechanism. If we divorce the two (*g* and cognition), then there is no way back to explaining the very phenomena that make *g* a potentially interesting psychological construct in the first place. Perhaps even more fundamentally, Cronbach was correct in wanting to merge the two psychologies because there is only one mind, and it must be one and the same mind that underlies both our universal capacities and the ways in which we systematically differ. So I agree with Cronbach that the goal of our study of intelligence must be to unify these approaches under a common theory. But what of the point with which we started this section? Must such a theory be a unified theory of all aspects of cognition? I have already agreed that this is too broad a conception. But, equally, if we do not want to restrict our study of intelligence to *g* (Anderson, 2001), on what basis should it be restricted? Our theory of intelligence should be a theory that explains the range of cognitive phenomena that we believe to be germane to those aspects of individual differences and developmental changes in intelligence that we seek to explain. In other words, we have to set a research agenda that will both determine the scope of the theory and its level of explanation. It is this approach that laid the foundation for me to develop my own theory of intelligence and development.

A RESEARCH AGENDA FOR A THEORY OF INTELLIGENCE

My theory of intelligence and development (see Fig. 1), the theory of the Minimal Cognitive Architecture underlying individual differences and cognitive development (Anderson, 1992b), evolved through an attempt to answer what I saw as the central questions surrounding intelligence

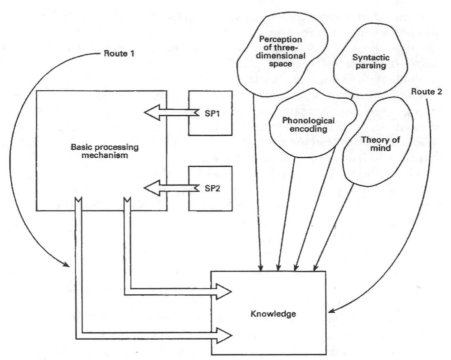

FIGURE 1. The theory of the minimal cognitive architecture underlying intelligence and development. Reproduced with permission from Anderson (1992b, p. 107).

and development. I assembled those questions as a series of agenda items that an adequate theory would have to address. The agenda items came in two clusters, one concerned with regularities in the data and the other with the exceptions to those regularities.

The regularities are (1) cognitive abilities increase with development, (2) individual differences in intelligence are remarkably stable with development, and (3) cognitive abilities covary (general intelligence).

In terms of our previous discussion, it should be clear that a biologically based theory is well equipped to explain such regularities by, for example, associating general intelligence (regularity 3) with variation in neural functioning, a parameter that in turn improves with age (regularity 1). The stability of individual differences (regularity 2) is less well accommodated without additional assumptions but, all in all, a biologically based, lower-level theory accommodates the regularities well. In other words, for the regularities on our agenda, a theory of intelligence need not be a cognitive theory. However, things change when we consider the exceptions to these regularities.

The major exceptions are (4) some individuals of normal or above-average general intelligence have specific problems or deficits in particular aspects of cognitive functioning, for example, in reading or spelling, (5) the corollary of item 4 is that there are individuals of very low IQ who are capable of remarkable cognitive feats (savants), (6) while some relatively simple problems are the very stuff of intelligence tests and beyond the reach of many individuals considered mentally retarded, those same individuals are capable of "everyday" cognitive activities such as acquiring language or seeing in three dimensions that are vastly more computationally complex.

Lower-level biologically based theory does not have the theoretical constructs to embrace both the regularities and the exceptions to those regularities. Rather, a higher level of description and explanation (a cognitive level) is necessary to embrace both clusters of agenda items. In this way, then, the explanatory agenda for a theory can be used to set the appropriate level of description and explanation and crucially alters the kind of research questions that can be asked and the methodologies that can be employed to answer them.

THE THEORY OF THE MINIMAL COGNITIVE ARCHITECTURE UNDERLYING INTELLIGENCE AND DEVELOPMENT

The theory has as its central focus the synthesis between general and specific abilities but also incorporates a developmental dimension to intelligence. The theory is framed within a general theory of cognitive architecture proposed by Fodor (1983), which makes the distinction between central processes of thought and dedicated processing modules.

While, as we have seen, intelligence tests measure intelligence through assessing knowledge, the theory proposes that knowledge itself is acquired through the two different routes proposed by Fodor. The major proposition is that these two processing routes are related to the two different dimensions of intelligence: individual differences and cognitive development.

The first route to knowledge is through *thought* (central processes). This is the route that is related to differences in IQ. Thoughtful problem solving can be done either by verbalizing a problem (using language-like propositions to think) or by visualizing it (using visuo-spatial representations to think). In the theory, this is accomplished by having two different kinds of knowledge-acquisition routines, each generated by one of two specific processors. The latent ability of each specific processor is normally distributed but uncorrelated in the population. So far these latent abilities look like the kinds of independent intelligences argued for by Gardner (1983). But there is another crucial part to this picture. In practice, the observed ability served by either specific processor is constrained by the speed of a basic processing mechanism – at slow speed only the simplest thoughts of either kind can be implemented (the speed of the basic processing mechanism can be estimated using tasks such as inspection time and reaction time).

It is this constraint that is the basis of general intelligence and the reason why manifest specific abilities are correlated (giving rise to the g factor).

It is in knowledge acquired through thought, then, that the relationship between general and specific *abilities* is accommodated. A particular feature of this processing route is that as speed of processing increases and the constraint on the specific processors decreases, manifest specific abilities will become less correlated. This predicts the differentiation of abilities (greater independence and importance of specific abilities) at higher levels of IQ (see Detterman & Daniel, 1989), and the complement – the pervasiveness and importance of difference in general intelligence at lower levels of IQ.

The second route for acquiring the knowledge that will influence intelligence test performance is through dedicated information processing *modules*; it is this route that is related to cognitive development. Modules have evolved to provide information about the environment that could not be provided by central processes of thought (route 1, knowledge acquisition) in an ecologically useful time frame. For example, if we had to think through all the perceptual information presented to us in order to construct a three-dimensional view of the world, we would be literally lost in thought. Because this activity is so important to us and requires great computational power and speed, evolution has created special modular devices to allow us to do this automatically. Other examples of likely modules are various language-acquisition devices, face recognition systems, the core computational procedures involved in acquiring a Theory of Mind, and the fetch and carry mechanisms of information processing (for example, inhibition) that might subserve "executive functions." In addition, modular processes can be acquired through extensive practice. The common features of both the acquired and the innate modules are that they operate automatically and independently of thought and are consequently unconstrained by the speed of the basic processing mechanism.

Perhaps the most important claim of the theory of *minimal cognitive architecture* is that there are two dimensions to g. The first is related to IQ differences within ages and is based on an unchanging speed of processing. The second is related to developmental changes in cognitive competence and is underpinned by the maturation and acquisition of modules. It is because modules function independently of variations in the speed of the basic processing mechanism that their operation is independent of differences in IQ. In turn, this means that individual differences and cognitive development represent two independent dimensions of intelligence. It also means that these complex cognitive functions are available to all non-brain-damaged individuals with intellectual disabilities.

Clearly this theory eschews the obvious possibility that speed of processing underlies differences in both individual differences and developmental *g*. The motives for the hypothesis that speed of processing does not change with development are several:

If it is true, then it shows the value of a cognitive level of analysis. Behaviorally, this theoretical possibility is invisible to the naked eye. So if we look at either intelligence test scores or RT and IT performance, there is no good reason to think that individual differences lie on a different dimension from developmental change (in short, lower IQ individuals are slower and score more poorly on intelligence tests than higher IQ individuals and the same is true when we compare younger with older children). But it is at least theoretically possible that the behavioral manifestations in these two domains are supported by quite different mechanisms. And, again, if true, that sets a different agenda for the neurophysiological task of looking for the underpinnings of this in the brain. For individual-differences dimensions, we would be looking for neural support for global differences in speed of processing. For developmental change, we should be looking for neural support for the development of information processing modules.

Of course, I happen to believe it is true and that there is empirical evidence to support the contention, if you are motivated to look closely enough. While it is clear that the major markers for speed of information processing, RT and IT, improve with cognitive development, I have written extensively how this is not enough to support the hypothesis that speed of processing improves during development (Anderson, 1992a, 1999). Quite simply, we do not want to fall into the trap of operational definitions (where speed of processing is defined as performance on those tasks) if for no other reason than the fact that there are no pure measures of any construct. I have also shown in a number of ways that both RT and IT tasks are likely to reflect both a speed and an executive/inhibitory component (Anderson, Nettelbeck, & Barlow, 1997) and that it is the latter, not the former, where developmental changes occur (Davis & Anderson, 1999, 2001).

Recent work by Duncan and colleagues (Duncan, 1995; Duncan et al., 1996, 2000) points to a specific mechanism that might be the causal basis of any general factor in cognitive development – the development of executive functions supported by the frontal lobes of the brain (Duncan, 1995). Of course, Duncan also argues that these processes underlie individual differences in Spearman's *g* in adults – but here speed of processing is a serious contender for that role. Ironically, perhaps, the hypothesis of two dimensions to *g* undermines Binet's great insight, with which we started. It argues that what truly distinguishes children of different ages is not that which distinguishes children of high and low intelligence within ages, or one adult from another.

Although the theory is intended to be a constrained theory of the mental architecture underlying individual differences and the development of intelligence (it is crucial that the theory posits the *minimal* architecture required to explain the data that are relevant to our research agenda), the evidence for the architecture is diverse and catholic. Some comes from the standard literature on individual differences and some from an experimental and developmental literature specifically designed to test the theory. Here are some examples: (1) the crucial data base on the relationship between measures of speed of processing, such as RT and IT, and IQ and developmental change (Anderson, 1986, 1988; Nettelbeck, 1987; Fairweather & Hutt, 1978; Kail, 1992; Nettelbeck & Wilson, 1985); (2) experimental tests of the relationship between IT, RT, and development (Anderson, 1989; Anderson, Nettelbeck, & Barlow 1987); (3) experimental evidence for the independence of modules from IQ (Moore et al., 1996; Anderson & Miller, 1998); (4) a set of longitudinal and cross-sectional studies (Project KIDS – see Anderson, Reid, & Nelson, 2001) that looks at many indices that estimate parameters of the architecture simultaneously in 240 children each year; (5) current experimental studies that use manipulations of key tasks based on predictions from the theory about the consequences of those manipulations for different clinical groups (e.g., adults with frontal-lobe damage, children born prematurely, children with autism, and children with Williams syndrome; see, for example Scheuffgen et al., 2000); (6) evidence from the differentiation of abilities and mental retardation, particularly experimental studies of savant syndrome (Anderson, O'Connor, & Hermelin, 1998). This methodological approach is sympathetic to Gardner's position that a theory of intelligence should be able to account for a rich data set rather than, say, a single association between an intelligence test and some quirky isolated laboratory task. The very diversity of the former constrains the theory because it has to satisfy so many different conditions with the same minimal architecture (a plethora of minitheories would be self-defeating and a scientific disaster). The pursuit of the latter may make researchers feel comfortable because they have a lot of company, but they are likely to be following a "Pied Piper" and going somewhere they do not really want to be. However, unlike Gardner, the explicit aim is to produce a coherent and, if possible, relatively simple theory of how a cognitive architecture could underlie these rich and complex data. More particularly, once an architecture is in place that makes a passable job of explaining the rich data set, the scientific goal must be to test the constructs of the theory (preferably experimentally) and not to endlessly search for yet more diversity. This brings me to my final section – a consideration of the most appropriate level of analysis and scientific strategy for understanding intelligence, much of which has been implicit in what I have discussed so far.

LEVELS OF DESCRIPTION AND METHODOLOGICAL STRATEGIES IN INTELLIGENCE RESEARCH

The dominant approach to understanding intelligence from an individual-differences perspective has been a psychometric one. The first half-century of research was conducted largely within a factor-analytic framework, where researchers hoped that the patterns of observed correlations among easy-to-observe intelligence test scores, coupled with a suitably ingenious statistical analysis, would discover the structure of the intellect. Famously, this general approach failed. Some 50 years later, the wide-eyed optimism that "if-only-we-get-our-measures-right-and-derive-reliable-replicable-associations-then-we-can-eschew-hot-air-speculations-about-the-nature-of-intelligence-and-get-on-with-the-job-of-normal-sciences-of-collecting-sensible-data-bit-by-bit" is still with us. A contemporary example is the following:

In the field of human intelligence so-called theories have done more harm than good . . . For some reason there has been a demand for fairly all-encompassing theories of intelligence differences, looked for as emerging whole from their originators (Guilford, 1956; Sternberg, 1990). In an area of study like psychology, where the error terms are so large and the valid constructs and laws so rare, it is absurd that one should be expected to come up with a broad theory that requires many constructs and their interrelations . . . a theory can keep one busy refuting or operationalizing its aspects instead of focusing on less immediately compelling, but fundamentally more important sensible empirical advances. (Deary, 2000, p. 108)

Science would be simpler indeed if there was a clear dichotomy between the available data and the scientific theories that are constructed to explain the data. Maybe then we could first gather all the relevant facts before we cloud our vision with attempts to explain them (theories). To imagine this is what happens in "normal" sciences is to be seduced by the schoolboy attraction for chemistry sets. There are no theory-free facts. Theories are not things that get in the way of facts; they are the things that give facts their meaning. It is hard to comprehend how we would know whether sensible empirical advances were being made (or even what that possibly could mean) without reference to some theoretical position. In short, generating theories is not some superfluous affectation but what science is all about. This is so because theories simply represent our current best understanding of the world, and understanding the world is what science is about – not unearthing new "facts," no matter how replicable. It is the failure of individual-differences researchers to take theories seriously that has impeded scientific progress in the field. In my view, this failure is the basis of the unhappy marriage with cognitive psychology. All this time, it turns out that the groom was never really interested in what the bride had to offer. While the bride has to come to the party by acknowledging that she has ignored the central interest of the husband for an indecently long time (Spearman's g), repairing the relationship requires the acknowledgment from the groom that the appropriate theoretical framework for understanding intelligence is a cognitive one. This might be a big ask for the old fellow.

When we meet any phenomenon in psychology, we have a number of levels of description and explanation available to us. The three major levels in the study of intelligence are the behavioral (including cultural), the cognitive/computational, and the biological/neurophysiological (including genetic). These different levels can be considered to range from high to low and map onto Eysenck's recipe (adapted from Hebb) on how to study intelligence scientifically. Eysenck (1988) divides constructs of intelligence into three distinct levels: intelligence A, which is its biological substrate; intelligence B, which is the conversion of intelligence A by cultural forces into what we know; and intelligence C, which is behavior manifested in intelligence test performance. Many would recognize these distinctions but Eysenck, for one, goes further in adopting a *reductionist* stance. He believes that a comprehensive theory of intelligence must first wait for a comprehensive theory of intelligence A (Eysenck, 1988). What this ordering implies is that the important aspects of intelligence will be best captured by a theory of its neurophysiological basis and, indeed, such theories are on offer (Henderickson & Hendrickson, 1980; Jensen, 1982).

Yet, as I have argued elsewhere (Anderson, 1992b), it is not at all obvious that discovering the precise neuronal basis of intelligence (even supposing this is possible independently of adequate descriptions at the other levels) is a prerequisite for studying intelligence B or intelligence as a cognitive construct. Indeed, I believe the opposite – there are no constraints that I can see on the cognitive theory of intelligence imposed by alternative physiological theories. However, I do agree with Eysenck that the other end of this explanatory dimension (intelligence C, or to quote Boring's famous dictum, "Intelligence is what the tests test") has run out of theoretical steam.

It is clear that others take an opposite view to Eysenck. For example, Gardner (1983), while accepting as nearly everyone does that there are biological correlates and perhaps determinants of intelligence, has argued that intelligence can only be considered in the social and cultural context in which it has evolved and functions. In other words, focusing on the biological loses sight of the very phenomenon of interest.

So what sets the level of description? In my view it is the questions that we want to answer. For me the central questions for the psychology of intelligence were laid out in my research agenda, and, as I argued above, the explanation of that agenda requires a theory that can address the relationship between general intelligence and knowledge – only cognitive psychology offers any hope that this can be done in a mechanistic fashion. Everything else is just correlations.

CONCLUSION

What constrains a theory of intelligence is neither a methodological approach nor any a priori belief that intelligence is a property of genes, neurophysiology, education, or culture but rather it is the research agenda for that theory – or more prosaically what it is that such a theory wants to explain. It is the research agenda that determines the level of description and explanation for that theory. For the psychology of intelligence and its development, that research agenda clearly requires a cognitive theory.

References

Anderson, J. R. (1983). *The architecture of cognition*. Cambridge, MA: Harvard University Press.

Anderson, M. (1986). Understanding the cognitive deficit in mental retardation. *Journal of Child Psychology and Psychiatry, 27*, 297–306.

Anderson, M. (1988). Inspection time, information processing and the development of intelligence. *British Journal of Developmental Psychology, 6*, 43–57.

Anderson, M. (1989). Inspection time and the relationship between stimulus encoding and response selection factors in development. In D. Vickers & P. L. Smith (Eds.), *Human information processing measures, mechanisms and models* (pp. 509–516). Amsterdam: Elsevier Science.

Anderson, M. (1992a). Intelligence. In A. P. Smith and D. M. Jones (Eds.), *Handbook of human performance* (Vol III, pp. 1–24). London: Academic Press.

Anderson, M. (1992b). *Intelligence and development: A cognitive theory*. Oxford, UK: Blackwell.

Anderson, M. (1999). *The development of intelligence*. Hove, UK: Psychology Press.

Anderson, M. (2000). An unassailable defense of *g* but a siren-song for theories of intelligence. *Psycoloquy, 11* (013).

Anderson, M. (2001). Conceptions of intelligence. *Journal of Child Psychology & Psychiatry, 42*(3), 287–298.

Anderson, M., & Miller, K. L. (1998). Modularity, mental retardation, and speed of processing. *Developmental Science, 1*, 239–245.

Anderson, M., Nettelbeck, T., & Barlow, J. (1997). Using reaction time measures of speed of information processing: Speed of response selection increases with age but speed of stimulus categorisation does not. *British Journal of Developmental Psychology, 15*, 145–157.

Anderson, M., O'Connor, N., & Hermelin, B. (1998). A specific calculating ability. *Intelligence, 26*, 383–403.

Anderson, M., Reid, C., & Nelson, J. (2001). Developmental changes in inspection time: What a difference a year makes. *Intelligence, 29*, 475–486.

Binet, A., & Simon, T. (1905). Upon the necessity of establishing a scientific diagnosis of inferior states of intelligence. *L'annee Psychologique, 11*, 163–191.

Bjorklund, D. F., & Harnishfeger, K. K. (1990). The resources construct in cognitive development: Diverse sources of evidence and a theory of inefficient inhibition. *Developmental Review, 10*, 48–71.

Case, R. (1985). *Intellectual development: Birth to adulthood*. London: Academic Press.

Ceci, S. J. (1990). *On intelligence . . . more or less. A bio-ecological treatise on intellectual development*. Englewood Cliffs, NJ: Prentice-Hall.

Cronbach, L. J. (1957). The two disciplines of scientific psychology. *American Psychologist, 12*, 671–684.

Davis, H., & Anderson, M. (1999). Individual differences in development – One dimension or two? In M. Anderson (Ed.), *The development of intelligence* (pp. 161–191). Hove, UK: Psychology Press.

Davis, H., & Anderson, M. (2001). Developmental and individual differences in fluid intelligence and speed of processing: Evidence against the unidimensional hypothesis. *British Journal of Developmental Psychology, 19,* 181–206.

Deary, I. J. (2000). *Looking down on human intelligence: From psychometrics to the brain.* Oxford, UK: Oxford University Press.

Deary, I. J., & Caryl, P. G. (1997). Neuroscience and human intelligence differences. *Trends in Neuroscience, 20,* 321–372.

Detterman, D. K., & Daniel, M. H. (1989). Correlations of mental tests with each other and with cognitive variables are highest for low IQ groups. *Intelligence, 13,* 349–359.

Duncan, J. (1995). Attention, intelligence, and the frontal lobes. In M. S. Gazzaniga (Ed.), *The cognitive neurosciences* (pp. 721–733). Cambridge, MA: MIT Press.

Duncan, J., Emslie, H., Williams, P., Johnson, R., & Freer, C. (1996). Intelligence and the frontal lobe: The organization of goal-directed behaviour. *Cognitive Psychology, 30,* 257–303.

Duncan, J., Seitz, R. J., Kolodny, J., Bor, D., Herzog, H., Ahmed, A., Newell, F., & Emslie, H. (2000). Neural basis for general intelligence. *Science, 289,* 457–460.

Eysenck, H. J. (1988). The concept of "intelligence": Useful or useless? *Intelligence, 12,* 1–16.

Fairweather, H., & Hutt, S. J. (1978). On the rate of gain of information in children. *Journal of Experimental Child Psychology, 26,* 216–229.

Fodor, J. A. (1983). *The modularity of mind.* Cambridge, MA: MIT Press.

Gardner, H. (1983). *Frames of mind: The theory of multiple intelligences.* London: Heinemann.

Gould, S. J. (1996). *The mismeasure of man.* Revised and expanded. New York: Norton.

Guildford, J. P. (1956). The structure of intellect. *Psychological Bulletin, 53,* 267–293.

Hale, S. (1990). A global developmental trend in cognitive processing speed. *Child Development, 61,* 653–663.

Halford, G. S. (1987). A structure-mapping approach to cognitive development. *International Journal of Psychology, 22,* 609–42.

Hendrickson, A. E., & Hendrickson, D. E. (1980). The biological basis for individual differences in intelligence. *Personality and Individual Differences, 1,* 3–33.

Herrnstein, R. J., & Murray, C. A. (1994). *The bell curve: Intelligence and class structure in American life.* New York: Free Press.

Hindley, C. B., & Owen, C. F. (1978). The extent of individual changes in IQ for ages between 6 months and 17 years, in a British longitudinal sample. *Journal of Child Psychology and Psychiatry, 19,* 329–350.

Howe, M. J. A. (1988). Intelligence as an explanation. *British Journal of Psychology, 79,* 349–360.

Howe, M. J. A. (1990). *The origins of exceptional abilities.* Oxford, UK: Blackwell.

Howe, M. J. A. (1997). *IQ in question: The truth about intelligence.* London, Sage.

Hunt, E. (1980). Intelligence as an information processing concept. *British Journal of Psychology, 71,* 449–474.

Hunt, E. (1995). Pulls and pushes on cognitive psychology: The view toward 2001. In R. L. Solso & D. W. Massaro (Eds.), *The science of the mind: 2001 and beyond* (pp. 258–273). Oxford, UK: Oxford University Press.

Hunter, J. E. (1986). Cognitive ability, cognitive aptitudes, job knowledge and job performance. *Journal of Vocational Behaviour, 29,* 340–362.

Jensen, A. R. (1982). Reaction time and psychometric *g.* In H. J. Eysenck (Ed.), *A model for intelligence* (pp. 93–102). Berlin: Springer-Verlag.

Jensen, A. R. (1984). Test validity: *g* versus the specificity doctrine. *Journal of Social and Biological Structures, 7,* 93–118.

Jensen, A. R. (1998). *The g factor: The science of mental ability.* Westport, CT: Praeger.

Jensen, A. R. (1999). Precis of: "The g factor: The science of mental ability." PSYCOLOQUY *10*(023).

Kail, R. (1986). Sources of age differences in speed of processing. *Child Development, 57,* 969–987.

Kail, R. (1991a). Processing time declines exponentially during childhood and adolescence. *Developmental Psychology, 27,* 259–266.

Kail, R. (1991b). Developmental change in speed of processing during childhood and adolescence. *Psychological Bulletin, 109,* 490–501.

Kail, R. (1992). Processing speed, speech rate, and memory. *Developmental Psychology, 28,* 899–904.

Karmiloff-Smith, A. (1992). *Beyond modularity: A developmental perspective on cognitive science.* Cambridge, MA: MIT Press.

Longstreth, L. E. (1984). Jensen's reaction time investigations of intelligence: A critique. *Intelligence, 8,* 139–160.

Moore, D., Hobson, R. P., & Anderson, M. (1995). Direct perception: Evidence for IQ-independent processing. *Intelligence, 20,* 65–86.

Moore, D. G., Hobson, P., & Anderson, M. (1995). Person perception: Does it involve IQ-independent perceptual processing? *Intelligence, 20,* 65–86.

Nettelbeck, T. (1987). Inspection time and intelligence. In P. A. Vernon (Ed.), *Speed of information processing and intelligence* (pp. 295–346). New York: Ablex.

Nettelbeck, T., & Wilson, C. (1985). A cross sequential analysis of developmental differences in speed of visual information processing. *Journal of Experimental Child Psychology, 40,* 1–22.

Richardson, K. (1999). *The making of intelligence.* London: Weidenfield & Nicolson.

Scheuffgen, K., Happé, F., Anderson, M., & Frith, U. (2000). High "intelligence," low "IQ"? Speed of processing and measured IQ in children with autism. *Development and Psychopathology, 12,* 83–90.

Spearman, C. (1904). "General Intelligence," objectively determined and measured. *American Journal of Psychology, 15,* 201–293.

Stern, W. (1912). *Die psychologische methoden der intelligenzprufung.* Leipzig: Barth.

Sternberg, R. J. (1983). Components of human intelligence. *Cognition, 15,* 1–48.

Sternberg, R. J. (1990). *Metaphors of mind.* Cambridge, UK: Cambridge University Press.

Yule, W., Gold, R. D., & Busch, C. (1982). Long-term predictive validity of the WPPSI: An 11-year follow-up study. *Personality and Individual Differences, 3,* 65–71.

15

From Description to Explanation in Cognitive Aging

Timothy A. Salthouse

Two different approaches have been employed in contemporary research to investigate the effects of aging on cognitive and intellectual abilities. One approach can be termed *process analysis* because it relies on task analyses or formal models to attempt to identify the specific processes in a cognitive task that are responsible for the observed age differences. This approach has used a variety of analytical methods such as subtraction, additive factors, and process dissociation to attempt to partition the variance in the target variable into theoretically distinct processes. Because the primary interest is in decomposing the variance in a single variable into different processes, process analysis research has typically involved comparing performance in one or more conditions in a single task, frequently in relatively small samples of young and old adults.

The second approach taken to investigate aging and cognition can be termed *covariance analysis* because it attempts to specify which combinations of variables covary together with respect to their age-related influences. A primary goal of this type of research is to partition the variance in the target variable into a portion not related to age, a portion related to age and shared with other variables, and a portion uniquely related to age. Covariance analysis research necessarily requires data from multiple variables and tasks and usually involves moderately large samples of adults across a wide age range.

One way to conceptualize the difference between the two perspectives is portrayed in Figure 1. The left side represents the process analysis perspective in which the variance in the target variable is partitioned into hypothesized processes, and the right side represents the covariance perspective in which the variance in the variable is partitioned according to age-related individual differences. Because the two approaches focus on different ways of partitioning variance in the same variable, they can be considered to address different questions, and thus it is not surprising that

288

Task   Person

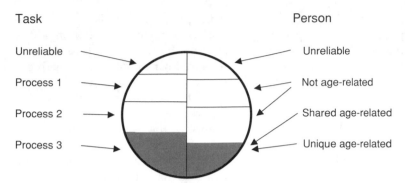

Unreliable   Unreliable

Process 1   Not age-related

Process 2   Shared age-related

Process 3   Unique age-related

FIGURE 1. Schematic illustration of different approaches to partitioning the variance in the variable of interest.

there is often little communication between researchers working within each perspective.

Much of my research has been motivated by the belief that when trying to understand age-related individual differences in cognitive functioning, it is important to combine the two approaches and to interpret age-related effects on variables representing processes hypothesized to be responsible for performance in a particular task in the context of age-related effects occurring on other variables. Another major assumption guiding my research is that before attempting to explain the phenomenon of cognitive aging, it is essential to have an accurate description of the phenomenon in terms of the number and nature of statistically distinct age-related influences that are operating because that will determine the scope of the explanations that will eventually be needed.

The point that an accurate description has implications for the explanation can be illustrated with examples from the sensory domain. Assume that age-related effects were found on measures of visual acuity (i.e., the smallest visual angle that can be resolved), visual accommodation (the closest distance at which one can see with clear focus), and color discrimination (distinguishing between colors such as blue and purple). The age-related effects on these variables could all be independent of one another in the sense that they are caused by separate and distinct mechanisms. However, these particular variables were selected because they could each be manifestations of the accumulation of dead cells in the lens of the eye, which leads to blurred vision (affecting visual acuity), reduced flexibility in altering the shape of the lens (affecting accommodation), and yellowing that selectively absorbs short wavelength light in the blue region of the spectrum (affecting color discrimination). In this example, therefore, a single age-related change in the structure of the lens may be able to account for age-related effects on what might, at least initially, appear to be quite different variables.

Of course, independent age-related influences could also occur. Consider the phenomena of presbyopia – the reduced accommodation ability of the lens that leads to a decreased ability to focus on near objects – and presbycusis – the reduced sensitivity to, and discrimination among, high-frequency tones. These are both age-related problems (as indicated by the common root presby, which refers to elders), but it is likely that they originate from different, and potentially independent, causes. That is, as just noted, presbyopia is largely a consequence of the accumulation of dead cells in the lens, whereas presbycusis is a disorder associated with degeneration of the bones of the middle ear and/or death of hair cells on the basilar membrane. The probability or rate that an individual develops presbyopia as he or she ages may therefore be unrelated to the probability or rate that he or she will develop presbycusis. If this is the case, such that knowledge of the effects of aging on one of these conditions is not informative about the effects of aging on the other condition, then they can be inferred to be independent with respect to their age-related influences. Because information of this type is critical for determining exactly what needs to be explained, and for specifying the most meaningful level of analysis in characterizing the phenomenon of cognitive aging, a major focus of my research has been to investigate the extent to which the age-related influences on different cognitive variables are independent of one another.

DESCRIPTION OF COGNITIVE AGING

Alternative analytical models that can be used to investigate age-related influences in cognitive functioning are schematically illustrated in Figure 2. The model in panel A represents the simple univariate approach because the focus is on a single variable. The remaining models in Figure 2 are multivariate in that age-related effects on the target variable are examined in the context of effects on other variables. However, it is important to note that process analyses of the target variable can still be conducted within the multivariate perspective, but because multiple variables are examined it is also possible to partition the variance in the target variable into portions shared with other variables and portions uniquely related to age. In each case, direct age–variable relations (represented in the figure by dotted lines) can be evaluated in the context of relations of age to other variables or constructs. Furthermore, only if the direct age relation is equal in magnitude to the observed (or total) age relation could one infer that age-related influences on the target variable are independent of age-related influences on other variables or constructs.

The model in panel B represents the hypothesis that the age-related effects on variable x are at least partially mediated through age-related effects on variable a. A relatively large number of studies have examined

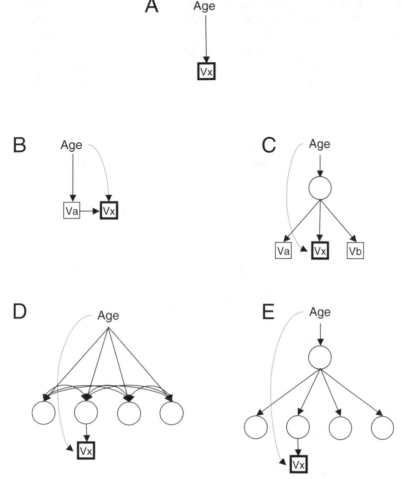

FIGURE 2. Alternative analytical models portraying relationships between age and cognitive variables. See text for details.

variants of this type of mediation model with measures of processing speed or working memory as the hypothesized mediator of age-related effects on other cognitive variables. In nearly every study the age-related variance in the target variable was considerably reduced when the variance in the hypothesized mediator variables was statistically controlled (e.g., Lindenberger, Mayr, & Kliegl, 1993; Park et al., 1996; Salthouse, 1996b, c, 1998; Salthouse et al., 1996b; Verhaeghen & Salthouse, 1997). Although this pattern of results has been interpreted as supporting the hypothesis that the controlled variable partially mediates the age-related effects on other cognitive variables, it is important to recognize that this is not the only possible interpretation. That is, causal direction is ambiguous in single-occasion correlational studies, and the effects on both variables could be attributable to an unknown third variable. However, the important point in the current context is that because results from mediational models indicate that the age-related influences on different cognitive variables vary according to the other variables included in the analysis, we can conclude that the age-related influences are not completely independent of one another.

The model portrayed in panel C in Figure 2 represents a shared influence model that differs from the mediational model in that it does not assume that any single variable or construct has special status, or causal priority, in terms of the age-related influences on different types of cognitive variables. Shared influence models are therefore agnostic about the existence or identity of mediators; instead they simply examine age-related effects on individual variables after controlling the age-related effects on an estimate of what is common to all variables. These types of models are sometimes referred to as common cause models because many variables are assumed to be influenced by a common cause, even though the specific nature of that common cause is unknown.

Several different types of analytical procedures have been used within shared influence models to partition the age-related effects on a target variable into a portion shared with other variables, and a portion unique to that variable. For example, the first principal component in a principal components analysis can be used to estimate the variance common to all variables, and then that estimate can be controlled in a hierarchical multiple regression analysis before examining age-related effects on the target variable. Alternatively, a structural equation model can be specified in which all variables are assumed to be influenced by a common factor, which in turn is influenced by age (e.g., Kliegl & Mayr, 1992; McArdle & Prescott, 1992; Salthouse, 1994). A variety of methods can also be used within shared influence methods to examine unique age-related influences. For example, the predicted age–variable correlation based on a single shared influence can be compared to the observed age correlation, with the difference between the two correlations inferred to be attributable to unique age-related influences. Alternatively, the path coefficient for a direct relation from age to the variable can be examined when age-related influences also operate through the shared or common factor.

Many different combinations of variables have been examined with shared influence analyses in different data sets from my laboratory (e.g., Salthouse, 1994, 1996a, b, 2001b; Salthouse & Czaja, 2000; Salthouse, Hambrick, & McGuthry, 1998; Salthouse et al., 1996b; Salthouse, McGuthry, & Hambrick, 1999; Salthouse et al., 1997; Verhaeghen & Salthouse, 1997) and in data sets from other laboratories (e.g., Anstey & Smith, 1999; Christensen et al., 2001; Hultsch et al., 1998; Lindenberger & Baltes, 1994;

Lindenberger et al., 1993; McArdle & Prescott, 1992; Park et al., 2002). A consistent finding in each of these studies has been that the unique age-related influences on cognitive variables are few in number and small in magnitude. Quantitative estimates of the magnitude of shared and unique age-related influences on a given variable have varied according to the method of estimating the common and unique variances and according to the particular combination of variables included in the analysis. However, it has almost always been the case that a relatively small proportion of the total age-related variance was unique to the target variable and independent of the age-related effects on other variables.

An interesting implication of shared influence models is that a systematic relation should exist between the degree to which a variable shares variance with other variables and the magnitude of the correlation of age with the variable. That is, if a large proportion of the age-related effects on a set of variables operates through the common factor that represents variance shared among the variables, then one would expect a strong relationship between the variable's relation to the common factor and the magnitude of the variable's relation to age. These predicted functions can be termed AR functions because they link the age (A) effects on the variables with the relatedness (R) of the variables to each other.

Examination of the correspondence between two sets of relations has been used in several areas of psychology as a means of investigating the pattern by which different variables are related to one another. For example, Hart and Spearman (1914) compared normal individuals and mental patients on a number of different variables and reported that an index of the "intellectual saturation" of a variable correlated .47 with the amount of impairment in the variable exhibited in the sample of mental patients. In the area of attention and performance, Duncan et al. (1992) examined a set of variables representing different aspects of driving performance and found a correlation of .67 between the variable's correlation with the score on an intelligence test and the degree to which performance on the variable was impaired when the research participant was simultaneously performing another task. In the field of behavioral genetics, Plomin et al. (1994) reported a correlation of .77 between loadings of a set of cognitive variables on the first (unrotated) principal component and estimates of the heritability of the variables. The most extensive use of this technique has been by Jensen (e.g., 1998), who termed it the *method of correlated vectors*. He has primarily used it as a method of determining the degree to which a factor affects intellectual g rather than specific abilities, and in different data sets he has reported positive correlations between a variable's g loadings and its correlation with factors such as head size, heritability, and reaction time.

The degree to which a variable is related to other variables can be assessed with a variety of indices, such as the median correlation of the variable with all other variables, the multiple correlation between that variable and other variables, the loading of the variable on the first principal factor in a factor analysis, or the loading of the variable on the first principal component in a principal components analysis. However, the estimates from each of these procedures tend to be highly correlated with one another (see Salthouse, 2001a, b), and hence only results with the method of assessing relatedness based on the first principal component loading will be described here. Positive AR functions have been reported in a number of different studies (e.g., Salthouse, 2001a, b), including a recent analysis of data from over 5,000 adults under the age of fifty (Schroeder & Salthouse, 2004). Re-analyses of thirty different data sets from my laboratory revealed that the phenomenon of positive AR functions appears to be quite robust because across these data sets the median rank-order correlation between the relation of a variable to age and the variable's relation to other variables was .80 (Salthouse, 2001b). Moreover, most of the exceptions with low correlations were interpretable in terms of restriction of range in either the relatedness dimension or the age correlation dimension. Additional analyses revealed that similar values of relatedness were obtained when estimates of the reliability of the variables, and of the relations of age to the variables, were statistically controlled before determining the degree to which the variables were related to one another (Salthouse, 2001a).

Figure 3 contains a summary AR function created by plotting the means (and standard errors) of the AR coordinates for variables that were assessed

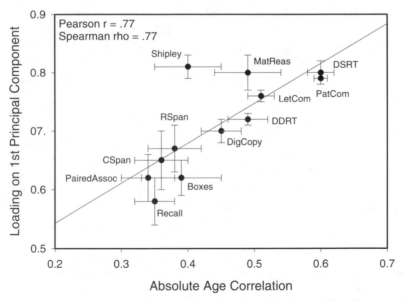

FIGURE 3. Means and standard errors of age correlations and loadings on the first principal component of variables included in at least five different studies.

in at least five studies from my laboratory. Notice that a positive AR function is evident even with these meta-analytic results. Although not portrayed here, a similar pattern was evident when the variables were represented in terms of percentiles of the A and R values from each data set (i.e., rho = .63) instead of absolute values of the loadings and correlations. The systematic relations apparent in AR analyses are intriguing because they raise the possibility that the ordering of variables along the AR function might be informative about the dimension underlying shared age-related influences. Although convincing interpretations of how variables at various positions along the AR function differ from one another are not yet available (but see Salthouse, 1994, 2001a, b, for speculations), the outcomes of shared influence analyses are clear in suggesting that, as was the case with mediational models, large proportions of the age-related influences on different cognitive variables are not independent of one another.

The model portrayed in panel D in Figure 2 is a correlated factors model in which the observed variables are structured into first-order latent factors, and then those factors are allowed to correlate with one another. This type of model does not allow a direct investigation of age-related influences that are shared across factors because the covariation among factors is represented by correlations instead of by a higher-order factor that could be examined with respect to its age relations. Nevertheless, the correlations among the factors are informative about the potential independence of age-related influences on the factors (and on the constituent variables) because the larger the correlations among the factors, the less likely the age-related influences are independent. That is, age-related effects can operate directly on the factors, or they can be indirect and operate through other factors with which the target factor is correlated. To the extent that the cognitive factors are moderately correlated with one another, therefore, it is unlikely that age-related effects upon them would be completely independent.

Evidence relevant to the interrelations of cognitive factors is contained in Table 1, which summarizes results from ten recent studies in my laboratory in which estimates of relations among age and cognitive factors could be obtained. Participants in each of the studies ranged from about 18 to 80 years of age, and most had completed at least some college education and reported themselves to be in good to excellent health. In each case, we analyzed the data with a model similar to that portrayed in panel D of Figure 2, except that direct relations of age to individual variables were ignored. All of the analyses provided reasonably good fits to the data (i.e., the median CFI was .99, and the median RMSEA was .07). Despite different samples of participants and combinations of variables, the results in Table 1 are quite consistent in indicating moderately strong correlations among the factors.

A crude indication of the extent of dependence among the age-related influences on the factors can be obtained by comparing the simple age

TABLE 1. *Correlations among Factors and Age in 10 Recent Studies*

Study	N	Age-g_f	Age-Mem	Age-Spd	Age-Voc	g_f-Mem	g_f-Spd	g_f-Voc	Mem-Spd	Mem-Voc	Spd-Voc
A	261	−.46	−.47	−.58	.36	.61	.56	.66	.51	.65	.50
B	204	−.50	−.61	−.79	.17	.61	.48	.71	.54	.66	.50
C	206	−.71	−.60	−.64	.00	.41	.47	.56	.25	.42	.36
D	220	−.76		−.66	.02		.66	.70			.52
E	229	−.78		−.67	.14		.61	.45			.56
F	207	−.46		−.45	.41		.42	.54			.38
G	380	−.46	−.40	−.64	.35	.53	.66	.54	.59	.51	.44
H	124		−.41	−.73	.40				.34	.33	.29
I	259	−.57	−.62	−.72	.22	.47	.64	.67	.40	.42	.46
J	178		−.64	−.77	.22				.75	.51	.46
Wt. Avg.		−.58	−.53	−.66	.26	.53	.57	.60	.50	.51	.46

A – Salthouse, Atkinson, & Berish (2002), g_f = Ravens, Letter Sets, Spatial Relations, Paper Folding, Form Boards; Mem = Recall across 4 trials, Logical Memory, Paired Associates; Speed = Digit Symbol, Letter Comparison, Pattern Comparison; Voc = Synonym Vocabulary, Antonym Vocabulary, WAIS III Vocabulary, Woodcock–Johnson Picture Vocabulary

B – Salthouse & Ferrer-Caja (2003), g_f = Analysis-Synthesis, Spatial Relations, Ravens, Paper Folding, Block Design; Mem = Recall across 4 trials, Recall on new list, Logical Memory, Paired Associates; Speed = Digit Symbol, Letter Comparison, Pattern Comparison; Voc = Synonym Vocabulary, Antonym Vocabulary, WAIS III Vocabulary, Woodcock–Johnson Picture Vocabulary

C – Salthouse (2001b), g_f = Ravens, Analysis-Synthesis, Paper Folding, Letter Sets; Mem = Recall on trials 1, 2, and 3, Paired Associates; Speed = Letter Comparison, Pattern Comparison; Voc = Synonym Vocabulary, Antonym Vocabulary, Knowledge 1, Knowledge 2

D – Salthouse (2001a, Study 1), g_f = Ravens, Figure Classification, Locations; Speed = Letter Comparison, Pattern Comparison; Voc = Synonym Vocabulary, Antonym Vocabulary

E – Salthouse (2001a, Study 2), g_f = Analytical Reasoning, Figure Classification, Locations; Speed = Letter Comparison, Pattern Comparison; Voc = Synonym Vocabulary, Antonym Vocabulary

F – Salthouse, Toth, et al. (2000), g_f = Ravens, Spatial Relations; Speed = Letter Comparison, Pattern Comparison; Voc = Synonym Vocabulary, Antonym Vocabulary

G – Salthouse et al. (1998), g_f = Ravens, Cube Assembly; Mem = Recall on trials 1, 2, 3, 4, and 5; Speed = Letter Comparison, Pattern Comparison; Voc = Synonym Vocabulary, Antonym Vocabulary

H – Salthouse, Toth, et al. (1997), Mem = CVLT Recall Trials 1 through 3, CVLT Recall on New List; Speed = Letter Comparison, Pattern Comparison; Voc = Synonym Vocabulary, Antonym Vocabulary

I – Salthouse et al. (1996a), g_f = Shipley Abstraction, Block Design, Object Assembly; Mem = Recall across 5 trials, Recall on new list, Paired Associates; Speed = Digit Symbol, Letter Comparison, Pattern Comparison; Voc = Shipley Vocabulary

J – Salthouse (1996b), Mem = Recall at 0.5, 1.0, and 2.0 sec rates; Speed = Letter Comparison, Pattern Comparison; Voc = Synonym Vocabulary, Antonym Vocabulary correlations with the partial age correlations in which the variance in one of the other factors is statistically controlled before examining the relation of age to the other factor. To illustrate, the weighted average correlation between age and the fluid intelligence (g_f) factor was $-.58$, but this was reduced to $-.42$ after partialling the variance in the episodic memory factor, and it was reduced to $-.33$ after partialling the variance in the perceptual speed factor. Because the partial correlations are considerably smaller than the simple correlations, and the corresponding proportions of variance even smaller, it can be inferred that the age-related influences on the factors are not independent of one another.

The model in panel E represents a hierarchical structure in which correlations among the first-order factors are interpreted in terms of one or more higher-order factors. That is, rather than representing the covariation among factors as correlations, which leave the relations unexplained in the context of the model, a hierarchical model attributes the covariation to the operation of higher-order factors. When variables with both positive (e.g., vocabulary and knowledge) and negative (e.g., reasoning, spatial visualization, episodic memory, and speed) age relations are included in the analysis, at least two distinct age-related influences are likely to be required. However, it is not yet clear whether it is more meaningful to think of the two influences as operating in opposite directions on factors at the same level in the hierarchy (as in models based on the distinction between fluid and crystallized abilities), or as a negative age-related influence operating at the highest level and a positive age-related influence, perhaps representing the benefits of experience, operating at an intermediate level in the hierarchy (as in models postulating a unitary g factor). Hierarchical models have also been applied in analyses restricted to variables with negative age-related influences to determine the number of independent age-related effects that may be operating on the factors and variables. Results from several data sets suggest that there are at least three statistically distinct age-related influences, one affecting the highest level of the hierarchy that represents what all factors and variables have in common, one affecting an episodic memory factor, and one affecting a perceptual speed factor (e.g., Salthouse, 2001b; Salthouse & Czaja, 2000; Salthouse & Ferrer-Caja, 2003). More research of this type with a broader range of variables is needed before definitive conclusions can be reached about the number and nature of distinct age-related influences. However, the important point in the current context is that because age-related effects have been found to operate at the highest level in the hierarchical structure, age-related influences on variables at lower levels can be inferred to be at least partially shared with one another.

To summarize, results from several different types of multivariate analyses conducted on data from my laboratory and from other laboratories have been consistent in suggesting that the age-related influences on a wide range of cognitive variables are not independent of the age-related influences on other variables. To the extent that this is an accurate description of the phenomenon of cognitive aging, a primary theoretical challenge is to explain age-related influences that are shared across different types of variables. It should be emphasized that acceptance of this goal does not deny the existence, or the importance, of unique age-related effects on individual variables or constructs. Rather, the point is that understanding shared age-related effects should be considered a high priority because such effects have a broader impact, and are frequently larger in magnitude, than age-related effects that are specific to particular variables or factors.

EXPLANATION OF COGNITIVE AGING

What types of explanations might be plausible to account for shared age-related influences on different types of cognitive variables? By definition, the mechanisms are unlikely to involve processes or strategies that are restricted to a small set of cognitive tasks. Instead, the relevant mechanisms must be broad enough to affect a wide variety of cognitive variables, ranging from those assessing perceptual speed to those assessing episodic memory and inductive reasoning.

Although there is little consensus at the current time with respect to how shared age-related effects are to be explained, a number of researchers have attempted to interpret individual differences on a variety of different cognitive variables in terms of constructs at the same level of analysis as the to-be-explained phenomena. For example, among the constructs that have been proposed to be critical with respect to individual differences in a variety of other cognitive variables are goal neglect (e.g., Duncan et al., 1996), context maintenance (e.g., Braver et al., 2001), controlled attention (e.g., Engle, Kane, & Tuholski, 1999), working memory (e.g., Kyllonen & Christal, 1990), processing speed (e.g., Salthouse, 1996c), and various types of inhibition (e.g., Hasher, Zacks, & May, 1999). Hypotheses of this type have often been accompanied by plausible theoretical arguments and intriguing experimental findings, but most share two important weaknesses.

First, the relevant construct has often been assessed with a single variable, with little or no evidence provided to indicate that the variable exclusively, and exhaustively, reflects that construct.[1] The correspondence between the variable and the theoretical construct has typically been justified by subjective judgments of face validity, and by arguments based on plausibility. However, in the absence of relevant empirical evidence,

---

[1] Some researchers have attempted to assess the same construct with different variables, but because the variables were usually examined in separate studies the relations among the variables could not be examined to determine whether they represented the same dimension of individual differences.

questions can be raised with respect to whether the variables actually represent the intended construct, and whether that construct is distinct from other constructs.

A second weakness of most of the existing theoretical explanations is that the empirical data offered in support of the hypothesis are frequently in the form of correlations between measures of the presumed critical construct and other cognitive variables. However, because one of the best-established results in all of psychology is that most cognitive variables are positively correlated with one another, a discovery of significant correlations involving the relevant variables is merely necessary, and is not sufficient, to establish that the hypothesized construct is responsible for effects on other variables. What is also needed is evidence that the critical construct is the primary cause of the individual differences in other variables and constructs. Unfortunately, it is difficult to determine causal priority when all of the data are of the same type – namely, observations of overt behavior at a single point in time.

The first weakness can be addressed with more sophisticated research designs that allow investigations of convergent and discriminant aspects of construct validity. That is, one way to investigate the validity of a theoretical construct is to determine whether the variables hypothesized to assess that construct have moderate to strong correlations with one another (i.e., exhibit convergent validity), but have weak to nonexistent correlations with variables representing other constructs (i.e., exhibit discriminant validity). Research of this type can be time-consuming and expensive because moderately large samples of participants with multiple measures of several constructs are required to allow patterns of correlations to be examined. Nevertheless, it is one of the few methods currently available for evaluating what variables actually represent and for determining the extent to which they assess something different from what is assessed by established constructs. An example of this type of research is a recent study (Salthouse et al., 2003) that we designed to investigate the construct validity of the neuropsychological concept of executive functioning, and of aspects of executive control corresponding to inhibition, updating, and time sharing. The major finding in the study was that nearly all of the individual-difference variance common to measures of the neuropsychological construct of executive functioning, and to measures of updating and time-sharing aspects of executive control, overlapped with the individual-difference variance in a fluid intelligence (g_f) construct. Such results are potentially important because they suggest that researchers who assume that they are investigating one theoretical construct may also, or instead, be investigating manifestations of another construct.

Determination of causal priority will likely require several different types of research. Two approaches that may prove informative involve the investigation of plausible neurobiological substrates and the investigation of lead–lag relationships with longitudinal comparisons.

Although brain–behavior relations have been the focus of considerable research, a fundamental assumption of the perspective outlined here is that it is important that the neurobiological substrate be at a level of analysis that is appropriate to account for broad age-related effects on cognitive performance. One possible candidate for the neural substrate of shared age-related influences is impairment in the effectiveness of a single neural structure responsible for coordinating or controlling multiple cognitive operations. The dorsal lateral prefrontal cortex has been mentioned as a possible site of the "CEO" of the cognitive system, but this or any other speculation must be accompanied by evidence that the structure is actually involved in many different cognitive tasks and that its efficiency or effectiveness is impaired with increased age. A second possible candidate to account for shared age-related effects is an alteration in the effectiveness of communication among different neural regions. That is, the critical age-related influences may not be on a discrete structure, but rather on the efficiency or effectiveness in communicating among different regions.

Both the critical structure and the communication deficiency hypotheses would benefit from somewhat different approaches to functional neuroimaging than the currently dominant discrete localization approach. For example, examination of patterns of activation that are common to several different cognitive tasks, which Price and Friston (1997) termed *conjunction analysis*, would likely be informative about which neuroanatomical structures are involved in multiple cognitive tasks. Furthermore, examination of co-activation patterns across different regions within a single cognitive task, in what has been termed *functional connectivity analysis* (e.g., Grady et al., 2002; Esposito et al., 1999; Nyberg & McIntosh, 2001), would likely be informative about the efficiency of cortical communication.

Ultimately, of course, research will have to determine why particular structures or circuits are affected by increased age. Among the possible candidates at a somewhat lower level of analysis are age-related differences in the density of receptors for the dopamine neurotransmitter (e.g., Backman et al., 2000; Kaasinen et al., 2000; Rinne et al., 1993; Volkow et al., 1998), and in the integrity of axonal myelination (e.g., Abe et al., 2002; Nusbaum et al., 2001; O'Sullivan et al., 2001). The particular level of reductionism that will eventually be most meaningful in interpreting age-related differences in cognitive functioning is not yet obvious. However, a key assumption motivating the search for neurobiological substrates is that mechanisms responsible for age-related changes in neural substrates are likely to be more primitive or fundamental than those responsible for changes at higher conceptual levels, such that investigation of neural substrates may help identify the sequence in which changes in relevant constructs occur.

A second type of research that might help establish causal priority among constructs is evidence from longitudinal comparisons that changes in different measures of the critical construct (including neurobiological measures if they are available) occur together and precede changes in the cognitive variables they are hypothesized to affect. Evidence of this type will probably be difficult to obtain because a broad variety of variables representing the critical construct and other cognitive constructs is needed, and the retest interval between successive measurements must be long enough to capture the phenomenon of interest, namely age-related changes occurring over a span of decades. Furthermore, the analytical methods should allow evaluation of whether age-related changes in the measures of the critical construct occur together and before changes in the cognitive variables they are presumed to mediate. Even with the appropriate data and suitable analytical methods, however, determination of the sequential order among relevant constructs will be challenging because little is currently known about the timing of the changes (e.g., do they begin at age 70, at age 20, or somewhere in between?), about the interval between changes in the critical construct and changes in the cognitive variables affected by that construct (e.g., is the lag on the order of days, years, or decades?), or about individual differences in these parameters (e.g., how much do people vary in the age at which the first changes occur, and in the interval between the initial and subsequent changes?).

STRENGTHS AND WEAKNESSES

The primary strength of the description-to-explanation approach that I have been pursuing is that the multivariate perspective provides a broader and more comprehensive assessment of the phenomenon of cognitive aging than that based on univariate research. Moreover, because of the greater amount of information about exactly what needs to be explained, explanations based on that data are more likely to be at the most meaningful level of analysis. However, a nontrivial weakness is that multivariate research is more difficult and expensive to conduct than the more typical type of research focusing on a single variable in relatively small samples of young and old adults. Not only does multivariate research require large samples with a continuous range of ages, but also more time is needed from each participant to allow the assessment of multiple variables, and the analytical procedures are frequently more complex. Partly because of this difficulty, the most progress made thus far has been in the description of the cognitive aging phenomenon rather than in its explanation.

FUTURE DIRECTIONS

One direction for future research is to revise and extend the methods of characterizing the nature, and estimating the relative magnitude, of shared and unique age-related influences on cognitive variables. A primary goal of these efforts should be a more refined assessment and characterization of each type of influence. Efforts in this direction are also valuable because all analytical methods require assumptions that may not be valid, and thus it is always desirable to converge on conclusions with analyses based on different combinations of assumptions and procedures.

A second direction for future research is to investigate relations between age-related influences identified from behavioral studies and possible neural substrates of those influences. As noted above, a key assumption of the current perspective is that progress in understanding brain–behavior relations involving aging is likely to be faster when the correspondence is examined at the appropriate level of analysis. In the cognitive domain this will not only be single variables, but also combinations of variables that share age-related variance, and in the neurobiological domain the neural substrates should be able to account for age-related effects that are shared across different types of cognitive variables.

A third direction for future research is to examine candidates for causal influences by investigating potential moderators of the relations between age and measures of cognitive functioning. Many factors have been found to be related to the level of cognitive performance; but to be plausible as a determinant of the age differences in cognition the factor should significantly interact with age, such that the relations between age and measures of cognitive functioning are moderated by the level of that factor.

Because the strongest evidence for causality is based on experimental manipulation, a final goal for future research is to examine interventions that might alter the course of age-related change in both cognitive constructs and their neurobiological substrates. The specific nature of the interventions are not yet obvious, but definitive conclusions about the causes of age-related differences in cognitive functioning will probably not be possible until interventions are available to eliminate those differences.

References

Abe, O., Aoki, S., Hayashi, N., Yamada, H., Kunimatsu, A., Mori, H., Yoshikawa, T., Okubo, T., & Ohtomo, K. (2002). Normal aging in the central nervous system: Quantitative MR diffusion-tensor analysis. *Neurobiology of Aging, 23,* 433–441.

Anstey, K. J., & Smith, G. A. (1999). Interrelationships among biological markers of aging, health, activity, acculturation, and cognitive performance in late adulthood. *Psychology and Aging, 14,* 605–618.

Backman, L., Ginovart, N., Dixon, R. A., Robins Wahlin, T-B., Wahlin, A., Halldin, C., & Farde, L. (2000). Age-related cognitive deficits mediated by changes in the striatal dopamine system. *American Journal of Psychiatry, 157,* 635–637.

Braver, T. S., Barch, D. M., Keys, B. A., Carter, C. S., Cohen, J. D., Kaye, J. A., Janowsky, J. S., Taylor, S. F., Yesavage, J. A., Mumenthaler, M. S., Jagust, W. J., & Reed, B. R. (2001). Context processing in older adults: Evidence for a theory relating cognitive control to neurobiology in healthy aging. *Journal of Experimental Psychology: General, 130,* 746–763.

Christensen, H., Mackinnon, A., Korten, A., & Jorm, A. F. (2001). The "common cause hypothesis" of cognitive aging: Evidence for not only a common factor but also specific associations of age with vision and grip strength in a cross-sectional analysis. *Psychology and Aging, 16,* 588–599.

Duncan, J., Emslie, H., Williams, P., Johnson, R., & Freer, C. (1996). Intelligence and the frontal lobe: The organization of goal-directed behavior. *Cognitive Psychology, 30,* 257–303.

Duncan, J., Williams, P., Nimmo-Smith, I., & Brown, I. (1992). The control of skilled behavior: Learning, intelligence and distraction. In D. E. Meyer & S. Kornblum (Eds.), *Attention and Performance XIV* (pp. 322–341). Cambridge, MA: MIT Press.

Engle, R. W., Kane, M. J., & Tuholski, S. W. (1999). Individual differences in working memory capacity and what they tell us about controlled attention, general fluid intelligence, and functions of the prefrontal cortex. In A. Miyake & P. Shah (Eds.), *Models of working memory: Mechanisms of active maintenance and executive control* (pp. 102–134). New York: Cambridge University Press.

Esposito, G., Kirkby, B. S., Van Horn, J. D., Ellmore, T. M., & Berman, K. F. (1999). Context-dependent, neural system-specific neurophysiological concomitants of ageing: Mapping PET correlates during cognitive activation. *Brain, 122,* 963–979.

Grady, C. L., Bernstein, L. J., Beig, S., & Siegenthaler, A. L. (2002). The effects of encoding task on age-related differences in the functional neuroanatomy of face memory. *Psychology and Aging, 17,* 7–23.

Hart, B., & Spearman, C. (1914). Mental tests of dementia. *Journal of Abnormal Psychology, 9,* 217–264.

Hasher, L., Zacks, R. T., & May, C. P. (1999). Inhibitory control, circadian arousal, and age. In A. Koriat & D. Gopher (Eds.), *Attention and Performance XVII* (pp. 653–675). Cambridge, MA: MIT Press.

Hultsch, D. F., Hertzog, C., Dixon, R. A., & Small, B. J. (1998). *Memory change in the aged.* New York: Cambridge University Press.

Jensen, A. (1998). *The g-factor: The science of mental ability.* Westport, CT: Praeger Press.

Kaasinen, V., Vilkman, H., Hietala, J., Nagren, K., Helenius, H., Olsson, H., Farde, L., & Rinne, J. O. (2000). Age-related dopamine D2/D3 receptor loss in extrastriatal regions of the human brain. *Neurobiology of Aging, 21,* 683–688.

Kliegl, R., & Mayr, U. (1992). Commentary (on Salthouse, 1992). *Human Development, 35,* 343–349.

Kyllonen, P. C., & Christal, R. E. (1990). Reasoning ability is (little more than) working-memory capacity?! *Intelligence, 14,* 389–433.

Lindenberger, U., & Baltes, P. B. (1994). Sensory functioning and intelligence in old age: A strong connection. *Psychology and Aging, 9,* 339–355.

Lindenberger, U., Mayr, U., & Kliegl, R. (1993). Speed and intelligence in old age. *Psychology and Aging, 8,* 207–220.

McArdle, J. J., & Prescott, C. A. (1992). Age-based construct validation using structural equation modeling. *Experimental Aging Research, 18,* 87–115.

Nusbaum, A. O., Tang, C. Y., Buchsbaum, M. S., Wei, T. C., & Atlas, S. W. (2001). Regional and global changes in cerebral diffusion with normal aging. *American Journal of Neuroradiology, 22,* 136–142.

Nyberg, L., & McIntosh, A. R. (2001). Functional neuroimaging: Network analyses. In R. Cabeza & A. Kingstone (Eds.), _Handbook of functional neuroimaging of cognition_ (pp. 49–72). Cambridge, MA: MIT Press.

O'Sullivan, M., Jones, D. K., Summers, P. E., Morris, R. G., Williams, S. C. R., & Markus, H. S. (2001). Evidence for cortical "disconnection" as a mechanism of age-related cognitive decline. _Neurology, 57_, 632–638.

Park, D. C., Lautenschlager, G., Hedden, T., Davidson, N. S., Smith, A. D., & Smith, P. K. (2002). Models of visuospatial and verbal memory across the adult life span. _Psychology and Aging, 17_, 299–320.

Park, D. C., Smith, A. D., Lautenschlager, G., Earles, J. L., Frieske, D., Zwahr, M., & Gaines, C. L. (1996). Mediators of long-term memory performance across the life span. _Psychology and Aging, 11_, 621–637.

Plomin, R., Pedersen, N. L., Lichtenstein, P., & McClearn, G. E. (1994). Variability and stability in cognitive abilities are largely genetic later in life. _Behavior Genetics, 24_, 207–215.

Price, C. J., & Friston, K. J. (1997). Cognitive conjunction: A new approach to brain activation experiments. _Neuroimage, 5_, 261–270.

Rinne, J. O., Hietala, J., Ruotsalainen, U., Sako, E., Laihinen, A., Nagren, K., Lehikoinen, P., Oikonen, V., & Syvalahti, E. (1993). Decrease in human striatal dopamine D2 receptor density with age: A PET study with [^{11}C] Raclopride. _Journal of Cerebral Blood Flow and Metabolism, 13_, 310–314.

Salthouse, T. A. (1994). How many causes are there of aging-related decrements in cognitive functioning? _Developmental Review, 14_, 413–437.

Salthouse, T. A. (1996a). Constraints on theories of cognitive aging. _Psychonomic Bulletin & Review, 3_, 287–299.

Salthouse, T. A. (1996b). General and specific speed mediation of adult age differences in memory. _Journal of Gerontology: Psychological Sciences, 51B_, P30–P42.

Salthouse, T. A. (1996c). The processing speed theory of adult age differences in cognition. _Psychological Review, 103_, 403–428.

Salthouse, T. A. (1998). Independence of age-related influences on cognitive abilities across the life span. _Developmental Psychology, 34_, 851–864.

Salthouse, T. A. (2001a). Attempted decomposition of age-related influences on two tests of reasoning. _Psychology and Aging, 16_, 251–263.

Salthouse, T. A. (2001b). Structural models of the relations between age and measures of cognitive functioning. _Intelligence, 29_, 93–115.

Salthouse, T. A., & Czaja, S. (2000). Structural constraints on process explanations in cognitive aging. _Psychology and Aging, 15_, 44–55.

Salthouse, T. A., & Ferrer-Caja, E. (2003). What needs to be explained to account for age-related effects on multiple cognitive variables? _Psychology and Aging, 18_, 91–110.

Salthouse, T. A., Atkinson, T. M., & Berish, D. E. (2003). _Executive functioning as a potential mediator of age-related cognitive decline in normal adults. Journal of Experimental Psychology. General, 132_, 566–594.

Salthouse, T. A., Fristoe, N., Rhee, S. H. (1996a). How localized are age-related effects on neuropsychological measures? _Neuropsychology, 10_, 272–285.

Salthouse, T. A., Hambrick, D. Z., & McGuthry, K. E. (1998). Shared age-related influences on cognitive and non-cognitive variables. _Psychology and Aging, 13_, 486–500.

Salthouse, T. A., Hancock, H. E., Meinz, E. J., & Hambrick, D. Z. (1996b). Inter-relations of age, visual acuity, and cognitive functioning. *Journal of Gerontology: Psychological Sciences, 51B*, P317–P330.

Salthouse, T. A., McGuthry, K. E., & Hambrick, D. Z. (1999). A framework for analyzing and interpreting differential aging patterns: Application to three measures of implicit learning. *Aging, Neuropsychology, and Cognition, 6*, 1–18.

Salthouse, T. A., Toth, J., Daniels, K., Parks, C., Pak, R., Wolbrette, M., & Hocking, K. (2000). Effects of aging on the efficiency of task switching in a variant of the Trail Making Test. *Neuropsychology, 14*, 102–111.

Salthouse, T. A., Toth, J. P., Hancock, H. E., & Woodard, J. L. (1997). Controlled and automatic forms of memory and attention: Process purity and the uniqueness of age-related influences. *Journal of Gerontology: Psychological Sciences, 52B*, P216–P228.

Schroeder, D. H., & Salthouse, T. A. (2004). Age-related effects on cognition between 20 and 50 years of age. *Personality and Individual Differences, 36*, 393–404.

Verhaeghen, P., & Salthouse, T. A. (1997). Meta-analyses of age–cognition relations in adulthood: Estimates of linear and non-linear age effects and structural models. *Psychological Bulletin, 122*, 231–249.

Volkow, N. D., Gur, R. C., Wang, G-J., Fowler, J. S., Moberg, P. J., Ding, Y-S., Hitzemann, R., Smith, G., & Logan, J. (1998). Association between decline in brain dopamine activity with age and cognitive and motor impairment in healthy individuals. *American Journal of Psychiatry, 155*, 344–349.

16

Unifying the Field

Cognition and Intelligence

Jean E. Pretz and Robert J. Sternberg

In 1957, Lee Cronbach called on psychologists to integrate research on cognition and intelligence, and this volume has been dedicated to presenting a progress report of the work in this field. This final chapter will summarize and synthesize the work reported in this volume, and will conclude with an evaluation of our status with respect to Cronbach's call and suggestions for future work in the field.

Research on cognition and intelligence can be characterized as either bottom-up or top-down. Bottom-up approaches focus on identifying the basic information processes, usually measured by elementary cognitive tasks, that underlie individual differences in traditional psychometric tests of cognitive ability. In contrast, top-down approaches study the relationship of intelligence to complex cognitive tasks such as complex problem solving, decision making, and transfer. Each approach brings with it theoretical and methodological strengths and weaknesses, research questions it can and cannot answer. In some ways, these two distinct approaches complement each other, but it is also true that the differences in the research programs' methodologies and assumptions often make it difficult to compare results and synthesize an understanding of the role of cognition in intelligence.

The future of research on cognition and intelligence depends on the willingness of researchers to agree on a set of ground rules and to stretch their comfort zones in terms of their research methods and assumptions. Regardless of whether this ideal is achieved, researchers will do best to attempt to consider the results of research of various perspectives and synthesize those data with their own to devise more pointed research hypotheses for future work in the field. The purpose of this chapter is to begin to synthesize existing knowledge in the field with the goal of prompting new ideas for researchers in all areas of research on intelligence and cognition.

BOTTOM-UP APPROACH

Psychologists who take a bottom-up approach to studying cognition and intelligence have the advantage of being able to identify specific processes and mechanisms of intelligence. By examining simple processes and linking their variation to variation in intelligence scores, researchers can begin to understand the cognitive mechanisms behind intelligent behavior. Studies attempting to link lower-order cognition to intelligence have measured sensory and perceptual information processing using elementary cognitive tasks (ECTs). These tasks include the Hick paradigm and the inspection time paradigm. Participants must think quickly to do well on these tasks. The tasks themselves are not difficult or complex, but they do elicit individual differences in processing. Due to the precise nature of these tasks, they also lend themselves to replication, a methodological characteristic that is always highly desirable. One weakness of the bottom-up approach is that it is lacking in ecological validity. ECTs are criticized for their simple nature and dissimilarity to real-world tasks that require intelligence.

TOP-DOWN APPROACH

Top-down approaches to the study of intelligence include research on reasoning, problem solving, skill learning, decision making, and transfer. These studies also consider cognition in relation to psychometric measures of intelligence. In fact, Lohman (Chap. 12) points out that most intelligence measures are themselves reasoning tasks. However, higher-order approaches are often based on conceptions of intelligence that extend beyond the traditional psychometric definition. For example, researchers have pointed out the role of knowledge and context when observing intelligent behavior. The top-down approach to intelligence has advantages that complement the bottom-up approach in many respects. Research on complex cognition is often situated in real-world tasks such as everyday decision making or problem solving, providing a great deal of ecological validity. Naturally, contextualized approaches to the study of intelligence often must sacrifice generalizability for this better understanding of real-life intelligent behavior. Because the higher-order approach appreciates the complexity of intelligent behavior, it attempts to account for a variety of variables simultaneously rather than isolating a particular variable of interest. However, research involving more complex, real-world tasks trades off the precision and power to discover mechanisms that can be better achieved in research on simple, lower-order cognition.

To synthesize the results of research on cognition and intelligence, we will first review the findings from both lower-order and higher-order cognitive approaches. Following this summary and synthesis, we will evaluate the field's progress toward Cronbach's goal of integrating cognitive and differential approaches.

WHAT HAVE LOWER-ORDER COGNITIVE APPROACHES REVEALED ABOUT INTELLIGENCE?

Behavioral and neuroscientific research on the relationship between lower-order cognitive processes and scores on intelligence tests has led to a wealth of data on a great number of cognitive components affecting intelligence, including processing speed, neural efficiency, functional connectivity, and frontal lobe activation.

Processing Speed

Intelligent people are sometimes referred to as "bright," and less intelligent people are sometimes politely called "slow." Do the data prove that intelligence is simply speed of processing? Jensen (Chap. 2, this volume) and Stankov (Chap. 3) address this implicit theory of intelligence in their work on processing speed and psychometric intelligence.

Jensen's research demonstrates that reaction time is consistently negatively correlated with traditional measures of IQ. This relationship is small to moderate, depending on the difficulty of the reaction time (RT) task. The highest correlations range from −.40 to −.50 among moderately difficult RT tasks with RTs around 500–900 ms. Jensen explains that for these moderately difficult tasks, the relationship between IQ and RT is due to sheer processing speed. For the simpler tasks (those whose response times average less than one-third of a second), the relationship between RT and IQ is smaller because the influence of perceptual and motor factors is more apparent. For the more difficult tasks (those whose response times average over 1.2 seconds), the correlation is attenuated due to the effect of differences in strategy use.

While Jensen has concluded that processing speed underlies individual differences in IQ scores, other researchers do not find the evidence compelling. Most RT–IQ correlations average −.20 to −.30 (Jensen, Chap. 2). Similarly, correlations between sensory discrimination tasks and measures of g also average around .21 to .31 (Acton & Schroeder, 2001). Stankov has argued that the correlation between speed of processing and intelligence is not due to elementary cognitive processes, but rather to more complex cognitive processes, specifically decision time. For example, when the reaction time task requires the participant to make more complex choices, the correlation between RT and IQ increases. Consequently, Stankov suggests that future studies focus on the complexity rather than the "elementarity" of elementary cognitive tasks.

Neural Efficiency

More sophisticated research methods in cognition have led to a more sophisticated but related hypothesis regarding individual differences in intelligent information processing. The neural efficiency hypothesis proposes that more intelligent individuals have more efficient neural processing, measured as cortical activation. This hypothesis has been put forth by cognitive neuroscientists including Neubauer and Fink (Chap. 4) and Newman and Just (Chap. 5). Neubauer and Fink explain that studies of neural processing using positron emission tomography (PET) have produced support for this hypothesis. PET studies show that the glucose metabolism rate is negatively correlated ($-.44$ to $-.84$) with scores on Raven's Advanced Progressive Matrices, a standard intelligence test. Similarly, increased practice on cognitive tasks has also been shown to lead to decreases in glucose metabolism rate. Other measures of neural processing such as electroencephalogram (EEG) have revealed that the brains of more intelligent individuals show a pattern of more focused activation, consistent with an efficiency hypothesis. One particularly interesting finding is that the efficiency effect is most apparent for tasks on which participants perform well. For example, men showed the effect on a figural-spatial task, while females showed the effect on a verbal task.

Data from functional magnetic resonance imaging (fMRI) studies corroborate these findings. Newman and Just explain that cortical activation was found to be lower in specific brain areas for participants with higher scores on relevant specific ability tests. For example, participants who scored high on verbal measures also showed relatively less cortical activation in brain regions associated with verbal functioning (in this case, Broca's area). Similarly, participants with high visual-spatial abilities had relatively reduced cortical activation in the left parietal cortex.

Functional Connectivity

Functional connectivity refers to the extent to which various brain regions operate together to perform a particular function. Newman and Just (Chap. 5) explain that this neural synchrony has been found to increase with the difficulty and demands of a cognitive task. Findings from fMRI studies have shown evidence that connectivity is correlated with increases in task performance as well. Essentially, functional connectivity is a larger-scale example of the Hebbian principle: Cells that fire together, wire together. While connectivity has not been shown to correlate with intelligence measures, diffusion tensor imaging (DTI) studies demonstrating anatomical connections between brain regions have shown that differences in white matter tracts are strongly related to individual differences in cognitive tasks such as reading. Furthermore, Stankov mentions findings that may be interpreted as support for the functional connectivity hypothesis. The synchronicity of various brain regions in cognitive tasks is also related to intelligence scores. To the extent that neural functioning is well orchestrated and tuned to the task at hand, the person is found to be more intelligent. Obviously, further research is required to confirm these hypotheses.

Frontal Lobe

Neuroimaging studies have tied executive function in working memory and other control processes to frontal lobe processing. Given the relationship between these functions and intelligence, can we conclude that frontal lobe activity is the seat of intelligence in the brain? This hypothesis has been tested by Duncan and colleagues. One study found that participants with higher *g* showed greater activation in the frontal cortex than did participants with lower *g* (Duncan et al., 2000). More specifically, the process in the frontal lobe that is more strongly related to *g* was identified as goal neglect and goal activation (Duncan, Emslie, & Williams, 1996). Newman and Just use this evidence to support their theory that intelligence reflects flexibility of processing. Their view is that more intelligent individuals make more efficient and flexible use of their brains.

WHAT HAVE HIGHER-ORDER COGNITIVE APPROACHES REVEALED ABOUT INTELLIGENCE?

Research focusing on higher-order cognitive processes in relation to intelligent behavior complements the results of lower-order approaches. This research has found that working memory and attention, cognitive control, flexibility of strategy use, learning ability, and context-based knowledge are strongly related to intelligence.

Working Memory and Attention

Much basic research in cognitive psychology in recent decades has focused on the construct of working memory. Intuitively, it would seem that intelligence is largely dependent on an individual's working memory, the amount of information an individual can keep in mind and manipulate simultaneously. Generally, research has found that variance in working memory can explain approximately 35% of the variance in fluid intelligence test scores.

Researchers such as Randall Engle (Chap. 6) and his colleagues have examined specifically the role of attentional processes as a component of working memory and their relationship to scores on intelligence tests. Their studies have found that fluid intelligence, as measured by abstract reasoning tasks, was positively correlated with working memory measures of attentional control but not to general short-term memory storage. Further investigation revealed that while verbal reasoning scores were well explained by memory storage capacity, fluid intelligence scores were uniquely predicted by working memory measures of "executive attention," indicating that intelligent functioning is related to an individual's ability to manipulate attention rather than store information for a short period of time.

Cognitive Control

Cognitive control refers generally to the metacognitive ability to exert influence over one's cognitive processes. For example, attention is a kind of cognitive control. Necka's (Chap. 7) studies of cognitive control have employed tasks such as the Stroop or Navon. These tasks require participants to suppress automatic responses in order to engage in more effortful processing. Efficiency of cognitive control is measured by subtracting reaction time of the prepotent response from the [longer] reaction time of the suppressed response. To the extent that the difference between these two reaction times is small, a participant's cognitive control is deemed efficient. That is, if you can suppress a prepotent response easily, you have a relatively great amount of control over your cognitive processes. Necka showed that this reaction time measure of cognitive control was associated with performance on Raven's Progressive Matrices (correlations of reaction time to intelligence scores were $-.21$ to $-.33$). Shorter reaction times were related to higher intelligence test scores. Similarly, gifted adolescents were found to have higher cognitive control abilities than peers in a control group. In studies of creativity, cognitive control has been found to be related to originality indices. Individuals with a strong cognitive control ability were better able to distinguish between novel ideas that were worthless and those that were truly purposeful and original.

Flexibility of Strategy Use

Just as memory researchers have found that intelligence is not simply storage capacity, but rather the ability to use that capacity, studies of metacognition have shown that intelligence is related not to knowledge of a particular strategy, but to flexibility in strategy application. MacLeod, Hunt and Mathews (1978) have shown that individuals with higher psychometric intelligence were better able to switch from one strategy to another, depending on which was most suited to the testing conditions. Other research corroborates this finding, showing that more intelligent individuals use a variety of strategies, depending on their appropriateness (Kyllonen, Lohman, & Woltz, 1984).

Learning Ability

One intuitive prediction that has existed in the intelligence literature from its inception is the hypothesis that intelligence is the ability to learn. Some psychologists have investigated the relationship between intelligence and skill learning, while others have examined its relationship with learning in the context of problem solving.

One implicit theory is that individuals who learn quickly are highly intelligent. Parents often express pride at the intelligence of their infant when the baby seems to catch on quickly. Ackerman (Chap. 8) has studied extensively the relationship between intelligence and skilled performance in specific domains such as typing speed and accuracy. This work uses psychometric measures of intelligence to predict performance on simulation tasks such as TRACON (Terminal Radar Approach Control). Ackerman's research has shown that scores on tests of general cognitive ability are positively predictive of performance during skill acquisition, but that as skills become mastered, general intelligence is less and less strongly related. Essentially, smarter people learn faster, but performance can be mastered by individuals regardless of their level of intelligence. Specifically, skill-learning performance at later stages of acquisition is related to perceptual speed and psychomotor abilities. Ackerman explains that general intelligence is critical for early stages of conceptual learning, but that as a skill is mastered, more basic abilities such as processing speed and motor ability become key to predicting high levels of performance.

Intelligence has been studied extensively with respect to elementary cognitive tasks and simple problem-solving tasks; however, is intelligence related to more complex problem solving? One main source of data on this question is the tradition of work on complex problem-solving (CPS) tasks involving computerized scenarios in which participants learn to control inputs and outputs to achieve a particular goal. Wenke, Frensch, and Funke (Chap. 9) have reviewed the literature on complex problem solving with respect to intelligence measures. They explain that most CPS studies found no significant relationship between problem-solving performance and intelligence. However, they point out that the existence of this relationship becomes more apparent when the task is more transparent (participants are given a diagram of the input–output model), when the goal is more specific (the experimenter breaks down the goal into specific subgoals), and when the semantic content of the problem is not misleading. Wenke, Frensch, and Funke conclude that complex problem solving is not related to global intelligence, but is moderately related to intelligence components such as processing capacity, reasoning ability, and learning potential. It appears that current methods of measuring intelligence and problem-solving ability may be obscuring any true relationship that may exist.

Contextualized Intelligence

Traditional measures of intelligence are designed to be decontextualized, free of specifics that may bias scores of individuals with more or less knowledge and experience. Several researchers have challenged this notion, contending that every test comes with a context and that knowledge and environment shape intelligent behavior.

Intelligent Heuristics

An alternative to traditional methods of estimating intelligent behavior is Raab and Gigerenzer's study (Chap. 10) of intelligent heuristics. The authors explain that the mind is a Swiss Army knife of specific tools that are well adapted to various environmental conditions. They posit that intelligence is a toolbox of cognitive strategies, including various adaptive heuristics identified in their research on decision making under conditions of uncertainty. Their perspective hinges on the assumption that cognition and environment are integrally interconnected and should not be considered in isolation. The appropriateness, or intelligence, of a cognitive strategy is dependent on the conditions and constraints of the environment. Their goal is to model the interaction of the mind and the world, and this has led them to conclude that, by nature, smart heuristics are domain-specific. Traditional methods of measuring cognitive abilities including psychometric and information processing approaches have failed to systematically examine the effect of the environment on performance. This criticism points to a difference between cognitive and differential approaches. Cognitive research recognizes the role of the environment, whereas differential research has attempted to decontextualize its measures and methods. This method is radically different from traditional intelligence research in that it seeks to model the mechanism by which people act intelligently using heuristics rather than to factor-analyze test scores.

Knowledge and Intelligence

Others who emphasize the interrelated nature of context and cognition are Barnett and Ceci (Chap. 11). They explain that intelligence can be studied fruitfully in very specific contexts with tasks that rely heavily on experience-based knowledge. Their method enables them to maximize their chance of observing high levels of intelligent behavior. For example, in Ceci and Bronfenbrenner's (1985) study of prospective memory for removing cupcakes from the oven or disconnecting a battery charger, children behaved more intelligently when in a familiar home environment than when in an unfamiliar laboratory environment. At home, children calibrated their clock-watching so that they were able to enjoy an interim activity while waiting to remove the cupcakes or disconnect the battery. In contrast, children in the laboratory checked the clock more frequently and were less able to participate in an interim activity. This study shows that the highly contextualized measure of intelligent behavior revealed children's ability to use a relatively sophisticated strategy that was not observed in the laboratory environment.

In a similar vein, Lohman (Chap. 12) highlights the importance of knowledge in reasoning and intelligence. Reasoning researchers have long observed the effect of knowledge on reasoning performance. To the extent that intelligence tests rely on reasoning abilities, knowledge should affect intelligence scores as well. Lohman argues that reasoning ability and knowledge reside on a two-way street. Not only is reasoning on a particular task affected by previous knowledge, but also the acquisition of knowledge itself is affected by reasoning ability.

SYNTHESIS OF RESULTS

So what do we know about the relationship between cognition and intelligence? Research from a lower-order cognitive perspective has determined that cognitive components of intelligence include perceptual speed, neural efficiency, functional connectivity, and frontal lobe activation. Findings from a higher-order cognitive perspective have revealed that intelligence is related to attention, cognitive control, flexibility of strategy use, learning ability, and context-based knowledge. Based on the summary of research reported in this volume, we can conclude that intelligence is related to (1) efficiency of basic cognitive processes (speed of perception and focused brain activity) and (2) metacognitive control and flexibility of cognitive processes (attention, cognitive control, strategy flexibility).

As with all forms of higher cognition, intelligence is dependent on basic cognitive processes. Researchers including Jensen have long emphasized the role of basic perceptual speed in intelligent performance, and the data show at least a modest relationship between reaction time and IQ scores. However, new data from neuroimaging studies corroborate and clarify this relationship. More intelligent individuals show more focused patterns of brain activation than those who score lower on traditional measures of intelligence. In fact, increased practice has also been found to lead to more efficient neural processing. These two approaches appear to be tapping a common phenomenon that more intelligent behavior is caused by better-orchestrated brain functioning, which is reflected in faster responses. It remains unclear, however, if intelligence is the cause or result of these observed differences in behavior and processing. Future research should continue to clarify the causality of this relationship.

Both lower- and higher-order approaches have revealed a relationship between intelligence and cognitive control. According to research on neuroimaging, attention, cognitive control, and strategy use, intelligence seems to be a metacognitive ability, the ability to selectively attend, to focus one's cognitive processes, and to switch processing as conditions change. Intelligence is more than just good cognition; it is the ability to use that cognitive ability adaptively. This characteristic of intelligence is most apparent in studies of higher-order cognition, perhaps because those studies include problems complex enough to require this kind of flexibility of processing. Even neuroimaging studies suggest that most intelligent people cope with difficult tasks by using whatever brain area is most suitable. Future studies using bottom-up methods would do well to consider basic processes in more complex tasks to further investigate the hypothesis that intelligence is due to cognitive flexibility.

As mentioned earlier, an advantage of the bottom-up approach to intelligence research is its ability to identify mechanisms of cognition. The unique contribution of current lower-order approaches is that this mechanism may be neural efficiency. A critical, open question remains, however, about the causality of this connection. Neuroscientists who are interested in intelligence may further test this mechanism by including broader measures of intelligence in their designs.

Top-down approaches are complementary to bottom-up approaches in their ability to examine intelligent behavior in a more ecologically valid context. In fact, this has led to a critical point made in the research reviewed here. Studies of cognition in context have revealed the importance of context-based knowledge in intelligent behavior. Decontextualized laboratory measures of intelligence do not necessarily elicit a participant's highest ability. Lohman, Raab & Gigerenzer, and Barnett & Ceci contend that knowledge is integral to cognition and that studies of intelligence must acknowledge that fact. Future studies of situated cognition will be a source of confirmation of current knowledge about cognition and intelligence, and may very well expand our understanding as well.

A source of innovation of interest to all intelligence researchers is Embretson's development of intelligence test items using the methods of artificial intelligence. Using this method, adaptive testing of intelligence becomes more viable. Given a large test bank of items, examiners can tailor each intelligence test to each test-taker, yielding a more accurate and reliable measure of ability. Embretson's method, reported in Chapter 13, points to an exciting future of research on intelligence all around.

CRONBACH'S CALL

In pursuing these data, in what way has the field responded to Cronbach's call for the integration of cognitive and differential approaches? As the research reviewed in this volume suggests, cognitive psychologists have done a great deal of work relating information processing components to scores on psychometric measures of intelligence. These studies have increased our knowledge of the relationship between intelligence and particular cognitive processes, but these approaches have not yet succeeded in describing the causal relationship between intelligence and cognition.

Future work may combine experimental with differential variables in designs that can estimate their interactive effects. For example, do certain treatment variables lead to different results for individuals at various levels of intelligence? Many studies have compared individuals with high intelligence to those with lower intelligence test scores; however, this comparison neglects the possibility of nonlinear relationships between the two. Future studies should combine cognitive and intelligence variables as independent variables in a single study to better understand how these two may interact.

FUTURE WORK IN COGNITION AND INTELLIGENCE

What is next? How do we proceed productively in the study of cognition and intelligence? Many suggestions for future work have already been given in this and previous chapters. Overall, we should strive to reconcile the findings from both bottom-up and top-down studies of intelligence.

An example of a theoretical synthesis that already exists in the field is Anderson's (Chap. 14) theory of minimal cognitive architecture. This theory of intelligence and cognitive development links the main findings of lower- and higher-order approaches, arguing that general intelligence is comprised of two factors: stable individual differences in speed of processing and the development of cognitive modules that may underlie executive functioning. Anderson explains that central processes that comprise thought (verbal and visuo-spatial abilities) are constrained by the speed of the processing mechanism, and this constraint underlies individual differences in intelligence. Additionally, the theory proposes that intelligence is influenced by acquired and innate cognitive modules that process information automatically and expediently (e.g., perceptual modules and language-acquisition modules). Anderson points out that these modules may also serve executive functions such as inhibition. Future work that focuses on confirming this theory can also contribute to the synthesis of current knowledge about cognition and intelligence.

Stankov has made suggestions for researchers taking a bottom-up approach to the study of cognition in intelligence. He laments the lack of systematic study of information processing tasks, pointing out that the choice of ECTs as correlates of intelligence has been restricted to a few tasks whose selection has seemed somewhat arbitrary. There has been no unified research agenda aimed at identifying the information processing–intelligence link via comprehensive measures of both constructs. Future research should rectify this problem by including multiple measures of both intelligence and information processing, preferably in more than one modality.

It appears that a fruitful future direction would be to continue to discover the neural underpinnings of intelligence as measured more broadly and diversely. Newman and Just are eager to explore the functional connectivity hypothesis more thoroughly as DTI methods are improved. In addition, Raab and Gigerenzer have suggested we seek the biological underpinnings of intelligent heuristics. Another characteristic of intelligence to be explored in neuroimaging research is cognitive flexibility. Behavioral research provides a strong case that cognitive control and flexibility in strategy use are key to intelligence, so we would expect converging evidence from neuroscience to be especially encouraging.

Future studies in both lower- and higher-order approaches should include examples of cognition in context to increase the chance of observing maximally intelligent behavior. For example, Hambrick, Kane, and Engle have already begun to study the effect of working memory and attention in a study using baseball game broadcasts. Barnett and Ceci suggest using knowledge-rich tasks in real-world contexts to study intelligence. They propose that while such studies often lack generalizability, there are domains in which common experience will allow for comparisions to be made across samples. Future work can further explore the suitability of various contexts for studying the role of context-based experiential knowledge in intelligent behavior.

Another future direction proposed by several researchers who take a higher-order approach is to broaden the range of variables studied in relation to intelligence measures, and to examine their interactive and joint effect on intelligence. Salthouse's (Chap. 15) work on cognitive aging is an example of research that examines several variables simultaneously in a single design. His work has shown that cognitive aging affects global intelligence, as well as episodic memory and perceptual speed. This lifespan developmental approach to the study of intelligence deserves to be further developed, as its findings are a unique source of converging evidence for more traditional methods of intelligence research.

In addition, the use of contextualized methods provides an ideal opportunity to examine a broader set of variables in relationship to intelligence. For example, many suggest that future work on intelligence include measures of personality, affect, and motivation. Such variables will be best understood in a real-world context. Similar to Stankov's hope for future research using lower-order approaches, research designs are more powerful and produce more meaningful results when they include many variables simultaneously rather than in isolation. Intelligence is a complex construct and will only benefit from such future work.

References

Acton, G. S., & Schroeder, D. H. (2001). Sensory discrimination as related to general intelligence. *Intelligence, 29*(3), 263–271.

Ceci, S. J., & Bronfenbrenner, U. (1985). "Don't forget to take the cupcakes out of the oven": Prospective memory, strategic time-monitoring, and context. *Child Development, 56*(1), 152–164.

Cronbach, L. J. (1957). The two disciplines of scientific psychology. *American Psychologist, 12,* 671–684.

Duncan, H., Emslie, H., & Williams, P. (1996). Intelligence and the frontal lobe: The organization of goal-directed behavior. *Cognitive Psychology, 30,* 257–303.

Duncan, J., Seitz, R. J., Kolodny, J., Bor, D., Herzog, H., Ahmed, A., Newell, F. N., & Emslie, H. (2000). A neural basis for general intelligence. *Science, 289,* 457–460.

Kyllonen, P. C., Lohman, D. F., & Woltz, D. J. (1984). Componential modeling of alternative strategies for performing spatial tasks. *Journal of Educational Psychology, 76,* 1325–1345.

MacLeod, C. M., Hunt, E., & Mathews, N. N. (1978). Individual differences in the verification of sentence–picture relationships. *Journal of Verbal Learning and Verbal Behavior, 17,* 493–507.

Author Index

Subject Index